THE SACRED BOOKS OF THE EAST

F. MAX MULLER (ED.)

LIST OF THE 50 VOLUMES

1. Upanishads.
2. Sacred Laws of Aryas.
3. Texts of Confucianism.
4. Zend-Avesta.
5. Pahlavi Texts.
6. Qur'an.
7. Institutes of Vishnu.
8. Bhagavadgita, & c.
9. Qur'an.
10. (i) Dhammapada.
10. (ii) Sutta-Nipata.
11. Buddhist Suttas.
12. Satapatha-Brahmana.
13. Vinaya Texts.
14. Sacred Laws of Aryas.
15. Upanishads.
16. Texts of Confucianism.
17. Vinaya Texts.
18. Pahlavi Texts.
19. Fo-sho-hing-tsanking.
20. Vinaya Texts.
21. Saddharma Pundarika.
22. Gaina-Sutras.
23. Zend-Avesta.
24. Pahlavi Texts.
25. Laws of Manu.
26. Satapatha-Brahmana.
27. Texts of Confucianism (Li Ki).
28. Texts of Confucianism (Li Ki).
29. Grihya-Sutras.
30 Grihya-Sutras.
31. Zend-Avesta.
32. Vedic Hymns.
33. Minor Law-Books.
34. Vedanta-Sutras.
35. Milinda.
36. Milinda.
37. Pahlavi Texts.
38. Vedanta-Sutras.
39. Texts of Taoism
40. Texts of Taoism
41. Satapatha-Brahmana
42. Atharva-veda.
43. Satapatha-Brahmana.
44. Satapatha-Brahmana.
45. Gaina-Sutras.
46. Vedic Hymns.
47. Pahlavi Texts.
48. Vedanta-Sutras.
49. (i) Buddhakarita.
49. (ii) Mahayana Texts.
50. A General Index

The Sacred Books of the East, Vol. 24

PAHLAVI TEXTS

Edited by

F. MAX MULLER

Translated by

E. W. WEST

PART-III

DINA-I MAINOG-I KHIRAD
SIKAND-GUMANIK VIGAR
SAD DAR

GYAN

Published by

Gyan Publishing House
5, Ansari Road
Daryaganj, New Delhi-110002
Phone: 011-47034999, 9811692060
E-mail: books@gyanbooks.com

Distribution Network
gyanbooks.com
India, USA, Canada, UK, Australia, France

ISBN : 978-81-212-2937-1 (Set)
ISBN : 978-81-212-2825-1 (PB)
First Published, 1884

2nd Impression 2021

Printed at: Gyan Press, Delhi.

The Sacred Books of the East, Vol. 24

Pahlavi Texts, Part-III
Edited by: F. Max Muller, Translated by: E. W. West

THE

SACRED BOOKS OF THE EAST

TRANSLATED

BY VARIOUS ORIENTAL SCHOLARS

AND EDITED BY

F. MAX MÜLLER

VOL. XXIV

Oxford

AT THE CLARENDON PRESS

1885

PAHLAVI TEXTS

TRANSLATED BY

E. W. WEST

PART III

DÎNÂ-Î MAÎNÔG-Î KHIRAD
SIKAND-GÛMÂNÎK VIGÂR
SAD DAR

Oxford
AT THE CLARENDON PRESS
1885

CONTENTS.

INTRODUCTION.

TRANSLATIONS.

INTRODUCTION.

1. THE DÎNÂ-Î MAÎNÔG-Î KHIRAD.

THE Pahlavi phrase Dînâ-î Maînôg-î Khira*d*, 'Opinions of the Spirit of Wisdom,' is a name applied to sixty-two enquiries, or series of enquiries, on subjects connected with the religion of the Mazda-worshippers, made by an anonymous wise man and answered by the Spirit of Wisdom. But, as this name is only found prefixed to a manuscript, written in A.D. 1569, in which the first part of the work is missing[1], it is doubtful whether it be the original name of the book, or not, although it is very suitable to the general character of the work.

Regarding the reading of this name, here adopted, it must be observed that the correct pronunciation of the Pahlavi word maînôg, 'spirit,' is uncertain; the traditional reading is madônad, which is a possible pronunciation of its letters, but is otherwise inexplicable; Haug proposed to read maînivad or mînavad, but, in that case, the word ought to end with *d*=t, or with nd; some of the present Dastûrs read mînôê, but this would be written mînôêk in Pahlavi; the Pâzand writers have mainyô, but this is evidently an imitation of Av. mainyavô, and does not correspond with the Pahlavi letters. As the word is manû or minô in the Sasanian inscriptions, and mînû in Persian, to which words a final k would be added in Pahlavi, it seems probable that the final letter of the Pahlavi word is not d or ê, but g, a corruption of k, and that we ought to read mînôg or maînôg. At the same time it should be noticed that a very old copy of the Pahlavi Farhang, in the library of Dastûr Jâmâspji Minochiharji in Bombay, has the word written with an extra medial stroke, so that it might be

[1] See p. 3, note 1.

read mînavand, as required by Haug's hypothesis, although this copy of the Farhang gives madonend as the traditional reading.

The subjects discussed by the Spirit of Wisdom are of a very miscellaneous character, and their discussion is evidently intended to furnish an outline of the tenets, legends, and morality of the religion with which they deal; but it forms by no means a complete, or systematic, treatise on these subjects, and it is remarkably silent with regard to all details of religious rites and ceremonies, which are only occasionally mentioned. This silence may, perhaps, be due to the fact that the author was a layman, as seems clear from the account he gives of his doubts and enquiries in Chap. I, 14-56. Any incompleteness of the treatise may also be explained by the apparent loss of the latter end of the work, as the sixty-second reply (Chap. LXIII) terminates the extant text of the treatise abruptly, and without any trace of peroration.

By the Spirit of Wisdom the author means the innate wisdom of Aûharmazd (Chap. LVII, 4), the âsna khratu of Yas. XXII, 29, XXV, 18, through which the spiritual and worldly creations were produced (Chaps. I, 49, 51, LVII, 5). It was originally created by Aûharmazd (Chap. VIII, 3, 8), and is superior to the archangels (Chap. I, 53); it can appear in a personal form, and undertake to be an instructor (Chap. I, 57, 60, 61); and it can likewise be used as a defence (Chap. XLIII, 6).

With regard to the author of this treatise, and the age in which he lived, we have no further information than can be gathered from the contents of the book itself. The author was evidently a devoted Mazda-worshipper, and probably a layman, as has been already remarked, but he has given us no further hints about himself. Whether he wrote before or after the Arab conquest of Persia is doubtful. There are only two passages that might be strained into allusions to Muhammadanism: one in Chap. I, 18, which alludes to some heterodox religion injuring the property of the orthodox faith, but the author has just been talking of many sects, and the grievance here mentioned is much too common to be considered as applicable only to the Arabs; the other passage is Chap. XVI, 37–48, which describes the advantages of 'the moderate drinking of wine,' and might be supposed to be written in indirect opposition to the Muhammadan prohibition of such indulgence. In either case the allusion is certainly far too obscure to form a fair basis for argument. On the other hand, Chap. XIII, 13, 14, speaks of the sovereignty of Vistâsp existing in connection with the most powerful sect or form of devotion, which statement might be strained to imply that the government was still orthodox; and the definitions of good and bad government in Chap. XV, 12–39 could hardly have been written after the Arab conquest. The allusion to the continued conflict of the Arûmans and Tûrânians with the Irânians, in Chap. XXI, 23–26, may possibly refer to some troublesome wars carried on by the Greeks and Turks against the Persians in the time of the author, and the late Dr. A. D. Mordtmann has suggested A.D. 580–590 as a probable period for such remarks, but, here again, the allusion is too obscure to be relied on.

Very few of the author's quotations can be identified, but this is no argument for a greater age than eight or ten centuries, as we know, from passages quoted in the Shâyast Lâ-shâyast, Dâdistân-î Dînîk, and other works, that some of the lost Nasks must have been still extant as recently as that. The Avesta is quoted only twice by name, in Chaps. I, 27, XVI, 15; the former passage has not been identified, but the latter may perhaps be from the Pâzag Nask. Several quotations, however, are made from the dînô or 'revelation,' a term which, when it refers to writings, is often applied by Pahlavi writers to the Avesta only. Of these passages Chap. XLIV, 18–23 is from the Vendîdâd, Chap. XXI, 24–26 may be from the *K*idrast Nask, and six other quotations have not been identified. In other cases the quotations are merely prefaced by the phrase '*it is* declared.' And of these the passage in Chap. LVII, 24–28 appears to be derived from the Vendîdâd, and that in Chap. II, 155, 156 from the so-called Hâdôkht Nask, while eight other passages are unidentified. In this last class the quotations seem to be rather paraphrases than accurate translations of the original texts.

Of the original Pahlavi text of the Dînâ-î Maînôg-î Khira*d* only two manuscripts are yet known to exist; one of these (K43) is contained in No. 43 of the Irânian manuscripts in the University Library at Kopenhagen, and the other (TD2) belongs to Mr. Tehmuras Dinshawji Anklesaria of Bombay.

The manuscript K43 is a small quarto volume of 178 folios, of which the Dînâ occupies fols. 2–37, written fifteen lines to the page. The first and second folios also contain the conclusion of the larger Bundahi*s*, of which the first 129 folios are missing from this codex, as described in SBE, vol. v, introd. pp. xxxix–xli. And the latter part of the codex contains about one-fifth of the Dînka*rd*, in several detached fragments, and four-fifths of the Bahman Ya*s*t. This manuscript was brought from Persia by the late Professor Westergaard in 1843 [1], and the Pahlavi text of the Dînâ, which it contains, was published in facsimile by Andreas in 1882 [2].

In this codex the text of the Dînâ-î Maînôg-î Khira*d* begins in the middle of Chap. I, 28; but, as the copyist has prefixed an introductory heading to this imperfect text, it is evident that he, or some predecessor of his, must have copied the work, in this imperfect state, from some manuscript whose first folio had been lost. Besides this deficiency, ten folios of the text have been lost from this particular codex; nine of these were occupied by Chaps. XIV, 1–XXVII, 49, and the tenth contained Chaps. XXXIX, 31–XL, 17. At the end of the work, Chap. LXIII is followed by a colophon to the following effect:—'Completed in peace and pleasure and joy on the day Shatvai*r*ô of the month Â*v*ân of the year 938 of Ya*zd*aka*rd*, king of kings, [26th May 1569]. I, Mit*r*ô-âpân Anôshak-rûbân Rûstâm Shat*r*ô-îyâr, wrote *it* for my own possession. From the copy

[1] See Zend-Avesta, or the Religious Books of the Zoroastrians, edited by N. L. Westergaard (Kopenhagen, 1852–54), vol. i, introd. p. 8, note 3.

[2] The Book of the Mainyô-i-Khard, also an old fragment of the Bundehesh, edited by F. C. Andreas (Kiel, 1882).

of Dastûr Gadman-pîrû*g* Aspendiyâr Gadman-pîrû*g*, and that from the copy of Dastûr Shat*r*ô-aîyyâr Vê*g*an Khûsrôî-shah, and that, as regards these several sayings, was written from the copy of the heavenly-destined Mâh-vindâ*d* Naremâhân *with* the righteous soul, and comes unto us from the realm of the Hindûs. May even our writing be in accordance with the will of the sacred beings.' In addition to the date, the chief matter of interest in this colophon is its acknowledgment of the fact that the work had come from India, where the original Pahlavi text appears to have since become extinct. We have, therefore, in this text, merely so much of the work as had reached India, on which the Pâzand-Sanskrit version of Nêryôsang, described below, was undoubtedly based; and the possibility of hereafter finding the latter part of the work in Persia should not be overlooked. It is, however, upon the text contained in K43, so far as it is preserved, that the translation of the Dînâ-î Maînôg-î Khira*d* in this volume is founded.

Of the other Pahlavi manuscript, TD2, nothing further is known to the translator than a copy of the passages corresponding to those contained in the ten folios lost from K43, upon which copy the translation of those passages has been based.

Besides these manuscripts of the original Pahlavi text, there exist other copies, in which the text has been merely reproduced from the Pâzand version described below; and, of these copies, K22 (No. 22 in the University Library at Kopenhagen) may be cited as a typical example. This manuscript is a large octavo volume of 56 folios of glazed Indian paper, probably about a century old, but without a date. The first 48 folios contain a corrupt Pahlavi text of the Dînâ-î Maînôg-î Khira*d*, alternating with the usual Sanskrit version described below, written nineteen lines to the page, and extending as far as Chap. XXVII, 41. The corruptions in the text consist of misuse of Huzvâri*s* equivalents, and errors in orthography which no old writer of Pahlavi would be likely to commit, such as writing ko*l*âvist for harvist, naf*s*manîdârîk for khvê*s*inî*d*ârîh, ba*r*â-gûmân for a*v*îgûmân, hamê for hamâî, a*v*a*s* for aûba*s*, lâ and mâ for *al*, denman instead of hanâ for Pâz. *e*, the constant use of the adjective suffix -îk for the abstract suffix -îh, and the frequent omission of the final k in such words as dânâk, a*v*istâk. It can be seen at once, by any one really acquainted with Pahlavi, that a text of this description is merely a modern transliteration of the Pâzand version by some one whose knowledge of Pahlavi was rather limited and artificial.

Most of the Indian manuscripts of this work contain only the Pâzand version written in short sentences, alternating with a word-for-word Sanskrit translation of each sentence; the Sanskrit being written upside down, for the sake of forming a continuous line with the reversely-written Avesta characters of the Pâzand. This Pâzand-Sanskrit version of the Mainyô-i Khard (as it is called in Pâzand) was compiled by Nêryôsang, son of Dhaval, a Parsi priest who is supposed to have lived some time in the fifteenth century, and evidently possessed a very good knowledge of Pahlavi, though not sufficient to avoid some few mistakes, especially in reading foreign names. His authorship is attested by a Sanskrit introduction, prefixed to most manuscripts of this version, to the following effect:—'Through the name and almighty power and assistance of the lord Ahura-mazda, the greatly wise, may the achievement be auspicious, *and be* the progress and success of the good Mazda-worshipping religion, and energy in body and long life for all the good *and* right-minded. This Pahlavi heavenly wisdom, called the Mainyô-i Khard, is translated by me, Nêryôsang son of Dhaval, from the Pahlavi language into the Sanskrit language, and written from the difficult Parsi letters[1] with the Avesta letters, for the joyful understanding of the good listeners to instruction, the true-minded. Salutation to the good, the pure-thinking, the true-speaking, the just-acting.'

Of this Pâzand-Sanskrit version the oldest manuscript that has been examined is L19, No. 19 of the Avesta and Pahlavi manuscripts in the India Office Library in London, one of the manuscripts brought from India by Dr. Samuel

[1] That is, from the ambiguous Pahlavi characters, used in all Persian writings before the Arab conquest.

Guise who was head surgeon of the general hospital at Surat from 1788 to 1795, and obtained several manuscripts from the widow of Dastûr Dârâbji, the instructor of Anquetil Duperron. It is a small octavo volume, containing 148 folios of old Indian paper, of which the first 132 are occupied by the Pâzand-Sanskrit Mainyô-i Khard, written fifteen lines to the page. At the beginning of the text the folio containing Nêryôsang's Sanskrit introduction (described above) has been lost, but the text itself is complete. At the end of the work is a Pâzand-Sanskrit postscript which may be reasonably attributed to Nêryôsang himself, and can be translated as follows:—'Completed for the peace and pleasure, happiness and dominion of all the good who are virtuous. To him for whom *it is* written may it be well-resulting and well-omened, *and*, after a hundred and fifty years, may he be a transmitter *of it* to his own religious children's children, through the will of the sacred beings. Of whomsoever the best ability is not wisdom, that best ability of his is *even* then owing to it. Wisdom which is without learning is poor, and learning which is without wisdom is helpless.' After this postscript a Pahlavi colophon has been copied from some older manuscript to the following effect:—'Completed in peace, pleasure, and joy, and ended; written by me, a servant of the religion, the priest Shat*r*ô-aîyyâr, contemporary (?) of Nêryôsang.' And this is followed by a colophon in very corrupt Sanskrit, which states that this manuscript was completed, in the district of Nâgama*nd*ala[1], at a date corresponding to Friday, the 19th October 1520, by the teacher Mihrvân, son of Mahyâr and grandson of Padama, for the priest Bahrâm, son of Pâlhan. This manuscript of the Pâzand text is, therefore, nearly 49 years older than that of the original Pahlavi text (K43) upon which the present translation is based. It corresponds very closely with that Pahlavi text, and where it differs the variation is nearly always due to some mistake, or attempt at improvement, on the part of Nêryôsang. It must, however, be acknowledged that very few translators adhere so

[1] Probably an old name of Nausârî.

closely to their original texts as this learned Parsi priest has done to his.

Other manuscripts of the Pâzand-Sanskrit version are PA10 and PB6. The former is No. 10 of the Anquetil Collection in the National Library at Paris, and was brought from Surat by Anquetil Duperron in 1761. It is an octavo volume, in which the Mainyô-i Khard occupies the first 211 folios, and commences with Nêryôsang's Sanskrit introduction, translated above, but does not contain the postscript. The date of its colophon appears to correspond to the 7th December 1649, new style. The latter manuscript, PB6, is No. 6 of the Burnouf Collection in the same library, and is probably about a century old.

The Pâzand version also occurs alternating with a Gugarâti translation in K23, No. 23 of the Irânian manuscripts in the University Library at Kopenhagen. It is an octavo volume of 168 folios of glazed Indian paper, of which the first 162 contain the Pâzand-Gugarâti text, written fifteen lines to the page, and the remaining six folios contain an index stating the contents of each chapter. A colophon, at the end of the text, has a date corresponding to the 25th August 1663, new style; and another, at the end of the index, states that the manuscript was written by the priest Yazad-yâr, son of Vikaji, of Sangân, and finished at a date corresponding to the 17th October of the same year.

In another class of Pâzand manuscripts of the Mainyô-i Khard the Pâzand text is written in the Perso-Arabic character, and accompanied by a Persian translation, forming what may be conveniently termed a Pârsî-Persian version. One example of this version is contained in MH7, No. 7 of the Haug Collection in the State Library at Munich, of which it occupies the first 70 folios, written fifteen lines to the page. Most of the Persian translation is written in sentences alternating with those of the Pârsî text, in which case the translation is merely a paraphrase of the Pârsî; but some of the translation is interlined, and this is much more literal, each Pârsî word having its Persian equivalent written below it. This manuscript contains several other texts, and from two colophons, one near the middle, and the other near the end of the volume, it appears that it was written by Dârâshâh, son of Mihrbânji, and the first half of the volume was completed at a date corresponding to Wednesday the 9th August 1809.

Another example of the Pârsî-Persian version is found in No. 2769 of the Persian manuscripts in the India Office Library in London, in which manuscript it occupies 75 folios, written eleven lines to the page, and is not dated, though probably written early this century. In this copy the Pârsî text is tolerably complete, but long passages of the Persian translation are omitted; when given, the Persian is usually identical with that in MH7, though some instances of independent translation occur.

In addition to the Pahlavi, Pâzand, Sanskrit, Gugarâti, Pârsî, and Persian texts of the prose Dînâ-î Maînôg-î Khira*d*, the popularity of the work is further evinced by the existence of two versions in Persian verse. One of these was described by Professor Sachau in the Journal of the Royal Asiatic Society, new series, vol. iv, pp. 229–283, from a manuscript in the library of that Society in London, written probably near the end of last century. The author of this metrical Persian paraphrase appears to have been a native of Râvar in Sindh, named Marzubân, who composed it from a Pârsî version of the original text, bequeathed to him by his teacher while he was studying the old traditions at Yazd; and the date of his composition seems to have been A.D. 1612. His verses contain only fifty-four questions and answers, but these contain the substance of the greater part of the Mînôkhirad, as the work is called in Persian, with some few additions from other sources.

A copy of the other metrical Persian Mînôkhirad occupied fols. 527–550 in the second volume of B29, a two-volume quarto Rivâyat, No. 29 in the Bombay University Library. It is doubtful whether the original number of folios were twenty-four or twenty-six, but only twenty-two now remain. These contain 497 couplets of introductory matter, 1060 representing the text of the work, and 190 of epilogue; and from 160 to 330 further couplets of the text are missing. According to statements in the introduction and epilogue the verses appear to have been composed, from Nêryôsang's Pâzand-Sanskrit text, by the priest Hormazyâr and his son Dârâb, the latter being the actual writer, and the former being a son of Farâmruz[1], son of Qavâmu-d-dîn, son of Kaî-Qubâd, son of Ham*k*ârapadam[1] of San*g*ân, of the family of the priest Nêryôsang Dhaval. The work was commenced on the 7th November 1676, new style, and completed in thirty-five days; and the copy in B29 was finished on the 21st November 1679, new style. The order of the subjects discussed in this metrical version differs, in some respects, from that followed in the prose texts, and the 1060 couplets of extant text represent only forty chapters of the work, though several of the others were, no doubt, represented in the missing couplets. Another copy of this later metrical version appears to exist in pp. 231–248 of No. 12 of Anquetil's Collection in the National Library at Paris.

Of the Pâzand text of the Mainyô-i Khard, Chaps. LVII, XXVII, LXII, I, 51–61, VII, 9–12 have been published, with German translations, by Professor Spiegel, in his 'Grammatik der pârsi Sprache,' pp. 128–155, 161–173, 185, 186, 188, 189. He has also published German translations of Chaps. II, 110–193, VIII, XXXVII, XLII in his 'Traditionelle Literatur der Parsen,' pp. 138–144, 147–150. And the complete Pâzand-Sanskrit texts, with an English translation, Pâzand glossary and grammar, were published by the present translator in 1871. Since that date the original Pahlavi text of the Dînâ-î Maînôg-î Khira*d* has been discovered, from which the present translation has been made.

In connection with this account of the various versions of the 'Opinions of the Spirit of Wisdom,' it should be noticed that an abridgement of the work also exists in Persian prose, and is called the 'Other Mînôkhirad.' A copy of this abridgement is contained in fols. 71–78 of MH7 (described above), and consists of a very free Persian translation of the Pâzand texts of Chaps. I, 14–II, 64, III–VII, XIV, XV,

[1] A variation of this pedigree is quoted in p. xlii.

XXI, XXV, followed by a variety of short statements about thankfulness towards the sacred beings, the supreme heaven, male and female angels and demons, wealth and poverty, &c., and concluding with the names of the first sovereigns of the world, the descent of mankind from Gayômard, and of the 292[1] species of animals from the primeval ox. Another copy of this abridgement appears to be contained in fols. 80–84 of No. 15 of Anquetil's Collection in the National Library at Paris.

2. THE *S*IKAND-GÛMÂNÎK VI*G*ÂR.

The term *S*ikand-gûmânîk Vi*g*âr, 'doubt-dispelling explanation,' is the Pahlavi name applied to a controversial work by its author. The chief object of the work is to prove the correctness of the fundamental doctrine of the Mazda-worshipping religion, that good and evil do not proceed from the same source, and to show that other religions, while professing to believe in the unity of creation, can only account for the origin of evil, either by degrading the character of the sacred being, or by attributing evil to a corrupting influence which is really a second being. In other words, the author's object is to show that all people, who believe in an all-good and omnipotent creator, must logically admit the existence of an independent origin of evil, whatever they may say to the contrary. In the course of his arguments, he naturally finds it easier to attack the inconsistencies of other beliefs than to defend his own, and much of his attention is, therefore, given to pointing out apparent inconsistencies and seemingly delusive statements in the scriptures of the Muhammadans, Jews, Christians, and Mânîchaeans.

The author's name was Mar*d*ân-farukh, son of Aûha*r*ma*zd*-dâ*d* (Chap. I, 35), and his account of his enquiries (§§ 36, 37) bears much resemblance to what is said of the wise man's proceedings in Mkh. I, 34–36. He determines to

[1] Bd. X, 3, XIV, 13 mention 282 (or 272 in some copies).

write a treatise for removing religious doubt, and calls it the *S*ikand-gûmânîk Vi*g*âr (Chap. I, 38). He is also careful in stating that he has selected many of his facts and arguments from older writings, such as those of Âtû*r*-pâ*d*îyâvand [1], which he had found in the Dînka*rd* [2] compiled by Âtû*r*-frôbag, son of Farukh-zâ*d*. In this statement he must be referring to the first two books of the Dînka*rd*, which have not yet been discovered, as the other seven books, which are extant, do not contain the matters to which he alludes. He also mentions the Rôshan manuscript compiled by Rôshan [3], son of Âtû*r*-frôbag, a writer who is often quoted in the Pahlavi commentaries on the Avesta [4]. And he begins his religious discussion by replying to some difficulties that had been suggested to him, in a friendly manner, for solution by Mit*r*ô-aîyyâr, son of Mahmâ*d*, of Ispahân [5].

His allusions to Muhammadanism are of a very guarded character, though sufficiently clear to leave no doubt as to the religion he means. Like all Pahlavi writers, he never mentions that religion by name, but when, in the position of a Zoroastrian in Persia, he states that he did not admire the religion that was then in supremacy [6], there can be little doubt that he refers to Muhammadanism. And any such doubt would be dispelled, not only by such vague references to passages in the Qur'ân as occur in Chap. XI, 4, 5, 269–271, but also by the distinct quotation of a striking legend, from the same source, regarding the fallen angel in §§ 52–60, 248 of the same chapter, and by the use of the term Mûtazalîk (Ar. mu'htazil) with reference to a certain sect in § 280.

With regard, therefore, to the age of the *S*ikand-gûmânîk Vi*g*âr, we may be quite certain that it was written long after the Arab conquest of Persia; and from the names mentioned by the author, as stated above, it is evident that he lived after the time of Rôshan, son of Âtû*r*-frôbag, son of

[1] See Chaps. I, 38, IV, 106, IX, 2, X, 52.

[2] See Chaps. IV, 107, IX, 1, 4, X, 57.

[3] See Chap. X, 53, 54.

[4] See Sls. I, 4 n.

[5] See Chap. II, 1, 2.

[6] See Chap. X, 45.

Farukh-zâd. Now, according to a Pahlavi tale[1], the accursed Abâlis[2], the Zandîk, had a religious disputation with Âtûr-frôbag, son of Farukh-zâd, in the presence of the Khalîfah Al-Mâmûn who reigned A.D. 813–833; it is, therefore, hardly possible that Rôshan, son of Âtûr-frôbag, could have written his commentary before the middle of the ninth century. We also know, from the last chapter of the third book of the Dînkard, that Âtûr-frôbag was not the last editor of that work, but was succeeded by his son Zaratûst, and, later still, by Âtûrpâd, son of Hêmîd, who appears to have given the book its final revision. Of Âtûrpâd's work the author of the Sikand-gûmânîk Vigâr does not speak, and it is, therefore, reasonable to suppose that it had not been completed in his time. But, according to Bd. XXXIII, 10, 11, this Âtûrpâd was a contemporary of Zâd-sparam who was living in A.D. 881[3], and his revision of the Dînkard was, therefore, probably in progress by the end of the ninth century. From these facts we may conclude that the Sikand-gûmânîk Vigâr was written after the middle, but before the end, of the ninth century; unless we were to suppose that, although its author consulted only the first two books of the Dînkard (as mentioned above), the remaining seven books may have existed as a separate work unknown to him. Considering, however, that Âtûrpâd, son of Hêmîd, was so important a personage as 'the leader of those of the good religion' of his time, this supposition would not be very probable.

There is probably nothing new to defenders of Christianity in Mardân-farukh's attacks upon the apparent inconsistencies of their scriptures, with regard to the origin of evil and the existence of unity in trinity, subjects that are more usually admitted without investigation than seriously discussed. This is not, however, the mode in which such subjects are likely to be treated by outsiders, and missionaries will no doubt find among Mardân-farukh's arguments many that they must become accustomed to hear from educated

[1] A copy of which is contained in the very old codex No. 20 in the University Library at Kopenhagen, fols. 148–152.

[2] The reading of this name is uncertain, but this is the Pâzand form.

[3] See Ep. III, 2, 17, 21.

men of other faiths. And, if they engage in controversy, as they ought to do, they must expect to hear them stated in less considerate language than this author uses.

An interesting question, for any one who possesses special information on the subject, would be to ascertain from what version of the Old and New Testaments Mar*d*ân-farukh drew his quotations. There seems every probability that his translation of the passages, though it may not be altogether literal, is yet sufficiently so to admit of the particular version being identified, if its peculiarities of wording were carefully considered. The peculiar Pahlavi spelling of the name Isaac in Chap. XIV, 42, as deduced from its corruption in Pâzand, points to a Syriac version of one of the legendary works consulted by the author.

In his discussion of the tenets of the Mânîchaeans Mar*d*ân-farukh is dealing with a subject that is far less known than the other faiths he attacks, and the information he gives may be valuable. Unfortunately the latter part of this discussion is missing, although the loss of text is probably not very extensive.

The original Pahlavi text of the *S*ikand-gûmânîk Vi*g*âr has not yet been discovered, although there are several existing copies of a Pahlavi version of the earlier part of the work, which are evidently reproductions from the Pâzand text. These pseudo-Pahlavi manuscripts usually end with the fifth chapter, and are certainly superior to the similiar reproductions of the Dînâ-î Maînôg-î Khira*d*, represented by K22 (see p. xix). Yet they generally use the adjective suffix -îk for the abstract suffix -îh, because both these suffixes become -î in Pâzand; they often have kabed, 'much,' for afa*s*, 'and by him,' when the Pâzand has vas by mistake for va*s*; they also substitute the Pâzand misreading ainâ for the true Pahlavi adîna*s*; besides adopting other occasional miswritings for which the Pâzand version alone is responsible. Such manuscripts could be of no critical value, unless they had descended from some family of Pâzand manuscripts which had left no surviving representatives in Pâzand, and this does not appear to be the case.

A specimen of these Pahlavi reproductions is contained

in the last 36 folios of L15, No. 15 of the Avesta and Pahlavi manuscripts in the India Office Library in London. It commences with the words 'all the angels' in Chap. I, 4, and ends with Chap. V, 71; the handwriting being the same as that in L26, a manuscript that contains a date corresponding to A.D. 1737.

In fols. 9–16 of BM. No. 22,378 of the Additional Oriental manuscripts in the British Museum Library, there is a modern fragment of this reproduced Pahlavi text, interlined with a transliteration in the Persian character, and alternating with a Persian paraphrase. This fragment contains only Chap. I, 1–31.

The reproduced Pahlavi text also occurs, in parallel columns with the usual Pâzand and Sanskrit versions and a Persian paraphrase, in R, an imperfect polyglot manuscript given to the late Mr. J. Romer by a Dastûr in Surat. Of this foolscap-folio manuscript Mr. Romer sent pp. 16–31 (with the first fifteen pages of a Pahlavi-Persian Bundahi*s*) to the late Professor M. J. Müller, through Mr. Poley; he also sent pp. 32–63, 82–93 to the late Professor H. H. Wilson on 3rd December 1836, who afterwards transferred them to Professor Max Müller; and he gave pp. 64–81, 99–143 to the late Mr. Norris. The first of these fragments, together with that of the Bundahi*s* now constitute No. 10 of the Müller Collection in the State Library at Munich; the next two fragments were presented to the India Office Library, and the two last mentioned were acquired by it, in 1876. It is most probable that the first fifteen pages of this polyglot manuscript were not given to Mr. Romer, but the first fifteen pages of the Bundahi*s* were substituted for them. The portion extant (pp. 16–143) contains all four versions of Chaps. I, 28–V, 57, with the Sanskrit and Persian versions of Chap. I, 25–27, and the Pahlavi and Pâzand versions of Chap. V, 58–62; and the latter two versions are everywhere interlined with a transliteration in Persian characters. This manuscript is modern and of no particular critical value; but, as the combination of the four versions is rare, if not unique, it would be very desirable to discover the rest of the manuscript.

In another manuscript, No. 18 of the Anquetil Collection in the National Library at Paris, the reproduced Pahlavi text has the usual Pâzand version written above it. This manuscript, which is in the form of a roll, begins at the same point as L15 (see p. xxix) and ends with Chap. V, 95, which is said to be the usual extent of other manuscripts of this class in India. A copy of this manuscript is No. 23 of the Müller Collection in the State Library at Munich.

An extension of the same reproduced Pahlavi text, with the Pâzand version written above it, and alternating with the Sanskrit version, is contained in K28, No. 28 of the Irânian manuscripts in the University Library at Kopenhagen. It is an imperfect octavo manuscript, of which only 66 folios remain, written eleven lines to the page, and, in its present state, it is undated, but seems to be fully 150 years old. The portions of the text that it still contains are only Chaps. I, 1–II, 8; III, 1–25; III, 36–IV, 106; VIII, 103–IX, 16; IX, 30–X, 13; X, 71–XI, 28; XI, 55–61; so that more than half the text that ought to be included within its extreme limits is missing; but its original extent, within the same limits, was more than double the usual length of the reproduced Pahlavi text, as stated above. In this particular, of unusual length, only one other manuscript of that text seems to be known in India that resembles it, in addition to the imperfect copy next described. K28 contains Nêryôsang's usual Sanskrit introduction (see p. xxxiii), and differs from the oldest Pâzand manuscript AK in only two or three instances, and these variations can be explained as corrections made on the authority of the Sanskrit version.

An imperfect and modern copy of the Pahlavi-Pâzand-Sanskrit texts is also contained in twenty-two folios prefixed to AK (described below). This copy commences with Nêryôsang's Sanskrit introduction, and includes only Chaps. I, 1–IV, 100 and X, 71–XI, 47. Its writer has intended to give the three versions in successive sentences, but, after Chap. I, 23, the Pâzand and Sanskrit sentences are less and less frequently written, till they cease altogether after I, 43, with the exception of one or two isolated sections. In several cases he has also substituted the correct abstract suffix -îh for the usual incorrect -îk, but this correction is generally confined to abstract nouns in common use.

As none of these Pahlavi manuscripts can be considered otherwise than as reproductions from the Pâzand, it is to the Pâzand-Sanskrit version of Nêryôsang that we must still look for the nearest approach to the original text of the work. It is in this version, too, that we find the greatest extent of text still extant, although the *S*ikand-gûmânîk Vigâr seems to possess the peculiarity of wearying out all its copyists at some point or other, so that not only is there no complete copy of the work known, but also nearly every copyist has stopped his work at a different place.

The oldest known manuscript of the Pâzand-Sanskrit version belongs to Dastûr Hôshangji Jâmâspji of Poona, and is called AK, because it is supposed to have been written by Âsadîn, son of Kâkâ. In its present state this manuscript consists of seventy-seven small quarto folios of very old, discoloured, Indian paper, written sixteen lines to the page, and containing the Pâzand version in short sentences, alternating with a word-for-word Sanskrit translation of each sentence; the Sanskrit being written upside down, for the sake of forming a continuous line with the reversely-written Avesta characters of the Pâzand. From other manuscripts it is known that this Pâzand-Sanskrit version was compiled by Nêryôsang, son of Dhaval, but in this manuscript his usual Sanskrit introduction is lost with the first three folios of the text, and the existing seventy-seven folios contain only Chaps. I, 16–XI, 145. As this extends only one folio beyond the middle of the whole of the text that is extant, it is supposed that this old manuscript was divided into two nearly equal moieties on the occasion of some division of property, of which the earlier moiety has been preserved, and the later one either lost, or destroyed, or buried in some inaccessible library.

In consequence of the imperfect state of this manuscript it bears no date, but an old Sanskrit colophon has been copied by the writer of JE (one of the more modern manuscripts that are evidently derived from AK through one or more intermediate copies), and this may be fairly assumed to be the colophon of AK. This colophon may be translated as follows:—'In the Sa*m*vat year 1625, in the current *S*âka *year* 1490, on the present day (?), the fourth day Shahrîvar of the eleventh month Bahman, in the district of Nâga-ma*nd*ala[1], in the royal reign of king Sul*t*ân Mu*th*-affar-shâh, the book named *S*ikand-gûmânîk Vi*g*âr is written, for the use of Amalshâh *K*angashâh[2], by the priest Âsadîn[3], son of the priest Kâkâ. May it become auspicious! may it be beneficial!'

The date indicated by this colophon seems to correspond to the 23rd September 1568[4], but it may, of course, be doubted whether it originally belonged to AK, because the text to which it is appended in JE is incomplete. If it were attached to AK, the text in that manuscript must either have been originally incomplete, or some of the later folios must have been lost, while the last one, containing the colophon, was still preserved. If it did not belong to AK, it must have belonged to some later manuscript, because there is no doubt that JE has descended from AK, and could not, therefore, contain the colophon of an older manuscript than AK, unless it had been written in AK itself, or obtained in an irregular manner from some unrecorded source. For these reasons there seems little doubt that AK was written either in 1568, or earlier; and the general appearance of its folios favours this assumption. So far as it extends this is the best manuscript of the *S*ikand-gûmânîk Vi*g*âr that is known to exist, and the present translation has, therefore, been based upon its texts,

[1] Probably an old name of Nausârî.

[2] This *K*angashâh was probably a grandson of the *K*angashâh at whose instigation the Parsis in India carried on a correspondence with those in Persia in A.D. 1478-81, which is still preserved in the Persian Rivâyats. And his father may have been the Mâ*n*ekshâh *K*angashâh who was the head of the Parsi laymen in Nausârî in 1531, when he was 70 years old, as appears from the Hâdesâ Nâmu (Bombay, 1831).

[3] In a Gu*g*arâti memorandum, recently appended to JE, it is stated that the colophon of a Yasna Sâdah, written in A.D. 1572 or 1576, gives the pedigree of this copyist as follows:—Âsadîn, son of Kâkâ, son of Dharpâl, son of Lakhmidar, son of Môbad Kâmdîn, son of Zaratû*s*t, son of Môbad Hormazdyâr, son of Râmyâr.

[4] Or it may be 1569, as the *S*âka date has been altered from 1491 into 1490.

which are, no doubt, very nearly in the same state as when edited by Nêryôsang; the Sanskrit version, especially, is far more correct than in the later copies. Many of the Pâzand sections in Chaps. V–VIII are written in Pahlavi only, or in Pahlavi with the Pâzand written above it; but, in all cases, this Pahlavi is as corrupt as that of the reproduced Pahlavi manuscripts.

The most complete manuscripts of the Pâzand-Sanskrit version are JJ and JE, of which JJ is the oldest and best, but it has not yet been thoroughly examined. It is a small quarto volume of 182 folios of Indian paper, written fifteen to seventeen lines to the page, and belongs to Dastûr Khurshêdji Jamshêdji of Nausârî. From certain blunders and peculiarities, which its writer has copied, it is certain that this manuscript has descended from AK, and, also, that it has derived a few variations from some other source. Its Sanskrit text is not written inverted, as it is in AK, and it commences with Nêryôsang's usual Sanskrit introduction, as translated in p. xx, but with the clause containing the names altered to the following effect:—'This book, named *S*ikand-gûmânîk Vi*g*âr, is translated by me, Nêryôsang son of Dhaval, from the Pahlavi language into the Sanskrit language, and written from the difficult Parsi letters with the Avesta letters, for the joyful understanding of the good listeners to instruction, the true-minded.' The texts in JJ are of the same extent as the translation in this volume, and are followed by a colophon in Persian, Sanskrit, and imperfect Pahlavi, which states that the manuscript was written by Dastûr Jamshêd, son of Jâmâsp, son of Âsâ, son of Frê*d*ûn, inhabitants of Nausârî, and completed on the day Srôsh of the month Vohûman, A.Y. 1137 (corresponding to the 28th August 1768).

The other manuscript, JE, which is as complete as the translation in this volume, is a foolscap-folio volume of 132 folios, written eighteen lines to the page, and belongs to Dastûr Hôshangji Jâmâspji of Poona. It corresponds very closely with JJ, but its Sanskrit (which is not written inverted) is rather more corrupt; and it contains the same indications of descent from AK as that manuscript does, with the same variations derived from some other source. It commences with Nêryôsang's usual Sanskrit introduction, and at the end of the text it has the old Sanskrit colophon translated above, and supposed to belong to AK. And this is followed by a Persian colophon, written on the day Hôrmazd of the month Bahman, A. Y. 1211 (corresponding to the 26th July 1842), and stating that this manuscript was copied from that of Âsadîn, son of Kâkâ, in Bombay, by Jamshêd, son of Edalji, son of Bahmanji, son of the writer of JJ. From this it might be too hastily assumed that the old manuscript AK was still complete as recently as 1842; but, if such were the case, it would be difficult to understand why Dastûr Hôshangji could learn nothing about its missing moiety some twenty-five years afterwards, when he made searching enquiries on the subject; and it would be still more difficult to explain the variations in JE, already mentioned as derived from some other source than AK. It is more probable that the writer of JE found the old colophon of AK copied at the end of a more recent manuscript, which led him to believe that the latter was written by Âsadîn, son of Kâkâ.

That the first folio of AK had already been lost, considerably more than a century ago, appears from PB3, No. 3 of the Burnouf Collection in the National Library at Paris, which was evidently copied from a copy of AK, and is certainly more than a century old, judging from the general appearance of the paper on which it is written. This manuscript, which was given to Burnouf by Mr. Mâ*n*ekji Khurshêdji of Bombay, is a small octavo volume of 125 folios of Indian paper, written twelve to sixteen lines to the page, and contains the Pâzand-Sanskrit text of Chaps. I, 5–53, and II, 5–X, 66: the Sanskrit being written upside down, as in AK. The loss of Nêryôsang's Sanskrit introduction and Chap. I, 1–4 of the text indicates that the first folio of AK was already missing when the original of PB3 was copied, and several lacunae in the earlier folios, which have been filled up in red ink from some other source, indicate the torn condition of the earlier folios of AK. The loss of Chaps. I, 54–II, 4 is due to two folios being absent between folios 11 and 12 of PB3; and after Chap. X, 66 all further folios have been lost. In some sections in Chaps. VI and VIII, where the Pâzand text is written above its Pahlavi equivalent in AK, much confusion has been occasioned in PB3 by reading the Pâzand and Pahlavi versions as two successive lines of text; and it is evident that this confusion originated in some manuscript intermediate between AK and PB3, though it has been increased by further blundering on the part of the writer of PB3 itself.

The Pâzand version of Nêryôsang also occurs in short sentences alternating with a Gugarâti translation in MH19, No. 19 of the Haug Collection in the State Library at Munich. This manuscript, which was given to Haug by Dastûr Kaî-Khusrô at Surat in 1864, is a small quarto of 124 folios of old Indian paper, of which the first 110 folios contain the Pâzand-Gugarâti version of Chaps. I, 1–XI, 201, written thirteen to nineteen lines to the page. Towards the latter end of the manuscript blank spaçes are left for the Gugarâti version of many of the sections; and several of the passages that are written only in Pahlavi in AK are similarly written in MH19. From this and other peculiarities it is evident that MH19 has descended from AK, but probably through some intermediate manuscript that must have been written when AK was more complete than it is now. Judging from the appearance of the paper of MH19 it can hardly be less than 150 years old, but it contains no date or colophon of any description.

Another manuscript, which contains a large portion of the Pâzand version of Nêryôsang, without his Sanskrit translation, is L23, No. 23 in the India Office Library in London. It is an octavo volume of eighty folios of Indian paper, written ten to twelve lines to the page, in the same handwriting as L15 and L26 (see p. xxix), which last manuscript contains a date corresponding to A. D. 1737. L23 contains the Pâzand text of Chaps. I, 34–VIII, 23, and many of the passages written in Pahlavi in AK are similarly written in L23, which indicates the descent of the latter manuscript from the former; an indication which is confirmed by the repetition of other peculiarities.

From this account of all the manuscripts of the *S*ikand-gûmânîk Vigâr, that have been examined by the translator, it appears probable that no manuscript independent of AK has yet been discovered. The few variations which indicate another source can easily be explained as emendations by some later copyist, who had noticed, or imagined, some deficiencies in the text of that manuscript.

The *S*ikand-gûmânîk Vigâr has not been hitherto translated into any European language, but an edition of its Pâzand and Pahlavi texts was prepared by Dastûr Hôshangji about fifteen years ago, and arrangements have been made for the publication of these texts, with the Sanskrit version, at an early date.

3. The Sad Dar.

As its name implies the Sad Dar is a treatise on 'a hundred subjects' connected with the Zoroastrian religion. The word dar, literally 'door, or gate,' being also applied to the 'chapters' of a book, and to the 'matters, or subjects,' of which it treats. This work is not a Pahlavi text, being written in Persian with an admixture of about four per cent. of Arabic words; it is, however, more quoted than any other work by the Parsi compilers of the Persian Rivâyats, or religious 'traditions,' in the seventeenth century. In one of its recensions it is also found written in Avesta characters, and the Avesta-Persian sentences alternate with an old Gugarâti translation, in imitation of the Pâzand-Sanskrit versions of Pahlavi texts compiled by Nêryôsang. In consideration of the existence of this pseudo-Pâzand recension, together with the general acceptance of the work as an important authority, and its being a convenient summary of many of the religious customs handed down by Pahlavi writers, this work may be offered as a suitable appendix to the true Pahlavi texts, connecting them with the Persian writings that are too modern to be accepted as authorities in religious matters.

The Sad Dar NaTHr, or prose Sad Dar, which is here translated, appears to be first mentioned in the introduction to the Sad Dar-i Ba'hr-i *T*avîl [1], or long-metre Sad Dar, in which the versifier states that the prose Sad Dar was compiled by three celebrated high-priests, named Mêdyômâh, Vardast, and Siyâvakhsh, near the time of the Arab conquest of Persia. This, however, really means little more than that the prose Sad Dar was considered a very old work at the time when the long-metre Sad Dar was composed from it. It appears, from Dastûr Jâmâspji's preface to his Gu*g*arâti translation of the long-metre Sad Dar, that this metrical version was composed in A.D. 1531 by Mullâ Rustam Isfendiyâr of Khurâsân and Mullâ Behzâd Rustam [2]. It may, therefore, be concluded that the prose Sad Dar had the reputation of being a very old work in the early part of the sixteenth century.

Another version of the work, called the Sad Dar Na*th*m, or metrical Sad Dar, had already been composed in Kirmân by Îrân-shâh [3], son of Malik-shâh, as early as the 14th October, A. D. 1495. In his introduction he does not mention the source whence he drew his information, though he speaks of 'renovating the old mysteries,' but whether this phrase refers to the old prose Sad Dar, which he must undoubtedly have used, or to the original Pahlavi sources of that work, is uncertain. A Latin translation of this metrical Sad Dar was published by Hyde, in his History of the Religion of the Ancient Persians [4].

The contents of the Sad Dar are of a very miscellaneous character, and are not very systematically arranged. They treat of a great variety of duties and customs, but all from a strictly religious point of view, though the work is evidently

[1] See Sad-dare Behere Tavîl, translated into Gugarâti by Dastûr Jâmâspji Minochiharji Jâmâsp-Âsâ-nâ; 2nd edition; Bombay, 1881.

[2] Possibly a son of the preceding Mullâ. In the preface to his second edition Dastûr Jâmâspji calls him Rustam Behzâd.

[3] So stated in his introduction, but in his postscript (as printed by Hyde) he calls himself Mard-shah.

[4] Historia religionis veterum Persarum (Oxon. 1700), p. 433.

intended rather for the guidance of the laity than for the information of the priesthood. The almost total absence of any reference to government or national life, other than complete submission to priestly control, seems to indicate a period of subjection to men of another faith, too dangerous, or too odious, to be mentioned, unless it were to forbid all voluntary social intercourse with them, as in Chap. XXXVIII. The allusions to the existing scarcity of priests in Chap. LVIII, 12, and to a rigorous levying of poll-tax in Chap. LX, 7, might also give some clue to the period when the work was compiled, if we were better acquainted with the minute details of Parsi history. Where temporal penalties for crimes are prescribed (as in Chaps. IX, LXIV) they were, no doubt, such as were recognised by the government of the time; and, in such matters, change of government has altered the law. Some other customs have also probably changed to some extent, but by far the greater part of the rules and duties prescribed in this work are still in force, though they may not be always very strictly attended to.

Of the numerous quotations from the sacred books, which the Sad Dar contains, only a few can be identified, and nearly all of these are in the form of translations which are merely paraphrases of the original texts. Avesta passages are quoted from the Vendîdâ*d* and Yasna in Chap. XIV, 3, and from an unknown section of the Hâ*d*ôkht Nask in XL, 4. The commentary of the Vendîdâ*d* is six times quoted by name, but only four of the passages[1] have been identified; and an unknown passage is quoted from the commentary of the Hâ*d*ôkht in Chap. XXII, 3, 4, and three others[2] from the commentary of the Avesta. Four statements are said to be 'declared in the good religion,' but have not been identified; and out of thirty quotations from 'revelation' only five have been identified, of which those in Chaps. LXXII, 2, 3, LXXXII, 2 belong to the Vendîdâ*d*, and those in IV, 3–11, XVI, 3, XVIII, 3 belong to the Spend Nask, which is no longer extant. The large

[1] Chaps. XII, 3–5, LXVII, 3–6, LXXI, 2, 3, LXXXVI, 2.
[2] Chaps. XXVIII, 4, XCIV, 3, 4, XCVII, 3.

proportion of quotations that cannot be now identified, or are no longer extant, is a strong argument in favour of the work being several centuries older than the oldest manuscripts in which it is now found.

The translation of the prose Sad Dar, published in this volume, is based upon the text of La, the oldest manuscript of the work with which the translator is acquainted. This is No. 3043 of the Persian manuscripts in the India Office Library in London, which was presented to the East India Company's Library, on the 31st August 1837, by Mr. J. Romer, who had brought it from India, most probably from Surat. This manuscript is an octavo volume, containing 144 folios of light-brown Indian paper which may be as much as three centuries old. The volume was last bound and repaired some time subsequent to 1818, as several English foolscap fly-leaves bear that date as a water-mark. Its Persian text has the peculiarity of being written in Avesta characters, in short sentences alternating with an old Gugarâti translation in Devanâgarî characters which, for the sake of running in a continuous line with the reversely-written Avesta-Persian, is written upside down; each page containing generally thirteen lines. This Avesta-Persian is not Pâzand, either in verbal forms or syntactical arrangement, but its orthography is as irregular and uncertain as in most Pâzand texts written in Avesta characters. The text commences with a Sanskrit introduction, copied verbatim from that used by Nêryôsang as a preface to all his Pâzand-Sanskrit texts (see p. xx), with the clause containing the names altered as follows:—'This book, named Sad Dar, is brought together by me, the priest Râma, son of Kanhaksha, *and* translated from the Parsi language into the Gugar language, and written from the difficult Parsi letters with the Avesta letters by his son, the priest Padama.' And this preface is followed by the Pâzand invocation that commences the Persian introduction, as translated on p. 255; which introduction contains a passage (§ 6) probably interpolated in the prose Sad Dar after the composition of the metrical version.

The last chapter of the text in La is followed by two

Persian couplets in Avesta characters, with their translation in Gugarâti; and, after a few more verses in Sanskrit, the colophon concludes with Sanskrit to the following effect:—'In the Samvat year 1631, the ninth *day* in the light half of *the month* Gyaishtha, on Wednesday, the Uttarâ [Ashâdhâ ?] lunar mansion; in the Parsi Samvat year 944, the 27th day Âsmân, the sixth month Shahrîvar [18th May 1575][1], the Uzayêirina period (the afternoon), the book Sad Dar *is* completely written *by* an inhabitant of Bhrigu-kakkha[2]. Brought together by the priest Râma, son of Kanhaksha, *and* written in the handwriting of the priest Padama, his son, the book Sad Dar *is* completed. Written, by another, for the purpose of reading *and* for the purpose of reciting by Hîrâka of the good religion, son of . . .[3] of the good religion, and also by Âdaraka of the good religion, son of Gâyâ of the good religion; may it become auspicious and beneficial!' Followed by 'may it be healthful! may it be excellent! so may it be! *and* more so may it be!' in Pâzand.

It is possible that this colophon may have been copied from an older manuscript, but there are certainly some reasons for supposing that La is the original manuscript completed in 1575. In the first place, the appearance of the paper, on which it is written, favours such a supposition, and enquiries, made in Bombay, have not succeeded in discovering the existence of any other copy of this recension. Again, there are a few defects and inconsistencies in the Gugarâti translation which are best explained by supposing that the translation was made at the time this manuscript was written. Thus, the greater part of Chap. LXXIII, after having been written on one side of a folio, is repeated by mistake on the other side of the same folio with several variations, most of which are alterations in the Gugarâti translation, as if the writer were making the trans-

---

[1] As the manuscript was written in India, the calendar used would be the Rasmî one.

[2] The old name of Bhrôk.

[3] This name, with one or two epithets, has to be extracted from the corrupt Sanskrit compound gnâtîvyavyagihilûâ.

lation at the time when he wrote it. Also, in Chap. LXXVII, a blank having been left for some illegible word in the Avesta-Persian text, a similar blank has been left in the Gugarâti translation, although it is hardly possible that any mere copyist would have found the same word illegible in both versions.

With regard to the source whence the Avesta-Persian text of La was derived, there can be little doubt that it was originally transliterated from a manuscript written in the Perso-Arabic character, as there are several blunders in La which can be best explained as owing to the mutual resemblance of certain letters in that character. Thus, the fact that the modern Persian letters b, n, t, y differ only in the number and position of certain dots, which are sometimes omitted or misplaced, accounts for such blunders as bâ and yâ for tâ, khâna for '*h*âyah. While, owing to similar resemblances, the transliterator has written kustî for gêtî, muluk for balkih, guza for gôsh, and having been doubtful, in one place, whether to read rô*z* or *z*ôr, he has written both words, one above the other.

Somewhat more recent than this Avesta-Persian manuscript is Lp, No. 2506 of the Persian manuscripts in the India Office Library in London, which was presented to the Library by Mr. J. Romer at the same time as La. This manuscript is a small octavo volume, in which the prose Sad Dar occupies the first forty-six folios of Indian paper, written generally fifteen lines to the page in the Perso-Arabic character. In its present state it contains no date, the last folio of the colophon being lost, but the paper is not much newer than that of La. The colophon is written in the Avesta character, and is to the following effect:—'This book is the book Sad Dar, a Nask of the religion of Zarathustra, the good religion of the Mazda-worshippers. *These* hundred questions of the proper and improper are extracted from this good *religion* of the Mazda-worshippers, *and* Îrân-shâh, son of Yazad-yâr, . . .;' the rest being lost.

Another important copy of the Persian text of the prose Sad Dar is contained in B29, a two-volume, quarto Rivâyat,

No. 29 in the Bombay University Library. In this Rivâyat, or miscellany of traditional lore, the prose Sad Dar occupies fourteen folios (17–30) in the first volume, each page containing twenty-one closely-written lines. The Persian colophon at the end of the last chapter is to the following effect:—'This book of the prose Sad Dar is completed on the day Âstâd of the auspicious month Daî of the year 1048 of Yazdagard, the king of kings of happy Îrân, of the race of Sâsân. And the writer of the lines *am* I, the servant of the good religion of the Mazda-worshippers, the priestly-born priest Dârâb, son of the priest Hormazyâr, son of Qavâmu-d-dîn, son of Kaî-Qubâd, son of Hormazyâr[1] of the surname Sangânâ, of the family of the priest Nêryôsang Dhaval.' The date mentioned in this colophon corresponds to the 28th September 1679, new style.

A third copy of the Persian text is contained in J15, a small quarto volume, No. 15 in the library of Dastûr Jâmâspji Minochiharji in Bombay. In this volume the prose Sad Dar occupies the last thirty-six folios, and is written thirteen lines to the page, but is not dated. This manuscript has been consulted in only a few passages, and usually where the other copies differ considerably.

Regarding the variations in the text of these manuscripts it will be noticed, on reference to the foot-notes to the translation, that there is usually considerable agreement among the three Persian manuscripts (Lp, B29, J15[2]) when they differ from the Avesta-Persian text of La. In a few cases the text of La is undoubtedly defective, and then Lp or B29 may perhaps supply the original reading which has come down to them through some collateral line of descent. But, in the great majority of instances, their variations (especially those of B29) seem to be intended either to make the text more intelligible, or to correct some statement that the copyist thought doubtful. That none of these three manuscripts is derived from La is proved by the fact that they all contain a passage (Chap. XIX, 4–6) which

[1] A variation of this pedigree has already been quoted in p. xxiv.

[2] Allowing for the fact that this last has been only occasionally used.

the writer of La has omitted by mistake. There is, however, more agreement with La to be found in Lp than in the other two manuscripts.

The arrangement of the chapters in La is confused by the accidental combination of a portion of Chap. XLVIII with a portion of Chap. L, while Chap. XLIX, omitted in its proper place, has been subsequently added at the end of the work. In Lp Chap. XLIX follows Chap. LIII, and, Chaps. L and LV being omitted, the full number of a hundred chapters is obtained by repeating Chaps. XLIX and C at the end of the work. As this confusion in Lp occurs in the same portion of the work as that in La, though it differs somewhat in its details, and as it has been shown above that Lp cannot have been derived from La, it is reasonable to suppose that La and Lp were both derived from some older manuscript, in which some portion of the middle of the work had been omitted or lost, and that the writers of La and Lp adopted different modes of supplying the deficiency from other manuscripts. This confusion does not occur in B29 and J15, which two manuscripts agree in arranging the chapters as they are placed in this volume; they must, therefore, be derived from the original prose Sad Dar through some collateral line of descent, independent of the manuscript in which the confusion originated.

In the metrical Sad Dar nine of the later chapters are scattered about among the earlier ones, thus the 82nd chapter occurs next after the 16th, the 83rd after the 23rd, the 84th after the 24th, the 85th after the 27th, the 86th after the 57th, the 87th after the 58th, the 88th after the 70th, the 89th after the 72nd, and the 90th after the 73rd. And, besides this variation, a chapter about the advantage of daily ceremonies in honour of the guardian spirits follows the 65th chapter, a very long chapter about the season festivals is substituted for the 93rd chapter, and the 100th chapter is omitted.

So far as five of the scattered chapters (85–89) are concerned, the reason for their change of position was probably to bring them into closer connection with other chapters treating of similar subjects; but this explanation will not apply to the remaining four chapters (82–84, 90). It might be argued that the more methodical arrangement of the five chapters (85–89) favours the supposition that the metrical Sad Dar may be older than the prose one, but, independent of the fact that this argument does not apply to the four other chapters, it is quite as reasonable to suppose that the later editor would endeavour to improve the arrangement of his text, and to remedy whatever he thought defective. The pre-existence of the prose Sad Dar may be fairly assumed on the positive evidence afforded by the statement of the long-metre Sad Dar, mentioned in p. xxxvii, in default of any clear statement by the author of the metrical Sad Dar as to the originality of his work.

Since the above was written, the translator has had an opportunity of examining a Persian text of the prose Sad Dar, written in Persia by Rustam Gustâsp Ardashîr, and completed on the 19th July 1706. In this manuscript, the introductory chapter is practically the same as in La, with a few variations. Thus, the invocation in § 1 is as follows:—'In the name of the sacred being, administering justice. The beginning of the book Sad Dar; may it be a good gift!' And § 6 runs as follows:—'On this occasion I, Bahman, a servant of the religion, *am* confirmed by the book of the môbad of môbads Îrân-shâh, son of Yazad-yâr, son of Tistar-yâr, son of Âdar-bâd, so that every one who reads *it* and orders duty *to be done* brings a reward to the souls of those *persons*.' The arrangement of the chapters is the same as in the metrical Sad Dar[1], and the text differs from La in many more small details than in B29; it often inserts additional sentences, and is generally more diffuse, without giving more information to the reader. The Avesta of the passage quoted in Chapter XL, 4 is omitted, and only the first three words of that quoted in Chapter XIV, 3 are given. Notwithstanding their numerous variations, the resemblance of Bahman's text to that of La is too great

[1] As far as the long chapter about the season festivals (see p. xliii), but this is subdivided into six chapters (one for each festival) which conclude the work. The same arrangement also occurs in the Gugarâti translation of the long-metre Sad Dar.

to permit the assumption that they are two different prose versions of Îrân-shâh's metrical Sad Dar. It seems more probable that Bahman merely collated the prose Sad Dar with the metrical version, and made many alterations in the former to bring it into closer correspondence with the latter. This manuscript, therefore, throws no fresh light upon the origin of the prose version in La, but, as it confirms the fact that the Îrân-shâh whose name occurs in the introductory chapter was a son of Yazad-yâr, it raises a doubt whether this was the same person as the Îrân-shâh, son of Malik-shâh (or Mard-shah), who composed the metrical version.

In conclusion, it is desirable to notice that another Persian work exists, similar in form and character to the Sad Dar, but entirely distinct in its details, which is usually called the Sad Dar Bundahis. A complete copy of it is contained in Anquetil's Old Rivâyat in the National Library in Paris, and it is frequently quoted in the Bombay Rivâyat (B29) mentioned in p. xli. In this latter manuscript its name is written صد در بند هش twenty-five times, صد در بند هوش eighteen times, and صد در بند هُش thrice. And the only plausible reading applicable to all these three forms is Sad Darband-i Hush (or Hûsh), 'the hundred door-bolts of the understanding,' a very possible name for a book. The Sad Dar Bundahis is, therefore, most probably a misnomer.

E. W. WEST.

April, 1885.

ABBREVIATIONS USED IN THIS VOLUME.

Acc. for accusative case; A.D. for Anno Domini; Âf. for Âfrîngân; AK for Âsadîn Kâkâ's MS. of Sg.; Aog. for Aogemadaêkâ, ed. Geiger; app. for appendix; Ar. for Arabic; AV. for the Book of Ardâ-Vîrâf, ed. Hôshangji and Haug; Av. for Avesta; A.Y. for Anno Yazdagardi; B29 for Persian Rivâyat MS. No. 29 of the Bombay University Library; Bd. and Byt. for Bundahis and Bahman Yast, as translated in vol. v of this series; BM. for No. 22,378 additional Oriental MS. in the British Museum; Chap. for chapter; Dan. for Daniel; Dd. for Dâdistân-î Dînîk, as translated in vol. xviii of this series; Deut. for Deuteronomy; ed. for edition or edited by; Ep. for Epistles of Mânuskîhar, as translated in vol. xviii of this series; Ex. for Exodus; Eze. for Ezekiel; fol. for folio: Gen. for Genesis; Gesch. Pers. Sas. for Geschichte der Perser und Araber zur Zeit der Sasaniden; Göt. gel. Anz. for Göttingische gelehrte Anzeigen; Haug's Essays for Essays on the Sacred Language, Writings, and Religion of the Parsis, by M. Haug, 2nd ed.; Heb. for Hebrew; Hn. for Hâdôkht Nask, as published with AV.; Huz. for Huzvâris; introd. for introduction; Is. for Isaiah; J15 for Dastûr Jâmâspji Minochiharji's MS. No. 15 of Sd.; JE for Jamshêdji Edalji's MS. of Sg.; JJ for Jamshêdji Jâmâspji's MS. of Sg.; Jos. for Joshua; J.R.A.S. for Journal of the Royal Asiatic Society; K22, K23, K28, K43 for Iranian MSS. Nos. 22, 23, 28, 43 in the University Library at Kopenhagen; L15, L19, L23, L26 for Avesta and Pahlavi MSS. Nos. 15, 19, 23, 26 in the India Office Library in London; La, Lp for Persian MSS. Nos. 3043 and 2506 in the same library; Mat. for Matthew; MH7, MH10, MH19 for MSS. Nos. 7, 10, 19 of the Haug Collection in the State Library in Munich; Mkh. for Maînôg-î Khirad, as translated in this volume; MS. for manuscript; n. for foot-note; Na. for Nahum; Nêr. for Nêryôsang; Num. for Numbers; Ost. Kul. for Ostîrânische Kultur im Altertum, von W. Geiger; p. for page; PA10 for MS. No. 10 of the Anquetil Collection in the National Library in Paris; Pahl. for Pahlavi; Pâz. for Pâzand; PB3, PB6 for MSS. Nos. 3, 6 of the Burnouf Collection in the National Library at Paris; Pers. for Persian; Ps. for Psalms; R. for Mr. Romer's polyglot MS. of Sg. (see p. 116); Rev. for Revelation; Rom. for Romans; Sam. for Samuel; Sans. for Sanskrit; Sd. for Sad Dar, as translated in this volume; Sg. for *S*ikand-gûmânîk Vi*g*âr, as translated in this volume; Sîr. for Sîrôzah; Sls. for Shâyast-lâ-shâyast, as translated in vol. v of this series; Syr. for Syriac; TD2 for Mobad Tehmuras Dinshawji's MS. of Pahl. Mkh.; Vend. for Vendîdâ*d*; vol. for volume; Yas. for Yasna; Yt. for Ya*s*t; Zarat. for Zaratû*s*t; Zor. Stud. for Zoroastrische Studien, von Windischmann.

DÎNÂ-Î MAÎNÔG-Î KHIRA*D*,

OR

OPINIONS

OF THE

SPIRIT OF WISDOM.

OBSERVATIONS.

1. The division into chapters corresponds with the beginnings of the questions, and the sections are divided according to the alternating Pâzand-Sanskrit text of Nêryôsang.

2. Italics are used for any English words that are not expressed, or fully understood, in the original text, but are added to complete the sense of the translation.

3. Italics occurring in Oriental words, or names, represent certain peculiar Oriental letters (see the 'Transliteration of Oriental Alphabets' at the end of this volume). The italic *d*, *l*, *n*, *r*, *v* may be pronounced as in English; but *g* should be sounded like j, *hv* like wh, *k* like ch in 'church,' *s* like sh, and *z* like French j.

4. In Pahlavi words the only vowels expressed in the original text are those circumflexed, initial a, and the letter ŏ; italic *d* is written like t, *r* and *l* like n or the Avesta o, *v* and *z* like *g*, and *zd* like â in the Pahlavi character.

5. In the translation, words in parentheses are merely explanatory of those which precede them.

6. For the meanings of the abbreviations used in the notes, see the end of the Introduction.

7. The manuscripts mentioned are:—

K43 (written A.D. 1569) Pahlavi, No. 43 in the University Library at Kopenhagen; upon the text of which, so far as it extends, this translation is based.

L19 (written A.D. 1520) Pâz.-Sans., No. 19 in the India Office Library at London.

MH7 (written A.D. 1809) Pârsî-Pers., No. 7 of the Haug Collection in the State Library at Munich.

MH10, a Persian Rivâyat, No. 10 of the same Collection.

PA10 (written A.D. 1649) Pâz.-Sans., No. 10 of the Anquetil Collection in the National Library at Paris.

PB6, Pâz.-Sans., No. 6 of the Burnouf Collection in the same library.

TD2, Pahlavi, belonging to Mobad Tehmuras Dinshawji Anklesaria at Bombay; upon a copy of which this translation chiefly relies in the passages (XIV, 1–XXVII, 49 and XXXIX, 31–XL, 17) missing from K43.

DÎNÂ-Î MAÎNÔG-Î KHIRAD.

THROUGH the name and power and assistance of the creator Aûharmazd, the archangels *who are* good rulers and good performers, and all the angels of the spiritual and the angels of the worldly *existences*, by a happy dispensation (dahisn) and well-omened we write the Opinions of the Spirit of Wisdom through the will of the sacred beings[1].

CHAPTER I[2].

[1. In the name and *for* the propitiation of the all-benefiting creator Aûharmazd, (2) of all the angels of the spiritual and worldly creations, (3) *and* of the learning of learnings, the Mazda-worshipping

---

[1] This heading is prefixed to the original Pahlavi text in K43, a facsimile of which was published by Andreas in 1882; as, however, the text which follows it, in that codex, begins in the middle of Chap. I, 28, this heading must have been composed by some copyist, after the first folio of the text had been lost from some previous copy. It is, therefore, doubtful whether the name he gives to the work, 'Opinions (or decisions) of the Spirit of Wisdom,' be the original title, or not; but it is, at any rate, preferable to the modern appellation, 'the Spirit of Wisdom.' In Pâzand this title is Mainyô-i Khard; but regarding the Pahlavi word maînôg, see the Introduction.

[2] The beginning of this chapter, enclosed in brackets, as far as § 28 (being lost from the Pahlavi text of K43, and no copy of it from TD2 being available) is here taken from the Pâzand version contained in L19. The division into sections, adopted throughout, is that of the alternating Pâz.-Sans. text of Nêryôsang.

religion, (4) forth from which this, *which is* such a source of wisdom, is a selector[1]. 5. Through the glory and will of the creator Aûharmazd—*who is* promoting the prosperity of the two existences[2]—(6) and of all the greatly powerful angels, (7) and *through* the completely calm repose of the sacred beings, the princely[3], purpose-fulfilling sages, (8) presentations of various novelties for the appropriation of wisdom, (9) through largely acquiring reasoning thought[4], are most wholesome for the body and soul *in* the two existences.

10. As in the pure marvel of marvels, the unquestionable and well-betokened good religion of the Mazda-worshippers, by the words of the creator, Aûharmazd, and Zaratûst the Spîtamân[5], it is in

[1] That is, this work is a selection of wisdom from the religion. The Pâz. vas is a misreading of Pahl. agas, 'from it,' which is identical in form with Pahl. afas, the correct equivalent of Pâz. vas.

[2] This world and the next.

[3] The angels are here compared to the vâspûharakân, the highest class of Sasanian nobles, called barbêtân, 'sons of the house,' in Huzvâris (see Nöldeke's Gesch. Pers. Sas. pp. 71, 501). As these nobles ranked next to the royal house, so do the archangels and angels rank next to Aûharmazd. The title vâspûhar is evidently connected with the ancient Pers. equivalent of Av. vîsô puthra, 'son of the village or town,' which, as Darmesteter points out (Études Iraniennes, II, p. 140), is used in Vend. VII, 114 as the title of a person who has to pay the same medical fees as the zantu-paiti, 'tribe-ruler,' mentioned in the earlier § 108, and who must, therefore, have been a man of equal rank.

[4] Reading vîrmat, both here and in § 13, instead of the Pâz. nîrmad, which is a misreading of the same letters.

[5] Av. Zarathustra Spitama, the great apostle of the Mazda-worshippers, whose conversations with Ahura Mazda (Pahl. Aûharmazd) constitute a considerable portion of the Avesta, or scripture of the Mazda-worshippers.

many places decided, (11) that he, who is the all-good creator, created these creatures through wisdom, (12) and his maintenance of the invisible revolutions[1] is through wisdom; (13) and the imperishable and undisturbed *state*, in that which is immortality *for* ever and everlasting, he reserves for himself by means of the most deliberative[2] means of wisdom. 14. For the same reason *it* is declared, (15) that *there* was a sage who said, (16) that 'if this be known, that the religion of the sacred beings (ya*zd*ân) is truth, and *its* law is virtue, and *it* is desirous of welfare and compassionate as regards the creatures, (17) wherefore are *there* mostly many sects, many beliefs, and many original evolutions[3] of mankind? 18. And, especially, that which is a sect, law, and belief, causing harm to the property (khêl) of the sacred beings[4], and is not good? 19, 20[5]. And this, too, *one has* to consider, that, in order to become a chooser in this matter, trouble is to be undergone; (21) and it is necessary to become acquainted with this matter, (22) because, in the end, the body is mingled with the dust, and reliance is on the soul. 23. And every one is to undergo trouble for the soul, (24) and is to become acquainted with duty and good works; (25) because that good work which a man does unwittingly is little of a good work, (26) and that sin which a man

[1] Of the spheres, or firmaments, which are supposed to carry along the heavenly bodies.

[2] Reading vîrmat-hômandtûm.

[3] Reading bûn ga*s*t (see Sg. IV, 73 n).

[4] It may be questioned whether this allusion to a heterodox religion injuring the property of the orthodox faith is sufficient to identify the former with Muhammadanism.

[5] These two sections are improperly separated by Nêryôsang.

commits unwittingly amounts to a sin in *its* origin[1]. 27. And *it* is declared by the Avesta[2] (28) thus:] [3]"Nothing *was* taken by him by whom the soul *was* not taken (29) hitherto, and he takes nothing who does not take the soul (30) henceforward likewise[4]; (31) because the spiritual and worldly *existences* are such-like as[5] two strongholds, (32) one *it* is declared certain that they shall capture, and one it is not possible to capture."'

33. After *being* replete *with* those good actions *of*[6] which *it* is declared certain that it is not possible to capture, (34) and when he[7] surveyed the incitement for this, (35) he started forth (fravaftŏ), in search of wisdom, into the various countries and various districts of this world; (36) and of the many[8] religions and beliefs of those people who are superior in their wisdom he thought and enquired, and he investigated and came upon *their* origin[9]. 37. And when he saw that they are so mutually afflicting (hanbêshin) and inimical among

---

[1] The original text was, no doubt, vinâs pavan bûn va*l* yehevûnê*d*, which would be gunâh pa bun ô bahô*d* in Pâzand; but L19 has omitted the p in pa, and Nêr. has mistaken the preposition va*l* for the pronoun valman, which blunders have misled the writers of later MSS. into a variety of inconsistent readings.

[2] The sacred literature of the Parsis in its original language.

[3] The extant Pahlavi text of K43 commences at this point.

[4] By this division of §§ 28–30 Nêr. found himself compelled to add another Sanskrit clause in explanation, which would have been unnecessary if he had separated them as here pointed.

[5] K43 omits 'as.'

[6] L19 has 'after those good actions of a store.'

[7] The sage mentioned in § 15.

[8] L19 has 'every.'

[9] L19 omits 'origin,' having merely va*g*ôst, 'investigated,' instead of bun *g*ûstŏ, 'investigated the origin.'

one another, (38) he then knew that these religions and beliefs and diverse customs, which are so mutually afflicting among one another in this world, are not worthy to be from the appointment of the sacred beings; (39) because the religion of the sacred beings is truth, and *its* law is virtue. 40. And through this he became without doubt that, *as to* whatever[1] is not in this pure religion, *there* is then doubtfulness for them in everything, (41) and in every cause they see distraction.

42. After that he became more diligent in the enquiry and practice of religion; (43) and he enquired of the high-priests who have become wiser in[2] this religion and more acquainted *with* the religion, (44) thus: 'For the maintenance of the body *and* preservation of the soul what thing[3] is good and more perfect?'

45. And they [spoke[4]], through the statement [from revelation, (46) thus: 'Of the[5] benefit which happens to men] wisdom is good; (47) because it is possible to manage the worldly *existence* through wisdom[6], (48) and it is possible to provide also the spiritual *existence* for oneself through the power of wisdom. 49. And this, too, is declared, that Aûhar*mazd* has produced these creatures and creation, which are in the worldly *existence*, through innate

[1] L19 has 'every one who,' having read ko*l*â mûn instead of ko*l*â maman. The meaning, however, is that all details of foreign faiths that are not found in the Ma*zd*a-worshipping religion are doubtful.

[2] K43 has 'of,' by omitting pavan, 'in.'

[3] L19 has 'what one thing.'

[4] K43 omits the words in brackets, by mistake.

[5] Sans. has 'this.'

[6] L19 has 'through the power of wisdom.'

wisdom[1]; (50) and the management of the worldly and spiritual *existences* is also through wisdom.'

51. And when, in that manner, he saw the great advantage and preciousness of wisdom, he became more thankful unto Aûharmazd, the lord, and the archangels of[2] the spirit of wisdom; (52) and he took[3] the spirit of wisdom as a protection. 53. For the spirit of wisdom *one* is to perform more homage and service than *for* the remaining archangels. 54. And this, too, he knew, that it is possible to do for oneself every duty and good work and proper action through the power of wisdom; (55) and it is necessary to be diligent for the satisfaction of the spirit of wisdom. 56. And, thenceforward, he became more diligent in performing[4] the ceremonial of the spirit of wisdom.

57. After that the spirit of wisdom, on account of the thoughts and wishes of that sage, displayed *his* person unto him. 58. And he spoke to him (59) thus: 'O friend *and* glorifier! good from perfect righteousness! (60) seek advancement from me, the spirit of wisdom, (61) that I may become thy guide to the satisfaction of the sacred beings and

[1] The âsnô khiradô (Av. âsnô khratus) is 'the durable or innate wisdom' supposed to be implanted in one's nature, as distinguished from the Av. gaoshô-srûtô khratus, 'the ear-heard or acquired wisdom,' obtained by experience.

[2] That is, 'produced by' this spirit, as mentioned in § 49 regarding the world, and here extended to the archangels. L19 omits the particle î, so as to convert this spirit into the wisdom of Aûharmazd and the archangels. It is very probable, however, that we ought to read 'and the spirit of wisdom.'

[3] L19 has 'made;' these two verbs being written alike in Huzvâris.

[4] L19 has 'to perform,' by omitting 'in.'

the good[1], and *to* the maintenance of the body in the worldly *existence* and the preservation of the soul in the spiritual *one*.'

CHAPTER II.

1. The sage asked the spirit of wisdom (2) thus: 'How is it possible to seek the maintenance and prosperity of the body [without injury of the soul, and the preservation of the soul without injury of the body[2]]?'

3. The spirit of wisdom answered (4) thus: 'Him who is less than thee consider as an equal, and an equal as a superior, (5) and a greater than him as a chieftain[3], and a chieftain as a ruler. 6. And among rulers *one* is to be acquiescent, obedient, and true-speaking; (7) *and* among accusers[4] be submissive, mild, and kindly regardful.

8. 'Commit no slander; (9) so that infamy and wickedness *may* not happen unto thee. 10. For it is said (11) that slander is more grievous than witchcraft; (12) and in hell the rush of every fiend[5] is to the front, *but* the rush of the fiend of slander, on account of the grievous sinfulness, is to the rear.

13. 'Form no covetous desire; (14) so that the

---

[1] Meaning, specially, the priests.

[2] The passage in brackets is omitted by K43, and is here supplied from L19.

[3] In L19 the text is corrupt, but has nearly the same meaning.

[4] L19 has 'associates,' which seems equally appropriate; the two words are much alike in Pahlavi writing.

[5] The word drûg, 'fiend,' is usually supposed to mean a female demon, and is often understood so in the Avesta, perhaps because it is a feminine noun. It is usually an impersonation of some evil passion (see Chap. XLI, 11).

demon of greediness *may* not deceive thee, (15) and the treasure of the world *may* not be tasteless to thee, and that of the spirit unperceived.

16. 'Indulge in no wrathfulness; (17) for a man, when he indulges in wrath, becomes then forgetful of his duty and good works, of prayer and the service of the sacred beings, (18) and sin and crime of every kind occur unto his mind, and[1] until the subsiding of the wrath (19) he[2] is said *to be* just like Aharman[3].

20. 'Suffer no anxiety; (21) for he who is a sufferer of anxiety becomes regardless of enjoyment of the world and the spirit, (22) and contraction happens to his body and soul.

23. 'Commit no lustfulness; (24) so that harm and regret *may* not reach thee from thine own actions.

25. 'Bear no improper envy; (26) so that thy life *may* not become tasteless.

27. 'Commit no sin on account of [disgrace][4]; (28) because happiness and adornment[5], celebrity (khanîdîh) and dominion, skill and suitability are not through the will and action of men, but through the appointment, destiny, and will of the sacred beings.

29. 'Practise no sloth; (30) so that the duty and good work, which it is necessary for thee to do, *may* not remain undone.

31. 'Choose a wife who is of character; (32)

---

[1] L19 omits 'and.'

[2] L19 has 'wrath;' making § 19 a separate sentence.

[3] The evil spirit, Av. angra mainyu.

[4] K43 omits 'disgrace,' by mistake.

[5] L19 omits 'adornment.'

because that *one* is good who in the end is more respected.

33. 'Commit no unseasonable chatter[1]; (34) so that grievous distress *may* not happen unto Ho*r*vada*d* and Ame*r*oda*d*, the archangels[2], through thee.

35. 'Commit no running about uncovered[3]; (36) so that harm *may* not come upon thy bipeds and quadrupeds, and ruin upon *thy* children.

37. 'Walk not with one boot[4]; (38) so that grievous distress *may* not happen to thy soul.

---

[1] A free translation of the name of the sin which is usually called drâyân-*g*ûyi*s*nîh, 'eagerness for chattering;' here, however, K43 omits the latter y, so that the name may be read drâyân-*gal*i*s*nîh, 'chatteringly devouring,' and a similar phrase is used in AV. XXIII, 6. The sin consists in talking while eating, praying, or at any other time when a murmured prayer (vâ*g*) has been taken inwardly and is not yet spoken out; the protective spell of the prayer being broken by such talking. If the prayer be not taken inwardly when it ought to be, the same sin is incurred (see Sls. V, 2, Dd. LXXIX, 8).

[2] Instead of amah*r*aspend, 'the archangel,' L19 has Mâr-spe*n*d, the angel of the 'righteous liturgy;' but this is probably a misreading, due to the fact that, when the chattering interrupts prayer, the angel of the liturgy would be as much distressed as the archangels Ho*r*vada*d* and Ame*r*oda*d*, who protect water and vegetation (see Sls. XV, 25–29), would be when it interrupts eating and drinking. These archangels are personifications of Av. haurvatâ*d*, 'completeness or health,' and ameretâ*d*, 'immortality.'

[3] That is, moving about without being girded with the Kustî or sacred thread-girdle, which must not be separated from the skin by more than one thin garment, the sacred shirt (see Sls. IV, 7, 8).

[4] We should probably read 'without a boot,' as aê-mûkŏ and amûkŏ are much alike in Pahlavi; otherwise we must suppose that walking with only a single covering for the feet, and without outer boots, is meant. At any rate, walking or standing on unconsecrated ground with bare feet is a serious sin for a Parsi, on account of the risk of pollution (see Sls. IV, 12, X, 12).

39. 'Perform no discharge of urine (pêsâr-vâr) *standing* on foot[1]; (40) so that thou mayst not become a captive by a habit of the demons, (41) and the demons may not drag thee to hell on account of that sin.

42. 'Thou shouldst be (yehevûnes) diligent and moderate, (43) and eat of thine own regular industry, (44) and provide the share of the sacred beings and the good; (45) and, thus, the practice of this, in thy occupation, is the greatest good work.

46. 'Do not extort from the wealth of others; (47) so that thine own regular industry *may* not become unheeded. 48. For it is said (49) that: "He who eats anything, not from his own regular industry, but from another, is such-like as *one* who holds a human head in *his* hand, and eats human brains."

50. 'Thou shouldst be an abstainer from the wives of others; (51) because all these three would become disregarded by thee, alike wealth, alike[2] body, and alike[2] soul.

52. 'With enemies fight with equity. 53. With a friend proceed with the approval of friends. 54. With a malicious[3] man carry on no conflict, (55) and do not molest him in any way whatever. 56. With a greedy man thou shouldst not be a partner, (57) and do not trust him with the leadership. 58. With

---

[1] Whereby an unnecessary space of ground is polluted; hence the sin.

[2] K43 has hômanam, 'I am,' the Huzvâris of am, used by mistake for ham, 'alike,' which is written exactly like am in Pahlavi.

[3] K43 has kîkvar, instead of kênvar, but this is doubtless a miswriting.

a slanderous man do not go to the door of kings. 59. With an ill-famed man form no connection. 60. With an ignorant man thou shouldst not become a confederate and associate. 61. With a foolish man make no dispute. 62. With a drunken man do not walk on the road. 63. From an ill-natured man take no loan.

64. 'In thanksgiving unto the sacred beings, and worship, praise, ceremonies, invocation, and performing the learning of knowledge thou shouldst be energetic and life-expending. 65. For it is said (66) that: "In aid of the contingencies (*g*ahis*n*ŏ)[1] among men wisdom is good; (67) in seeking renown and preserving the soul liberality is good; (68) in the advancement of business and justice complete mindfulness is good; (69) and in the statements of those who confess (khûstîvân)[2], with a bearing on the custom of the law[3], truth is good. 70. In the progress of business energy is good, (71) for[4] every one to become confident therein steadfastness is good, (72) and for the coming of benefit thereto thankfulness is good. 73. In keeping oneself untroubled (anaîrang)[5] the discreet speaking which is in the path of[6] truth is good; (74) and in keeping away the disturbance of the destroyer[7] from oneself employment is good. 75.

[1] L19 has zahis*n*, 'issue, proceedings.'

[2] L19 has read aûstîkân, 'the steadfast,' by mistake.

[3] Reading dâ*d*ŏ-khûk-baris*n*ŏîhâ. L19 has 'conveying intercession (*g*âda*n*gô=dâ*d*ŏ-gôk);' this small difference in reading may be a clerical error in K43. The Sans. version omits the phrase altogether.

[4] L19 omits pavan, 'for.'

[5] Nêr. has 'unblemished.'

[6] L19 omits 'path of;' and it may possibly be superfluous.

[7] Or it may be 'the destroyer and adversary,' as in L19; the last word being defective in K43.

Before rulers and kings discreet speaking is good, and in[1] an assembly good recital; (76) among friends repose and rational friends[2] are good; (77) and with an associate to one's own deeds the giving of advantage (sûkŏ) is good. 78. Among those greater than one (*agas* masân) mildness and humility are good, (79) and among those less than one flattery[3] and civility are good. 80. Among doers of deeds speaking of thanks and performance of generosity are good; (81) and among those of the same race the formation of friendship (hûmânŏîh)[4] is good. 82. For bodily health moderate eating and keeping the body in action are good; (83) and among the skilled in thanksgiving performance is good. 84. Among chieftains unanimity and seeking advantage are good; (85) among those in unison and servants good behaviour and an exhibition of awe are good; (86) and for having little trouble in oneself contentment is good. 87. In chieftainship to understand thoroughly the good in *their* goodness and the vile in *their* vileness is good; *and* to make the vile unseen, through retribution[5], is good. 88. In every place and time to restrain oneself from sin and to be diligent in meritorious work are good; (89) and every day to consider *and* keep in remembrance Aûha*r*ma*zd*, as regards creativeness, and Aharman, as regards destructiveness, is good. 90. *And* for dishonour not to come unto one a knowledge of oneself is good." 91. All these are proper

[1] L19 omits pavan, 'in.'

[2] L19 has 'friendship.'

[3] Or 'adaptation.'

[4] L19 has humatî, 'good intention.'

[5] L19 has 'to cause the reward of the good and the punishment of the vile.'

and true and of the same description, (92) but occupation and guarding the tongue (pâ*d*-hûzvânîh)[1] above everything.

93. 'Abstain far from the service of idols[2] and demon-worship. 94. Because *it* is declared (95) that: "If Kaî-Khûsrôî[3] should not have extirpated the idol-temples (aûgdês-*k*âr) which *were* on the lake of *K*ê*k*ast[4], then in these three millenniums *of* Hûshê*d*ar, Hûshê*d*ar-mâh, and Sôshâns[5]—of whom one of them comes separately at the end of each millennium, who arranges again all[6] the affairs of the world, and utterly destroys the breakers of promises and servers of idols who are in the realm—the adversary[7] would have become so much more violent, that it would not have been possible to produce the resurrection and future existence."

96. 'In forming a store[8] of good works thou

---

[1] L19 has 'preserving pure language.'

[2] More correctly 'temple-worship,' as aûzdês means 'an erection.'

[3] Av. Kavi Husravangh, the third of the Kayân kings, who reigned sixty years, and was the grandson of his predecessor, Kâî-Ûs, and son of Sîyâvakhsh (see Bd. XXXI, 25, XXXIV, 7).

[4] The present Lake Urumiyah according to Bd. XXII, 2. This feat of Kaî-Khûsrôî is also mentioned in Bd. XVII, 7, and his exploits in the same neighbourhood are stated in Âbân Yt. 49, 50, Gô*s* Yt. 18, 21, 22, Ashi Yt. 38, 41, 42; but it is possible that the Avesta name, *K*aê*k*asta, may have been transferred to Lake Urumiyah in later times.

[5] The three future apostles who are supposed to be sons of Zaratû*s*t, whose births have been deferred till later times (see Bd. XXXII, 8). Their Avesta names are Ukhshya*d*-ereta, Ukhshya*d*-nemangh, and Saoshyãs.

[6] L19 omits 'all.'

[7] The evil spirit.

[8] L19 has 'in always doing;' having read hamvâr, 'always,' instead of ambâr, 'a store.'

shouldst be diligent, (97) so that it *may* come to *thy*[1] assistance among the spirits.

98. 'Thou shouldst not become presumptuous through any happiness of the world; (99) for the happiness of the world is such-like as a cloud that comes on a rainy day, which one does not ward off by any hill.

100. 'Thou shouldst not be *too* much arranging the world; (101) for the world-arranging man becomes spirit-destroying.

102. 'Thou shouldst not become presumptuous through much treasure and wealth; (103) for in the end it is necessary for thee to leave all.

104. 'Thou shouldst not become presumptuous through predominance; (105) for in the end it is necessary for thee to become non-predominant.

106. 'Thou shouldst not become presumptuous through respect and reverence; (107) for respectfulness does not assist in the spiritual *existence*.

108. 'Thou shouldst not become presumptuous through great connections and race; (109) for in the end thy[2] trust is on thine own deeds.

110. 'Thou shouldst not become presumptuous through life; (111) for death comes upon thee[3] *at* last, (112) the dog and the bird lacerate the corpse[4], (113) and the perishable *part* (segînakŏ)[5] falls to the ground. 114. During three days[6] and nights

---

[1] K43 omits 'thy.' [2] L19 omits 'thy.'

[3] L19 omits 'thee.'

[4] Referring to the mode of disposing of the dead adopted by the Parsis (see Sls. II, 6n, Dd. XV, 5, XVII, 17, XVIII, 2-4).

[5] L19 has ast, 'bone.'

[6] Including the day of death. The fate of the soul after death, as detailed in §§ 114-194, is also described in Vend. XIX, 90-112, Hn. II, III, Aog. 8-19, AV. IV-XI, XVII.

the soul sits at the crown of the head of the body[1].
115. And the fourth day, in the light of dawn—with the co-operation of Srôsh the righteous, Vâê the good, and Vâhrâm the strong[2], the opposition of Astô-vîdâd[3], Vâê the bad[4], Frazîstô the demon, and Nizîstô the demon[5], and the evil-designing action of Aeshm[6], the evil-doer, the impetuous assailant—

---

[1] Reciting a passage from the Gâthas or sacred hymns (see Hn. II, 4, 5, III, 3, 4, AV. IV, 9–11, XVII, 6, 7).

[2] These three angels are personifications of Av. sraosha, 'listening, obedience,' vaya or vayu, 'the upper air (uncontaminated by the evil spirit),' and verethraghna, 'victorious, triumphant;' the last is more literally 'demon-smiting,' that is, 'smiting Verethra (the demon),' Sans. vritrahan.

[3] Av. Astô-vîdhôtu, 'the bone-dislocator,' or demon of death who binds the parting soul (see Vend. V, 25, 31); in later writings, such as the Book of Dâdâr bin Dâd-dukht, he is said to throw a noose over the neck of the soul to drag it to hell, but if its good works have exceeded its sins, it throws off the noose and goes to heaven; and this noose is also mentioned in Bd. III, 22, Dd. XXIII, 3. In Bd. XXVIII, 35 this demon is said to be the same as the bad Vâê, but all other authorities consider them as distinct beings. It may be noted that a different demon of death is usually mentioned when the soul is wicked (see § 161).

[4] Av. vaya or vayu, 'the lower air (vitiated by the evil spirit).' Just as the wind (vâd) may be either an angel or a demon, according as its strength makes it a refreshing breeze or a violent hurricane, so may the air be a good or evil being, according as it retains its original purity or has been vitiated by the evil spirit. That the angel Vâê is the upper air appears from its epithet uparô-kairya, 'working aloft,' in the Râm Yt.; and that it is only the lower air that is vitiated by the evil spirit is in accordance with the division of the sky into three thirds, of which the uppermost is inaccessible to the evil spirit (see Dd. XXXVII, 24–31). But this distinction between a good and bad Vâê is not made in Vend. V, 25, 31, where we are told that Vayô conveys the soul when bound by Astô-vîdhôtu.

[5] These two demons have not been recognised elsewhere.

[6] The demon of wrath, Av. Aêshmô daêva, appears to be the Asmodeus of the Book of Tobit.

[it goes][1] up to the awful, lofty *K*indvar[2] bridge, to which every one, righteous and wicked, is coming[3]. 116. And many opponents have watched there, (117) with the desire of evil of Aeshm, the impetuous assailant, and of Astô-vîdâ*d* who devours creatures of every kind and knows no satiety, (118) and the mediation of Mit*r*ô[4] and Srôsh and Rashnû, (119) and the weighing of Rashnû, the just, (120) with the balance[5] *of* the spirits, which renders no favour (hû-girâî) *on* any side[6], neither for the righteous nor yet the wicked, neither for the lords nor yet the monarchs. 121. As much as a hair's breadth it will not turn, and has no partiality; (122) and he who is a lord and monarch[7] it considers equally, in *its* decision, with him who is the least *of* mankind.

123. 'And when a soul of the righteous passes upon that bridge, the width of the bridge becomes as it were a league (parasang)[8], (124) and the

[1] K43 omits this verb.

[2] Or, perhaps, *K*ingvar, a partial translation of Av. *K*inva*d* (gv being a mispronunciation of v or w, as in gvâ*d* for vâ*d*, 'wind;' and Pers. var translating Av. va*d*). The Pâzand writers have *K*a*n*dôr. It is the bridge of ever-varying breadth which leads to heaven (see Vend. XIX, 100, 101, AV. III, 1, IV, 7, V, 1, 2, XVII, 1, Bd. XII, 7, Dd. XX, XXI), but it is not mentioned in Hn.

[3] Literally, 'is a comer.'

[4] The angel of the sun's light; being a personification of friendship and good faith he is specially concerned in calling the soul to account (see Dd. XIV, 3).

[5] In which the actions of men are weighed by Rashnû, the angel of justice, to ascertain whether the good or the evil preponderate.

[6] L19 has 'who makes no unjust balance of the spirits on either side.'

[7] K43 adds ra*d*, 'master,' but this is evidently an abortive beginning of the next word, levatman, which has been left unerased.

[8] Nine spears (about 126 English feet) in AV. V, 1, Dd. XXI, 5.

righteous soul passes over with the co-operation of Srôsh the righteous. 125. And his own deeds of a virtuous kind[1] come to meet him in the form of a maiden, (126) who is handsomer and better than every maiden in the world.

127. 'And the righteous soul speaks (128) thus: "Who mayst thou be[2], that a maiden who is handsomer and better than thee *was* never seen by me in the worldly *existence?*"

129. 'In reply that maiden form responds (130) thus: "I am no maiden, but I am thy virtuous deeds, *thou* youth who *art* well-thinking, well-speaking, well-doing, *and* of good religion! 131. For when thou sawest in the world *him* who performed demon-worship, then thou hast sat down, and thy performance *was* the worship of the sacred beings. 132. And when *it was* seen by thee that *there was* any one who caused oppression and plunder, and distressed *or* scorned a good person, and acquired wealth by crime, then thou keptest back from the creatures their own *risk of* oppression and plunder; (133) the good person *was* also thought of by thee, and lodging and entertainment provided; and alms *were* given by thee *to him* (134) who came forth from near and *him*, too, who *was* from afar; and wealth which *was* due to honesty *was* acquired by thee. 135. And when thou sawest *him* who practised

The parasang is probably used here as an equivalent for Av. hâthra, 'a mile.'

[1] L19 has 'his own virtuous deeds.' The conscience of the soul meets it in the form of a damsel, beautiful in proportion to the goodness of its deeds. In AV. IV, 18–36, Dd. XXIV, 5, XXV, 5 the conscience meets the soul before it attempts the bridge.

[2] More literally, 'what may be thou?' as the verb is in the third person here, though not so in the similar phrase in § 169.

false justice and taking of bribes, and false evidence *was* given by him, then thou hast sat down, and the recitation of truth and virtue[1] *was* uttered by thee. 136. I am this of thine, the good thoughts, the good words, and the good deeds which *were* thought and spoken and done by thee. 137. For when I have become commendable, I am then made altogether more commendable by thee; (138) when I have become precious, I am then made altogether still more precious by thee; (139) and when I have become glorious, I am then made altogether[2] still more glorious by thee."

140. 'And when he walks onwards from there, a sweet-scented breeze comes then to meet him, which is more fragrant than all perfume. 141. The soul of the righteous enquires of Srôsh (142) thus: "What breeze is this, that never in the world so fragrant a breeze came into contact with me?"

143. 'Then Srôsh, the righteous, replies to that righteous soul (144) thus: "This breeze is from heaven, which is so fragrant."

145. 'Afterwards, on *his* march, the first step is set[3] on *the place of* good thoughts, the second on *that of* good words, the third on *that of* good deeds[4], (146) and the fourth step reaches up unto the endless light[5] which is all-radiant. 147. And angels

[1] Meaning probably the recitation of the Avesta texts.

[2] K43 omits bar*â*, 'quite, altogether,' in this third clause.

[3] L19 has 'afterwards, he rests the first step;' but awar ârâme*d*, 'he rests,' is a misreading of madam khârâm dâ*d*, 'on the march is set.'

[4] These are the three lowermost grades of heaven, hûmat, hûkht, and hûvar*s*t (see Chap. VII, 12).

[5] The highest grade of heaven, where Aûhar*m*a*zd* and the angels are supposed to dwell (see Chap. VII, 11).

and archangels of every description come to meet him, (148) and ask tidings from him (149) thus: "How hast thou come, from that which is a perishable, fearful, *and* very miserable existence, to this which is an imperishable existence that is undisturbed, *thou* youth who *art* well-thinking, well-speaking, well-doing, *and* of good religion?"

150. 'Then Aûhar*m*a*zd*, the lord, speaks (151) thus: "Ask ye from him no tidings; for *he has* parted from that which *was* a precious body, and has come by that which is a fearful road. 152. And bring ye unto him the most agreeable of eatables, that which is the midspring butter[1], (153) so that he *may* rest his soul from that bridge of the three nights, unto which he came from Astô-vîdâ*d* and the remaining demons[2]; (154) and seat him upon an all-embellished throne."

155. 'As *it is* declared (156) that: "Unto[3] the righteous man[4] and woman, after passing away[5], they bring food[6] of the most agreeable of eatables—

[1] The Maidhyô-zarm rôghan, which is explained in Dd. XXXI, 14 as the spiritual representative of butter made during the Maidhyô-zaremaya, 'mid-verdure,' festival, which was considered the best of the year. This festival is held on the forty-fifth day of the Parsi year, which was about 4th May when the year was fixed to begin at the vernal equinox as described in Bd. XXV, 3–7, 20. The heavenly food which goes by this name is not to be confounded with the Hûsh which is expected to be prepared at the resurrection, from the fat of the ox Hadhayôs and the white Hôm, for the purpose of making mankind immortal (see Bd. XXX, 25); although some such confusion appears to exist in AV. X, 5. K43 has rûbân, 'soul,' instead of rôghan, 'butter.'

[2] See §§ 114–123.

[3] K43 omits 'unto.'

[4] Literally, 'male.'

[5] L19 adds 'from the body and consciousness.'

[6] Reading kazag, instead of kazad, both here and in the next clause of the sentence. L19 has 'the angels of the spiritual *exist-*

the food of the angels of the spiritual *existences*— that which is the midspring butter[1]; and they seat them down on an all-embellished throne. 157. For ever and everlasting they remain in all glory with the angels of the spiritual *existences* everlastingly."

158. 'And when he who is wicked dies, his soul then rushes *about for* three days and nights in the vicinity of the head of that wicked *one*, and sobs[2] (159) thus: "Whither do I go, and now what do I make[3] as a refuge?" 160. And the sin and crime of every kind, that *were* committed by him in the worldly *existence*, he sees with *his* eyes in those three days and nights. 161. The fourth day Vîzaresh[4], the demon, comes and binds the soul of the wicked with the very evil noose[5]; (162) and with the opposition of Srôsh, the righteous, he leads *it* up to the *K*indvar bridge[6]. 163. Then Rashnû[7], the just, detects that soul of the wicked through *its* wickedness.

164. 'Afterwards, Vîzaresh, the demon, takes that

---

ences bring the most agreeable of eatables,' by omitting the first kazag, and misreading the second one.

[1] K43 has rûbân again, as in § 152, for rôghan. Although this sentence resembles Hn. II, 38, 39, it is evidently quoted from some other source, as its difference is more striking than its resemblance.

[2] This verb is Huz. bekhûnê*d*=Pâz. giryê*d*, but Nêr. has read bângînê*d*, 'laments,' and has written vãgine*d*.

[3] Or it may be 'take,' as these two verbs are written alike in Huzvâri*s*. This exclamation is a quotation from the Gâthas or sacred hymns, being the first line of Yas. XLV, 1.

[4] The Av. Vîzaresha of Vend. XIX, 94, who carries off the souls of the wicked; he is also mentioned in Bd. XXVIII, 18, Dd. XXXII, 4, 7, XXXVII, 44.

[5] Reading saryâtar *s*û*l*an. L19 has va*d* ba*n*d, 'an evil tie.'

[6] See § 115.

[7] See §§ 119, 120.

soul of the wicked, and mercilessly and maliciously beats *and* maltreats *it*. 165. And that soul of the wicked weeps with a loud voice, is fundamentally horrified[1], implores with many supplicating[2] entreaties, and makes many struggles for life disconnectedly[3]. 166. Whom[4]—when his struggling and supplication are of no avail whatever, and no one comes to his assistance from the divinities (bagân)[5], nor yet from the demons—moreover, Vîzaresh, the demon, drags miserably[6] to the inevitable[7] hell.

167. 'And then a maiden who is not like unto maidens comes to meet him. 168. And that soul of the wicked speaks to that evil maiden (169) thus: "Who mayst thou be, that never in the worldly *existence was* an evil maiden seen by me, who *was* viler and more hideous than thee?"

170. 'And she[8] speaks in reply to him (171) thus: "I *am* not a maiden, but I am thy deeds[9], *thou* monster who *art* evil-thinking, evil-speaking, evil-doing, *and* of evil religion! 172. For even when thou sawest[10] *him* who performed the worship of the sacred beings, still then thou hast sat down, and demon-worship *was* performed by thee, (173) and the demons and fiends *were* served. 174. And also when thou sawest *him* who provided lodging and

---

[1] Instead of burz-vângîhâ bekhûnê*d*, bun râmê*d*, L19 has burzâva*n*dihâ văgîne*d* u vârâme*d*, 'loudly shrieks and weeps.'

[2] Reading lâpakŏ-karîhâ.

[3] Instead of apa*d*vandîhâ, L19 has apatûihâ, 'fruitlessly.'

[4] L19 has 'and.'

[5] L19 has vehă, 'the good.'

[6] Instead of âk-hômandîhâ, L19 has anaom*e*dihâ, 'hopelessly.'

[7] Reading nagirz, but this is uncertain; L19 has az*e*r, 'lower.'

[8] L19 has 'that evil maiden.'

[9] L19 has 'evil deeds.'

[10] L19 adds 'in the world.'

entertainment, and gave alms, *for* a good person who came forth from near and *him*, too, who *was* from afar[1], (175) then thou actedst scornfully and disrespectfully *to* the good person, and gave no alms, and even shut up the door. 176. And when thou sawest *him* who practised true justice, took no bribe, gave true evidence, and uttered virtuous recitation, (177) even then thou hast sat down, and false justice *was* practised by thee, evidence *was* given by thee with falsehood, and vicious recitation *was* uttered by thee. 178. I am this of thine, the evil thoughts, the evil words, and the evil deeds which *were* thought and spoken and done by thee. 179. For when I have become uncommendable, I am then made altogether still more uncommendable by thee; (180) when I have become unrespected, I am then made altogether still more unrespected by thee; (181) and when I have sat in an eye-offending[2] position, I am then made altogether still more really eye-offending (*k*ashm-kah-î*k*tar-i*k*) by thee."

182. 'Afterwards he enters[3], the first step on *the place of* evil thoughts, the second on *that of* evil words, the third step on *that of* evil deeds[4], (183) and the fourth step rushes into the presence of the

[1] In L19 the words 'near' and 'afar' change places.

[2] Literally, 'eye-consuming,' the reading adopted by Nêr., but, though it gives a satisfactory meaning, it is not quite certain that it represents the Pahlavi text correctly.

[3] For dên vazlûnê*d*, 'he goes in,' L19 has a*n*dar zrôve*d*, indicating that the first letter, va, of vazlûnê*d* had been omitted in the Pahl. MS. used by Nêr., which misled him into reading the remaining letters as a new Pâz. verb zrôve*d*, as already remarked by Nöldeke in Göt. gel. Anz. 1882, p. 975.

[4] These are the three uppermost grades of hell, dû*s*-hûmat, dû*s*-hûkht, and dû*s*-hûvar*s*t (see Chap. VII, 20).

wicked evil spirit and the other demons[1]. 184. And the demons make ridicule and mockery of him (185) thus: "What was thy trouble and complaint, as regards Aûharmazd, the lord, and the archangels, and the fragrant and joyful heaven, when thou approachedst for a sight of Aharman and the demons and gloomy hell, (186) although we cause thee misery therein and do not pity, and thou shalt see misery of long duration?"

187. 'And the evil spirit shouts to the demons (188) thus: "Ask ye no tidings from him (189) who is parted *from*[2] that which *was* a precious body, and has come on by that which is a very bad road. 190. But bring ye unto him the foulest and vilest of eatables, the food which is nurtured in hell."

191. 'They bring the poison and venom of[3] the snake and scorpion and other noxious creatures that are in hell, (192) and give him to eat. 193. And until the resurrection and future existence he must be in hell, in much misery and punishment of various kinds[4]. 194. Especially that it is possible to eat food there only as though by similitude[5].'

195. The spirit of innate wisdom spoke to the sage (196) thus: 'This which *was* asked by thee, as to the maintenance of the body *and* concerning the preservation of the soul, is also spoken about by me, and thou art admonished. 197. Be virtuously

[1] In the lowermost grade of hell (see Chap. VII, 21).

[2] L19 has 'for *he has* parted from,' as in § 151.

[3] L19 has 'and.'

[4] L19 has 'he is in much misery and punishment of kinds worthy of hell.'

[5] So that starvation is one of the punishments of hell. L19 has 'and especially that the food there can be only like putrid blood.'

assiduous about it, and keep *it* in practice; (198) for this is thy chief way for the maintenance of the body *and* preservation of the soul.'

CHAPTER III.

1. The sage asked the spirit of wisdom (2) thus: 'Is liberality good, or truth[1], (3) or gratitude[2], or wisdom, (4) or complete mindfulness[3], or contentment?'

5. The spirit of wisdom answered (6) thus: 'As to the soul *it is* liberality, as to all the world *it is* truth, (7) unto the sacred beings *it is* gratitude, as to a man's self[4] *it is* wisdom, (8) as to all business *it is* complete mindfulness, and as to the comfort of the body and the vanquishing of Aharman and the demons contentment is good.'

CHAPTER IV.

1. The sage asked the spirit of wisdom (2) thus: 'Which is a good work *that is* great and good?'

3. The spirit of wisdom answered (4) thus: 'The greatest good work is liberality, and the second is truth and next-of-kin marriage[5]. 5. The third is

---

[1] K43 has 'or thy truth.' [2] L19 has 'or is gratitude good.'

[3] L19 has 'or is complete mindfulness good.'

[4] Literally, 'the body of a man.'

[5] This was the meaning of the term khvêtûk-das when this work was written, but some centuries ago such marriages were discontinued, and the term was then confined to marriages between first cousins, as at present (see Sacred Books of the East, vol. xviii, app. III).

keeping the season festivals[1], *and* the fourth is *celebrating* all the religious rites[2]. 6. The fifth is the ceremonial of the sacred beings, and the providing of lodging for traders[3]. 7. The sixth is the wishing of happiness for every one. 8. *And* the seventh is a kind regard for the good[4].'

Chapter V.

1. The sage asked the spirit of wisdom (2) thus: 'Which land is the happier[5]?'

3. The spirit of wisdom answered (4) thus: 'That land is the happier, in which a righteous man, who is true-speaking, makes his abode. 5. The second,

---

[1] Of which there are six, each held for five days. These Gâsânbârs or Gâhambârs end, respectively, on the 45th, 105th, 180th, 210th, 290th, and 365th days of the Parsi year; and when that year was fixed to begin at the vernal equinox, they celebrated the periods of midspring, midsummer, the beginning of autumn, the beginning of winter, midwinter, and the beginning of spring (see Sls. XVIII, 3). In modern times they have been supposed to commemorate the several creations of the sky, water, earth, vegetation, animals, and man; but this idea must have been borrowed from a foreign source.

[2] The periodical ceremonies which are obligatory for all Parsis (see Dd. XLIV, 2 n).

[3] Literally, 'for the producers of business.'

[4] That is, for the priests. The Parsi-Persian version divides these good works into nine items, by counting 'next-of-kin marriage' as the third, and 'providing of lodging' as the seventh. For a fuller detail of good works, see Chap. XXXVII.

[5] This chapter is an imitation of Vend. III, 1–20, where it is stated that the five most pleasing spots on the earth are, first, where a righteous man performs ceremonies; second, where he has built his house and keeps his fire, cattle, family, and retainers; third, where the land is best cultivated; fourth, where most oxen and sheep are produced; and fifth, that which is most manured by oxen and sheep.

in which they make the abode of fires. 6. The third, when oxen and sheep repose upon it. 7. The fourth is uncultivated and uninhabited land when they bring *it* back to cultivation and habitableness. 8. The fifth, from which they extirpate the burrows of noxious creatures. 9. The sixth, on which exist the ceremonies and coming of the sacred beings, and the sitting of the good[1]. 10. The seventh, when they make populous that which *was* desolate. 11. The eighth, when from the possession of the bad it comes into the possession of the good. 12. The ninth, when of the produce and yield (bê*d*ŏ) which arise from it they provide the share of the sacred beings, the good, and the worthy. 13. *And* the tenth, in which they provide holy-water and ceremonies.'

Chapter VI.

1. The sage asked the spirit of wisdom (2) thus: 'Which land is the unhappier[2]?'

3. The spirit of wisdom answered (4) thus: 'That land is the more afflicted, in which hell is formed[3]. 5. The second, when they slay in it a righteous man who is innocent. 6. The third, for whose sake[4]

---

[1] That is, the ceremonial precinct where the priests sit to conduct the ceremonies.

[2] This chapter is an imitation of Vend. III, 21–37, where it is stated that the five most unpleasing spots on the earth are, first, the ridge of Arezûra, on which the demons congregate from the pit of the fiend; second, where most dead dogs and men lie buried; third, where most depositories for the dead are constructed; fourth, where there are most burrows of the creatures of the evil spirit; and fifth, where the family of a righteous man is driven into captivity.

[3] Bd. III, 27 states that 'hell is in the middle of the earth.'

[4] Reading mûn . . . rûnŏ-î pa*das*. Instead of drû*g*ân rûnŏ,

the demons and fiends work. 7. The fourth, in which they construct an idol-temple. 8. The fifth, when a wicked man, who is an evil-doer, makes an abode in it. 9. The sixth, when the interment of a corpse is performed below[1]. 10. The seventh, in which a noxious creature has a burrow. 11. The eighth, when from the possession of the good it comes into the possession of the bad. 12. The ninth, when they make desolate that which *was* populous. 13. *And* the tenth, in which they make lamentation and weeping[2].'

Chapter VII.

1. The sage asked the spirit of wisdom (2) thus: 'How is heaven, and how many? 3. How are the ever-stationary (hamîstân), and how many? 4. And how is hell, and how many? 5. What is the decision *about* the righteous in heaven, and from what is *their* happiness? 6. What are the misery and affliction of the wicked in hell? 7. And what and how is the decision *about* those who are among the ever-stationary?'

8. The spirit of wisdom answered (9) thus: 'Heaven is, first, from the star station unto the

Nêr. has read drûg hanrûnŏ, and assumed the last word to be equivalent to Av. handvarena, 'concourse;' so as to obtain the meaning, 'in which the demons and the fiend form a congress.' But Av. handvarena is Pahl. ham-dûbârisnîh (see Pahl. Vend. VII, 137).

[1] Or 'when much interment of corpses is performed,' as it is doubtful whether we ought to read avîr, 'much,' or azîr, 'below.'

[2] That is, for the dead. Such outward manifestations of mourning being considered sinful by the Parsis, as they ought to be by all unselfish people who believe in a future existence of happiness.

moon station; (10) second, from the moon station unto the sun; (11) *and*, third, from the sun station unto the supreme heaven (garô*d*mânô), whereon the creator Aûha*r*ma*z*d is seated. 12. Of heaven the first *part* is *that of* good thoughts (hûmatô), the second is *that of* good words (hûkhtô), and the third is *that of* good deeds (hûvar*s*tô).

13. 'The righteous in heaven are undecaying and immortal, unalarmed, undistressed, and undisturbed. 14. And, everywhere [1], they are full of glory, fragrant, and joyful, full of delight and full of happiness. 15. And, *at* all times, a fragrant breeze and a scent which is like sweet basil come to meet *them*, which are more pleasant than every pleasure, and more fragrant than every fragrance. 16. For them, also, there is no satiety owing to the existence in heaven. 17. And their sitting and walking, perception and enjoyment are with the angels and archangels and the righteous for ever and everlasting.

18. 'Regarding the ever-stationary *it* is declared, that *they are* from the earth unto the star station; (19) and its affliction for them is then [2] nothing whatever except cold and heat.

20. 'Of hell the first *part* is *that of* evil thoughts (dû*s*-hûmatô), the second is *that of* evil words (dû*s*-hûkhtô), and the third is *that of* evil deeds

[1] Nêr. has 'at all times,' which may be correct, as gâs means both 'time' and 'place.' It should be noticed, however, that the word used in § 15 is damân, which means 'time' only.

[2] Nêr. has 'their affliction is otherwise,' by mistaking Huz. adîna*s*-*s*ân, 'then its . . . for them,' for a supposed Pâz. ainâ*s*ã, 'otherwise their,' which seems to have no real existence, as wherever he reads ainâ, 'otherwise,' the Pahl. text has adîna*s*, 'then its.'

(dûs-hûvarstô)[1]. 21. *With* the fourth step the wicked person arrives at that which is the darkest hell; (22) and they lead him forwards to the vicinity of Aharman, the wicked. 23. And Aharman and the demons, thereupon, make ridicule and mockery of him (24) thus[2]: "What was thy trouble and complaint, as regards Aûharmazd and the archangels, and the fragrant and joyful heaven, when thou approachedst for a sight of us and gloomy hell, (25) although we cause thee misery therein and do not pity, and thou shalt see misery of long duration?" 26. And, afterwards, they execute punishment and torment of various kinds upon him.

27. 'There is a place[3] where, as to cold, *it* is such as that of the coldest frozen[4] snow. 28. There is a place where, as to heat, *it* is such as that of the hottest and most blazing fire. 29. There is a place where noxious creatures are gnawing them, just as a dog *does* the bones. 30. There is a place where, as to stench, *it* is such that they stagger about (barâ larzênd)[5] *and* fall down. 31. And the dark-

---

[1] These names, as here written, mean literally 'evil good thoughts, evil good words, and evil good deeds,' as if they implied that these places are for those whose best thoughts, words, and deeds are evil; but it is not quite certain that the Pahlavi names are spelt correctly.

[2] As already stated in Chap. II, 183–186.

[3] L19 has 'he is experienced' in §§ 27–30, owing to Nêr. having read dânâk, 'knowing, experienced,' instead of dîvâk, 'a place.'

[4] Literally, 'stone-possessing, stony' if we read sang-dâr, as seems most plausible; but we might read sôkhâr and consider Pers. khasâr or khasar, 'ice,' as a corruption of it, by transposition. L19 has 'ice (yah) and snow.'

[5] L19 has be rezend, 'they vomit up,' which is evidently a misreading.

ness is always such-like as though it is possible for them to seize upon *it* with the hand[1].'

CHAPTER VIII.

1. The sage asked the spirit of wisdom (2) thus: 'How and in what manner *has* Aûharmazd created these creatures and creation? 3. And how and in what manner *were* the archangels and the spirit of wisdom formed and created by him? 4. And how are the demons and fiends [and also the remaining corrupted *ones*][2] of Aharman, the wicked, miscreated? [5. How do every good and evil happen which *occur* to mankind and also the remaining creatures?] 6. And is it possible to alter anything which is destined, or not?'

7. The spirit of wisdom answered (8) thus: 'The creator, Aûharmazd, produced these creatures and creation, the archangels and the spirit of wisdom from that which is his own splendour, and with the blessing of unlimited time (zôrvân). 9. For this reason, because unlimited time is undecaying and immortal, painless and hungerless, thirstless and undisturbed; and for ever and everlasting no one is able to seize upon *it*, *or* to make *it* non-predominant as regards his own affairs.

10. 'And Aharman, the wicked, miscreated the demons and fiends, and also the remaining corrupted

---

[1] 'Even darkness *which* may be felt' (Ex. x. 21).

[2] K43 omits the phrase in brackets, as well as § 5; but these passages are supplied from L19, merely substituting yahidakân, 'corrupted ones,' as in § 10, for the vashûdagã, 'miscreations,' of L19.

ones[1], by his own unnatural intercourse. 11. A treaty of nine thousand winters[2] in unlimited time (damân) *was* also made by him with Aûharmazd; (12) and, until it *has* become fully completed, no one is able to alter *it* and to act otherwise. 13. And when the nine thousand years *have* become completed, Aharman is quite impotent; (14) and Srôsh[3], the righteous, will smite Aeshm[3], (15) *and* Mitrô[4] and unlimited time and the spirit of justice[5], who deceives no one in anything, and destiny and divine providence[6] will smite the creatures and creation of Aharman of every kind, and, in the end, even Âzŏ[7], the demon. 16. And every creature and creation of Aûharmazd becomes again as undisturbed as those which *were* produced and created by him in the beginning.

---

[1] Reading yahidakân, but it may be yâtukân, 'wizards,' though the word requires an additional long vowel to represent either term correctly. L19 has vashûdagã, 'miscreations.'

[2] According to the Bundahis, time consists of twelve thousand years (see Bd. XXXIV, 1). In the beginning Aûharmazd created the spiritual prototypes (Bd. I, 8) who remained undisturbed for the first three thousand years, when Aharman appeared and agreed to a conflict for the remaining nine thousand years (Bd. I, 18), during the first three of which Aûharmazd's will was undisputed, while during the next three Aharman is active in interference, and during the last three his influence will diminish till, in the end, it will disappear (Bd. I, 20). The nine thousand years of the conflict were supposed to extend from about B.C. 5400 to A.D. 3600 (see Byt. III, 11 n, 44 n).

[3] See Chap. II, 115.

[4] See Chap. II, 118.

[5] Probably the angel Rashnû (see Chap. II, 118, 119).

[6] Assuming that the vâgô-bakhtô of K43 is equivalent to the baghô-bakht, 'divine appointment,' of L19.

[7] Av. âzi of Yas. XVII, 46, LXVII, 22, Vend. XVIII, 45, 50, Âstâd Yt. 1, âzu of Yas. LII, 7, and the demon of 'greediness' in Chap. II, 13, 14, XVIII, 5, &c., Bd. XXVIII, 27, and modern Persian, who seems to be a being distinct from Av. azi, 'serpent.'

17. 'Every good and the reverse[1] which happen to mankind, and also the other creatures, happen through the seven *planets* and the twelve *constellations*[2]. 18. And those twelve constellations are such as in revelation are[3] the twelve chieftains who are on the side of Aûharmazd, (19) *and* those seven planets are called the seven chieftains who are on the side of Aharman. 20. Those seven planets pervert every creature and creation, and deliver *them* up to death and every evil. 21. And, as *it were*, those twelve constellations and seven planets[4] are organizing and managing the world.

22. 'Aûharmazd is wishing good, and never approves nor contemplates evil. 23. Aharman is wishing evil, and does not meditate nor approve anything good whatever. 24. Aûharmazd, when he wishes it, is able to alter as regards the creatures of Aharman; and Aharman, too, it is, who, when [he wishes][5] it, *can do so* as regards the creatures of Aûharmazd, (25) but *he* is *only* able to alter so that in the final effect *there may* be no injury of Aûharmazd, (26) because the final victory is Aûharmazd's own. 27. For it is declared, that "the Yim[6] and

---

[1] L19 has 'evil.'

[2] The zodiacal signs.

[3] L19 has 'are called in revelation.' The authority, here quoted, was not the Bundahis, because that book speaks of seven chieftains of the constellations opposed to the seven planets (see Bd. V, 1).

[4] L19 omits 'and seven planets,' but has a blank space at this place in both texts, Pâzand and Sanskrit.

[5] K43 omits the words in brackets, which may, perhaps, be superfluous in the Pahlavi text.

[6] Av. Yima or Yima khshaêta of Vend. II, the Jamshêd of the Shâhnâmah, some of whose deeds are mentioned in Chap. XXVII, 24–33, Yas. IX, 13–20. He was the third of the Pêsdâd dynasty, and is said to have been perverted by Aharman in his old

Frê*d*ûn[1] and Kâî-Ûs[2] of Aûha*r*ma*zd* are created immortal, (28) and Aharman so altered *them* as is known. 29. *And* Aharman so contemplated that Bêvarâsp[3] and Frâsîyâk[4] and Alexander[5] *should* be immortal, (30) *but* Aûha*r*ma*zd*, for great advantage, so altered *them* as that which is declared."'

CHAPTER IX.

1. The sage asked the spirit of wisdom (2) thus: 'Is it possible to go from region to region[6], or not?

---

age, when he lost the royal glory (see Dd. XXXIX, 16, 17), and was overthrown by the foreign dynasty of Az-î Dahâk.

[1] Av. Thraêtaona, who conquered Az-î Dahâk (see Chap. XXVII, 38–40, Yas. IX, 24–27). He was misled by Aharman into dividing his empire between his three sons, two of whom revolted and slew the third (see Chaps. XXI, 25, XXVII, 42).

[2] Av. Kava Usan or Kavi Usadhan, the Kaî-Kâvûs of the Shâhnâmah, misread Kahôs in Pâzand. He was the second monarch of the Kayân dynasty, and made an unsuccessful attempt to reach heaven, mentioned in Bd. XXXIV, 7, to which he may be supposed to have been instigated by Aharman, but he was also unfortunate in many other enterprises.

[3] A title of Az-î Dahâk in the Shâhnâmah, literally, 'with a myriad horses.' This king, or dynasty, is said to have conquered Yim and reigned for a thousand years, but was overthrown by Frê*d*ûn. In the Avesta (Yas. IX, 25, Âbân Yt. 34, Âf. Zarat. 3) Az-î Dahâk, 'the destructive serpent,' is described as hazangra-yaokhs*t*i, 'with a thousand perceptions,' a term analogous to baêvare-spasana, 'with a myriad glances,' which is usually applied to Mithra, the angel of the sun. From this latter, if used for the former, bêvarâsp might easily be corrupted.

[4] Av. Frangrasyan, the Afrâsiyâb of the Shâhnâmah, a Tûrânian king who conquered the Irânians for twelve years during the reign of Mânû*sk*îhar (see Bd. XXXIV, 6).

[5] Alexander the Great, misread Arasa*n*gar by Nêr.

[6] The earth is supposed to be divided into seven regions, of which the central one is as large as the other six united; two of

3. From what substance is the sky made? 4. And how and in what manner is the mingling of the water in the earth?'

5. The spirit of wisdom answered (6) thus: 'Without the permission of the sacred beings, or the permission of the demons, it is then[1] not possible for one to go from region to region[2].

7. 'The sky is made from the substance of the blood-stone[3], such as they also call diamond (almâst).

8. 'And the mingling of the water in the earth is just like the blood in the body of man.'

Chapter X.

1. The sage asked the spirit of wisdom (2) thus: 'Can *there* be any peace and affection whatever of Aharman, the wicked, and his demons and miscreations, with Aûharmazd and the archangels, one with the other, or not?'

3. The spirit of wisdom answered (4) thus: '*There* cannot be, on any account whatever; (5) because Aharman meditates evil falsehood and its deeds, wrath and malice and discord, (6) and Aûharmazd meditates righteousness and its deeds, good works

---

the six lie to the north, two to the south, one to the east, and one to the west; and they are said to be separated by seas or mountains, difficult to cross (see Bd. XI). For their names, see Chaps. XVI, 10, XXVII, 40.

[1] Instead of adînas, 'then for one,' Nêr. has manufactured a word ainâ, 'otherwise' (see also Chap. VII, 19 n).

[2] This information is derived from Pahl. Vend. I, 4 *a*.

[3] Or 'ruby,' referring to the rosy tints of dawn and sunset. The same statement is made in Bd. XII, 6. Nêr. has 'steel,' and the word can be translated 'blood-metal.'

and goodness and truth. 7. And everything can change, except good and bad nature. 8. A good nature cannot change to evil by any means whatever, and a bad nature to goodness in any manner. 9. Aûharmazd, on account of a good nature, approves no evil and falsehood; (10) and Aharman, on account of a bad nature, accepts no goodness and truth; (11) and, on this account, *there* cannot be for them any peace and affection whatever, one with the other.'

CHAPTER XI.

1. The sage asked the spirit of wisdom (2) thus: 'Is wisdom good, or skill, or goodness [1]?'

3. The spirit of wisdom answered (4) thus: 'Wisdom with which *there* is no goodness, is not to be considered as wisdom; (5) and skill with which *there* is no wisdom, is not to be considered as skill.'

CHAPTER XII.

1. The sage asked the spirit of wisdom (2) thus: 'Wherefore is *it* when the treasure of the spiritual *existence* is allotted so truly, *and* that of the worldly *existence* so falsely?'

3. The spirit of wisdom answered (4) thus: 'The treasure of the worldly *existence* was [2] allotted as truly, in the original creation, as that of the spiritual *existence*. 5. And the creator, Aûharmazd, provided the

[1] L19 omits the last two words, but they are evidently referred to in the reply.

[2] Literally, 'is.'

happiness of every kind, that is in these creatures and creation, for the use (bûn) of the sun[1] and moon and those twelve constellations which are called the twelve chieftains[2] by revelation; (6) and they, too, accepted *it* in order to allot *it* truly and deservedly.

7. 'And, afterwards, Aharman produced those seven planets, such as are called the seven chieftains of Aharman, for dissipating[3] *and* carrying off that happiness from the creatures of Aûharmazd, in opposition to the sun and moon and those twelve constellations. 8. And *as to* every happiness which those constellations bestow on the creatures of Aûharmazd, (9) those planets take away as much of it as *it* is possible for them (the constellations) to give[4], (10) and give *it* up to the power of the demons[5] and fiends and the bad.

11. 'And the treasure of the spiritual *existence* is so true on this account, because Aûharmazd, the lord, with all the angels *and* archangels, is[6] undisturbed, (12) and they make the struggle with Aharman and the demons, and also the account of the souls of men, with justice. 13. And the place of *him* whose good work is more is in heaven, (14) the place of *him* whose good work and sin are equal is among the ever-stationary[7], (15) and when the crime is more, his path is then to hell.'

---

[1] Literally, 'Mitrô,' the angel of the sun.

[2] See Chap. VIII, 17–21.

[3] By omitting one letter K43 has 'miscreating.'

[4] By omitting this verb L19 has 'possible for them (the planets).'

[5] So understood by Nêr., but all the best MSS. omit the relative particle, as if 'the powerful demons' were meant.

[6] Literally, 'are.'

[7] See Chap. VII, 18.

Chapter XIII.

1. The sage asked the spirit of wisdom (2) thus: 'Wherefore is *it* when oxen and sheep, birds, flying creatures, and fish are, each one, properly learned in that which is their own knowledge, (3) and men, so long as they bring no instruction unto them, and they do not perform much toil and trouble (an*g*înŏ)[1] about it, are not able to obtain and know the learning of the human race?'

4. The spirit of wisdom answered (5) thus: 'Men have been so wise, in the original creation, that, *as to* the good works and crime which *were* performed by them, the recompense of the good works and the punishment of the crime *were* then seen by them with their own eyes, (6) and no crime whatever proceeded from men. 7. *But*, afterwards, Aharman, the wicked, concealed the recompense of good works and the punishment of sin. 8. And on this account, moreover, it is said in revelation (9) that: "[These][2] four [things are worse and more grievous] than every evil which the accursed evil *one*, the wicked, committed upon the creatures of Aûha*r*ma*zd*, (10) [that is, when the reward of good works and] punishment [of sin], the thoughts of men, and the consequence of actions *were* quite concealed [by him][3]."

---

[1] Nêr. has read khva*z*înak, and taken it as equivalent to Pers. khazînah, 'treasury,' in the sense of 'expenditure;' but this is very doubtful.

[2] The words in brackets, in §§ 9, 10, are taken from the Pâzand version, as the passage containing them has been omitted by mistake in K43.

[3] The Pandnâmah of Buzurg-Mihir states 'this, too, is declared, that the evil spirit committed even this very grievous thing upon

11. 'And, for the same reason, he made many devotions and improper creeds current in the world. 12. And, on account of men's not knowing of duty and good works, every one believes that most, and considers *it* as good, which his teaching in devotion has included. 13. And that devotion, in particular, is more powerful[1], with which sovereignty exists. 14. But that one is the lordship and sovereignty of Vistâsp[2], the king of kings, (15) by whom, on account of knowing *it* unquestionably and certainly (aêvarîhâ), the perfect and true religion, which is in the word of the creator Aûharmazd, was received from the unique Zaratûst, the Spîtamân[3], (16) who has manifested clearly, explicitly, and unquestionably the treasure of the worldly and spiritual *existences*, of every kind, from the good religion of the Mazda-worshippers. 17. There is then[4] no *other* creed, through which it is possible for one to obtain and know the treasure of the worldly and spiritual *existences* so explicitly and clearly, (18) but, on account of much controversy[5], they are so cut up (âgîstakŏ)

the creatures of Aûharmazd, when the reward of good works and punishment of sin *were* quite concealed by him, in the thoughts of men, as the consequence of actions.'

[1] Nêr. has 'purer,' by connecting pâdîyâvandtar with pâdîyâv, 'ablution;' but this is hardly possible, whereas the former word can be readily traced to Av. paiti+yâ+vant, with the meaning 'resistant, stubborn, strong;' compare Pers. pâyâb, 'power.'

[2] Av. Vîstâspa, Pers. Gustâsp, the fifth king of the Kayân dynasty, who adopted the religion of Zarâtust in the thirtieth year of his reign, and is said to have reigned 120 years (see Bd. XXXIV, 7).

[3] See Chap. I, 10 n.

[4] Instead of 'then for one,' Nêr. has 'otherwise,' as in Chap. IX, 6.

[5] Reading vigûftakîh. Nêr. has 'by much contemplation,'

and entangled, that the statements of their beginning are much unlike to the middle, and the middle to the end.'

CHAPTER XIV.

1. The sage asked the spirit of[1] [wisdom (2) thus: 'Which protection is the more defensive? 3. Which friend[2] (4) and which supporter of fame are good? 5. Which helper of enjoyment is good? 6. Which wealth is the pleasanter? 7. And which is the supremest pleasure of all pleasures[3]?'

8. The spirit of wisdom answered (9) thus: 'The sacred being is the more defensive protection. 10. A virtuous brother is a good friend. 11. A child, who is virtuous and an upholder of religion, is a good supporter of fame. 12. A virtuous wife, who is well-disposed, is a good helper of enjoyment. 13. That wealth is better and pleasanter which is collected by honesty, *and one* consumes *and* maintains with duties and good works. 14. *And* the pleasures which are superior to all pleasures are health of body, freedom from fear, good repute, *and* righteousness[4].'

---

having read vênaftakîh. Both words are very uncommon, and it is doubtful which of them is the more appropriate to the context.

[1] From this point to Chap. XXVII, 49 the Pahlavi text of K43 is missing, owing to the loss of nine folios in that MS., but a copy of the missing passage, made by Dastur Hoshangji Jamaspji from TD2, has been consulted for the purpose of controlling the Pâz. version of L19.

[2] L19 inserts 'is good?'

[3] TD2 has 'which is the friend who is the supremest of friends;' but this does not correspond well with the reply in § 14.

[4] TD2 adds '*and* are good.'

CHAPTER XV.

1. The sage asked the spirit of wisdom (2) thus: 'Is poverty good, or opulence[1]?'

3. The spirit of wisdom answered (4) thus: 'Poverty which is through honesty is better than opulence which is from the treasure of others. 5. For it is stated (6) thus: "*As to* him who is the poorest and most secluded (armêsttûm)[2] person, whenever he keeps his thoughts, words, *and* deeds honest, and in duty to the sacred beings, for him even *there* is lawfully a share of all the duties and good works which mankind shall do in the world[3]. 7. *As to* him, too, who is opulent, who is a man of much wealth, when the wealth is not produced by honesty, though he takes trouble (angînakŏ) in[4] duties and good works and righteous gifts, his good work is then not his own, (8) because the good work is his from whom *the wealth* is abstracted[5]."

---

[1] L19 adds 'or sovereignty,' to account for §§ 12–39.

[2] Av. armaêsta, applied to water, means 'most stationary, stagnant;' Pahl. armêst (Av. airima) is applied to the place of 'seclusion' for impure men and women, and in Sls. VI, 1 it seems to refer to 'helpless' idiots or lunatics; Nêr. explains it in Sanskrit as 'lame, crippled, immobility,' but 'secluded, immured, helpless' are terms better adapted to the context, whether the word be applied to persons, as it is here and in Chaps. XXXVII, 36, XXXIX, 40, or to learning and character, as in Chap. LI, 7.

[3] Persons who are wholly unable to perform good works are supposed to be entitled to a share of any supererogatory good works performed by others (see Sls. VI, 1, 2), but the allotment of such imputed good works seems to be at the discretion of the angels who keep them in store (see Sls. VIII, 4).

[4] Nêr. has 'makes expenditure on,' by reading khvazînak, as in Chap. XIII, 3.

[5] § 8 does not occur in L19, but is found in TD2, PA10, and MH7.

9. 'And *as to* that much wealth which is collected by proper exertion, and *one* consumes and maintains with duties and good works and pleasure, even that is no better thereby, (10) because it is necessary to consider that as perfect. 11. But *as to* him who is a man of much wealth, whose wealth is collected by proper exertion, and he consumes and maintains *it* with duties and good works and pleasure, he is great and good and more perfect[1].

12. 'And regarding even that which is sovereignty they state (13) thus: "What is[2] good government in a village is better than what is[2] bad government in a realm. 14. Because the creator Aûha*r*ma*z*d produced good government for effecting the protection of the creatures, (15) and Aharman, the wicked, has produced bad government as the adversary of good government."

16. 'Good government is that which maintains *and* directs a province flourishing, the poor untroubled, *and* the law *and* custom true, (17) *and* sets aside improper laws and customs. 18. It well *maintains* water and fire by law[3], (19) *and* keeps in progress the ceremonial of the sacred beings, duties, and good works. 20. It causes friendliness

---

[1] That is, the proper use of wealth does not make the wealth itself any better, but only the rightful possessor of it. This is, however, probably only an emendation of Nêr., as the copy of TD2 gives merely the following, for §§ 9-11: 'But *as to* him who is a man of much wealth, by whose proper exertion it is collected, *and* he consumes *and* maintains *it* with duties, good works, and pleasure, he is no better thereby, because it is necessary to consider him as perfect.'

[2] L19 omits 'what is' in both places.

[3] TD2 omits 'maintains,' as it is sufficiently expressed by the same Pahl. verb 'keeps' in § 19; and L19 omits 'by law.'

and pleading[1] for the poor, (21) and delivers up itself, *and* even that which is its own life, for the sake of the good religion of the Maz*d*a-worshippers. 22. And if there be any one who desists from the way of the sacred beings, then it orders *some one* to effect his restoration thereto; (23) it also makes him a prisoner, *and* brings *him* back to the way of the sacred beings; (24) it allots, out of the wealth that is his, the share of the sacred beings *and* the worthy, of good works *and* the poor; (25) and delivers up the body for the sake of the soul[2]. 26. A good king, who[3] is of that kind, is called equal to the angels and archangels.

27. 'Bad government is that (28) which destroys the true and proper law and custom, (29) and brings[4] oppression, plunder, and injudiciousness into practice. 30. It dissipates the treasure of the spiritual *existence*, (31) *and* considers duty and good works a vexation, through greediness[5]. 32. It keeps back a person performing good works from doing good works, (33) and he thereby becomes a doer of harm. (34) Its disbursement[6], too, of every kind is for its own self, (35) the administration of[7] the treasure

[1] Reading dâ*d*ŏ-gôbîh, 'pronouncing the law,' or 'speaking of gifts,' instead of Pâz. *g*âda*n*gôî, a misreading of Nêr. for Pahl. yêdatô-gôbîh, 'speaking of the sacred being.'

[2] The usual way of treating nonconformists in all ages and all sects, when party spirit is strong. TD2 has 'delivers *him* up for the sake of body and soul.'

[3] TD2 has 'good government which.'

[4] TD2 has 'keeps;' but the two verbs are much alike in Huzvâri*s*.

[5] Because nearly all such works entail expenditure.

[6] Nêr. has 'accumulation,' but this is the meaning of andôzi*s*n, rather than of the andâzi*s*n in the text.

[7] So in TD2.

of the worldly existence, (36) the celebrity[1] *and* exaltation of the vile, (37) the destruction *and* neglect of the good, (38) *and* the annihilation of the poor. 39. A bad king, who[2] is of that kind, is called equal to Aharman and the demons.'

Chapter XVI.

1. The sage asked the spirit of wisdom (2) thus: 'Of the food which men eat, and the clothing which men put on, which are the more valuable and good?'

3. The spirit of wisdom answered (4) thus: 'Of the food which men eat, the milk of goats is produced good. 5. Because, *as to* men and quadrupeds, who are born from a mother, until the *time* when food is eaten by them, their growth *and* nourishment are then from milk, (6) *and* on milk they can well live. 7. And if men, when they withdraw from the milk of the mother, make thorough experience of the milk of goats, (8) then bread is not necessary for use among them. 9. Since it is declared, (10) that "the food of mankind, who are in Arzah and Savah, Frada*d*afsh and Vîda*d*afsh, Vôrûbar*s*t and Vôrû*g*ar*s*t[3], is the milk of goats and cows; (11) other food they do not eat." 12. *And* he who is a milk-consuming man is healthier and stronger, and even the procreation of children becomes more harmless.

---

[1] Reading khanî*d*îh as in TD2 and Chap. II, 28.

[2] TD2 has 'bad government which.'

[3] The six outermost regions of the earth, of which Arzah lies to the west, Savah to the east, Frada*d*afsh and Vîda*d*afsh to the south, and Vôrûbar*s*t and Vôrû*g*ar*s*t to the north of the central region (see Bd. V, 8, XI, 3).

13. 'Of grains wheat is called great and good, (14) because it is the chief of grains[1], (15) *and* even by the Avesta its name is then specified in the chieftainship of grains[2].

16. 'And of fruit the date *and* grape are called great and good. 17. When bread has not come, it is necessary to consecrate the sacred cake by means of fruit[3]; (18) when the fruit to consecrate is the date or grape, it is allowable to eat every fruit; (19) *and* when those have not come, it is necessary to eat that fruit which is consecrated[4].

20. 'Regarding wine *it* is evident, that it is possible *for* good *and* bad temper to come to manifestation through wine[5]. 21. The goodness of a man is manifested in anger, the wisdom of a man in irregular desire[6]. 22. For *he* whom anger hurries on (aûs-

[1] It is called 'the chief of large-seeded grains' in Bd. XXIV, 19.

[2] Possibly in the Pâzag Nask, part of which was 'about the thirty-three first chieftainships of the existences around, that is, how many of which are spiritual *and* how many worldly *existences*, and which is the second, and which the third of the spiritual *and* worldly *existences*;' as stated in the eighth book of the Dînkard.

[3] That is, when a cake cannot be made, fruit can be substituted for it in the ceremony of consecrating the sacred cakes. The sacred cake, or drôn, is a small, round, flexible pancake of unleavened wheaten bread, about the size of the palm of the hand, which, after consecration, is tasted by all those present at the ceremony (see Sls. III, 32 n).

[4] Fruit and wine are usually consecrated and eaten, in the Âfrîngân ceremony, after the completion of the Drôn ceremony, but sometimes the Âfrîngân is celebrated alone. Both ceremonies are performed in honour of some angel, or the guardian spirit of some deceased person (see Haug's Essays, pp. 407–409).

[5] TD2 has 'through the nature of wine;' but âs, 'wine,' is written mas.

[6] TD2 has 'the good of a man is in anger, and the wisdom of a man in lust exciting viciousness.'

tâ*v*ê*d*) is able to recover himself from it[1] through goodness, (23) *he* whom lust hurries on is able to recover himself from it through wisdom, (24) *and he* whom wine hurries on is able to recover himself from it through temper.

25. 'It is not requisite for investigation, (26) because he who is a good-tempered man, when he drinks wine, is such-like as a gold *or* silver cup which, however much more they burn *it*, becomes purer and brighter. 27. It also keeps *his* thoughts, words, *and* deeds more virtuous; (28) and he becomes gentler and pleasanter unto wife and child, companions and friends[2], (29) and is more diligent in every duty and good work.

30. 'And he who is a bad-tempered man, when he drinks wine, thinks *and* considers himself more than ordinary. 31. He carries on a quarrel with companions, displays insolence, makes ridicule and mockery, (32) *and* acts arrogantly *to* a good person. 33. He distresses his own wife and child[3], slave and servant; (34) and dissipates the joy of the good, (35) carries off peace, *and* brings in discord.

36. 'But every one must be cautious as to[4] the moderate drinking of wine. 37. Because, from the moderate drinking of wine, thus much benefit happens to him: (38) since it digests the food, (39) kindles the *vital* fire[5], (40) increases the understanding and intellect, semen and blood, (41) removes vexation, (42) *and* inflames the complexion.

[1] Reading a*g*a*s*, instead of afa*s* (Pâz. va*s*); these two words being written alike in Pahlavi.

[2] TD2 has 'he becomes more friendly, gentler, and pleasanter unto wife and child and companions.' It also omits § 29.

[3] TD2 inserts 'hireling.'

[4] Or 'must become intelligent through.'

[5] The animal heat, called the Vohu-fryãn fire in Bd. XVII, 1.

43. It causes recollection of things forgotten, (44) *and* goodness takes a place in the mind. (45) It likewise increases the sight of the eye, the hearing of the ear, and the speaking of the tongue; (46) *and* work, which it is necessary to do *and* expedite, becomes more progressive. 47. He *also* sleeps pleasantly in the sleeping place[1], *and* rises light. 48. And, on account of these contingencies, good repute for the body, righteousness for the soul, and also the approbation of the good[2] come upon him.

49. 'And in him who drinks wine more than moderately, thus much defect becomes manifest, (50) since it diminishes his wisdom, understanding and intellect, semen and blood; (51) it injures the liver[3] and accumulates disease, (52) it alters the complexion, (53) and diminishes the strength and vigour. 54. The homage *and* glorification of the sacred beings become forgotten. 55. The sight of the eye, the hearing of the ear, and the speaking of the tongue become less. 56. He distresses Hor*v*adad and Amer*o*dad[4] (57) *and* entertains a desire of lethargy[5]. 58. That, also, which it is necessary for him to say and do, remains undone; (59) *and* he sleeps in uneasiness, *and* rises uncomfortably. 60. *And*, on account of these contingencies, himself[6],

---

[1] Nêr. has 'at sleeping time,' and the word gâs means either 'time' or 'place,' but usually the latter. TD2 has bâ*s*n gâs, probably for bâli*s*n gâs, 'bed place.'

[2] Nêr. inserts the words 'greatly increase' in the Sanskrit version, but they do not occur in TD2.

[3] These four words occur only in TD2.

[4] The two archangels who are supposed to be injured by improper eating and drinking (see Chap. II, 34 n).

[5] Bûshâsp (Av. Bûshyãsta), the fiend of slothful sleep.

[6] Or it can be translated 'his own body.'

wife, and child, friend *and* kindred are distressed *and* unhappy, (61) and the superintendent of troubles[1] and the enemy are glad. 62. The sacred beings, also, are not pleased with him; (63) and infamy comes to his body, and even wickedness to *his* soul.

64. 'Of the dress which people possess *and* put on[2], silk is good for the body, and cotton for the soul. 65. For this reason, because silk arises from a noxious creature[3], (66) and the nourishment of cotton is from water, and *its* growth from earth[4]; and as a treasure of the soul it is called great and good and more valuable.'

CHAPTER XVII.

1. The sage asked the spirit of wisdom (2) thus: 'Which is that pleasure which is worse than unhappiness?'

3. The spirit of wisdom answered (4) thus: 'Whoever has acquired wealth by crime, and he becomes glad of it thereby[5], then that pleasure is worse for him than unhappiness.'

CHAPTER XVIII.

1. The sage asked the spirit of wisdom (2) thus: 'Wherefore do people consider these very little,

[1] Meaning probably the evil spirit.

[2] The Sanskrit version omits the former verb, and TD2 the latter.

[3] Caterpillars are creatures of Aharman, because they eat and injure vegetation which is under the special protection of the archangel Amer*o*da*d*.

[4] Water and earth, being both personified as angels, would impart somewhat of their sacred character to the cotton arising from them.

[5] 'Glad of the crime on account of the wealth' is probably meant.

these four things which it is necessary for them to consider more, as warnings (dakhshak), (3) the changeableness of the things of the worldly *existence*, the death of the body, the account of the soul[1], *and* the fear of hell?'

4. The spirit of wisdom answered (5) thus: 'On account of the delusiveness (nîyâzânîh) of the demon of greediness[2], and of discontent.'

Chapter XIX.

1. The sage asked the spirit of wisdom (2) thus: 'Is living in fear *and* falsehood worse, or death?'

3. The spirit of wisdom answered (4) thus: 'To live in fear and falsehood is worse than death. 5. Because every one's life is necessary for the enjoyment *and* pleasure of the worldly *existence*, (6) and when the enjoyment *and* pleasure of the worldly *existence* are not his, and fear and even falsehood[3] are with him, it is called worse than death.'

Chapter XX.

1. The sage asked the spirit of wisdom (2) thus: '*For* kings which is the one thing more advantageous, and which the more injurious?'

3. The spirit of wisdom answered (4) thus: 'For kings conversation with the wise *and* good is the

---

[1] That is, the account to be rendered by the soul after death.

[2] See Chap. VIII, 15 n.

[3] These being considered as fiends; the latter, mîtôkht, being the first demon produced by the evil spirit (see Bd. I, 24, XXVIII, 14, 16).

one thing more advantageous, (5) and speaking *and* conversation with slanderers *and* double-dealers are the more injurious for them.'

CHAPTER XXI.

1. The sage asked the spirit of wisdom (2) thus: 'What is the end of the world-arranging *and* spirit-destroying man? 3. What is the end of him who is a scoffing man? 4–6. What is the end of the idle, the malicious, and the lazy man? 7. What is the end of a false-hearted *one*, (8) and the end of an arrogant *one*[1]?'

9. The spirit of wisdom answered (10) thus: 'He who is a world-arranging *and* spirit-destroying man is as injured, in the punishment of the three *nights*[2], as a raging fire when water comes upon it.

11[3]. 'Of him who is a scoffing man *there* is no glory in body and soul; (12) *and* every time when he opens *his* mouth his wickedness then increases. 13. All the fiends, too, become so lodged in his body, that they leave no goodness whatever for his body; (14) and he makes mockery of the good, and glorification of the vile. 15. Also in the worldly *existence* his body is infamous, and *in* the spiritual *existence his* soul is wicked. 16. And, for effecting *his* punishment in hell, they deliver him over to

[1] L19 has 'What is the end of him who is an idle man?' in § 4, and repeats the same formula in each of the §§ 5–8.

[2] Referring to the three days and nights of final punishment, reserved for those specially wicked, at the time of the resurrection (see Bd. XXX, 12–16).

[3] In TD2 the remaining sections are arranged in the following order:—§§ 18, 27–33, 19–26, 34–44, 11–17.

the scoffing fiend; (17) *and* that fiend inflicts a ridicule and a mockery upon him with every single punishment.

18. '*As to* him who is an idle man, yet devoid of wickedness, mostly when[1] death comes on in the worldly *existence*, he thereupon (a*g*a*s*) begets pleasantly for the sake of another.

19. 'The bridge[2] which is for the soul of him who is a malicious man is more difficult than *for* the other wicked who are in hell. 20. For this reason, because malice proceeds by lineage; (21) *and* it is possible to manage every sin better than malice, (22) because malice will abide in a lineage. 23. There are *instances* when it adheres[3] until the renovation *of the universe;* (24) for *it* is clearly declared by the pure revelation, (25) that the origin of the estrangement (anîrânîh) of the Arûmans, *and* even the Tûrânians, *from* the Irânians, was owing to that malice which *was* generated by them through the slaughter of Aîrî*k*[4]; (26) *and it* always adheres until the renovation.

---

[1] L19 inserts 'misery and.'

[2] The *K*indvar bridge (see Chap. II, 115, 162), which is supposed to resemble a beam with many unequal sides, the side turned uppermost being narrower in proportion as the soul, intending to pass along it, is more wicked; so that the difficulty of the transit increases with the sin of the soul (see Dd. XXI, 3–5).

[3] Or 'continues.'

[4] Pâz. *E*raz, one of the three sons of Frê*d*ûn, the Pê*s*dâ*d* sovereign, who divided his empire among them, giving the Arûman provinces to Salm, the Tûrânian to Tû*g*, and the Irânian to Aîrî*k*. The last was slain by his two brothers, and his death was subsequently avenged by his descendant Mânû*sk*îhar (see Chap. XXVII, 41–43, Bd. XXXI, 9–12). Though these sons are not mentioned in the Avesta now extant, their history appears to have been related in the *K*i*d*rast Nask (see Sls. X, 28 n).

27. 'He who is a lazy man is said *to be* the most unworthy of men. 28. Because *it* is declared by revelation, (29) that the creator Aûha*r*ma*zd* produced no corn for him who is a lazy man; (30) for him who is a lazy man *there* is then no giving of anything in gifts and charity[1]; (31) and lodging and entertainment are not to be provided for him. 32. For this reason, because that food which a lazy man eats, he eats through impropriety and injustice; (33) and, on account of his laziness and unjust eating, his body then becomes infamous and the soul wicked.

34. 'He who is a false-hearted man is as dubious in good *things* as in bad; (35) *he* is dubious as to the treasure of the spiritual and worldly *existences*, and also as to the ceremonial, invocation, *and* service of the sacred beings. 36. And, on account of these circumstances, the angels *and* archangels shall accept little of the ceremonial *and* invocations which he performs, (37) and give unto him little of the gain, too, which he seeks. 38. And in the mouth of the good *man he* is always infamous, (39) and his soul becomes wicked.

40. 'The friends of him who is an arrogant man are few, and his enemies many. 41. And even of the gifts which he gives to any one, *and* the ceremonial, too, which he performs for the sacred beings, they shall accept little, on account of *his* arrogance, (42) and give little of the gain, too, which he seeks. 43. And in hell they deliver him to the fiend of arrogance, in order to inflict punishment upon *his* soul; (44) and the fiend of arrogance inflicts punishment of various kinds upon it, *and* is not pacified.'

[1] L19 has 'he then gives nothing *as* his living, which is through gifts and charity.'

CHAPTER XXII.

1. The sage asked the spirit of wisdom (2) thus: 'Is it possible to provide, for one's own hand, the treasure *and* wealth of the worldly *existence* through exertion, or not?'

3. The spirit of wisdom answered (4) thus: 'It is not possible to provide for one's self, through exertion, that benefit which is not ordained; (5) but a morsel (kazd) of that which is ordained comes on by means of exertion. 6. Yet the exertion, when it is fruitless in the worldly *existence*, through the sacred beings not *being* with it[1], still comes, afterwards, to *one's* assistance in the spiritual *existence*, *and* outweighs in the balance[2].'

CHAPTER XXIII.

1. The sage asked the spirit of wisdom (2) thus: 'Is it possible to contend with destiny through wisdom *and* knowledge, or not?'

3. The spirit of wisdom answered (4) thus: 'Even with the might and powerfulness of wisdom *and* knowledge, even then it is not possible to contend with destiny. 5. Because, when predestination as to virtue, or as to the reverse[3], comes forth, the wise becomes wanting (nîyâzân) in duty, and the astute in evil *becomes* intelligent; (6) the faint-hearted *becomes* braver, and the braver *becomes* faint-hearted;

---

[1] TD2 has 'time not *being* with it.'

[2] The balance in which men's actions are weighed by the angel Rashnû (see Chap. II, 119–122).

[3] L19 has 'vileness.'

(7) the diligent *becomes* lazy, and the lazy acts diligently[1]. (8) Just as is predestined as to the matter, the cause enters into it, (9) *and* thrusts out everything else.'

Chapter XXIV.

1. The sage asked the spirit of wisdom (2) thus: 'On account of the begging of favours, and the practice and worthiness of good works, do the sacred beings also grant anything to men otherwise[2], or not?'

3. The spirit of wisdom answered (4) thus: 'They grant; (5) for *there are* such as they call thus: "Destiny *and* divine providence." 6. Destiny is that which is ordained from the beginning, (7) *and* divine providence is that which they also grant otherwise. 8. But the sacred beings provide and manifest in the spiritual *existence* little of that grant, on this account, because Aharman, the wicked[3], through the power of the seven planets extorts wealth, *and* also every other benefit of the worldly *existence*, from the good *and* worthy, *and* grants *them* more fully to the bad *and* unworthy.'

Chapter XXV.

1. The sage asked the spirit of wisdom (2) thus: 'Of the rich who is the poorer, and of the poor who is the richer?'

[1] L19 has 'becomes diligent.'

[2] That is, otherwise than by destiny, as mentioned in the previous chapter, and in consequence of prayer and merit.

[3] TD2 inserts 'through that cause.'

3. The spirit of wisdom answered (4) thus: 'Of the rich he is the poorer who is not content with that which is his, (5) and suffers anxiety for the increase of anything.

6. '*And* of the poor he is the richer who is content with that which has come, (7) and cares not for the increase of anything.'

Chapter XXVI.

1. The sage asked the spirit of wisdom (2) thus: 'Is a blind eye worse, or a blind mind (dîl)? 3. Is the ill-informed worse, or the bad-tempered?'

4. The spirit of wisdom answered (5) thus: 'He who is blind-eyed, when he has understanding in anything, *and* accomplishes learning, is to be considered as sound-eyed. 6. *And* he who is sound-eyed, when he has no knowledge *and* understanding[1], and even that which they teach him he does not accept, then that is worse than even a blind eye.

7. 'The ill-tempered is less evil[2] than the ill-informed; (8) because the ill-tempered, except by a decree, is not able to seize anything away from any one; (9) and *as to* the ill-informed man, his desire of every kind is then[3] for oppression and plunder. 10. Concerning him who is ill-informed *it* is declared that, apart from predestination, he is born *free* from fresh understanding[4].'

---

[1] L19 has 'when he has no knowledge of anything.'

[2] L19 has 'is better.'

[3] That is, when he has a decree in his favour.

[4] § 10 is found only in TD2. It probably means that an ill-informed man is not likely to acquire any knowledge beyond that which is unavoidable.

CHAPTER XXVII.

1. The sage asked the spirit of wisdom (2) thus: 'Wherefore have the people who *were* from Gâyômar*d*[1], *and* those, too, who *were* lords and monarchs, from Hôshâng[2], the Pês*d*â*d*, even unto Vi*s*tâsp[3], the king of kings, been such doers of *their own* wills? 3. Much benefit *was* also obtained by them from the sacred beings, (4) *and* they have been mostly those who *were* ungrateful unto the sacred beings, (5) and there are *some* even who have been very ungrateful, promise-breaking, *and* sinful. 6. For what benefit then have they *been* severally created, (7) and what result and advantage proceeded from them?'

8. The spirit of wisdom answered (9) thus: 'That which thou askest concerning them, *as to* benefit, or as to the reverse[4], thou shouldst become aware of and fully understand. 10. Because the affairs of the world of every kind proceed through destiny and time and the supreme decree of the self-existent eternity (zôrvân), the king and long-continuing lord. 11. Since, at various periods, it happens unto every one, for whom it is allotted, just as that which is necessary to happen. 12. As even from the mutual connection of those ancients, who are passed

---

[1] Av. Gaya-maretan, the primeval man from whom the whole human race is supposed to have sprung, and who lived for thirty years after the advent of the evil spirit (see Bd. III, 22, XXXIV, 2).

[2] Av. Haoshyangha, the first monarch of the Irânian world, and founder of the Pês*d*â*d* (Av. paradhâta, 'early law') dynasty. He was the great-grandson of Mâshya, the first earthly man that sprang from Gâyômar*d*, and is said to have reigned for forty years (see Bd. XV, 21–28, XXXI, 1, XXXIV, 4).

[3] See Chap. XIII, 14 n.

[4] L19 has 'evil.'

away, it is manifest (13) that, ultimately, that benefit arose which was necessary to come from them to the creatures of Aûharmazd.

14. 'Because the advantage from Gâyômard was this, (15) first, the slaying of Ârzûr[1], and making delivery of his own body, with great judiciousness, to Aharman[2]. 16. *And* the second advantage was this, (17) that mankind and all the guardian spirits of the producers of the renovation *of the universe*, males[3] *and* females[4], *were* produced from his body. 18. *And*, thirdly, this[5], that even the metals *were* produced *and* formed[6] from his body[7].

19. 'And the advantage from Hôshâng, the Pêsdâd, was this, (20) that, of three parts, he slew two parts of the demons of Mâzendar[8], who *were* destroyers of the world.

21. 'The advantage from Tâkhmorup[9], the well-

---

[1] Written Aîrzûr in TD2. It has been suggested by Windischmann (Zor. Stud. p. 5) that this was the name of a demon, afterwards applied to the Arezûr ridge at the gate of hell (see Bd. XII, 8), but this requires confirmation. Regarding this ridge the following explanation occurs in the Pahlavi Rivâyat which precedes Dd. in many MSS.:—'They say that hell is the ridge (pûstŏ) of Arekzûr; and hell is not the ridge of Arekzûr, but that place where the gate of hell *exists* is a ridge (grîvakŏ) such as the ridge named Arekzûr, and owing to that they assert that *it is* the ridge (pûstŏ) of Arekzûr.' The explainer appears to mean that the ridge at the gate of hell was named after the other Mount Arezûr, in Arûm (see Bd. XII, 16).

[2] Compare Bd. III, 21–23.

[3] L19 has 'righteous males.'

[4] Fifteen of each, as stated in Bd. XXX, 17.

[5] L19 has 'this advantage.'

[6] L19 omits the former verb.

[7] See Zs. X, 2, Dd. LXIV, 7.

[8] See Dd. LXV, 5, referring probably to the demon-worshippers of Mâzendarân, south of the Caspian.

[9] Av. Takhmô-urupa, the Tahmûras of the Shâhnâmah; he

grown, was this, (22) that the accursed evil *one*, the wicked, *was* kept by him thirty years as a charger[1]. 23. *And* the writing of penmanship of seven kinds, which that wicked *one* kept in concealment, he brought out to publicity.

24. 'The advantage from the well-flocked Yimshêd[2], son of Vîvangha, was this, (25) that an immortality of six hundred years, six months, and sixteen days[3] is provided by him for the creatures and creation, of every kind, of the creator Aûharmazd; (26) *and* they are made unsuffering, undecaying, *and* undisturbed[4]. (27) Secondly, this[5], that the enclosure formed by Yim[6] *was* made by him; (28) *and* when that rain of Malkôs[7] occurs—since *it* is declared in revelation that mankind and

---

is said to have been a great-grandson of Hôshâng, whom he succeeded on the throne, and to have reigned thirty years (see Bd. XXXI, 2, XXXIV, 4). Written Takhmôrîdô in TD2.

[1] See Râm Yt. 12, Zamyâd Yt. 29.

[2] Av. Yima khshaêta, 'Yim the spendid;' he was a brother of his predecessor, Tâkhmorup, and the Bundahis states that he reigned six hundred and sixteen years and six months in glory, and one hundred years in concealment (see Chap. VIII, 27, Bd. XXXI, 3, XXXIV, 4).

[3] TD2 has only 'three hundred years,' by the accidental omission of a cipher; it also omits the months and days.

[4] See Vend. II, 16, Râm Yt. 16, Zamyâd Yt. 33.

[5] L19 has 'this advantage.'

[6] See Chap. LXII, 15–19. The formation of this enclosure is ordered by Aûharmazd in Vend. II, 61–92, for the preservation of mankind, animals, and plants from the effects of a glacial epoch which he foretells, and which is here represented as the rain of Malkôs.

[7] This term for 'deluging rain' may be traced either to Chald. מַלְקוֹשׁ 'autumnal rain,' or to Av. mahrkûsô, the title of a demon regarding whom nothing is yet known (see Dd. XXXVII, 94 n and SBE, vol. xviii, p. 479).

the other creatures and creations of Aûharmazd, the lord, are mostly those which shall perish[1]—(29) *one* shall afterwards open the gate of that enclosure formed by Yim, (30) *and* the people *and* cattle, and other creatures and creations of the creator Aûharmazd, shall come out from that enclosure, (31) and arrange the world again. 32. Thirdly, (33) when[2] he brought back the proportion of the worldly *existences*, which that evil-producing wicked *one*[3] had swallowed, from his belly[4]. Fourthly, when a goat (gôspend) *was* not given by him to the demons in the character of an old man[5].

34. 'And the advantage from Az-î Dahâk, the

[1] L19 has merely 'shall mostly perish,' in place of these last six words.

[2] L19 has 'thirdly, this advantage, that.'

[3] L19 adds 'who is Aharman.'

[4] According to a legend preserved in the Persian Rivâyats (see MH10, fol. 52) Aharman, while kept as a charger by Tâkhmorup, induced the wife of the latter to ascertain from her husband whether he ever felt fear while riding the fiend, and, acting upon the information thus obtained, he threw the king from his back while descending from the Alburz mountains, and swallowed him. Information of this event was conveyed to Yim by the angel Srôsh, who advised him to seek the fiend and propitiate him. Yim, accordingly, went into the wilderness singing, to attract Aharman, and, when the fiend appeared, Yim ingratiated himself into his favour and, taking advantage of an unguarded moment, he dragged Tâkhmorup out of the fiend's entrails, and placed the corpse in a depository for the dead. In consequence of this feat his hand was attacked with leprosy, from which he suffered greatly until it was accidentally washed in bull's urine, which healed it. This legend is related for the purpose of recommending the use of bull's urine for purification of the body.

[5] Or, perhaps, 'as a substitute for an old man.' This fourth advantage is found only in TD2, where the text is as follows:— '*K*ahârûm, amata*s* gôspend pavan gôharîk-î pîr va*l* *s*êdân lâ yehabûntô.'

Bêvarâsp[1], and the accursed Frâsîyâk of Tûr[1] was this, (35) that, if the dominion should not have come to Bêvarâsp *and* Frâsîyâk, the accursed evil spirit would then have given that dominion unto Aeshm[2]; (36) and when it would have come unto Aeshm, it would not have been possible to take *it* away from him till the resurrection *and* future existence, (37) for this reason, because he has no bodily existence[3].

38. 'And the advantage from Frê*d*ûn[4] was this, (39) such as the vanquishing *and* binding of A*z*-î Dahâk, the Bêvarâsp[5], who *was* so grievously sinful. 40. And, again too, many demons of Mâzendar[6] were smitten by him, and expelled from the region of Khvanîras[7].'

41. 'And the advantage from Mânûs*k*îhar[8] was this, (42, 43) that, in revenge for Aîrî*k*, who was his grandfather, Salm and Tû*g* *were* kept back by him from disturbing the world[9]. 44. From the land of

[1] See Chap. VIII, 29.

[2] The demon of wrath (see Chap. II, 115).

[3] And would, therefore, have continued to live and reign till the resurrection.

[4] See Chap. VIII, 27. He is said to have reigned for five hundred years (see Bd. XXXIV, 6), but this period includes the lives of ten generations of his descendants who did not reign (see Bd. XXXI, 14).

[5] He is said to have been confined in Mount Dimâvand (see Bd. XXIX, 9).

[6] See § 20.

[7] The central region of the earth, containing all the countries best known to the Irânians, and supposed to be as large as the six outer regions united (see Bd. XI, 2–6).

[8] The successor of Frê*d*ûn, who reigned one hundred and twenty years (see Bd. XXXIV, 6). He was a descendant, in the tenth generation, from Aîrî*k*, one of the sons of Frê*d*ûn, who had been slain by his brothers Salm and Tû*g* (see Bd. XXXI, 9–14).

[9] L19 has 'that he slew Salm and Tû*g*, who were his great-

Padashkhvârgar[1] unto the beginning of Dûgakŏ[2], such as Frâsîyâk[3] had taken, by treaty (padmânŏ)[4] he seized back from Frâsîyâk, *and* brought *it* into the possession of the countries of Irân. *And as to* the enlargement of the sea of Kânsât[5], such as Frâsîyâk supplied, he also expelled the water from it.

45. 'And the advantage from Kaî-Kavâd[6] was

---

uncles, in revenge for Aîrîk, *and* kept *them* back from disturbing the world.'

[1] The mountainous region in Taparistân and Gîlân, south of the Caspian (see Bd. XII, 17).

[2] L19 has 'hell.' This Dûgakŏ may possibly be meant for the Duzakô of Vend. I, 34, of which Vaêkereta was the chief settlement, and this latter is identified with Kâvûl (Kâbul) by the Pahlavi translators. The name can also be read Gangakŏ, which might be identified with Canzaca, but this would not correspond so well with the legend, alluded to in the text, which relates how Mânûskîhar, having shut himself up in the impregnable fortress of Âmul in Taparistân, could not be conquered by Frâsîyâk, who was compelled to come to terms, whereby all the country within an arrow-shot east of Mount Dimâvand should remain subject to Mânûskîhar. The arrow was shot and kept on its flight from dawn till noon, when it fell on the bank of the Oxus, which river was thenceforward considered the frontier of the Irânians. This frontier would fully include all the territory between Taparistân and Kâbul mentioned in the text. In Bd. XXXI, 21 the success of Mânûskîhar is attributed to some dispute between Frâsîyâk and his brother, Aghrêrad.

[3] See Chap. VIII, 29 n.

[4] L19 has 'such as was made the portion (padmânŏ) of Frâsîyâk.'

[5] Called Kyânsîh in Bd. XIII, 16, XX, 34, where it is stated that it was formerly fresh, but latterly salt, and that Frâsîyâk diverted many rivers and streams into it. It is the brackish lake and swamp now called Hâmûn, 'the desert,' or Zarah, 'the sea,' in Sîstân. In the Avesta it is called Kãsu, and the future apostles of the Mazda-worshipping faith are expected to be born on its shores.

[6] Av. Kavi Kavâta, the Kaî-Qubâd of the Shâhnâmah. He

this, (46) that he became a thanksgiver unto the sacred beings. 47. Dominion, also, *was* well exercised by him, (48) *and* the family and raçe of the Kayâns proceeded again from him.

49. 'And the advantage from Sâhm][1] was [this], (50) that the serpent Srôvar[2] and the wolf Kapû*d*[3], which they also call Pêhînŏ[4], the watery demon Gandarep[5], the bird Kamak[6], and the deluding demon *were* slain by him. 51. And he also performed many other great and valuable actions, (52) and kept back much disturbance from the world, (53) *as to* which, when one of those disturbances, in particular, should have remained behind, it would not have been possible to produce the resurrection and future existence.

54. 'And the advantage from Kâî-Ûs[7] was this,

---

was the founder of the Kayân dynasty, and reigned fifteen years (see Bd. XXXI, 24, 25, XXXIV, 7).

[1] The brackets indicate the end of the passage taken from TD2 and the Pâzand version, in consequence of the nine folios containing Chaps. XIV, 1-XXVII, 49 being lost from K43. From this point the translation follows the text of K43. Sâhm (Av. Sâma) was the family name of the hero Keresâsp (see Fravar*d*în Yt. 61, 136), who was a son of Thrita the Sâman (see Yas. IX, 30, 31). For the legends relating to him, see SBE, vol. xviii, pp. 369-382. His name is written Sâm in Pâzand.

[2] Av. azi srvara (see Yas. IX, 34-39, Zamyâ*d* Yt. 40).

[3] Or 'the blue wolf;' not yet identified in the Avesta.

[4] Darmesteter (SBE, vol. xxiii, p. 295, note 4) identifies this name with Pathana of Zamyâ*d* Yt. 41, which seems to mean 'highwayman;' but this identification appears to depend merely on similarity of sound.

[5] Av. Ga*n*darewa of Âbân Yt. 38, Râm Yt. 28, Zamyâ*d* Yt. 41.

[6] A gigantic bird mentioned in the Persian Rivâyats as overshadowing the earth and keeping off the rain, while it ate up men and animals like grains of corn, until Keresâsp killed it with arrows shot continuously for seven days and nights.

[7] See Chap. VIII, 27 n. He was a grandson of Kaî-Kavâ*d*,

(55) as Sîyâvakhsh[1] *was* produced from his body. 56. Many other actions also proceeded from him.

57. 'And the advantage from Sîyâvakhsh was this, (58) such as the begetting of Kaî-Khûsrôî[2], and the formation of Kangde*z*[3].

59. 'And the advantage from Kaî-Khûsrôî was this, (60) such as the slaying of Frâsîyâk[4], (61) the extirpation of the idol-temples which *were* on the lake of *K*ê*k*ast[5], (62) and the management of Kangde*z*. 63. And *he* is able to do good through his assistance of the raising of the dead[6] *by* the restorer of the dead, the triumphant Sôshâns[7], which is in the future existence.

64. 'And the advantage from Kaî-Lôharâsp[8] was

whom he succeeded, and is said to have reigned a hundred and fifty years (see Bd. XXXI, 25, XXXIV, 7), but perhaps this period may have included the reign of his father, whom tradition has nearly forgotten.

[1] Av. Syâvarshân, the Siyâvush of the Shâhnâmah. Though both his father and son were kings, he did not reign himself. L19 has Kaî-Syâvash.

[2] See Chap. II, 95.

[3] Av. Kangha. A fortified settlement said to have been 'in the direction of the east, at many leagues from the bed of the wide-formed ocean towards that side,' and on the frontier of Aîrân-vêg (see Chap. LXII, 13, Bd. XXIX, 10).

[4] See Chap. VIII, 29. This name must have been applied rather to a dynasty than to a single individual, as he reigned in Irân in the time of Mânûs*k*ihar, nearly two hundred years earlier.

[5] See Chap. II, 95.

[6] He is expected to assist in the renovation of the universe at the resurrection, together with Keresâsp and other heroes (see Chap. LVII, 7, Dd. XXXVI, 3).

[7] See Chap. II, 95.

[8] Av. Kavi and Aurva*d*aspa. He was a descendant of Kaî-Kavâ*d* in the fifth generation, being a second cousin once removed of his predecessor, Kaî-Khûsrôî, and reigned a hundred and twenty years (see Bd. XXXI, 25, 28, XXXIV, 7).

this, (65) that dominion was well exercised by him, (66) and he became a thanksgiver unto the sacred beings. 67. He demolished the Jerusalem of the Jews[1], and made the Jews dispersed *and* scattered; *and* the accepter of the religion, Kaî-Vistâsp[2], *was* produced from his body.

68. 'And the advantage from Vistâsp was this, (69) such as the acceptance and solemnization of the good religion of the Mazda-worshippers, (70) through the divine voice (bakân aêvâz) *of* the Ahunavar[3], the word of the creator Aûharmazd; (71) the annihilation and destruction of the bodies of the demons and fiends; (72) and the pleasure and comfort of water and fire and all the angels and spirits of the worldly *existences*[4]. 73. And *he was* full of the hope of the good and worthy, (74) through a virtuous desire for his own determination, (75) the compensation (nôs dasnŏ)[5] and gratification of Aûharmazd, with the archangels, (76) and the affliction and destruction of Aharman and the[6] miscreations.'

---

[1] Aûrîsalêm-i Yahûdânŏ. The first fourteen words of § 67 do not occur in the Pâz.-Sans. version, but a corresponding statement is found in a Persian metrical version, described by Sachau in his Contributions to the Knowledge of Parsee Literature (J.R.A.S., New Series, vol. iv, pp. 229–283), also in the works of several Arab writers of the tenth century (see Nöldeke, Göt. gel. Anz. 1882, p. 964).

[2] See Chap. XIII, 14 n.

[3] The most sacred formula of the Mazda-worshippers, consisting of twenty-one words, forming three metrical lines of sixteen syllables each, beginning with yathâ ahû vairyô, 'as a patron spirit is desirable.' It is supposed to have been uttered by Aûharmazd, for the discomfiture of Aharman, on the first appearance of that evil spirit in the universe (see Bd. I, 21).

[4] L19 has 'all the angels of the spiritual and worldly *existences*.'

[5] L19 has u shnâisn, 'and the propitiation.'

[6] L19 has 'his.'

CHAPTER XXVIII.

1. The sage asked the spirit of wisdom (2) thus: 'Who is the more forgiving (vakhshayânîktar)? 3. What is the more in strength? 4. What is the swifter[1]? 5. What is the happier? 6. What is the more miserable[2]?'

7. The spirit of wisdom answered (8) thus: 'Aûharmazd, the lord, is the more forgiving. 9. He saw[3] the nine thousand years' mischief[4] among his own creatures, owing to Aharman, yet afterwards, through justice and forgiveness, he does not then smite him *for* it[5].

10. 'And the *celestial* sphere is the more in strength. 11. The intellect[6] of mankind is the swifter. 12. The souls of the righteous are the happier. 13. *And* those of the wicked are the more penitent[7].'

CHAPTER XXIX.

1. The sage asked the spirit of wisdom (2) thus: 'What is it necessary to keep with more regard and more protection?'

---

[1] Or 'sharper.'

[2] L19 adds 'what is the more hopeless?'

[3] L19 has 'who sees.'

[4] The period appointed for the conflict between the good and evil spirits (see Chap. VIII, 11).

[5] Reading êdînasas, which Nêr. has misread ainâs, 'otherwise him.' L19 has 'yet then, except with justice and patience, he does not smite him otherwise.' It is also possible to read 'he does not smite him without listening (agûshas).'

[6] L19 has 'the thought.'

[7] L19 has 'the more miserable and more hopeless.'

3. The spirit of wisdom answered (4) thus: 'It is necessary to keep a young serving-boy (rasîk)[1], a wife, a beast *of burden*, and a fire with more protection and more regard.'

Chapter XXX.

1. The sage asked the spirit of wisdom (2) thus: 'Which of any living *existence* (zîvêndag-1) is the worse? 3. And in wisdom who is the more unforeseeing[2]?'

4. The spirit of wisdom answered (5) thus: 'A life of him is the worse, who lives in fear and falsehood[3]. 6. And in wisdom he is the more unforeseeing, who does not provide for[4] the spiritual *existence*, and attends to the worldly *one*.'

Chapter XXXI.

1. The sage asked the spirit of wisdom (2) thus: 'What is the business of the priests, warriors, and husbandmen[5], each separately?'

3. The spirit of wisdom answered (4) thus: 'The business of the priests is to maintain the religion properly; (5) and to perform the ceremonial and invocation of the sacred beings well *and* with atten-

[1] L19 has 'a young boy (r*e*dak).'

[2] Literally, 'more unforeknowing (apa*s*dânîktar).' L19 has 'more unapprovable (apasa*n*da*s*nîtar).'

[3] See Chap. XIX, 6.

[4] L19 has 'does not believe in.'

[5] The three classes which are often mentioned in the Avesta as constituting the Maz*d*a-worshipping community. For their vices, see Chap. LIX.

tion, (6) and[1] the decrees, decisions[2], custom, and control[3], as revealed by the pure, good religion of the Mazda-worshippers. 7. To make people aware of the goodness of good works[4]; (8) and to show the way to heaven, and the danger and avoidance of hell.

9. 'The business of the warriors is to defeat the enemy; (10) and to keep their own country and land (bûm)[5] unalarmed and tranquil.

11. 'And the business of the husbandmen is to perform tillage and cultivation; (12) and, to the extent of *their* ability, to keep the world invigorated and populous.'

Chapter XXXII.

1. The sage asked the spirit of wisdom (2) thus: 'What is the business of the well-endeavouring[6], the artizans?'

3. The spirit of wisdom answered (4) thus: 'The business of the artizans is this, (5) that *as to* that work which they do not understand, they do not bring a hand to it; (6) and that which they well[7]

---

[1] L19 inserts 'to keep true.'

[2] K43 has dâd dâdistân, 'decisions of the law;' but the repetition of the syllable dâd is probably a clerical blunder.

[3] L19 omits va band, 'and control.'

[4] L19 has 'aware of good works and sin.'

[5] L19 has vîmand, 'frontier.'

[6] The hûtûkhshân (Av. hûiti) are the fourth class of the community, and are very rarely mentioned in the Avesta, possibly because they were originally enslaved outcasts or aborigines, as in other ancient communities. The passage where they are specially mentioned (Yas. XIX, 46) is probably taken from the Bagh Nask (see Sls. X, 26 n; XIII, 1 n, 9 n).

[7] L19 omits 'well.'

understand (hû-dânend), they perform well *and* with attention; (7) and they demand wages lawfully. (8). For *as to him* who persists in doing that work which[1] he does not understand, it is *he by* whom that work is spoiled and becomes useless; and when, moreover, he is a man whose work makes himself satisfied, it then becomes even an origin of sin for him.'

CHAPTER XXXIII.

1. The sage asked the spirit of wisdom (2) thus: '*As to* a ruler[2], (3) a chieftain, (4) a friend, (5) a kinsman, (6) a wife, (7) a child, (8) and a country, which is the worse?'

9. The spirit of wisdom answered (10) thus: 'That ruler is the worse, that is not able to keep the country unalarmed, and the people untroubled. 11. That chieftain is the worse, who is defective in ability, unthankful unto agents (ka*rd*ârân), and no helper and interceder for a servant (a*s*âk)[3]. 12. That friend is the worse, who is not fit to be relied upon. 13. That kinsman is the worse, who is no helper in illness (khastânak)[4]. 14. That wife is the worse, with whom it is not possible to live with pleasure. 15. That child is the worse, who is no bringer of renown. 16. And that country is the worse, in which it is not possible to live in happiness, fearlessness, and permanence.'

---

[1] L19 omits 'work,' and K43 omits 'which.'

[2] L19 makes §§ 2–7 each a separate question, by adding 'which is the worse' to each, as in § 8.

[3] L19 has a*s*âgardân, 'disciples.'

[4] Or, 'in accident (hastânak).'

Chapter XXXIV.

1. The sage asked the spirit of wisdom (2) thus: '*Has* the creator Aûharmazd produced the creation of anything whatever for the worldly *existence*[1], unto which Aharman is not able to bring disturbance?'

3. The spirit of wisdom answered (4) thus: 'To him who is a wise and contented man it is *but* little possible to bring disturbance.'

Chapter XXXV.

1. The sage asked the spirit of wisdom (2) thus: 'How many are those people whom it is necessary to consider as rich, and how many are those who are poor?'

3. The spirit of wisdom answered (4) thus: 'These are the people it is necessary to consider as rich:—(5) one is he who is perfect in wisdom; (6) the second, whose body is healthy, and he lives fearlessly; (7) the third, who is content with that which has come; (8) the fourth, he whose destiny is a helper in virtue; (9) the fifth, who is well-famed in the eyes of the sacred beings, and *by* the tongues of the good; (10) the sixth, whose trust is on this one, pure, good religion of the Mazda-worshippers; (11) *and* the seventh, whose wealth is from honesty.

12. 'And these are the people to be considered as poor:—(13) one is he *with* whom there is no wisdom; (14) the second, whose body is not healthy; (15) the third, who lives in his fear, terror[2], and falsehood; (16) the fourth, who is not ruling in his

[1] L19 omits these four words.

[2] L19 omits 'terror.'

own body; (17) the fifth, whose destiny is no helper; (18) the sixth, who is infamous in the eyes of the sacred beings, and *on* the tongues of the good; (19) *and* the seventh, who is old, *and* no child and kindred exist.'

CHAPTER XXXVI.

1. The sage asked the spirit of wisdom (2) thus: 'Which sin is the more heinous?'

3. The spirit of wisdom answered (4) thus: 'Of the sin which people commit, unnatural intercourse is the more heinous. 5. The second is *he* who *has* suffered *or* performed intercourse with men. 6. The third, who slays a righteous man. 7. The fourth, who breaks off a next-of-kin marriage[1]. 8. The fifth, who destroys the arrangement of an adopted son (satôr)[2]. 9. The sixth, who smites the fire of Varahrâm[3]. 10. The seventh, who kills a water-beaver[4]. 11. The eighth, who worships an idol.

---

[1] See Chap. IV, 4 n.

[2] If a man has not appointed an adopted son during his lifetime, and leaves property producing an income of eighty-four rûpîs or more, but no privileged wife, or child, or domesticated brother, fit for the duty of guardianship, then an adopted son must be appointed by his nearest relations after his death (see Dd. LVI–LX).

[3] The sacred fire, named after the angel Varahrâm or Vâhrâm (see Chap. II, 115).

[4] The baprakŏ-î â*v*ik is the Av. bawri*s* upâpô, with whose skins Ardvîsûra, the angel of water, is said to be clothed (Âbân Yt. 129). It is said to have been 'created in opposition to the demon which is in the water' (see Bd. XIX, 29). Whether it is the same as the Av. udra upâpa, 'water-otter,' is not quite certain; but killing the latter was considered (for some reason not clearly ascertained) a very heinous sin, for which the proper atonement is fully detailed in Vend. XIV.

12. The ninth, who believes and wishes to worship in every religion. 13. The tenth, who consumes anything which is received into his custody, and becomes an embezzler. 14. The eleventh is he who, through sinfulness, provides support for wickedness[1]. 15. The twelfth, who does no work, but eats unthankfully and unlawfully. 16. The thirteenth, who commits heresy (zandîkîh)[2]. 17. The fourteenth, who commits witchcraft. 18. The fifteenth, who commits apostasy (aharmôkîh)[3]. 19. The sixteenth, who *commits*[4] demon-worship. 20. The seventeenth, who *commits* theft, or abetting (a*v*âgî*d*îh) of thieves. 21. The eighteenth, who *commits* promise-breaking[5]. 22. The nineteenth, who *commits* maliciousness. 23. The twentieth, who commits oppression to make the things of others his own. 24. The twenty-first, who dis-

[1] L19 has 'falsehood.'

[2] The term zandîk, according to Mas'aûdî (chap. xxiv), was first applied to the Manicheans, and afterwards to all others who followed the commentary (zand) in preference to the Avesta; finally, however, the Arabs applied the term to the Persians, probably with its acquired meaning of 'heretic' or 'infidel.' A different explanation of the term is given in Pahl. Yas. LX, 11, where it is stated that 'Zand is the apostle of the wizards, *and* through Zand it is possible to perform witchcraft.' The Sanskrit version here adds, 'that is, he thinks well of Aharman and the demons;' and in PA10 it continues thus: 'the atheist's religion, the wicked way *that* there is no creator, there is no heaven, there is no hell, there is no resurrection, *and* so on; such is the meaning.'

[3] From Av. ashemaogha, 'disturbing righteousness.' Nêr. adds in Sanskrit, 'that is, having thoroughly known the meaning of the Avesta, he becomes deceived.'

[4] As the verb in § 23 can apply, in Pahlavi, to any number of preceding sections, it is omitted by K43 in §§ 19–22. The verb is also omitted by K43 in § 25 for a similar reason.

[5] Or 'breach of contract.'

tresses a righteous man. 25. The twenty-second, who *commits* slander. 26. The twenty-third, who commits arrogance. 27. The twenty-fourth, who goes to a professional courtezan[1]. 28. The twenty-fifth, who commits ingratitude. 29. The twenty-sixth, who speaks false and untrue[2]. 30. The twenty-seventh, who causes discontent as to the affairs of those who are departed[3]. 31. The twenty-eighth, whose pleasure is from viciousness *and* harassing the good. 32. The twenty-ninth, who considers sin as to be urged on, and a good work as a day's delay[4]. 33. *And* the thirtieth, who becomes grieved by that happiness which is provided by him for any one.'

Chapter XXXVII.

1. The sage asked the spirit of wisdom (2) thus: 'Through how many ways and motives of good works do people arrive most at heaven?'

3. The spirit of wisdom answered (4) thus: 'The first good work is liberality[5]. 5. The second, truth. 6. The third, thankfulness. 7. The fourth, contentment. 8. The fifth, wanting to produce welfare for the good, and becoming a friend to every one. 9. The sixth, being without doubt as to this, that the

---

[1] Such appears to be the meaning of zanô-î kârân. L19 has zan-î kasân, 'the wives of others.'

[2] Or 'irreverent,' according as we read arâstô or anâstô.

[3] L19 has 'secluded and departed,' similar to Chap. XXXVII, 23.

[4] It is doubtful whether sîpang, 'a halting-place,' or sîpôg, 'setting aside,' should be read; but the meaning is practically the same.

[5] Compare Chap. IV, which divides good works into seven classes.

sky and earth and every benefit of the worldly and spiritual *existences* are owing to the creator Aûhar*m*a*zd*. 10. The seventh, *being so* as to the unquestionableness of this[1], that all misery and affliction are owing to Aharman the wicked, who is accursed. 11. The eighth, freedom from doubt as to the resurrection and future existence. 12. The ninth, who for love of the soul effects[2] a next-of-kin marriage. 13. The tenth, who arranges adoption[3]. 14. The eleventh, who practises regular industry. 15. The twelfth, who is without doubt in this pure, good religion of the Ma*zd*a-worshippers. 16. The thirteenth, who is kindly regardful as to the ability and means of every one. 17. The fourteenth, who perceives[4] the kind regard of the good, and becomes himself, also, kindly regardful as to the goodness which *one* wants among the good. 18. The fifteenth, who seeks the affection of the good. 19. The sixteenth, who keeps malice and uncharitableness far from *his* mind. 20. The seventeenth, who bears no improper envy. 21. The eighteenth, who forms no desire of lust. 22. The nineteenth, who produces no discord with any one. 23. The twentieth, who brings no distress into the affairs of a departed and unassisted *one* (avi*g*î*d*)[5]. 24. The twenty-first, who

---

[1] By the transposition of two words L19 has 'freedom from doubt as to this.'

[2] Whether for himself, or for another, is uncertain (see Chap. IV, 4n).

[3] Nêr. explains in Sanskrit, thus: 'that is, whoever becomes a spirit childless, maintains any man, with his wealth, for his fame and his lineage, then thus the soul, too, is for an increase of good works.'

[4] L19 transposes the two verbs, 'perceives' and 'wants.'

[5] Nêr. reads *hv*azî*d*, which he identifies with Pers. '*h*azîd, 'con-

lets[1] no wrath into *his* body. 25. The twenty-second, who commits no sin on account of disgrace[2]. 26. The twenty-third, who forms no desire of lethargy on account of laziness. 27. The twenty-fourth, who is without doubt as to the sacred beings. 28. The twenty-fifth, who is without doubt as to the existence of heaven and hell, and the account which is *to be rendered* by the soul, the glory which is in heaven, and the misery which is in hell. 29. The twenty-sixth, who abstains[3] from slander and envious looks. 30. The twenty-seventh, who causes the happiness of himself, and gives happy advancement also to others. 31. The twenty-eighth, who becomes the help[4] of the good, and accuser of the bad. 32. The twenty-ninth, who restrains himself from deceit and evil (dûsîh)[5]. 33. The thirtieth, who does not speak false and untrue[6]. 34. The thirty-first, who restrains himself firmly from promise-breaking. 35. The thirty-second, who, for the sake of seeking his own benefit and happiness, causes the abstinence of others from evil. 36. *And* the thirty-third, who provides lodging accommodation for the sick and secluded[7] and traders.'

Chapter XXXVIII.

1. The sage asked the spirit of wisdom (2) thus: 'Wherefore *is it* when they do not allot the happiness

cealed, secluded;' and which might also be taken in the sense of one who has 'crawled,' meaning a young child; but the identification is doubtful.

[1] L19 has 'keeps.'

[2] That is, 'for fear of disgrace.'

[3] L19 has 'restrains himself.'

[4] L19 has 'helper.'

[5] L19 has *hvad*-dôshî, 'self-conceit.'

[6] See Chap. XXXVI, 29 n.

[7] See Chap. XV, 6 n.

of the worldly *existence* according to worthiness, and they make the soul a seizer upon the spiritual *existences* by worthiness of action?'

3. The spirit of wisdom answered (4) thus: 'On account of the compassion of Aûharmazd, the lord, as regards the creatures, he allots all happiness alike among the good and alike among the bad. 5. But when it does not always come upon them, *it is* on account of the oppression of Aharman and the demons, and the extortion of those seven planets[1].

6. 'And they make *one*[2] a seizer upon the spiritual *existences*, by worthiness of action, on this account, because the wickedness of any[3] one arises through the performance of his own actions.'

Chapter XXXIX.

1. The sage asked the spirit of wisdom (2) thus: 'Which power is the more seemly? 3. In wisdom who is the more complete? 4. And in disposition who is the more faithful? 5. Whose speech is the more proper? 6. In whose mind is the goodness little[4]? 7. And as a friend who is the worse? 8. In whose mind is the pleasure little? 9. In heart who is the more seemly? 10. In endurance who is the more approvable? 11. Who is not to be considered as faithful? 12. What is that which is worth keeping with every one? 13. And what

---

[1] Which are supposed to be agents of Aharman for causing misfortune to the creatures (see Chaps. VIII, 19, 20; XII, 7–10).

[2] L19 has 'the soul.'

[3] L19 has 'every.'

[4] L19 has 'much the more,' to correspond with a different reply in § 26.

is that which is not to be kept with any one? 14. What is to be preserved in conversation? 15. Who is he that is not to be accepted as a witness? 16. And unto whom is it necessary to be obedient? 17. What is it more necessary to mind and to keep praising? 18. What is that which is not to be made unrespected in any way? 19. What is he who, in his own degree, is said *to be* such as Aûharmazd and the archangels? 20. And what is he who, in his own degree, is[1] such as Aharman and the demons?'

21. The spirit of wisdom answered (22) thus: 'In power he is the more seemly who, when he indulges his wrath, is able to allay the wrath, and not commit sin and gratify himself. 23. And in wisdom he is the more complete who is able to preserve his own soul. 24. In disposition he is the more faithful, in whom there is nothing whatever *of* deceit and pretence. 25. The speech of him is the more proper who speaks more true. 26. Goodness is little in the mind of a man of wrath[2]. 27. As a friend, a malicious man who is a fighter is worse. 28. And pleasure is little in the mind of him who is an envious man. 29. In heart he is the more seemly who abandons the worldly *existence* and seizes the spiritual *one;* (30) and by his own will accepts righteousness as a yoke (val kavarman)[3]. 31. And in endurance he is the more approvable who[4],

[1] L19 has 'is said *to be*.'

[2] L19 has 'goodness is more in an humble-minded man,' so as to correspond with the difference in its question in § 6.

[3] Literally, 'for the neck.' Nêr. has misread val-ik valman (Pâz. ô-ka ôi), and has 'by his own will for it, also accepts righteousness.'

[4] From this point to Chap. XL, 17, the Pahlavi text of K43 is missing, owing to the loss of one folio in that MS. The copy of

[contentedly and with a will, accepts, as a yoke[1],] the misery and affliction which [come upon] him [from Aharman and the demons and the vile; (32) *and* it, in no way, harasses his own soul. 33. He is not to be considered as faithful who has no fear of the sacred beings, *nor* shame as to mankind. 34. Those which are worth keeping with every one are peace and affection. 35. And those which are not to be kept with any one whatever are malice *and* discord. 36. All[2] these three are to be preserved in conversation: good thoughts, good words, *and* good deeds in one's own thinking, speaking, *and* doing. 37. These three are not to be accepted as a witness: a woman[3], a young serving-boy[4], and a man-slave. 38. These are such as must be personally obedient *and* do service: (39) the wife unto the husband, (40) and the child unto the father and mother, the chieftain[5] and high-priest, the teacher[6], the adopted son[7], and secluded[8] kindred. 41. *And* unto rulers, chieftains, *and* teachers *one* is also to be obedient. 42. The sacred beings it is more necessary to mind and to keep praising. 43. And one's own soul is not to be made[9] unrespected in any mode, (44) *and* is always to be kept

TD2 is, therefore, followed, and its translation is enclosed in brackets.

[1] See § 30 n.

[2] L19 omits 'all.'

[3] Or 'a wife,' as both meanings are expressed by the same word, and, in fact, every woman is expected to become a wife.

[4] L19 has 'a young boy,' as in Chap. XXIX, 4.

[5] The word sardâr (Pâz. sâlâr) also means 'guardian.'

[6] L19 inserts 'and fire.'

[7] See Chap. XXXVI, 8 n. As the adopted son takes the place of the deceased father, he must be obeyed accordingly by the whole family.

[8] See Chap. XV, 6 n.

[9] L19 has 'considered.'

in remembrance. 45. The judge who exercises true justice, *and* takes no bribe, is[1], in his own degree, such as Aûharmazd and the archangels. 46. And he who exercises false justice is said *to be*, in his own degree, such as Aharman and the demons.'

CHAPTER XL.

1. The sage asked the spirit of wisdom (2) thus: 'What is the colder and what is the warmer? 3. What is the brighter and what is the darker? 4. What is the fuller and what is the emptier[2]? 5. What end is the more fruitless[3]? 6. What is that thing of which no superfluity arises *for* any one? 7. What is that which no one is able to deprive *one of?* 8. What is that thing which it is not possible to buy at a price? 9. What is that thing with which every one is always[4] satisfied? 10. What is that with which no one[5] whatever is satisfied? 11. What is that one wish that Aûharmazd, the lord, *contemplates*[6] as regards men? 12. What is that one wish that Aharman, the wicked, contemplates as regards men? 13. What is the end of the worldly *existence* and what is the end of[7] the spiritual *one?*'

14. The spirit of wisdom answered (15) thus: 'The heart of the righteous is the warmer, and that

[1] L19 has 'is said *to be*.'

[2] Reading tôhîktar, both here and in § 17; L19 has ta*n*gîtar, as if for tangtar, 'narrower,' in both places.

[3] TD2 has 'fearless,' but this does not correspond with § 18.

[4] L19 omits 'always.'

[5] L19 has 'nothing.'

[6] The verb in § 12 is sufficient in Pahlavi for this section also.

[7] L19 omits these five words.

of the wicked the colder. 16. Righteousness is the brighter, and wickedness the darker. 17. The hope *and* protection which *pertain* to the sacred beings][1] are the fuller, and those which *pertain* to the demons are the emptier[2]. 18. The end of the world-arranging *and* spirit-destroying man is the more fruitless. 19. It is knowledge of which no one knows a superfluity. 20. It is learning and skill which no one is able to deprive *one of*. 21. It is understanding and intellect which it is not possible to buy at a price. 22. It is wisdom with which every one and one's own self are untroubled and satisfied. 23. It is stupidity and ignorance with which every one and even one's own self are troubled and not satisfied.

24. 'That one wish which Aûharmazd, the lord, contemplates as regards men is this, (25) that "ye shall fully understand me; for every *one* who fully understands me, comes after me and strives for my satisfaction." 26. And that one wish which Aharman contemplates as regards men is this, (27) that "ye shall not understand me;" for he knows that whoever fully understands that wicked *one*, does not go after his evil deeds[3], (28) and nothing whatever of power and help for him arises[4] from that man.

29. 'And *as to* that which is asked by thee concerning the spiritual and worldly *existences*, the worldly *existence* is, in the end, death and disappearance, (30) and of the spiritual *existence*, in the end,

[1] From this point the translation again follows the Pahlavi text of K43.

[2] See § 4 n.

[3] L19 has 'for whoever fully understands me *as* wicked, *his* deeds do not go after me.'

[4] L19 has 'nothing whatever of advantage and help comes to me.'

that of a soul of the righteous is undecaying, immortal, and undisturbed, full of glory and full of enjoyment, for ever and everlasting, with the angels and archangels and the guardian spirits[1] of the righteous. 31. And the bridge[2] and destruction[3] and punishment of the wicked in hell are for ever and everlasting[4]. 32. And the wicked soul, apart from the punishment, contemplates the existence, and even the appearance[5], with the demons and fiends just as, in the worldly *existence*, a healthy man *does that* with him who is very grievously sick.'

CHAPTER XLI.

1. The sage asked the spirit of wisdom (2) thus: 'Which man is the mightier? 3. Which road is the more dreadful? 4. Which account is the more

[1] The guardian spirits are the spiritual representatives of each individual being and thing of the good creation, which are supposed to have been all created by Aûharmazd in the beginning (see Chap. XLIX, 23, Bd. I, 8).

[2] That is the investigation into the character of the soul at the *K*indvar bridge (see Chap. II, 115, 162). L19 omits this mention of the bridge.

[3] Reading drû*s*, as in L19, but this is doubtful.

[4] This phrase can be used either with reference to time or to eternity. Time which lasts for ever must end at the resurrection, as in this case (see Chap. II, 193), because time then ceases to exist. But eternity which lasts for ever can never end. If this phrase had the same meaning here as in § 30, it would contradict all the other statements regarding the fate of the wicked, which are to be found in Pahlavi literature, including those of the author himself.

[5] L19 has 'the wicked soul contemplates being apart from the punishment, and also apart from appearance.'

perplexing? 5. Which tie[1] is the pleasanter? 6. Which work is the more regretable? 7. And which gift is the more unprofitable?'

8. The spirit of wisdom answered (9) thus: 'That man is the mightier who is able to struggle with his own fiends[2]; (10) and, in particular, *he* who keeps these five fiends far from *his* person, (11) which are such as greediness, wrath, lust, disgrace, and discontent. 12. The road in passing over the *K*indvar bridge[3] is the more dreadful. 13. The account for a soul of the wicked is the more perplexing. 14. The tie of children is the pleasanter and more desirable. 15. That work is the more regretable which they do for the ungrateful. 16. *And* that gift is the more unprofitable which they give to the unworthy[4].'

Chapter XLII.

1. The sage asked the spirit of wisdom (2) thus: 'How many kinds of man are *there*?'

3. The spirit of wisdom answered (4) thus: '*There* are three kinds of man, (5) one is man, one is demi-man, and one is demi-demon.

6. 'A man is he who is without doubt as to the creativeness of Aûha*r*ma*zd*, the destructiveness of Aharman, and the existence of the resurrection and future existence; and also *as regards* every other happiness and misery, in the worldly and spiritual

[1] K43 has bôî, 'scent,' which is distinguished from band, 'tie,' only by diacritical marks in Pahlavi.

[2] His own passions and failings personified as fiends.

[3] See Chap. II, 115, 162.

[4] L19 has 'to the ungrateful and unworthy.'

existences, (7) that *its* origin is from both of those *beings*, from Aûharmazd and Aharman. 8. And his belief is in this one pure, good religion of the Mazda-worshippers; (9) and he does not believe in, and does not hearken unto, any heterodoxy.

10. 'A demi-man is he who performs the affairs of the worldly and spiritual *existences* according to his own opinion, self-conceitedly and obstinately; (11) be they duties and good works by the will of Aûharmazd, *or* be they by the will of Aharman, they proceed from him.

12. 'A demi-demon is he in whom *there* is only as *it were* the name of man[1] and the human race, *but* in his doing of every action *he* is then like unto a two-legged demon. 13. He understands no worldly and no spiritual *existence*, (14) he understands no good work and no sin, (15) he understands no heaven and no hell, (16) and even the account which is *to be rendered* by the soul he does not think of.'

CHAPTER XLIII.

1. The sage asked the spirit of wisdom (2) thus: 'How is it possible to make Aûharmazd, the archangels, and the fragrant, well-pleasing heaven more fully for oneself? 3. And how is it possible to make Aharman, the wicked, and the demons confounded, and to escape from hell, the depreciated[2] and dark?'

4. The spirit of wisdom answered (5) thus: 'To make Aûharmazd, the lord, and the archangels, and

[1] L19 has 'humanity.'

[2] Reading dûs-vahâk. Nêr. has misread the word dus-gand, 'evil-smelling,' both here and in §§ 5, 14.

the fragrant, well-pleasing heaven for oneself, and[1] Aharman, the wicked, and the demons confounded, and to escape from hell, the dark and depreciated, are possible thus: (6) that is, when they make the spirit of wisdom a protection for the back (pûstîk-pânakîh), (7) and wear the spirit of contentment on the body, like arms and armour and valour, (8) and make the spirit of truth[2] a shield, (9) the spirit of thankfulness a club, (10) the spirit of complete mindfulness a bow, (11) and the spirit of liberality an arrow; (12) and they make the spirit of moderation like a spear, (13) the spirit of perseverance a gauntlet, and they put forth the spirit of destiny as a protection[3]. 14. In this manner it is possible to come to heaven and the sight of the sacred beings, and to escape from Aharman, the wicked, and hell, the depreciated.'

CHAPTER XLIV.

1. The sage asked the spirit of wisdom (2) thus: 'How are the sky and earth arranged? 3. How are the flow and arrangement of the water in the world? 4. Whereon do the clouds rest? 5. Where is the demon of winter more predominant? 6. And which country is the more undisturbed?'

7. The spirit of wisdom answered (8) thus: 'The sky and earth and water, and whatever else is within

[1] L19 repeats 'to make,' but this is no more necessary in Pahlavi than in English.

[2] L19 inserts 'like' in §§ 8–11, and omits the verb 'make' in §§ 8, 12.

[3] §§ 6–13 bear some resemblance to Isaiah lix. 17 and Ephesians vi. 14–17, so far as mode of expression is concerned.

them[1] are egg-like (khâîyak-dîs), just as *it were*[2] like the egg of a bird. 9. The sky is arranged above the earth[3], like an egg, by the handiwork of the creator Aûharmazd; (10) and the semblance of the earth, in the midst of the sky[4], is just like as *it were* the yolk amid the egg; [(11) and the water within the earth and sky is such as the water within the egg.][5]

12. 'And the flow of the water of every kind which is in the world is from the region of Arzah[6] (13) there where the sun comes up[7]; and *its* downward surge (nîgun bâlisnŏ)[8] is towards the region of Savah (14) where[9] the sun goes down; and the

[1] L19 has 'within the sky.'

[2] L19 has 'are so arranged as.' The reading of dîs, 'like,' is rather uncertain.

[3] L19 adds 'and below the earth.'

[4] L19 has 'and the earth within the sky.'

[5] § 11 is taken from PB6, but is not found in any other Pâzand or Pârsî MS. consulted, nor in the Pahlavi text of K43; it is, therefore, probably an interpolation.

[6] See Chap. XVI, 10 n.

[7] This clause and the corresponding one in § 14 seem to be at variance with the statements of Bd. V, 8, XI, 3, that Arzah is in the west, and Savah in the east; Nêryôsang has, therefore, transferred the conjunction 'and' to the beginning of the section in both cases, so as to make the eastern waters flow towards Savah, and the western waters into the sea. If, however, we understand 'there' to mean 'in those places,' and not to refer to the region whose name it follows, we may conclude that the statement here is to the effect that in the east the water flows from Arzah (the western region), and in the west towards Savah (the eastern region), which might be true if we place the east in China or Bengal, and the west in Armenia or Mesopotamia, but it is more probably meant merely to imply that the whole of the water flows through the central region of Khvanîras.

[8] L19 has anbârisnŏ, 'accumulation,' both here and in § 14.

[9] L19 has 'there where;' and we must understand '*in those places* where,' as in § 13.

surging on (âbâlisnŏ) of the water is into the sea Pûtîk[1], (15) and from the sea Pûtîk it goes back to the sea Varkash[2].

16. 'The abode and seat of the clouds are on Albûrz[3].

17. 'The demon of winter is more predominant in Aîrân-vêgô[4]. 18. And *it* is declared by revelation[5], (19) that in Aîrân-vêgô *there* are "ten months winter and two months summer," (20) *and* "even those" two months of warm weather "are cold *as to* water, cold *as to* earth, and cold *as to* plants." 21. And their adversity[6] is the winter, (22) and the snakes therein are many, (23) while their other adversity is little.

24. '*It* is declared that Aûharmazd created Aîrân-vêgô better than other places and districts[7].

---

[1] Av. Pûitika, which Bd. XIII, 8–11 appears to identify with the Persian Gulf, but in early times, if not altogether mythic, it was probably some inlet of the Caspian or Aral.

[2] Av. Vouru-kasha; in Pahlavi it is usually called 'the wide-formed,' and in Bd. XIII, 1, 8–10 it is identified with the ocean; but in early times it was probably a term for the Caspian and Aral, when not applied to the mythic sea of the sky.

[3] Av. hara berezaiti, 'a lofty mountain-range,' which is said, in Chap. LVII, 13 and in the Bundahis, to surround the world and to be the origin of all mountains (see Bd. V, 3–5, XII, 1–4). In early times it appears to have been the name of mountains to the east of the first Irânian settlements, before it was transferred to the mountain range south of the Caspian (see Geiger's Ost. Kul. pp. 42–45).

[4] Av. Airyanem vaêgô, the first settlement of the Irânians, which Geiger (Ost. Kul. pp. 30–33) places on the upper waters of the Zarafsân river, and which Bd. XXIX, 12 describes, in accordance with late tradition, as 'in the direction of Âtûr-pâtakân (Âdarbîgân).'

[5] Vend. I, 9, 10.

[6] Produced by the evil spirit (see Vend. I, 7, 8).

[7] This is inferred from Vend. I, 2–4.

25. And its goodness is this, that the life of the people is three hundred years[1], (26) and of the oxen and sheep one hundred and fifty years. 27. Their pain and sickness, also, are little; (28) they fabricate (drûgênd)[2] no lies, (29) they make no lamentation and weeping, (30) and the domination of the demon of greediness (âz) in their bodies is little. 31. When they eat one loaf among ten men, they are satisfied. 32. And in every forty years one child is born from one woman and one man[3]. 33. Their law, also, is goodness, and *their* religion the primitive faith[4]; (34) and when they die they are righteous[5]. 35. Their *spiritual* chief (ratû), likewise, is Gôpaîtô[6], and *their* lord and king is Srôsh[7].'

CHAPTER XLV.

1. The sage asked the spirit of wisdom (2) thus: 'By what does Aharman most deceive and lead people to hell? 3. And from what is his pleasure most? 4. Where is the place he has a foundation?

---

[1] Compare Chap. LXII, 18.

[2] L19 has drenzinend, 'they cause to repeat.'

[3] Compare Chap. LXII, 17.

[4] Av. paoiryô-dkaêsha, a term applied to the true Mazda-worshipping religion of all ages, both before and after the time of Zaratûst.

[5] That is, they go at once to heaven, as the righteous soul does (see Chap. II, 123–157).

[6] L19 has Gôpatshâh, 'the king of Gôpat' (as in Chap. LXII, 8, 31), which land is described in Dd. XC, 4 as 'coterminous with Aîrân-vêgô.' Aghrêrad and his son are called kings of Gôpat in Bd. XXIX, 5, XXXI, 22; and Gôk-patô is said to be 'in the non-Aryan countries,' in the Sûdkar Nask (see Dd. XC, 8 n).

[7] Apparently the angel Srôsh (see Chap. II, 115).

5. Where, also, is his coming, *together* with the demons, most? 6. And from what is his food?'

7. The spirit of wisdom answered (8) thus: 'Aharman deceives people most by prosperity and adversity[1], the fiend of apostasy, scepticism, and covetousness. 9. His pleasure, also, is most from the discord of men. 10. And his food is from the impenitence[2] and reticence of men. 11. He has a foundation in the malicious[3]. 12. And his coming and going are most with the wrathful.'

Chapter XLVI.

1. The sage asked the spirit of wisdom (2) thus: 'Which is the one[4] oppression, as regards men, *that* Aharman considers as the more injurious and great?'

3. The spirit of wisdom answered (4) thus: 'Aharman, when he wrings life and wife and child and worldly happiness of every kind away from men, does not consider, as to this, that any injury whatever is inflicted by him upon that person; (5) but when he wrings away the soul of a single *individual*, and makes it utterly depraved, he then considers, as to this, that "an injury which is complete would thereby be inflicted by me," because this is done by him through his own depravity of wish and action[5].'

[1] Or 'superfluity and scarcity.'

[2] Assuming that apatôtakîh stands for apatîtakîh, 'non-renunciation *of sin*.' L19 has 'immoderate eating.'

[3] L19 has 'in the slanderous and malicious.'

[4] L19 omits 'one.'

[5] The last fourteen words occur only in the Pahlavi text of K43.

Chapter XLVII.

1. The sage asked the spirit of wisdom (2) thus: 'What is that thing *which* is the most perfect of all wealth? 3. What is that which is predominant over everything whatever? 4. And what is that from which no one is able to escape?'

5. The spirit of wisdom answered (6) thus: 'It is wisdom which is better than the wealth of every kind which is in the world. 7. It is destiny which is predominant over every one and everything. 8. And *it is* Vâê the bad[1] from whom no one is able to escape.'

Chapter XLVIII.

1. The sage asked the spirit of wisdom (2) thus: 'How is the dwelling of the understanding and intellect and seed of men in the body?'

3. The spirit of wisdom answered (4) thus: 'The place of the understanding and intellect and seed of men is in the brain of the head. 5. And when the brain of the head is sound, the understanding and intellect and seed are on the increase; (6) *but* when a person attains unto old age, the brain of the head remains only at a diminution. 7. And he who is an aged man, on account of the diminution of understanding and intellect, sees less and knows less of that which it is necessary to do with wisdom. 8. Wisdom, in the beginning, mingles with the marrow of the fingers of men's hands; (9) and, afterwards,

[1] The demon which conveys the soul to its account (see Chap. II, 115).

its seat and abode and place[1] are in the heart. 10. And its dwelling[2] in the whole body becomes such as the shape of the foot in various shoes (mûg-*k*akŏ).[3]'

CHAPTER XLIX.

1. The sage asked the spirit of wisdom (2) thus: '*As to* these stars which are apparent in the sky, and their number is so great, what is then their duty and influence? 3. And how is the motion of the sun and moon and stars?'

4. The spirit of wisdom answered (5) thus: 'Of the stars which are in the sky the first star is Tî*s*tar[4], which is said *to be* great and good, more valuable and more glorious[5]. 6. And prosperity of every kind and the fertility of the world are in the path of Tî*s*tar.

7, 8. 'And the star of water germs is for the increase of the star of plant germs[6]. 9, 10. And the star of plant germs is for the increase of cattle germs[7].

---

[1] L19 has 'its seat and abiding place.'

[2] L19 has 'and the dwelling of the soul.'

[3] L19 has 'in the shoe.'

[4] Av. Ti*s*trya, the eastern leader of the stars and special opponent of the planet Tîr (Mercury), which can be identified only with Sirius. It is personified as an angel who contends with the demon of drought and produces rain (see Bd. II, 7, V, 1, VII, 1-13).

[5] The usual Avesta epithets of Tî*s*tar are 'the radiant and glorious.'

[6] L19 has 'for the increase of water. And the star of earth germs is for the increase of earth.'

[7] L19 has 'for the increase of plants. And the star of cattle germs is for the increase of cattle.' The stars of water, earth, and plant germs are mentioned in the formula of dedication to Tî*s*tar (Sîr. 13), and the moon is said to possess the germs of cattle (Sîr. 12).

11. And water, fire[1], plant, and cattle germs are created for the increase of man germs[2].

12. 'And the star Vanand[3] is intrusted with the passes *and* gates of Albûrz[4]; (13) so that the demons and witches and fiends *may* turn from those gates and passes, (14) that *it may* not *be* possible for them to cut off and break up the road and passage of the sun and moon and stars[5].

15. 'And the star Haptôk-ring[6], with 99,999 guardian spirits of the righteous[7], is intrusted with the gate and passage of hell[8], (16) for the keeping

---

Reference is also made to all of them in Rashnu Yt. 29–31, 33, and to those of water germs in Vend. XXI, 33, Tîstar Yt. 39, 45, 46.

[1] L19 has 'earth.'

[2] L19 has 'for the increase of men.' As both the Pahlavi and Pâzand versions of §§ 7–11 are complete and consistent in themselves, it is uncertain which of them gives the original text. The Pâzand corresponds more closely to certain passages in the Avesta, but a wish to produce such a correspondence may have led Nêryôsang to alter the text. That the Pahlavi writer was thinking of some other passage, as yet unidentified, is evident from the omission of the star Satavês (which follows Tîstar in Sîr. 13) and from the details he gives concerning the others.

[3] The southern leader of the stars and special opponent of the planet Aûharmazd (Jupiter), which is perhaps best identified with Fomalhaut (see Bd. II, 7, V, 1). The Avesta mentions it in connection with Tîstar (Sîr. 13).

[4] See Chap. XLIV, 16 n.

[5] Which are supposed to rise and set through openings or passes in the mountain range of Albûrz, which encircles the world (see Bd. V, 5).

[6] Av. Haptôiringa, the northern leader of the stars and special opponent of the planet Vâhrâm (Mars), which corresponds to Ursa Major (see Bd. II, 7, V, 1). The Avesta mentions it, in connection with the other stars named in the text, in Sîr. 13.

[7] See Fravardîn Yt. 60. The number here mentioned is that generally used in the Avesta to express an indefinitely large number.

[8] Which is supposed to be in the north, so that the circumpolar

back of those 99,999 demons and fiends, witches and wizards, who are in opposition to the *celestial* sphere and constellations *of the zodiac*. 17. Its motion, also, is round about hell; (18) and its special business is this, as *it were* it holds the twelve signs of the zodiac by the hand, in *their* proper going and coming. 19. And those twelve constellations also proceed *in* like manner by the power and help of Haptôk-ring[1]; (20) and every single constellation, when it comes in at Albûrz, provides support for Haptôk-ring[2], (21) and begs protection from Haptôk-ring.

22. 'The remaining unnumbered and innumerable constellations[3] which are apparent are said *to be* the guardian spirits of the worldly *existences*. 23. Because, *as to* the creatures and creations of every kind, that the creator Aûharmazd created for the worldly *existence*, which are procreative and also which are developable (ârôdisnîk)[4], for every single body *there* is apparent its own single guardian spirit of a like nature.

24. 'And the motion of the sun and moon is the special illumination of the world, (25) and the maturing of procreations and growths of all kinds. 26. And the correct keeping of the day, month, and year, summer and winter, spring and autumn, and other calculations and accounts of all kinds which men ought to obtain, perceive, and understand, (27)

---

constellation of Ursa Major seems to revolve around it, and to remain on the watch.

[1] Written Haptâôrig in §§ 19–21 in K43.

[2] L19 has 'holds to Haptôk-ring by the hand.'

[3] L19 has 'stars.'

[4] L19 has azâisnî, 'unprocreative.'

are more fully defined by means of the setting (nisîvakŏ)[1] of the sun and moon.'

Chapter L.

1. The sage asked the spirit of wisdom (2) thus: 'Which is that opulent *person* who is to be considered as fortunate, and which is that *one* who is *to be considered* as evil-conditioned?'

3. The spirit of wisdom answered (4) thus: 'That *one* who has produced opulence by proper exertion is to be considered as fortunate; and that *one* who has produced *it* by dishonesty, as evil-conditioned.'

Chapter LI.

1. The sage asked the spirit of wisdom (2) thus: 'Wherefore *is it* when there are *instances* when a lazy, ignorant, and bad man attains to eminence and great welfare, (3) and there are *instances* when a worthy, wise, and good man attains to grievous misery, perplexity, and indigence?'

4. The spirit of wisdom answered (5) thus: '*As to* him who is a lazy, ignorant, and bad man, when his destiny becomes a helper, that laziness of his then becomes like unto diligence, that ignorance unto[2] knowledge, and that vileness unto[2] goodness. 6. And *as to* him who is a wise, worthy, and good man, when his destiny is an opponent, that wisdom of his then turns to stupidity and foolishness (alakîh), and that worthiness to ignorance; (7) and *his*

---

[1] Nêr. reads vaheza and translates 'new year's day.'

[2] L19 has 'like unto' in all three clauses.

knowledge, skill, and worthiness become manifestly secluded[1].'

CHAPTER LII.

1. The sage asked the spirit of wisdom (2) thus: 'How is it necessary to perform the ceremonial of the sacred beings and the thanksgiving for the welfare which is owing to the sacred beings? 3. *And* how is the renunciation *of sin* to be performed for the preservation of the soul?'

4. The spirit of wisdom answered (5) thus: 'That ceremonial of the sacred beings is good which they perform in this pure, good religion of the Maz*d*a-worshippers. 6. Its origin, also, is goodness and truth, and freedom from doubt in the sacred beings. 7. And for the little and the much that has come *there has* arisen thanksgiving unto the sacred beings; and *one* is to meditate upon the gratifications (shnû-makân) and prosperity which are owing to the sacred beings and to keep grateful[2]. 8. And even when perplexity and misery come on from Aharman and the demons, *he* is not to become doubtful as to the treasure of the sacred beings, (9) and not to diminish the thanksgiving unto the sacred beings. 10. And every disaster which springs up *he* is to give back[3] to the violence of Aharman and the demons. 11. *He* is not to seek his own welfare and advantage through the injury of any one else; (12) and he

[1] See Chap. XV, 6n. Nêr. has in Sans. 'are manifest in immobility.'

[2] The Pâzand version omits the latter half of this section, and also uses the present tense instead of the infinitive in several of the following sections.

[3] Perhaps 'trace back' may be meant, but this is uncertain.

becomes compassionate as regards the creatures of Aûharmazd. 13. In duty and good works *he* is diligent and striving[1]; (14) *and* especially in the care of water and fire[2] *he* is to persevere much. 15. And *he* is to be without doubt as to this, that, except happiness, the sacred beings do not then[3] give anything whatever, *as* a modification[4] of it, unto men; and Aharman and the demons, except misery, do not then[3] give them any happiness.

16. 'For the existence of renunciation *of sin* the special thing is this, that *one* commits no sin voluntarily; (17) and if, through folly, or weakness and ignorance, a sin occurs, he is then in renunciation *of sin* before the high-priests and the good. 18. And after that, *when*[5] he does not commit *it*, then that sin which is committed by him becomes thus a sweeping (êsvârakŏ)[6] from his body; (19) just as the wind which is hasty and mighty, when it comes swift and strong, sweeps so over the plain that it carries away every single blade of grass (gîyyâkî*k*akŏ-1) and anything which is broken *in* that place.'

CHAPTER LIII.

1. The sage asked the spirit of wisdom (2) thus: 'How are the homage and glorifying of the sacred beings to be performed?'

3. The spirit of wisdom answered (4) thus:

---

[1] L19 has 'he acts diligently and strivingly.'

[2] L19 adds 'and plants.'

[3] Reading êdînas; Nêr. has misread ainâ, 'otherwise.'

[4] Reading gvî*d*arîh; Nêr. has misread vatarî, 'an evil.'

[5] L19 has 'too,' and K43 omits the word.

[6] Misread a*v*âz, 'away,' by Nêryôsang.

'Every day three times, standing opposite the sun and Mitrô[1], as they proceed together[2], (5) and[3] the moon and fire of Vâhrâm[4], or the fire of fires[5], *in* like manner, morning, noon, and evening, homage and glorifying are performed, (6) and *one has* become grateful[6]. 7. And if a sin, or a deficiency (frôd-mând-1)[7], *has* occurred, especially[8] as regards the angels of the spiritual and worldly *existences*, men and beasts *of burden*[9], oxen and sheep, dogs and the dog species, and other creatures and creations of Aûharmazd the lord, (8) *one* is to become sorrowful, penitent, and in renunciation *of sin* before the sun and Mitrô, the moon and the fire of Aûharmazd[10]; (9) and, for the sake of atonement *for* the sin, good works are to be practised as much as is well possible.'

CHAPTER LIV.

1. The sage asked the spirit of wisdom (2) thus: 'Wherefore *is it* when an ignorant man—when they bring advancement to him—considers the learning

[1] The angel of the sun's light (see Chap. II, 118 n).

[2] L19 adds 'homage and glorifying are to be performed;' but this is unnecessary.

[3] L19 inserts 'opposite.'

[4] The sacred fire (see Chap. XXXVI, 9 n).

[5] A fire in which the remnants of all other fires are deposited from time to time.

[6] We ought probably to read '*one* is to perform homage and glorifying, and to be grateful.'

[7] L19 omits 'or a deficiency.'

[8] Reading fraêstô; Nêr. reads pargast and translates 'somewhat.'

[9] L19 omits the 'beasts *of burden*.'

[10] These are four out of the five existences to which the daily Nyâyises or supplications are addressed.

and advancement of the wise and good mostly so[1], through greediness, that to teach *it* to him is difficult?'

3. The spirit of wisdom answered (4) thus: 'For this reason, because the ignorant man considers, in thought, his own ignorance as good as the sage *does*, in thought, his own knowledge.'

Chapter LV.

1. The sage asked the spirit of wisdom (2) thus: 'Wherefore is he who is an ill-natured man no friend of the good, *nor* an untalented man of a talented *one*?'

3. The spirit of wisdom answered (4) thus: 'For this reason, because he who is an ill-talented[2] man is *at* [all][3] times *in* fear of the talented, (5) lest "they should trouble[4] us by *their* skill and talent, and, owing to that circumstance, shame *may* come upon *us* before the good and *our* opponents."

6. 'And the ill-natured are no friends of the good for this reason, because *there* is a time for their annihilation and destruction by the hands of the good.'

---

[1] L19 has 'such vexation,' by reading bêsh instead of vê*s*.

[2] L19 has 'untalented.'

[3] K43 omits 'all,' and its text may be translated thus:—'because the position of him who is an ill-talented man is *in* danger from the talented.'

[4] Reading aê ran*g*ênd. Nêr. has the doubtful reading airô*z*i-ne*n*d, 'they enlighten,' and also several other variations, so as to produce the following meaning:—'lest "these enlighten *others* by the skill and talent which are not mine," and shame come upon him before the good and *his* helpmates.'

CHAPTER LVI.

1. The sage asked the spirit of wisdom (2) thus: 'Wherefore are these mountains and rivers[1] made, which are in the world?'

3. The spirit of wisdom answered (4) thus: 'Of these mountains, which are in the world, there are *some* which are moderators of the wind, and there are *some* which are[2] warders off; (5) there are *some* which are the place and vent, the resting-place and support of the rainy cloud; (6) and there are *some* which are smiters of Aharman and the demons, and maintainers and vivifiers of the creatures and creation of Aûharmazd, the lord.

7. 'And these rivers, which are in the world, the creator Aûharmazd has formed, from the borders of Albûrz[3], for providing the protection and *for* the vivification of his own creatures and creation.'

CHAPTER LVII.

1. The sage asked the spirit of wisdom (2) thus: 'Wherefore *is it* when the knowledge and sagacity of the spiritual and worldly *existences*, both united, are connected with thee?'

3. The spirit of wisdom answered (4) thus: 'For this reason, because, from the first, I, who am the innate wisdom, *apart* from the spiritual and worldly existences, have been with Aûharmazd. 5. And

---

[1] Or it may be 'seas,' as the Sanskrit version translates the word, both here and in § 7, but this hardly agrees with the context.

[2] L19 omits these five words.

[3] See Chap. XLIV, 16 n.

the creator Aûharmazd created (âfrîdŏ) the angels of the spiritual and worldly creations, and all the other creatures and creations through the power and mightiness, the wisdom and sagacity of innate wisdom; and I produce[1] and he maintains and stimulates *them*. 6. And at the end of the renovation *of the universe* it is possible to cause the annihilation and destruction of Aharman and his miscreations more fully by the power of wisdom; (7) and Sôshâns[2], with Kaî-Khûsrôî[2], and those who cause the resurrection and future existence are able to act more fully, by means of the power and help of wisdom.

8. 'The knowledge and sagacity of the worldly *existence*, the learning and teaching in[3] every profession, and all advancement of temporal *beings*[4] are through wisdom. 9. The souls of the righteous, in escaping from hell[5] and coming[6] to heaven and the supreme heaven (garôdmân), arrive much better by means of the power and protection of wisdom. 10. And it is possible to seek the good living, pleasure, good repute, and every happiness of people in the worldly *existence*, through the power of wisdom.

11. 'And the maintenance of the seeds of men

---

[1] So in K43, but Nêr. has taken this verb in the third person, in place of the nearly synonymous âfrîdŏ, so as to state that the creator 'created, maintains, and stimulates the angels' and all other existences through the power of innate wisdom. The object of the Pahlavi text, however, seems to be to emphasize the fact that the creation was specially due to the innate wisdom of the creator, while its maintenance is dependent on all his powers and attributes.

[2] See Chaps. II, 95, XXVII, 63.

[3] L19 has 'of.'

[4] L19 has 'times.'

[5] That is, in escaping from the risk of being sent to hell.

[6] L19 omits 'and coming.'

and beasts *of burden*, oxen and sheep, and also every other creature and creation of Aûharmazd, the lord, the seating[1] *of them* in the womb, and making manifest what is their food in the womb, so that they shall not die from hunger and thirst, and the allotment and maturing of the limbs are effected[2] more fully by means of the durability (dôrângarîh) and great potency which are in the force[3] of wisdom.

12. 'The arrangement of the earth and the mingling of the water in the earth, the growth and increase of plants, colour of various kinds, and the scent, taste, and pleasantness of various things are allotted and produced more fully through wisdom. 13. And the arrangement of Albûrz[4] around the world, the manifestation of the earth of the seven regions[5] and the sky above the mountain of Albûrz, the motion of the sun and moon and twelve constellations[6], the six times of the season festivals (gâsânbâr)[7], the five times *devoted* to the guardian spirits (fravardîkân)[8], the heaven which is in the place of good thoughts, the place of good words, the place of good deeds, and the perfect supreme

[1] Nêr. has read shâyastan, 'possibility,' instead of nishâstanŏ, 'seating.'

[2] Reading vâdûnî-hênd. L19 has 'are possible to effect.'

[3] L19 has 'by means of the great potency and force.'

[4] See Chap. XLIV, 16 n.

[5] See Chap. IX, 2 n.

[6] The signs of the zodiac, whose apparent movement, due to the motion of the earth, is here alluded to.

[7] See Chap. IV, 5 n.

[8] The five supplementary days, named after the five Gâthas or sacred hymns, which follow the twelfth month in order to complete the Parsi year of 365 days. Together with the five preceding days they are specially devoted to the homage of the guardian spirits or Fravashis.

heaven (garôdmân) of all gloriousness[1], the path of the spirits and worldly *existences*, and the *K*indvar bridge[2] are produced and allotted through the power of wisdom.

14. 'The watery-looking[3] cloud's seizing water from the sea, advancing in the atmosphere, and gradually breaking away[4], drop by drop, to the earth, and Aûharmazd's[5] creatures' thoroughly understanding the nature of heaven and hell, the compassion of Aûharmazd, the archangels, and other angels as regards their own creatures, and the devastation and destructiveness of Aharman and the demons as regards the creatures of Aûharmazd it is possible to comprehend through the more complete power[6] of wisdom. 15. And the good religion of the Mazda-worshippers, the sayings and teaching of the spirits[7], and the demons' demolishing the worldly body *and* making *it* imperceptible by the sight of men are apprehended[8] more fully by means of the most perfect means of wisdom. 16. And even the struggle and warfare of Irân with foreigners (an-aîrân), and the smiting of Aharman and the demons it is possible to effect through the power of wisdom.

---

1 The four grades of heaven (see Chap. VII, 9–12).

2 See Chap. II, 115 n. By omitting 'and' Nêr. identifies this bridge with the path mentioned before it, but it forms only one portion of the path to the other world.

3 Assuming that mâ-vênakŏ stands for mayâ-vênakŏ.

4 Pahl. vîkhtanŏ is more probably connected with Pers. kîkhtan, 'to break,' than with Pers. pîkhtan, 'to sift.'

5 The Sanskrit version adds 'and Aharman's.'

6 L19 has 'more fully through the power.'

7 L19 has 'worldly *existences*.'

8 Reading girî-hastŏ. L19 has 'are effected.'

17. 'To occasion the sun's inspection of the hidden water also, below the earth, it is expedient to convey *it* for tillage and cultivation, and the advantage, comfort, and enjoyment of men and beasts *of burden*, oxen and sheep, through the power of wisdom. 18. The thorough understanding of the pain and sickness of men and beasts *of burden*, oxen, sheep, and other animals, and the bringing of medicine and remedies, health of body and comfort unto them are much more possible to effect[1] by means of the power of wisdom.

19. 'And *as to* every man whose participation in wisdom is much, his share of heaven is then much more. 20. Even *as to* Vi*s*tâsp[2], Zaratû*s*t[3], Gâyômar*d*[4], and those others whose share of heaven *was* much the more[5], *it was* on account of the much coming of wisdom unto them. 21. And *as to* Yim, Frê*d*ûn, Kâî-Ûs[6], and those other rulers who obtained splendour (var*g*ŏ) and mightiness (tagakîh)[7] from the sacred beings—just as the participation of Vi*s*tâsp and other rulers in the religion occurred[8]—and their not attaining to the religion, and also as to the *times* when they have become ungrateful unto their own lord[9], *it was* on account of the little coming of wisdom unto them.

22. 'And Aharman, also, and the demons deceive that man more, and lead *him* to hell, who is poorer

[1] L19 omits 'to effect.'
[2] See Chap. XIII, 14 n.
[3] See Chap. I, 10 n.
[4] See Chap. XXVII, 2 n.
[5] L19 has 'who more fully obtained a share of heaven.'
[6] See Chap. VIII, 27, where all three are mentioned.
[7] L19 has 'opulence.'
[8] This clause occurs only in K43.
[9] They all three suffered misfortunes in their old age, attributed by the priesthood to neglect of religion, which is here traced to diminution of intellect.

of wisdom and unsteadier in disposition. 23. And *it* is manifest, that, unto *him* who is virtuous in disposition, habit, and demeanour[1], praise is then *due*, owing to his maintenance of wisdom. 24. For *it* is declared, that Aharman shouted to Zaratûst thus[2]: "If thou desist from this good religion of the Ma*zd*a-worshippers, then I *will* give thee a thousand years' dominion of the worldly *existence*, (25) as *was* given to the Va*d*akân[3] monarch Dahâk[4]." 26. On account of complete wisdom, the virtuous disposition and demeanour of Zaratûst not *having* hearkened and not being deluded, he did not become deceived and longing through that temptation of the accursed evil *one*, the wicked[5]. 27. And he spoke to Aharman (28) thus: "I *will* shatter and cause to run (dûkânam)[6], and *will* make downcast (nigûîsâr) for thee[7], the bodies of your demons and fiends, wizards and witches, through the Hôm[8] *and* sacred twigs[9], and the good, true

---

[1] L19 has 'virtuous in disposition and virtuous of demeanour.'

[2] This is stated, in other words, in Vend. XIX, 23–32.

[3] As Va*d*ak is said (Dd. LXXII, 5) to have been the mother of Dahâk, this term may be a matronymic implying 'son of Va*d*ak.'

[4] See Chap. VIII, 29 n.

[5] This section is a good deal altered in the Pâzand version, but the general meaning is the same.

[6] L19 has va vânom, 'and I *will* smite.'

[7] L19 has 'and *will* make withered (nizâr).'

[8] A plant growing in Persia, small twigs of which are pounded in water, and the resulting juice is tasted by the priest during the ceremonial. It is a symbol of the mythic Hôm, the producer of immortality (see Chap. LXII, 28). Originally, no doubt, the Hôm (Av. haoma) and the Sans. soma were the same plant (see Dd. XLVIII, 16 n).

[9] The baresôm (Av. baresma) is a bundle of slender twigs or wires, prepared in a particular manner, to be held in the left hand

religion which the creator Aûharmazd *has* taught to me." 29. Aharman, when those words *were* heard by him, became confounded and stupefied, and rushed to hell, and remained confounded a long time.

30. 'This, too, is declared, that Aûharmazd, when Aharman, by agreement[1], had further operated[2] with his (Aûharmazd's) creatures and creation of every kind, afterwards formed an assembly with the angels and archangels of every kind[3], and the welfare (âvâdîh) due to his own wisdom *was* mentioned and recounted by him.

31. 'This, too, is declared, that *for* the nine thousand years of renovation[4], until the resurrection and future existence, wisdom maintains and stimulates the creatures and creation of every kind.

32. 'And this, too, is declared, that, *as to* him who is an ignorant and bad-tempered man, when he attains even to much eminence, opulence, and authority, even then he is not fit to elevate into that welfare and authority.'

---

of the priest while reciting certain parts of the liturgy (see Dd. XLIII, 5 n).

[1] The covenant between the good and evil spirits, by which their conflict was limited to nine thousand years (see Bd. I, 18, 19).

[2] That is, transformed and vitiated them. The Av. frâkerentad (Vend. I, 7), describing the modifying work of the evil spirit upon the creation, is here expressed by frâgô vâdûnd.

[3] Such an assembly is mentioned in Vend. II, 42, but its proceedings are not stated.

[4] So in all versions, but, as the renovation is generally considered as confined to the end of the nine thousand years, we ought perhaps to transpose the words and read '*for* the nine thousand years, until the renovation, resurrection, and future existence.'

Chapter LVIII.

1. The sage asked the spirit of wisdom (2) thus: 'Wherefore *is it* when *one* turns the ignorance and foolishness of an ignorant king back to knowledge and cleverness, on account of the sovereignty which is his; (3) and, *as to* a poor man, who is wise[1], *one* turns the knowledge and sagacity, which are his, back to foolishness and uselessness, on account of the poverty?'

4. The spirit of wisdom answered (5) thus: 'On account of the deceit and violence of the fiend[2] of greediness (6) men utter more words as to the manliness of every one whose wealth and power are more, and recount *his* deeds and actions more fully; (7) but, in the eyes of the angels and archangels, a poor *man* who is innocent and wise is better and more precious than a king *or* opulent *man*[3] who is ignorant.'

Chapter LIX.

1. The sage asked the spirit of wisdom (2) thus: 'What are the vices of priests? 3. What are the vices of warriors? 4. What are the vices of husbandmen? 5. And what are the vices of artizans[4]?'

6. The spirit of wisdom answered (7) thus: 'The vices of priests are heresy, covetousness, negligence,

---

[1] L19 adds 'and innocent.'

[2] L19 has 'demon.'

[3] L19 has 'than an opulent king.'

[4] Literally 'the well-endeavouring,' the lowest of the four classes of the community here mentioned (see also Chaps. XXXI, XXXII).

trafficking (sû*d*akîh)[1], attention to trifles, and unbelief in the religion.

8. 'The vices of warriors are oppression, violence, promise-breaking, unmercifulness (an-a*v*ôkhshâgâvandîh), ostentation (dakhshîh)[2], haughtiness, and arrogance.

9. 'The vices of husbandmen are ignorance, enviousness, ill-will, and maliciousness.

10. '*And* the vices of artizans are unbelief, want of thanksgiving, improper muttering *of prayers*, moroseness, and abusiveness.'

Chapter LX.

1. The sage asked the spirit of wisdom (2) thus: 'Of mankind which are more conversant with good and evil?'

3. The spirit of wisdom answered (4) thus: 'Of mankind *he* whose sojourn[3] and business are with the bad[4], and they provide him a name for good repute and goodness, is the man more conversant with good. 5. And he whose sojourn and business are with the good[5], and they provide him a name for disrepute, is the man more conversant with evil.

6. 'Because it is said, (7, 8) that whoever joins with the good brings good with *him*, and whoever

---

[1] Or, perhaps, 'usuriousness.' The Sanskrit version has 'laziness,' as if Nêr. had read âsû*d*akîh.

[2] Nêr. has read *g*ahî, and translated 'incontinence.'

[3] Reading ni*s*astô. L19 has 'whose business is most (vê*s*-ast), both here and in § 5.

[4] L19 has 'the good.'

[5] L19 has 'the bad.'

joins with the bad *brings*[1] evil—(9) just like the wind which, when it impinges on stench, is[2] stench, (10) and when it impinges on perfume, is perfume,—(11) *it* is, therefore, notorious[3], (12) that he whose business is with the good receives good, (13) and *he* whose business is with the bad *receives*[4] evil; (14) but, even then, both are to be considered as an experiment (aûzmâyisnŏ)[5].'

Chapter LXI.

1. The sage asked the spirit of wisdom (2) thus: 'Which is the chief of men? Which is the chief of women? 3. Which is the chief of horses? Which is the chief of flying creatures? 4. [Which is the chief of oxen?][6] Which is the chief of wild animals? Which is the chief of grains?'

5. The spirit of wisdom answered (6) thus: 'The man who is wise, who is steadfast in the religion, who is well-praising, who is true-speaking is chief over *his* associates.

---

[1] L19 has 'will bring with *him*' in both clauses, but the repetition is unnecessary in Pahlavi.

[2] L19 has 'will bring with *it*,' both here and in § 10.

[3] L19 has 'proper to know.'

[4] K43 does not repeat this verb.

[5] L19 has 'by the result (a*nz*âme*s*n).' The meaning is that, though a man's character is generally in accordance with the company he keeps, this must not be assumed without proof; and when the contrary is the case, as stated in §§ 4, 5, his own disposition must be of a very decided nature. Nêryôsang seems to have misunderstood the author's argument, and, supposing §§ 6–13 to contain a mere illustration of §§ 4, 5, he considered it necessary to transpose 'the bad' and 'the good' in §§ 4, 5, so as to make the illustration applicable.

[6] K43 omits the question in brackets.

7. 'The woman who is young[1], who is properly disposed, who is faithful, who is respected, who is good-natured, who enlivens the house, whose modesty and awe are virtuous, a friend of her own father and elders[2], husband and guardian, handsome and replete with animation[3] is chief over the women who are her own associates.

8. 'The ox which is glorious, which is tall-eared, which has a herd *of cows* is chief over oxen.

9. 'The *K*îharâ*v*[4] is the chief of birds. 10. The horse which is swift[5] is the chief of horses. 11. The hare[6] is the chief of wild animals; *and* wheat[7] is the chief of grains.'

Chapter LXII.

1. The sage asked the spirit of wisdom (2) thus: '*In* what place stands Kangde*z*? 3. Where is the enclosure formed by Yim constructed[8]? 4. *In* what

[1] L19 has 'talking, eloquent.'

[2] Nêr. translates nîyâk by 'father's brother,' an elder who is considered as a special protector in India.

[3] Reading namag-âkûn, which epithet is omitted in L19.

[4] A name of the Kar*s*ipt, who is said to be the chief of birds in this world (Pahl. Visp. I, 1, Bd. XXIV, 11), the Vi*s* Kar*s*ipta who brought the religion to the enclosure formed by Yim (see Vend. II, 138, 139), and which is said, in the Pahlavi version, to be 'a *K*ahârvâk (or *K*ahârnâk) who goes back into the existence of the spirits.' To determine the meaning of this name (which Nêr. translates by Sans. *k*akravâka, 'Brahmany duck') we have to consider not only the two forms *k*îharâ*v* and *k*ahârvâk, but also the term *k*ark, 'falcon,' used in Bd. XXIV, 11. The *k*âmrô*s* of Bd. XIX, 15, XXIV, 29 (the *k*înâmrô*s* of Chap. LXII, 40) is also said to be the chief of birds, but probably mythic birds are meant.

[5] L19 has 'white,' as in Bd. XXIV, 6.

[6] See Bd. XXIV, 9.

[7] See Bd. XXIV, 19.

[8] L19 omits 'constructed.'

place lies[1] the body of Sâhm? 5. Where is the abode of Srôsh? 6. *In* what place stands the three-legged ass? 7. Where is the Hôm grown, the preparer of the dead, with which they restore the dead and produce the future existence? 8. In which place is[2] Gôpaîtôshah? 9. With what work is the Kar fish intrusted? 10. Where has the griffon bird a nest (â*s*îyân)[3]? 11. *In* what place sits *K*înâmrô*s*, and what is his work?'

12. The spirit of wisdom answered (13) thus: 'Kangde*z*[4] is intrusted with the eastern quarter, near to Satavâyês[5], (14) on the frontier of Aîrân-vê*g*ô[6].

15. 'The enclosure formed by Yim[7] is constructed in Aîrân-vê*g*ô, below the earth[8]. 16. And every species and seed of all the creatures and creations of Aûha*r*ma*zd*, the lord, whatever is better and more select of man and beast *of burden*, *of* cattle and flying creatures is brought thither[9]. 17. And every forty years one child is born from one woman and one man[10] who are of that place; (18) their life,

---

[1] L19 has 'remains.'

[2] L19 has 'remains.'

[3] L19 has 'a resting-place.'

[4] See Chap. XXVII, 58, 62.

[5] Av. Satavaêsa, the western leader of the stars and special opponent of the planet Anâhî*d* (Venus), which may, perhaps, be identified with Antares (see Bd. II, 7, V, 1), though Geiger (Ost. Kul. p. 313) thinks Vega more probable. It also protects the southern seas, and its name is applied to the gulf of 'Umân in that direction (see Bd. XIII, 9–13, Zs. VI, 16, 18). But its connection with the east, as implied in our text, requires explanation, and throws some doubt upon the reading.

[6] See Chap. XLIV, 17–23.

[7] See Chap. XXVII, 27–31.

[8] So stated in Bd. XXXII, 5, and probably meaning that its position could no longer be discovered on earth. Bd. XXIX, 14 states that it is in the middle of Pârs, below Mount Yimakân.

[9] See Vend. II, 106–113.

[10] Perhaps we should understand 'from each woman and each

too, is three hundred years[1], (19) and their pain and disturbance are little[2].

20. 'The body of Sâhm[3] is in the plain of Pê*s*ândas[4], near to Mount Dimâvand[5]. 21. And on that plain, except corn and the eatable things they sow and reap *and* live upon, there is not so much as a single other tree[6], *or* shrub, *or* plant; (22) and its golden colour is mostly wormwood[7]. 23. And the angels and archangels have appointed 99,999 guardian spirits of the righteous as a protection for the body of Sâhm[8], (24) so that the demons and fiends *may* not injure it.

25. 'The abode of Srôsh[9] is mostly in Arzah[10], and afterwards also in Savah and the whole world.

man,' that is, a couple of children from each couple, which would agree with Vend. II, 134.

[1] Pahl. Vend. II, 136 has 150 years.

[2] The characteristics mentioned in §§ 17–19 are ascribed to the whole of Aîrân-vê*g*ô in Chap. XLIV, 25, 27, 32.

[3] See Chap. XXVII, 49.

[4] L19 has Pu*s*t Gu*s*tâspẫ, 'the ridge of Vi*s*tâsp,' which appears, from Bd. XII, 18, 34, XVII, 8, to have been somewhere in the central desert of Persia. In Bd. XXIX, 7–9, 11 we are told that Sâm lies asleep in the plain of Pê*s*yânsaî (evidently the Pê*s*ândas of our text) in Kâvulistân, till he is waked hereafter to slay Dahâk, who escapes from Mount Dimâvand. This legend may have led to the perplexing juxtaposition of Pê*s*ândas and Dimâvand in our text, and the perplexity occasioned by this may have led Nêr. to substitute Pû*s*t-î Vi*s*tâspân for the former name, as being nearer Dimâvand.

[5] The highest peak of the modern Albûrz, in which Dahâk is said to be confined (see Bd. XII, 31).

[6] Reading hânŏ drû-aê; L19 has han mûrd, 'another myrtle-bush.'

[7] With yellow blossoms.

[8] As stated in Fravar*d*în Yt. 61.

[9] See Chap. II, 115.

[10] The western region, as Savah is the eastern one (see Chap. XVI, 10).

26. 'The three-legged ass[1] sits[2] amid the sea Varkash[3]; (27) and *as to* water of every kind that rains on dead matter, the menstrual discharge, and other bodily refuse[4], when it arrives at the three-legged ass, he makes every kind clean and purified, with watchfulness.

28. 'The Hôm[5], which is the preparer of the dead, is grown in the sea Varkash, in that which is the deepest place; (29) and 99,999 guardian spirits of the righteous are appointed *as* its protection[6]. 30. The Kar fish[7], too, ever circles around it, and always keeps the frog and other noxious creatures away from it.

31. 'Gôpaîtôshah[8] is in Aîrân-vêgô, within the region of Khvanîras[9]. 32. From foot to mid-body *he* is an ox, and from mid-body to the top *he* is a man. 33. And *at* all times he sits on the sea-shore, (34) and always performs the ceremonial of the sacred beings, and pours holy-water into the sea. 35. On account of which[10], through the pouring of that holy-water, innumerable noxious creatures in

---

[1] A prodigious monster of benevolent character, described in Bd. XIX, 1–12; possibly some local divinity.

[2] L19 has 'stands,' as is also stated in Yas. XLI, 28.

[3] See Chap. XLIV, 15.

[4] L19 adds 'and pollution.'

[5] The white Hôm or Gôkarn, the tree of immortality (see Bd. XVIII, 1, XXVII, 4). It is 'the preparer of the dead,' because the elixir of immortality is expected to be prepared from it at the resurrection (see Bd. XXX, 25).

[6] Those who watch over the sea Vouru-kasha (see Fravardîn Yt. 59).

[7] Ten such fish, of enormous size and intense watchfulness, are said to be employed to protect the Gôkarn from a lizard or frog sent by Aharman to injure it (see Bd. XVIII, 2–6).

[8] See Chap. XLIV, 35 n.

[9] See Chap. XXVII, 40.

[10] L19 omits these four words.

the sea will die. 36. Because, if he does not specially perform that celebration of the ceremonial, and does not pour that holy-water into the sea—where those innumerable noxious creatures shall utterly perish[1]—then, whenever the rain shall rain, the noxious creatures *have* to rain just like rain.

37. 'The nest of the griffon bird[2] is on the tree opposed to harm, the many-seeded[3]. 38. Whenever he rises aloft a thousand twigs will shoot out from that tree, (39) and when he alights he breaks off the thousand twigs and bites the seed from them. 40. And the bird *K*înâmrô*s*[4] alights likewise *in* that vicinity; (41) and his work is this, that he collects those seeds which are bitten from the tree of many seeds, which is opposed to harm, and he scatters (pargandê*d*) *them* there where Tî*s*tar[5] seizes the water; (42) so that, while Tî*s*tar shall seize the water, *together* with those seeds of all kinds, he shall rain *them* on the world with the rain[6].'

---

[1] L19 has 'and those innumerable noxious creatures do not utterly perish.'

[2] The Sênô-mûrûv (Av. saênô mereghô) or Simurgh, a mythic flying creature said to suckle its young and to be of three natures like the bat (see Bd. XIV, 11, 24, XIX, 18).

[3] L19 has 'of all seeds.' This tree, from which all wild plants are supposed to spring, is said to grow in the sea near the Gôkarn tree, and also in Aîrân-vê*g*ô (see Bd. IX, 5, 6, XVIII, 9, XXVII, 2, XXIX, 5).

[4] The chief of mythic birds next to the Sênô-mûrûv; he is said to defend Irân from invasion by occasionally picking up foreign districts like grains of corn (see Bd. XIX, 15, XXIV, 29).

[5] The angel who personifies the star Tî*s*tar (Sirius, see Chap. XLIX, 5, 6), after a conflict with the demons of drought and thunder (see Bd. VII, 1–13), pours down rain from the cloud, in which he had brought the water from the sea.

[6] Originally, the archangel Ame*r*oda*d* (see Chap. II, 34) is said

CHAPTER LXIII.

1. The sage asked the spirit of wisdom (2) thus: 'Which is that good work which is greater and better[1] than [all[2]] good works, and no trouble (angînakŏ) whatever is necessary for its performance[3]?'

3. The spirit of wisdom answered (4) thus: 'To be grateful in the world, (5) *and* to wish happiness for every one. 6. This is greater and better than every good work, and no commotion (angegînakŏ) whatever is necessary for its performance[4].'

Peace and prosperity[5].

---

to have mingled the plants with the rain (see Bd. IX, 2); but afterwards this was done by the mythic bird (see Bd. XXVII, 3). This legend was evidently intended to account for the rapid appearance of wild plants after rain in dry climates, where all traces of vegetation often disappear during the summer droughts.

[1] L19 inserts 'more valuable and more advantageous.'

[2] K43 omits 'all.'

[3] L19 has 'no trouble and expense are necessary in it.'

[4] This reply is much altered by Nêr. and stands as follows, in L19:—'To wish happiness for every one; (5) to be grateful unto the sacred beings and the good; (6) in every position and time to consider and keep in remembrance Aûharmazd, as regards creativeness, and Aharman, as regards destructiveness; (7) and to be without doubt as to the existence of the sacred beings, the religion and soul, heaven and the account in the three *days*, and the reality of the resurrection and future existence. 8. This, most especially, is the good work which is greater and better, more valuable and more advantageous than all good works, and no trouble and expense are necessary in it.'

The text of all versions ends abruptly at this point, without any peroration.

[5] Only in K43.

*S*IKAND-GÛMÂNÎK VI*G*ÂR,

OR

THE DOUBT-DISPELLING EXPLANATION.

OBSERVATIONS.

1. For the division into chapters the translator is responsible, but the sections are divided according to the alternating Pâzand-Sanskrit text of Nêryôsang.

2–6. (The same as on page 2.)

7. The manuscripts mentioned are:—

AK (probably written A.D. 1568) Pâz.-Sans., belonging to Dastûr Hôshangji Jâmâspji of Poona; it is now defective, and contains only Chaps. I, 16–XI, 145, but this translation is based upon its text so far as it extends.

BM a modern fragment, Pahl.-Pers., in the British Museum (additional Oriental MS. No. 22,378), containing Chap. I, 1–31.

JE (written A.D. 1842, by Jamshedji Edalji) Pâz.-Sans., belonging to Dastûr Hôshangji and as complete as this translation, the latter half of which is based upon its text.

JJ (written A.D. 1768, by Jamshedji Jâmâsp Âsâ) Pâz.-Sans., belonging to Dastûr Khurshedji Jamshedji of Nâwsârî, and as complete as this translation.

K28 (about 150 years old) Pahl.-Pâz.-Sans., No. 28 in the University Library at Kopenhagen; it is now defective, but contains Chaps. I, 1–II, 8; III, 1–25; III, 36–IV, 106; VIII, 103–IX, 16; IX, 30–X, 13; X, 71–XI, 28; XI, 55–61.

L15 (written about A.D. 1737) Pahlavi, No. 15 in the India Office Library at London. It contains Chaps. I, 4–V, 71.

L23 (written by the same hand) Pâzand, No. 23 in the same library; containing Chaps. I, 34–VIII, 23.

MH19 (about 150 years old) Pâz.-Guj., No. 19 of the Haug Collection in the State Library at Munich. It contains Chaps. I, 1–XI, 201.

PB3 (more than a century old) Pâz.-Sans., No. 3 of the Burnouf Collection in the National Library at Paris. It contains Chaps. I, 5–X, 66.

R (modern) Pahl.-Pâz.-Sans.-Pers., formerly belonging to Mr. Romer, and now partly in the India Office Library at London, and partly in No. 10 of the Müller Collection in the State Library at Munich. It contains Chaps. I, 25–V, 57.

SIKAND-GÛMÂNÎK VIGÂR.

CHAPTER I.

1. *In* the name of Aûharmazd, the lord, the greatest and wise, [the all-ruling, all-knowing, and almighty, (2) who is a spirit even among spirits, (3) and from his self-existence, single in unity, *was* the creation of the faithful. 4. He also created, by his own unrivalled power, the seven supreme archangels[1],] all the angels of the spiritual *and* worldly *existences*, (5) and the seven worldly characteristics[2] which are man, animals, fire, metal, earth, water, *and* plants.

6. And man *was* created by him, as a control of the creatures, for the advancement of *his* will. 7. From him likewise came[3] *at* various times, through

---

[1] The passage in brackets is omitted in several Pahl. MSS., many of which commence at this point, but it is found in K28, BM, and others, and also in the Pâz. MSS. and Sans. version. The first epithet, 'all-ruling,' which it contains is likewise omitted in a few Pâz. MSS., while others add a further laudatory passage at that point, which is evidently a modern interpolation. The seven archangels include Aûharmazd himself (see Bd. I, 26 n).

[2] So in the Pahl. MSS. and Sans. version, and also in MH19 and PB3, which latter follows the oldest Pâz. MS. (AK) very closely; but §§ 1–16 have been lost from AK itself. Several other Pâz. MSS. substitute 'creations.'

[3] So understood by Nêryôsang, but the original Pahlavi could have been translated by 'he likewise sent,' because the Huzvâris yâtûnd, 'came,' and sedrund, 'sent,' are written alike.

his own compassion, mercifulness to his own creatures, religion, and a natural desire of the knowledge of purity *and* contamination. 8. So, also, *as to* the intellect, understanding, wisdom, knowledge, consciousness, *and* guardian spirit—which are the appliances of the soul that are seeking information of these spiritual appliances, the five which are the sight, hearing, smell, taste, *and* touch, (9) through the five worldly appliances, which are the eye, the ear, the nose, the mouth, and the rubbing surfaces of the whole body—(10) he likewise created man with the accompaniment of these appliances, for the management of the creatures.

11. He also created the religion of omniscience like an immense tree, (12) of which *there* are one stem, two branches, three boughs, four twigs, *and* five shoots[1]. 13. And its one stem is agreement. 14. The two branches are performance and abstinence. 15. The three boughs are Humat, Hûkht, *and* Huvarst, which are good thoughts, good words, *and* good deeds. 16. The four twigs are the four classes of the religion, by whom the religion *and* world are prepared, (17) which are priesthood, warriorship, husbandry, *and* artisanship. 18. The five shoots are the five rulers whose scriptural names are the house-ruler, the village-ruler, the tribe-ruler, the province-ruler, *and* the supreme Zaratûst. 19. And the one chief of chiefs, who is the king of kings, is the ruler of the world.

20. Likewise, the work manifested by him in the world—which is man—is in the likeness of these four

[1] The last two terms were, no doubt, Pahl. sâk and barg-gâh, of which the Pâz. dêsaa and brîsaa are merely misreadings.

classes of the world. 21. As unto[1] the head is priesthood, (22) unto the hand is warriorship, (23) unto the belly is husbandry, (24) *and* unto the foot is artisanship.

25. So, also, of the four capabilities (hunarân) that are in man—which are temper, ability, wisdom, *and* diligence—(26) unto temper (khîm) is priesthood, as the greatest duty of priests is the temper that they do not commit sin on account of shame and fear; (27) unto ability (hunar) is warriorship, that is, the most princely adornment of warriors is the ability which is expended, the manliness which is owing to self-possession (khva*d*îh); (28) unto husbandmen is the wisdom (khira*d*) which is strenuous performance of the tillage *of* the world, *and* continuance unto the renovation *of the universe;* (29) *and* unto artisans is the diligence (tukhshâkîh) which is the greatest advancement of their class.

30. This arrangement[2] of every kind is upon one stem, truth and agreement, opposing the fiend and his appliances which are co-existent. 31. These[3], which are recounted by me, are of many kinds *and* many species, as many are religious *and* many believing at a period that all are mutually afflicting[4],

---

[1] Or 'over.' This comparison of these four parts of the body to the four classes of men is mentioned several times in the Dînka*r*d, especially in the latter part of the fourth book.

[2] That is, the ordinances of religion (see §§ 11–13).

[3] The various heterodox religions, here assumed to be appliances of the fiend for misleading mankind, which the author discusses in the course of his arguments hereafter.

[4] Assuming that Pâz. a*n*basâ stands for Pahl. hanbêshin, as in Mkh. I, 37. It might be hû-bêshin, 'well-afflicting,' but this would not be so easily reconciled with the meaning 'inconsistent' which the word often assumes, as in Chaps. XIII, 145, 147, XV, 77, XVI, 42.

co-existent destroyers *and* injurers, one as regards the other. 32. *And* with the mutual afflictiveness, destructiveness, and combativeness which are theirs, one towards the other, they[1] afterwards also contend against the one truth co-operatively *and* with united strength.

33. The possession of truth is the one power of the faithful, through the singleness of truth. 34. The many kinds of falsehood, *which* must become confused *and* mutually afflicting to many, are, in the aggregate, from one source of deceitfulness.

35. *As to* that, this composition is provided by me, *who* am Mar*d*ân-farukh[2] *son* of Aûha*r*ma*zd*-dâ*d*, as I saw in the age much religiousness *and* much good consideration of sects (kêshân) of many species; (36) and I have been fervent-mindedly, *at* all times in my whole youthful career, an enquirer *and* investigator of the truth of them. 37. For the same reason I have wandered forth also to many realms and[3] the sea-shore. 38. And of these compendious statements which, owing thereto[4], are an enquiry of those desiring the truth, and[5] a collection and selection (vi*g*î*d*anŏ) of

---

[1] The heterodox religions.

[2] As this name has not been found elsewhere, nothing further is known about the author of this work than can be gathered from the few statements he has made in the work itself. He lived probably in the eighth or ninth century of the Christian era, as he mentions the Dînka*r*d edited by Âtûr-frôbag in Chaps. IV, 107, V, 92, IX, 1, 4, X, 57, XII, 1, and also the Rôshan commentary prepared by Âtûr-frôbag's son (see Chaps. X, 53, 54, XI, 213); but he does not allude to the later edition of the Dînka*r*d, prepared by Âtûr-pâ*d*, son of Hêmî*d*, who was living in the latter part of the ninth century (see Bd. XXXIII, 11 n).

[3] Sans. 'on.' This statement is very similar to that in Mkh. I, 35.

[4] Reading a*g*a*s*, instead of the similarly-written afa*s*, 'and of it.'

[5] Reading afa*s*, instead of a*g*a*s* here.

it, for these memoranda, from the writings and memoranda of the ancient sages *and* high-priests of the just—and especially those of the glorified Âtûr-pâdîyâvand[1]—the name Sikand-gûmânîk Vigâr[2] is appointed by me. 39. As it is very suitable for explaining away the doubts of new learners about the thorough understanding of the truth, the blessedness and truth of the good religion, and the inward dignity of those free from strife.

40. And it is composed and arranged by me not for the wise and talented, but *for* preceptors (farhangîkân)[3] *and* those newly qualified. 41. So that, while many become freer from doubt about the miraculousness and blessedness of the statements of the good religion and primitive faith, (42) I am still begging of distinguished sages, (43) that whoever wants to look, should not look[4] to the religion of the particular speaker *and* composer, but to the greatness of the truth, blessedness, and definite statements of the ancient sages. 44. Because I, who am the composer, do not hold the station of teaching, but that of learning.

45. And it seemed to me, through liberal thought, a statement, from that knowledge of the religion, destined and important even for new learners. 46. Because *he* who distributes to the worthy, out of the little knowledge which is his, is more acceptable than *he* who knows much *and* the worthy are without benefit *and* without help from him.

47. Since those ancient sages decided, (48) that liberality is of three kinds, of thought, of word, *and*

[1] See Chap. IV, 106.
[2] 'Doubt-dispelling explanation.'
[3] Sans. has 'students.'
[4] Sans. has 'you should not look.'

of deed. 49. Liberality of thought *being* that whose wishing of happiness for any others whatever, of a like disposition, is as much as for its own. 50. Liberality in word *being* that which teaches to the worthy *something* out of every virtuous knowledge and information which have come to it; (51) just as that which a *certain* sage said (52) thus: 'I desire that I *may* understand all information which is advantageous, and I *will* teach *it* to friends and acquire the result which is obtainable.' 53. *And* the liberality which is in deed *being* that which, out of any benefit whatever that has come to it, is a benefit to the worthy.

54. Again, *it* is a reminding of the good as to the preservation of the soul; (55) *and* for the same reason I *have* arranged that while the wise are kindly observant of me, through their own compassion, they *may* remember about the immortality of the soul. 56. Since it is said, that the eye of him who observes all good creatures with kind eyes is the eye of the sun; (57) because the sun is, indeed, an observer and beautifier with kind eyes for all creatures.

CHAPTER II.

1. The first subject (2) is about several questions *that* the ever-successful Mit*r*ô-aîyyâr[1], son of Mah-

[1] This person, who is not mentioned elsewhere, was probably a layman and evidently a Ma*zd*a-worshipper, although his father's name seems to be Muhammadan, either Ma'hmûd or Mu'hammad. The Parsis under a Muhammadan government often adopted Muhammadan names, as they also took Hindu names in India; but, in this case, it is perhaps more probable that the father had become

mâ*d*, from Spâhân[1], asked with good intent *and* not in search of defects, *and* the answer *thereto*.

3. *As to* that which is asked thus: 'Why did Aharman hurry on to the light[2], and how was it possible to be *so* when *he* is not *of* a like nature with it, though we always see that whatever is not *of* a like nature abstains from a different nature as much as water *does* from fire?' 4. The answer is this, that the cause itself of the hurrying on of Aharman, which *was* to the light, *was his* different nature. 5. And on account of the desire of a destroyer, which was perpetually in his nature, *he* is a destroyer of different natures.

6. Being injured *and* injuring, however they occur, do not take place except from difference of nature and those of a different nature. 7. Because *in* those of a like nature *there* exist similarity of will and unanimity, one towards the other, not injuring *and* being injured. 8. And those of a different nature, on account of *their* opposing nature, are destroyers *and* injurers, one of the other, however they come together. 9. Those of a like nature, on account of unanimity and similarity of nature, are lively[3], efficient, and mutually helping, when they come together.

10. The disintegration and separation of like natures is the disunion of different natures. 11. Just

---

a convert to Muhammadanism, and changed his name accordingly, after his son had grown up.

[1] The Pahlavi form of Ispahân.

[2] In Bd. I, 9, 10 we are told that when the evil spirit arose from the abyss, he rushed in to destroy the light which he then saw for the first time, but was frightened away by its bravery and glory.

[3] So understand by Nêr., but zîvihend may mean 'they are graceful,' or it may be a misreading of zênîhend, 'they are armed.'

as heat *and* cold which, on account of *their* opposing nature, are destroyers and injurers, resisting *and* disintegrating one another, through *their* perpetual nature. 12. Because every disintegration is owing to the laws (rastagân) of cold and dryness, heat and moisture, (13) and *their* destruction, injuring, *and* opposition of one another. 14. For the disintegration of bodies is owing to the perpetual struggling of heat and cold, dryness and moisture; (15) *and* owing to their struggling, one with the other, bodies are disintegrated *and* disabled.

16. Of water and fire, through their own nature, no injury whatever is manifest; (17) but the cold of *their* fraternization[1] is mingled with the moisture of the water, *and* is an opponent of the heat of the fire; (18) and the dryness of *their* fraternization is mingled with the heat of the fire, *and* is counteractingly an injurer of the moisture *of* the water.

Chapter III.

1. And *as to* that which is asked (2) thus: 'Why does not the creator Aûharmazd keep Aharman back from evil doing and evil seeking, when he is the mighty maker? 3. As I assert that no mighty maker is afterwards imperfect *nor* yet unresisting.'

4. The answer is this, (5) that the evil deeds of Aharman are owing to the evil nature and evil will which are always his, as a fiend. 6. The omnipotence of the creator Aûharmazd is that which is over all *that* is possible to be, and is limited *thereby*.

---

[1] When water comes in contact with fire.

7. That which is not possible to be is not stirred up *by* a capable *or* an incapable being. 8. Whoever says *it is so* is not within the limits of understanding the words. 9. Because, though he said that it is not possible to be, he says again that the sacred being is capable of it, *and* that *has* brought it out of the limits of *what* is not possible to be. 10. For then *it* is not the not-possible, but the possible to be.

11. As his capability is limited, so also is *his* will, thereby. 12. For *he* is sagacious, (13) and the will of a sagacious *being* is all for that which is possible to be, (14) and his will does not pass on to that which is not possible[1], (15) because he wills all that which is possible *and* fit to be.

16. If I say that the creator Aûharmazd is able to keep Aharman back from the evil which is his perpetual nature, (17) it is possible to change that nature which is demoniacal into a divine *one*, and that which is divine into a demoniacal *one*; (18) and it is possible to make the dark light, and the light dark.

19. *Of* the changing of a nature by its own self those not understanding nature speak, (20) who are uninformed of the nature of the result[2] in actions *and* propensities[3]; (21) and they account the wolf *and* noxious creatures as a benefit.

---

[1] Sans. adds 'to be,' and is followed by most of the modern MSS.

[2] Pâz. vazîhasn, probably a misreading of Pahl. uzdahisn.

[3] Pâz. gadasni, both here and in Chaps. IV, 56, VIII, 122, 123, 126, XII, 64, evidently means 'disposition, peculiarity.' It is probably a misreading of Pahl. guzinisn, occasioned by some writer connecting the two letters sn and so converting them into a t (*d*).

22. Since the harm and evil which *arise* from mankind and cattle are not naturally their own, but are owing to the havoc, deceit, solicitation, *and* deluding[1] of the fiend, (23) *they* are from the like vileness of other fiends who are such as the malice, wrath, and lust[2] which are mingled with mankind. 24. Just as the swallowing of bitter medicine, which is mingled with poison, is not the accomplishment of happiness, but for the removal of the pain and sickness which are owing to an extraneous nature (barâ gôhar). 25. As of a statement which is true *or* false—(26) though it *may* be that, connected with a false statement, a righteous man is preserved from much harm, and is ruined by that which is true—(27) mostly that benefit is not from the false statement, but from the removal of the destruction and evil which are mingled with the vile, (28) and that harm is not from the true statement, but from the evil which is mingled with the vile.

29. Also, as regards that which *happens* when opponents have appeared *in order* to remove each one its own competitor, (30) every one is unrestricted[3] *in* keeping away that which is its own opponent, (31) such as light *and* darkness, perfume *and* stench, good works *and* crime, erudition *and* ignorance. 32. That *which* is not unrestricted is the

---

[1] Nêr. reads vyâwãnî, which he understands to mean 'bewildering,' but it is doubtful if we can derive this meaning from vyâwãn, 'a waterless wilderness,' which word occurs in Chap. XIV, 30. The original Pahlavi word can be also read either nîyâzânîh, 'cause of longing, temptation,' or nihâzânîh, 'intimidation.'

[2] Evil passions which are personified as fiends (see Mkh. XLI, 10, 11).

[3] Reading atang, instead of the similarly-written âtûk which would be the equivalent of the Pâz. atû (Sans. sakta) used by Nêr.

light to keep away stench, nor the perfume darkness; (33) but they have each separately appeared *in order* to keep away their own opponent.

34. *As to* that, too, which they say[1], that in the dark night a righteous man is preserved from the lion, wolves, dogs, and robbers, (35) *while* in the light day he becomes a captive[2] in their hands, (36) it is not proper to consider that as a benefit owing to darkness, nor yet as an evil owing to light. 37. Because light is created for the removal of darkness, not for the keeping away of the lion, wolf, and noxious creatures. *And there are* many other *things* which are of this nature. 38. On account of tediousness *this* is collected *merely* as a summary; the virtue *and* understanding of you triumphant *ones* (39) are so much, that you *may* obtain more from revelation.

Chapter IV.

1. And *as to* that which is asked (2) thus: 'When I always see that all things ever arise from the *celestial* sphere and stars, (3) and who created this sphere, then it is like that *which* those of the Vîrôd[3] religion say, that he created good and evil. 4. If Aharman

---

[1] For the purpose of arguing that evils are sometimes advantageous, and may, therefore, form part of the design of a beneficent spirit.

[2] Or grôh may mean 'a hostage.'

[3] Compare Sans. viruddha, 'perverse, contradictory,' or Pers. bulûd, 'antiquity.' It is possible that Muhammadanism is alluded to, as that religion is hardly ever mentioned by name in Pahlavi writings, probably from motives of policy.

created *anything*, how did he become able to create the effect of these marvellous things, (5) *and* why *is it* when they are stars by which assistance of virtue is always bestowed? 6. If Aûharmazd and Aharman created in conference, then that way *it* is manifest that Aûharmazd is an accomplice *and* confederate, with Aharman, in the harm and evil which ever arise from the *celestial* sphere.' 7. The answer is this, (8) that the *celestial* sphere is the place of the divinities (baghân), who are the distributers of happiness, from which they always justly bestow their distribution of every happiness. 9. And the forms of the seven planets (star) are witches who rush below them, despoilers who are antagonistic distributers, (10) whose scriptural name is Gadûg[1].

11. *Through* the creator Aûharmazd *was* the arrangement of these creatures and creation, methodically *and* sagaciously, and for the sake of the continuance of the renovation *of the universe*. 12. As the evil spirit *was* entangled in the sky, that fiend, with evil astuteness *and* with lying falsehood, encompassed[2] *and* mingled with the light, *together* with the fiends of crimes of many kinds, who are those of a gloomy race, *thinking* thus: 'I *will* make these creatures *and* creation of Aûharmazd extinct, or I must make *them* for my own.'

13. Those luminaries, the highest of those of the

---

[1] Av. gadha, a term for 'a brigand' which is used in conjunction with witches and other evil beings in the Srôsh Yt. Hâdôkht, 5, 6.

[2] Supposing that the Pâz. frawast (fravast in § 16) stands for Pahl. parvast, as in Chaps. VIII, 96, 97, XIV, 73, XVI, 56, 60, 66–69, 71, 72; but as Nêr. uses Sans. prasarpita, pravish*t*a, pravartita, samudgata, and samutpatita to translate the word, he must have assumed that it stood for frazast (Pahl. fragast, 'sprang forth').

good *being*, became aware, by means of omniscience, of the blemishing operation and the lies *and* falsehoods of the fiend, (14) *and* of this too, that is, of what extent *was* this power of his, by which this blemishing operation and work of ruin creep on[1], (15) so that, henceforth, *there* exists no power whatever for its restoration, which is *free* from the complete daubing of restraint, pain, and entanglement that is inside the sky.

16. It is they[2] who are sagaciously mingled by him (the good being) with the substance of the luminaries, because that fiend encompassed and *was* entangled with his luminaries, therefore all his powers and resources are for the purpose of not allowing the fiends of crimes of many kinds their own performance of what is desirable for them each separately; (17) such as the fiendish venom of the noxious creatures which the four elements (zahakân), pertaining to Aûharmazd, [keep enveloped[3]. 18. For if this fiendish venom of the noxious creatures] does not remain entangled [with the four elements of the bodily formations pertaining to Aûharmazd]—which are water, fire, earth, and air—*it is* just as though they came to the sky *and* spiritual *existence*. 19.

---

[1] Sans. 'will retreat,' as if Nêr. understood the pronoun 'his' to refer to the good spirit, instead of the evil one; the application of the pronouns in §§ 14, 15 being by no means clear in the original text.

[2] The spiritual representatives of the luminaries, who are angels.

[3] The words in brackets are omitted in AK, PB3, L23, so that §§ 17, 18, in those MSS., stand as follows:—'Since the fiendish venom of the noxious creatures, that the four elements pertaining to Aûharmazd—which are water, fire, earth, and air—have not entangled, is just as though they (the creatures) came to the sky *and* spiritual *existence*.'

And if they attained to spirituality and a disembodied existence, it would not be possible for those creatures of Aûharmazd to avoid *and* escape from that demoniacal venom of theirs. 20. It would be in the grasp (grôhê)[1] and mingled with the breath (vâd) of mankind *and* the other creatures, *and their* restoration, support, increase, *and* growth would not be possible.

21. So they[2] also keep those planets enveloped in light, because the fiendish venom of the noxious creatures is in the substance of *those* luminaries. 22. On account of that, too, the existence of somewhat of advantage is manifest from the serpent species, which are dissolving venom from the multitudes of other wild animals *and* noxious creatures[3]. 23. So also from the planets; on account of the commingling of the inferior splendour of *those* luminaries, benefit is manifested by them.

24. A similitude of these planets *and* the benefit which they always bestow (25) is such as the brigands (gadûgân)[4] *and* highwaymen who interrupt the path of traders in a caravan. 26. They abstract important things *from* many, (27) *and* do not grant and give *them* to the diligent *and* worthy, but to sinners, idlers, courtezans, paramours, *and* the unworthy.

28. *Observe* this, too, that this performance of good works which astrologers compute and state from those planets is for this reason, (29) when they have not preferred the method of the divinities

---

[1] Or grôhê may mean 'an assemblage.'

[2] The angels of the luminaries.

[3] Which they eat, and thereby diminish the number of such objectionable creatures.

[4] See § 10 n.

(baghân) who are distributing welfare, and that, also, of the five constellations pertaining to Aûhar*mazd*—which are the great *one*[1] that is supreme and measurable[2], Haptôiring[3], created by Mazda[4], *and* the stars Vanand[5], Satavês[6], *and* Tistar[7]—as regards the brigands (gadûgân)[8] *and* distributers of evil. 30. And those are the five planets that rush below them in the shape of stars, and they keep *them* enveloped in light, which are Saturn, Jupiter, Mars, Venus, and Mercury. 31. Since the supreme constellation, the great *one* of the north-opposing[9] (32) Haptôiring, is opposing Saturn, (33) Haptôiring, created by Mazda, is opposing Jupiter, (34) Vanand, the smiter of noxious creatures, is opposing Mars, (35) the star Satavês is opposing Venus, (36) *and* the star Tistar is opposing the planetary Mercury[10], (37) the welfare, which they say is from those brigands (gadûgân), is from those five constellations per-

[1] Called 'the great *one* of the middle of the sky' in Bd. II, 8, V, 1, which has not yet been identified, but may be Regulus or Orion.

[2] Sans. 'very visible.'

[3] See Mkh. XLIX, 15–21, where it is called Haptôk-ring.

[4] This epithet is often applied to Haptôiring, Vanand, and Satavês.

[5] See Mkh. XLIX, 12–14.

[6] See Mkh. LXII, 13.

[7] See Mkh. XLIX, 5, 6.

[8] The planetary witches (see § 10).

[9] Or it may be 'planetary-opposing,' or 'north-accepting.' The dislocation, and probable corruption, of these sections is due to Nêr., who evidently considered the epithet mazdadhâta, 'created by Mazda,' as the name of one of the constellations, and 'great' and 'supreme' as mere epithets of Haptôiring. But he found it difficult to adapt the text to this opinion of his.

[10] These oppositions agree with those mentioned in Bd. V, 1, except that Haptôiring is there opposed to Mars, and Vanand to Jupiter.

taining to Aûharmazd, (38) as they obtain the triumph of much power *and* little injury.

39. And for the sake of not leaving these five planets to their own wills, they are bound *by* the creator, Aûharmazd, each one by two threads (gîk) to the sun (Mihir) and moon. 40. And their forward motion and backward motion are owing to the same cause. 41. There are *some* whose length of thread is longer, such as Saturn and Jupiter, (42) and there are *some of* which *it* is shorter, such as Mercury and Venus. 43. Every *time* when they go to the end of the threads, they draw *them* back from behind, (44) and they do not allow them to proceed by their own wills, (45) so that they *may* not injure the creatures.

46. And those two fiends that are greatly powerful, who are opponents of the planetary sun and moon, move below the splendour of *those* two luminaries[1]. 47. Another—even that which is called the brigand (gadûg) of the stars, as regards the welfare that exists[2]—is likewise confined below the splendour of the sun. 48. And when it[3] gets far from control, it commits damage and harm on the constellation into which it springs, *and* on the quarter which is the particular concern of that constellation, (49) until it

---

[1] Referring to the supposed cause of eclipses, which are said to be occasioned by two dark bodies revolving below the sun and moon, so as to pass between them and the earth whenever an eclipse occurs (see Dd. LXIX).

[2] Referring to the supposed injurious influence of comets which, as they usually appear one at a time to the unassisted eye, are here assumed to be a single evil being, the Mûspar of Bd. V, 1, 2.

[3] We should perhaps say 'she,' as a drûg, 'fiend,' is usually considered to be a female being, and the Mûspar or Mûs-pairika is a witch.

becomes again, a second *time*, bound *and* fettered *to* the sun.

50. The statement which they offer about it[1] (51) is this, the conflict of the superior beings within the star station. 52. Out of the inferior of those are the conflicts of Tis*tar and the demon Spenzagar[2], (53) *of* the fire Vâzist[3] and the demon Avâush[4], (54) *and of* other good spirits with gloomy ones, for the formation of rain and allotment of welfare to the creatures.

55. Below them are mankind and cattle, noxious creatures and deadly *ones*[5], and other creatures that are good and bad. 56. Because propensities (gadasni) are mingled with mankind, (57) which are greed, lust, malice, wrath, and lethargy, (58) wisdom, temper, skill, knowledge, understanding, and intellect, (59) as the good influences and bad influences are called, which are the causes of good works and sin.

60. All this welfare of the creatures[6] is specially owing to the creator of the creatures, (61) who is himself the healer and perfect ruler, the maintainer of protection, nourisher, and caretaker, preserving his own creatures. 62. And, for his own creatures, he

---

[1] Meaning, probably, the reason given by the astrologers for the good works mentioned in § 28.

[2] The demon of thunder (see Bd. VII, 12).

[3] The lightning (see Bd. XVII, 1).

[4] The demon of drought (see Bd. VII, 8, 10, 12, XXVIII, 39). These two conflicts represent the struggle between rain and drought, which culminates in the thunderstorm; Tistar (Sirius) being the bringer of rain.

[5] So in AK, PB3, MH19, but other MSS. have mâr, 'serpent,' instead of mar, though Nêr. uses Sans. nrisamsa.

[6] Which is manifest in the world around us.

has thoroughly created and taught the means of preservation from evil, and the appliances for abstaining from crime.

63. A semblance, too, of him is such as a wise orchard-owner and gardener who wishes to diminish the wild animals and birds which are mischievous and destructive for his orchard by spoiling the fruit of the trees. 64. And that wise gardener, effacing (padasâê) his own little trouble, for the sake of keeping those mischievous wild animals away from his own orchard, arranges the appliances which are necessary for the capture of those wild animals, (65) such as springes, traps, and snares for birds. 66. So that when a wild animal sees the snare, and wishes to proceed with suspicion of it, through unconsciousness of the springe and trap he is captured therein.

67. This is certain, that, when a wild animal falls into a trap, *it* is not a victory of the trap, but that of the arranger of the trap, (68) *and* through him the wild animal is captured in the trap. 69. The proprietor *and* orchard-owner, who is the arranger of the trap, is aware through sagacity that the wild animal is powerful, *and* to what extent and how long a time. 70. The power and strength of that wild animal, which are in its body, are exhausted and poured *out* by struggling, as much as it is able, in demolishing the trap and *in* endeavouring to destroy *and* spoil the springe. 71. And when, on account of imperfect strength, its power of struggling totters *and* is exhausted, that wise gardener then, by his own will and his own result of determination, wisely throws that wild animal out of the trap, with *its* existing nature *and* exhausted strength. 72. *And*

he consigns his own trap and springe, rearranged *and* undamaged, back to the storehouse.

73. Even like him is the creator Aûharmazd, who is the preserver of creations and arranger of creatures[1], the disabler of the evil original evolution[2] and protector of his own orchard from the injurer. 74. The mischievous wild animal, which is the spoiler of the orchard, is that accursed Aharman who is the hurrier *and* disturber of the creatures. 75. The good trap is the sky, in which the good creations are lodging, (76) *and* in which the evil spirit and *his* rudimentary[3] miscreations are captured. 77. And *pertaining* to the springe and trap of the wild animal, who is mischievous owing to his own wilfulness, is the exhauster (78) time that, for the struggling of Aharman and his powers *and* resources, is for the long period[4] (79) which, through the struggling of the wild animal in the springe and trap, is an exhaustion of its strength. 80. The sole[5]

[1] Nêr. has 'of the trap' in Sanskrit. The Pâz. dãm, meaning both 'creature' and 'trap.'

[2] Reading bûn gastak instead of bûn yastak, as the word has evidently no reference to any form of worship. It cannot be translated 'original perversion' (a possible meaning of the word) because there are two of them (see § 103 and Chap. VIII, 101), one competing with the other (see Chap. VIII, 1), which, as one of them is here said to be evil, implies that the other is good and cannot, therefore, be a perversion; nor would this term be applicable in Chap. VI, 6 or XV, 56.

[3] Or it may be 'primitive,' as kâdmon is the Huzvâris form of the Pâz. khâmast (superlative of Pers. *'h*âm, 'immature') here used.

[4] So in all the older MSS., but in Sans. it '*is* the long-time lord,' a common Avesta epithet of 'time,' and this alteration has been introduced into JE, R, and a few other modern MSS.

[5] Assuming that Pâz. awâs stands for *e*wâs. The word is omitted by Sans., K28, L15.

creator of the creatures arranges a preservation again, which is the preparation of an eternal happy progress *free* from his adversary, which that wise orchard-owner *does with* his own trap and springe [1].

81. Then [2] the scanty power and want of ability of that fiend for it, in his struggling for the luminaries, are manifest even from this. 82. When as with lying falsehood he thought thus [3]: 'I *will* make this sky and earth and the creatures of Aûharmazd extinct, or I *will* turn *them* from their own nature *and* bring *them* to my own,' (83) even then, with *all* the power, desire of destruction, and perpetual struggling of the fiend, no slaughter whatever *by* the demons is *free* from effectual limits; it is this earth and sky, and these creatures, (84) *that* are propagating from few to many, as is manifest, (85) and innumerable *persons* are convinced of it. 86. For, if in this struggling any victory should have specially occurred, it would have been impossible to attain from few to many.

87. Moreover, if the births of the worldly *existence* are mostly manifest through the occurrence of death therein, even then it is seen that that death is not a complete dissolution of existence, but a necessity of *going* from place to place, from duty to duty [4]. 88. For, as the existence of all these creations is *derived* from the four elements, *it* is manifest to the sight *that* those worldly bodies of theirs are to be mingled again with the four elements. 89. The spiritual *parts*, which are the rudimentary appliances of the life

[1] As stated in § 72.

[2] Reading adînas, 'then for it,' which is the original Pahlavi indicated by the Pâz. ainâ of Nêr. (see Mkh. IX, 6 n).

[3] See § 12.

[4] Compare Chap. XII, 79.

stimulating the body, are mingled with the soul—(90) on account of unity of nature they are not dispersed—(91) and the soul is accountable (amâr-hômand) for its own deeds. 92. Its treasurers[1], also, unto whom its good works and offences are intrusted, advance there for a contest. 93. When the treasurer of the good works is of greater strength, she preserves it, by her victory, from the hands of the accuser[2], *and* settles *it* for the great throne and the mutual delightfulness of the luminaries; (94) and it is assisted eternally in virtuous progress. 95. And when the treasurer of its offences is of greater strength, it is dragged, through her victory, *away* from the hands of the helper[3], (96) *and* is delivered up to the place of thirst and hunger and the agonizing abode of disease[4]. 97. And, even there, those feeble good works, which *were* practised by it in the worldly *existence*, are not useless to it; (98) for, owing to *this* same reason, that hunger and thirst and punishment are *inflicted* on it proportionately to the sin, *and* not lawlessly, (99) because *there* is a watcher[5]

[1] Nêr. divides the word gang*ô*bar, 'treasurer,' into the three words gang u bar, 'treasure and produce.' These treasurers are the female spirits who meet the soul after death, with its stores of good works and sins (see Dd. XXIV, 5, XXV, 5), and symbolize its good and bad conscience, represented by a beautiful maiden and a frightful hag, respectively.

[2] The accuser is any person or thing of the good creation that has been injured by any sin, and who must be satisfied by atonement before the sin can be remitted. The question, therefore, to be settled, when the account of the soul is rendered, is whether its good works are sufficient to atone for its sins. In this case the treasurer of offences represents the accusers.

[3] The treasurer of good works.

[4] That is, to the torments of hell.

[5] Either the treasurer of its good works, or the good works themselves.

of the infliction of its punishment. 100. And, ultimately, the compassionate creator, who is the forgiver of the creatures, does not leave any good creature captive in the hands of the enemy[1]. 101. *But*, one day[2], he saves even those who are sinful, *and* those of the righteous through atonement for sin, by the hands of the purifiers, *and* makes *them* proceed on the happy course which is eternal.

102. The conclusion is this, that the creator is the healer and perfect ruler, the maintainer and nourisher, protecting *and* preserving the creatures[3]; not a producer of the disease, a causer of the pain, and an inflicter of the punishment of his own creatures. 103. And it is more explicitly written below, with the arrangement of the two original evolutions[4], among the assertors of the non-existence of a sacred being[5], and the contemplators of unity[6].

104. As ordered and requested by you it is provided (padarâst); do you direct and observe *it* with kind regards. 105. Because, as written above[7] by us, I do not hold the station of teaching, but really that of learning. 106. Even this teaching of doctrines is that which *was* obtained by me, through the religion of wisdom[8], from the writing (nipîk) of Âtûr-pâ*d*îyâvand[9], and is here indicated. 107. And his teachings

---

[1] Compare Chap. XII, 59.

[2] Assuming that Pâz. *g*umê is a misreading of Huz. yôm-1.

[3] Compare § 61.

[4] See § 73 n, Chaps. V, 46–IX, 45.

[5] Chap. V. [6] Chap. X. [7] Chap. I, 44.

[8] It is doubtful whether this dîni-i-khard was the name of a book now unknown, as the phrase admits of reasonable translation.

[9] This writer is also mentioned in Chaps. I, 38, IX, 2, X, 52, but his name has not yet been found elsewhere. As he does not

are in the Dînka*r*d[1] manuscript (nipîk), which the supremely learned Âtûr-frôbag[2], son of Farukh-zâ*d*, who was the leader of those of the good religion, explained out of *his* knowledge of the religion, *and* which consists of a thousand subjects[3].

108. Of that, too, which is asked by you about unlimitedness and limitation, I have written below[4], through the will of the sacred beings.

CHAPTER V.

1. Another subject, among the assertors of the non-existence of a sacred being, is about the existence of the sacred being and his competitor.

2. Of the knowledge approvable by wisdom and the statements of the limits of evidence, *about* the existence of the sacred being and his competitor, (3)

---

appear to be mentioned in that portion of the Dînka*r*d known to be extant, his writings were probably embodied in the first two books of that work, which have not yet been discovered.

[1] The most extensive Pahlavi work in existence, of which only Books III–IX are extant; they contain about 170,000 words and are a summary of the religious opinions, customs, legends, and literature of the Ma*z*da-worshippers, compiled probably in or before the eighth century of the Christian era from earlier records.

[2] An early editor of the Dînka*r*d, 'acts of the religion.' His selections from various religious writings form the fourth and fifth books of that work. He appears to have been succeeded in the editorship by his son Zaratû*s*t. And when their manuscript became worn out, it was finally re-edited by Âtûrpâ*d*, son of Hêmî*d*, who lived in the latter part of the ninth century. All these three editors were 'leaders of the good religion,' and are mentioned in the last paragraphs of the third book of the Dînka*r*d.

[3] Pâz. daraa means rather 'subject' than 'chapter' (Pâz. dar).

[4] See Chap. XVI, 53–107.

this is a summary:—*One* knows it should be enjoined, that the supreme first knowledge, most *suitable* for the well-discerning, is comprehending the sacred being. 4. He, of whom this knowledge is not the leader of knowledge, is unaided by other knowledge. 5. Comprehending the sacred being is possible through undecayed[1] understanding, fervent intellect, and decisive wisdom.

6. Since comprehending the sacred being is not, thus far, more than *that one* knows that a sacred being exists, (7) because whoever is acquainted with the existence of a certain thing, and is unaware of its nature, is thinking thus, that that thing is good or bad, erudite or ignorant, antidote or poison, cold *and* frozen or hot and scorching, dry *and* withering or damp, (8) and, when unaware of its nature, his only knowledge of it is then useless—(9) for it is possible to cause the commendation and condemnation of any person *or* thing, not through *its* existence but through *its* nature—(10) *therefore one* knows this should be also enjoined, that a knowledge of[2] anything is *acquired* in three modes:—(11) by knowing *what* is inevitable, or by knowing *what* is analogous, or by *what* is possible *and* fit to exist.

12. Inevitable knowledge is such as once one is one, and twice two are four. 13. For within the bounds of the really inevitable it is not possible to say, (14) that *there* was *or will* be a time, or a place, where twice two are said *to be* five or three.

15. Knowledge *by* analogy is that which announces, from anything manifest, something which is not

[1] Assuming that Pâz. agunast (Sans. anâvila) stands for Pahl. agôndî*d*; but it may stand for Pahl. agûngî*d*, 'unsilenced.'

[2] Sans. inserts 'the nature of.'

manifest, (16) and brings, out of anything visible, something invisible, in the likeness of a hand put up [1], for the household service of the perception of wisdom, (17) through complete similarity, resemblance, *or* partial resemblance.

18. Complete similarity is such as *that of* a man of Pârs to a man of another district. 19. Resemblance is such as *that of* cheese to the white of an egg. 20. And partial resemblance is such as *that of* cheese to chalk, (21) since this is about the limit of partial resemblance, because cheese is like unto chalk only in whiteness, (22) *but to* the white of an egg in whiteness and also *as* food.

23. And there is also *that* which is called more resembling than resemblance, and more partially resembling *than* partial resemblance. 24. That which is more *than* complete similarity is not spoken about, (25) because completion does not become more complete.

26. By this mode *it* is set forth a second time at more length. 27. To demonstrate an invisible from a visible thing is such as from a thing made and maintained, which is not domestically serving the maker and maintainer, (28) and from a thing written, whose writer is not declared, (29) are manifest a maker of that *which is* made, a maintainer of that *which is* maintained, *and* a writer of that *which is* written, who are inevitable, (30) because that which is not manifest *and* is invisible is demonstrated by the thing which is manifest and visible.

31. Information of that which is within the possible *and* fit to exist is credible, (32) such as what *one*

[1] As a finger-post.

states thus: 'I saw a man by whom a lion, or a lion by whom a man, *was* slain outright.' 33. And this, *being* that which is within the limits of the possible *and* fit to exist, may be a lie. 34. But when a man announces that intelligence, who is renowned for truth and tested in judgment, it is within the limits of truth and reality. 35. If a man announces *it*, who is disgraced by falsehood and tested in misjudgment, it is within the limits of falsehood and unreality.

36. Another mode, outside of these *and* within the limits of the inevitable, is *by knowing what has* not occurred *and* is not possible; (37) such as what *one* states thus: 'It is possible to bring the world, in secrecy, into the inside of an egg,' (38) or 'it is possible *for* an elephant to pass into an eye of a needle,' (39) *in* such a manner *as* though one *of them* really becomes no greater and no less, (40) or *its* substance is something which is not a rudiment.

41. A struggle which should not be limited, (42) an existing thing which is not temporary and localised, (43) or is localised *and* not limited, (44) the working of a vain miracle, (45) and other *things* of this description of speaking *and* imagining are faulty and false and not possible.

46. Then[1] the knowledge of the existence of him who is the exalted sacred being, apart from tangibility of nature and other evidence, is through the inevitable and analogy, (47) as much visible before the sight of wisdom as from the prosperity[2], formation, and organization which are, according to dif-

[1] Reading adînas, 'then of him,' for Pâz. ainâ, as in Chap. IV, 81. Having explained the modes of arguing, in §§ 12–45, the author now returns to the argument itself.

[2] So in Sans., but bâhar-hômandîh also means 'divisibility.'

ferent statements of many kinds, the formation of the things of the world and mankind whose particles, *and* the appliances which are owing thereto, are such as the elements of the body *and* life, from which[1] they are prepared *and* formed, (48) which are fire, water, air, *and* earth, (49) that are, each separately, a stimulus so qualified and ennobled for their own operations, (50) that the operation of fire, through its own quality (*k*îharîh) and nobility (vâspûhara-kânîh), is such that the operations of water, air, *and* earth are not to stimulate unrestricted (atang)[2] by it. 51. Thus, also, the operation of water, through its own quality, is such that the operations of air, fire, *and* earth are not *unrestricted* by it. 52. So, also, of air, the operations of fire, water, *and* earth are not *unrestricted by it*. 53. So, also, of earth, the operations of these *others* are to stimulate not unrestricted *by it*. 54. But each separately is for its own operation, just as they are ennobled *and* qualified (55) by him who is, sagaciously *and* methodically, a qualifier, a constructor, and an ennobler. 56. *And* the organization is constructed, prepared, qualified, *and* ennobled as is suitable for those operations.

57. So, also, *as to* mankind and the other creatures, who are the germinating of these elements, (58) whose organization of bone, fat, sinew, veins, and skin, each separately (59) without sympathy, one for the other, is visible altogether. 60. Thus, too, are the nobility *and* qualification of the internal organs, (61) such as the liver, heart[3], lungs, kidneys, gall-bladder, *and*

---

[1] Reading mûn azas for Pâz. ke vas.

[2] See Chap. III, 30 n.

[3] Assuming that Pâz. dawur is a misreading of Pahl. dîl.

other appliances, *for* every one of which a function of its own is manifest. 62. They are qualified *and* ennobled for their defence by those functions which are their own.

63. So, also, is the qualification of the eye, ear, nose, tongue, mouth, teeth, hand, foot, *and* other external appliances, whose own functions are each separate. 64. And *it* is visibly manifest therein; inasmuch as, when one of these organs is disabled, any *one* of the rest is not suitable for the work of that other *one*, for which it is not qualified. 65. And when only the construction of one of the organs of the body is examined into—that is, how *it is*—it is wonderfully sagaciously constructed[1].

66. Such as the eye, which is of many natures of different names and different purposes, (67) as the eyelash, the eyelid, the white, the eyeball (khâyak), the iris (sâyak), *and* the pupil (tê*d*ak), (68) *in* such way that the white is fat[2], (69) the iris is water which *has* so stood in the prison[3] of fat that the turning of the eye, from side to side, occurs through it, (70) *and* the pupil, itself the sight, is like a view into the water. 71. The iris stands in the prison of white, like the standing of water in a prison of fat; (72) and the pupil is within the iris, like the view of a thing within clear water, (73) *or* the form of a column in

---

[1] So in Sans., but the Pahl. text may be translated 'how wonderful *it is*, it is sagaciously constructed.'

[2] Assuming that Pâz. p*e*gh, as well as pih in § 69 and peh in § 71, stands for Pahl. pîk (Pers. pî), 'fat.' It might also be connected with Pers. pikah, 'a veil,' as Nêr. seems to have understood it here; but 'fat' suits the whole context better.

[3] Reading lag, instead of rag, 'a vein,' which latter is adopted by Nêr. both here and in § 71.

a shining mirror. 74. And the arrangement of the white *in* the orbit is for the reason that the dust whirling from the atmosphere, when it arrives at the eye, shall not be concealed in it, (75) *but* shall turn to the lid (gumb) of the eye, (76) and shall not injure the sight of the eye. 77. Just as the construction of the tube (rag) of the ear is undilated (afâhal), for the reason (78) that whirls of dust and winged noxious creatures shall not rightly enter therein. 79. And the moisture of oneself, the secretion of the ear, and the venom of noxious creatures are manifestly as *useful*[1].

80. When the appliances of life and soul are observed—(81) such as the smell, hearing, sight, taste, and touch which are causing the intelligence of living beings, (82) as also the wisdom of every pontiff (ra*d*), *which* is pronounced decisive, (83) the knowledge which is acquiring, (84) the intellect which is a seeker *and* transmitter, (85) the understanding which is a treasurer *and* defender, (86) the consciousness which is itself the sight of the soul, (87) the guardian spirit (fravash) which is itself the nature that is a maintainer of the body, (88) the spiritual life (ahû) which is pure, (89) and the other spiritual *existences* that are maintaining the body, which are each separately qualified, in that manner[2], *for* their operation and duty—(90) they are perfect in their own operation, as to duty such as they are ennobled *and* qualified *for*. 91. As to that *for* which they are not qualified, they are not suitable.

92. The two *arguments* which are each separate

[1] As means of defence.

[2] By the assistance of the senses mentioned in § 81.

in the Dînka*rd* manuscript, as the supremely learned *one*[1] *has* explained *them* out of *his* knowledge of the religion, are here set forth at length. 93. *He* whose wish is to fully understand the wonderfulness of the Ma*zd*a-worshipping religion and the statements of the primitive faith, (94) examines into it in a manuscript of that character, (95) *and* shall understand more fully the wonderfulness and truth of the religion[2].

Chapter VI.

1. *As to* another delusion[3] of those asserting the non-existence of a sacred being—(2) whom they call atheistical (daharî)[4]—(3) that they are ordained *free* from religious trouble (alag) and the toil of practising good works, (4) and the unlimited twaddle (drâyisn)[5] they abundantly chatter, (5) you[6] should observe this:—6. That they account this world, with the much change and adjustment of description of its members *and* appliances, *their* antagonism to one another, and their confusion with one another, *as* an original evolution[7] of boundless time. 7. And this, too, that there is no reward of good works, no punishment of sin, no heaven and hell, and no stimulator of good works and crime. 8. Besides

---

[1] Âtûr-frôbag (see Chap. IV, 107).

[2] Nearly all the Pahlavi manuscripts of this work terminate here.

[3] Pâz. vyâwãnî (see Chap. III, 22 n).

[4] Sans. digambara refers this term to Buddhist ascetics, the nearest approach to atheists with which Nêr. was acquainted.

[5] A contemptuous term for the speech of evil beings.

[6] Or it may be '*one*,' as the Sanskrit uses the third person.

[7] See Chap. IV, 73 n.

this, that things are only worldly, and there is no spirit.

9. As I *have* written and shown above[1]—(10) that to be made without a maker, and decided without a decider, is as impossible as to prepare *what* is written without a writer, *or* a house without a mortar-mixer (râ*z*)[2] and building (dê*s*âk)—(11) things made, of all kinds, cannot arise without making.

12. And this worldly *existence* is owing to the mingling of competing powers. 13. So *its* numerous possessions are so constructed, selected, *and* made of diverse races (*k*îharân), diverse colours, diverse scents, diverse characteristics, *and* diverse species as I *have* stated above[3] about the body, (14) that it is constructed *and* made out of many things, such as bone, fat, sinew, veins, skin, blood, breath, hair[4], fundament[5], hand, foot, head, belly, *and* other members, internal and external, (15) in two series[6] of things of many kinds, of which *to be* never made by means of the diverse nature of diverse powers, (16) or to arise without a maker, the impossibility is certain.

17. And *in* like manner of the other creatures, plants *and* trees, water *and* fire, earth and air, their stimulus, too, which is not themselves, is to their own duty; and they are not stimulators, (18) but there is a stimulator, a building (dê*s*âk), and a making for

[1] Chap. V, 27–30.

[2] Sans. has 'carpenter.'

[3] Chap. V, 57–63.

[4] Assuming that Pâz. vas is a misreading of Pahl. varas. Nêr. has Sans. rasa, 'liquid secretion.'

[5] Supposing that Pâz. daryam (Sans. nish*th*â) stands for Pahl. dar-î dum.

[6] Literally 'columns.'

them. 19. And the usage (vâzâr) which is changing *and* urging them, from stimulus to stimulus, from statement to statement, *and* from time to time, is not according to the will and requirement of those made, but according to those that are stimulating and making.

20. Even so, indicative of the rotation of the years, months, days, *and* hours, is the revolution of the *celestial* sphere and stars which are settled (pasâkhtak), and *of* the sun and moon which are adjusted (nîvârdak), a well-horsed[1] progress *and* conspicuous revolution. 21. This, too, is an indication that the movements of every appearance (kîharîh) are owing to an exhibitor, by whom the movement of that appearance is exhibited.

22. Owing to other differences and different management in the worldly *existence* (23) it is possible to know, from the worldly *existence* at various times *and* various periods, that this worldly *existence* is not without a manager. 24. Or *that* its manager is not a sacred being[2], who is learned, acting reasonably, of unlimited power, and illumining[3] the sky, is also that which is visible when the development, decay, and death of the world are such, that the nature alike of mankind and animals, and alike of races and trees, is to come from youth to old age, *and* from old age to death. 25. No one whatever is seen *that has* come from old age back to youth, *or* from death back to life, and *it* is not

[1] Alluding to the supposed horses of the sun. Sans. has 'brilliant.'

[2] That is, the world cannot be controlled by a sacred being alone, on account of the evil it contains.

[3] Sans. has 'making,' another meaning of varz.

possible to say *so*. 26. Nor yet is it proper to think, say, *or* believe this, (27) that there is no recompense of good works and punishment of crime, (28) nor even an appearance of an attainable creator of all the creatures, and *of* the daubing of a destroyer.

29. Moreover, *as to* this *latter*, that is precious to those who are more friends of penury than *of* the comfort of ill-famed vileness—(30) because they produce their happiness thereby[1], and are grateful, (31) and when they see distress they become suppliants (32) even from this destiny and dispensation which cannot become spiritual except by the spirits—(33) even so, in the appearance of every one *of* the hungry, (34) *and* in every one hurrying and straitened[2], who is imploring favours, is a manifestation of the maintenance of a hope for a supreme inspection over mankind, *and*, indeed, over wild animals, birds, *and* quadrupeds.

35. *As to* this, too, which they call sophistical[3], (36) that there is no assurance of even one of *these* things, (37) because all are jaundiced[4]—(38) for whoever says that honey is bitter and honey is sweet, is right *in* both, (39) since *it* is bitter to those abounding in bile, *and* sweet to others; (40) also bread is pleasant and bread is unpleasant are both

---

[1] By performing the good work of charity, which is necessary for the future happiness of their own souls.

[2] Assuming that Pâz. *hv*as*t*âw u vada*n*g is a misreading of Pahl. aûs*t*â*v*ŏ va tang.

[3] Pâz. suwastâî (Sans. suvastâyîka) is evidently traceable to σοφιστικός through Pers. sûfis*t*âîyah.

[4] Paz. tahal (Sans. ka*t*uka) is transposed in Pers. tal'*h*, 'bitter,' in which sense the word is used in §§ 38, 39, and Chap. III, 24.

true, (41) since *it* is pleasant to the hungry, *and* unpleasant to the surfeited; (42) *and* many other *statements* of this description—(43) that *which* should be said in reply to their twaddle is summarily (44) such as the wise *have* told them (45) thus:—'Even this statement of you sophists, about the jaundiced nature of everything, is alike jaundiced, and there is no truth *in* it.'

46. Many other *things* are said among them; (47) and this that is indicated by us is the predominant information *for* you victors, (48) so that you *may* obtain more from revelation.

Chapter VII.

1. Another *subject* is about the existence of a competitor of a different nature, as shown above[1], (2) that, from the constructing, qualifying, *and* ennobling of things so sagaciously, *and* even from the circumstances of an unimproving (a*k*ârîk) hand put upon the concentrated light, *it* is manifest that its maker, constructor, concentrator, *and* qualifier is sagacious. 3. Also his constructing sagaciously is manifest, from each separately, through the qualifying *and* ennobling of his own works severally. 4. And his working sagaciously is an indicator that his work is purposed *and* caused, (5) because every one of the works of the sagacious ought to be purposed *and* caused. 6. The purpose and cause of a work arise first, the work *itself* afterwards.

7. From the many kinds of his work *it* is manifest that his work is willed and requisite. 8. For *there*

[1] Chaps. IV, 11, 12, V, 54–56.

are two modes of doing a work, (9) either the willed is *of* the many kinds which are his will, (10) or the quality is *of* one kind which is as it is qualified[1]; (11) *so* from the many kinds *of* work of the creator *it* is manifest that his work is willed and requisite. 12. And his will is owing to a necessity of different limit[2], (13) because his will *was* a requisite for the power of the original evolution.

14. The purpose and cause of a work are before the necessity, (15) because while the purpose of the necessity of a work does not occur, the necessity does not exist. 16. The purpose of a work arises from the cause, towards which the necessity of that work instigates. 17. The necessity *and* willing of a thing which is caused exist; (18) and a cause of the necessity of a thing owing to its own self is not well suited, (19) because the cause arises from progression, (20) concerning which an indicator is the purposed work that is sagacious. 21. The purpose is owing to a cause, the cause is owing to promptitude (aû*s*tâ*v*), the promptitude is owing to an exception (ba*r*â), the exception is owing to an injurer, and the injury is owing to an opponent, without *further* words.

22. I *have* also shown[3], on this subject, through inevitable knowledge and through analogy, the making and qualification of the world and its circumstances *and* appliances. 23. From the making and qualification of the world is manifested a maker and qualifier; (24) and[4] [through the purposely-made

---

[1] By necessity, and not exhibiting any freedom of will on the part of its maker.

[2] That is, not limited by anything in his work of creation.

[3] In Chap. V, 46–91.

[4] The passage in brackets is omitted by AK, PB3, MH19, L23,

work of the sagacious creator, (25) owing to] the purposely-made work[1], is manifested the existence of an injurer from without.

Chapter VIII.

1. Again, about the existence of a competing *and* different original evolution[2], *there* are these (2) that are manifest from the good and evil which are in the world, (3) and the particulars of *its* good maker which are self-limited. 4. Such as darkness and light, (5) erudition *and* ignorance, (6) perfume and stench, (7) life and death, (8) sickness and health, (9) order (dâ*d*) and disorder, (10) distress and freedom from care (â*z*â*d*îh), (11) *and* other co-existing[3] factors whose certain existence is visible in every district *and* land, and every age. 12. So that no district *or* land whatever is discovered, nor yet any age *has* existed *or* shall exist, (13) wherein these good and bad terms and particulars *have* not existed *or* do not exist. 14. And it is not possible to say, as to any place *or* age, that good and evil are changeable in themselves by their own nature.

15. So, moreover, of the other co-existences whose difference is not through different duty, through different species, *or* through different quality—(16) as the difference of those of a like nature among one another, such as male *and* female, (17) *of* the varieties

---

evidently by mistake, as it is necessary to complete the meaning of the sentence.

[1] Made for the purpose of frustrating the designs of the fiend, which he foresaw (see Chap. VIII, 51, 71).

[2] See Chap. IV, 73 n.

[3] And, therefore, competing, as their natures are different.

of scents *and* flavours, and *of* the sun *and* moon *and* stars, whose difference is not through different nature, but through different duty, through different qualification, and through different construction, which are such as are attainable for various duties—(18) the good and evil, light and dark, *and* other different natures are then their distinction not through different duty, but through different nature, (19) the incompatible quality and the injuriousness which are manifest *in* them, one towards the other. 20. Therefore, when good is there [1], the non-existence of evil is unquestionable; (21) when light *has* come, darkness is removed. 22. Even so *of* the other co-existences [2] whose incompatibility and injuriousness together are owing to the cause of difference of nature, (23) because, in the worldly *existence*, *there* is a manifestation of the competing nature and injuriousness of the things, one towards the other.

24. The worldly *existence* is the fruit of the spiritual, and the spiritual is its root, (25) because fruit is obtained through a root. 26. *In* like manner the giver of the evidence arisen among the intelligent is clear. 27. Of the worldly *existence being* the fruit, *and* the spiritual being the root, the evidence is this, (28) when the progress (ma*d*anŏ) of every visible *and* tangible thing from imperceptibility to perceptibility is explicitly manifest. 29. Because the arising of mankind and other creatures,

[1] Sans. has 'so that where (yatra) good is,' which has induced JE to insert Pâz. *e*dar for Sans. yatra, so as to make the author say 'when good is here (in this world), the non-existence of evil there (in the other world) is unquestionable.' A noteworthy instance of punctilious blundering, on the part of a revising copyist, making an author say more than he means.

[2] Mentioned in §§ 5–11; those in § 4 having been just referred to.

who are visible *and* tangible, from a spiritual *existence* which is invisible *and* intangible is known, (30) as much as the mirrored length *and* breadth of the body *being* an emanation of itself. 31. And the perceptibility of the body of man and other creatures was imperceptible *and* invisible in the semen which is *derived* from *their* fathers; (32) the semen itself, too, came into perceptibility, visibility, *and* tangibility in the skin[1] of the fathers.

33. It is now possible to know inevitably[2] that this worldly *existence*, which is visible *and* tangible, is produced *and* has arisen from a spiritual *existence* which is invisible *and* intangible. 34. *In* like manner the lapsing (yehevûntanŏ) from visibility *and* tangibility into invisibility *and* intangibility[3], which are themselves a spiritual *state*, is unquestionable.

35. When *these* are seen by us, in the worldly *existence*, the competing nature, formation, and injuriousness of one towards the other, even as to the property of the spiritual *existence*, (36) which is the root of the worldly *one;* (37) and, *in* like manner, *there* is no doubt of the existence of its fruit of worldly possessions; (38) this is that which is manifest as regards a competing nature. 39. Then[4] its purpose and cause *were* indicated by me above[5], which are the sagaciously working of the creator, (40) who created the creature which is an indicator *of* the existence of an opponent.

[1] That Nêr. thus read pôst is shown by his Sanskrit translation of the word, but the original word was probably pôst, 'the back.'

[2] See Chap. V, 12–14 for the technical meaning of this word.

[3] As in the case of death and decay.

[4] Reading adinasam, 'then its by me,' which is the Pahlavi form indicated by the Pâz. ainâum of Nêr. (see Mkh. IX, 6 n).

[5] Chap. VII, 4, 5, 19–21.

41. For *it* is known that work due to workers is *of* two kinds, designed or qualified. 42. That which is designed is *of* three kinds. 43. Two are due to the wise *and* sagacious; (44) either through seeking for their own working of advantage and benefit, (45) or *through* removing *and* keeping away the harm and evil which are from without. 46. And one is due to the ignorant *and* unwise, (47) *done* defectively *and* without a purpose. 48. From the wise *and* sagacious, work ought[1] not to arise without a purpose *and* without a cause.

49. As the sagacious creator, who is all-knowing, perfectly capable, *and* fully complete in his own self, *has* sought that which is not a necessity for any advantage and aggrandizement of his from without[2], (50) it is, therefore, necessary to understand that the purpose *and* causes of his works are *of* that one kind[3], (51) to remove *and* keep away the harm which is due to his opponent and the injurer who may arise from without, which is itself the purpose and cause of the creation of the creatures. 52. Also this, that that sagacious creator is good-willed, (53) and his will is all goodness. 54. The creatures *were* also created by him predominantly of his own will. 55. And the completely-stirring desire of him who is good-willed *and* sagacious is to subdue[4] evil *and* make *it* extinct, (56) for while evil is not subdued the

---

[1] Reading saz*ê*d, as in JE, because, although AK, PB3, MH19 have Pâz. sah*ed*, 'seems,' Nêr. uses Sans. *s*aknoti.

[2] And, therefore, cannot have been actuated by the design mentioned in § 44.

[3] Mentioned in § 45.

[4] Reading khvâftanŏ, instead of Pâz. anâftan, which is almost identical in writing; and making a similar correction in § 56.

will of him who is good-willed is not fulfilled. 57. *And* this, that the goodness of that sagacious creator is manifest from creativeness, cherishing, and protection, *and from* commanding *and* teaching the means of putting away the path of evil and causing forbearance from crime; (58) also from the qualities and powers of the body in pain and sickness from without.

59. And, as a cause of the body, (60) to remove and keep away the opponent who comes to the body, *and to be* the maintenance, the cause of maturity, and the cause of growth of animals *and* sprouting plants[1], through the power of maintaining *and* cherishing *their* qualities, *there* is a co-operator who is scripturally called the Fravash[2]. 61. And through those four powers that are accumulative, which are the powers of attracting, seizing, digesting, *and* extracting—(62) and which, owing to the creator's sagacity of every kind, are co-operators with proportionate power for keeping away the pain and sickness of various kinds which are owing to the opponent, who is working defectively *and* desirous of evil—(63) and *through* others *that* are of like strength *and* auxiliary, the good will of the creator is manifest.

---

[1] Pâz. rôdamãnã, which Nêr translates by the Sanskrit for 'trees and grains;' and the occurrence of the latter word has induced some reviser of AK to alter the following words zôr-i dârâ, 'power of maintaining,' into zôridâêã, 'grains,' which alteration has been adopted by MH19 and PB3, but the latter has also zôr-i dârâ inserted in the margin, while JE has both readings in the text which thus means 'through the power of maintaining *and* cherishing the quality of grains.'

[2] The guardian spirit or spiritual representative of each object created by Aûharmazd, which acts for that object in the spiritual world (see Mkh. XLIX, 23).

64. Of this, too, that this *one* is no creator of the pain and death which are dissipaters of the body, who is good-willed *and* a maintainer and cherisher of the body, (65) the evidence is even from this, when the sagacious creator is not a sufferer from sorrow (apakhshadâr) and performing penitence, (66) and is no dissipater and disabler of his own achievements[1], (67) because *he* is sagacious and all-knowing.

68. *As to* this *other and* the sorrow *and* penitence of the kind which is owing to his own work, it is fitting to speak about him *as* of deficient knowledge, incomplete wisdom, and inconclusive understanding. 69. As work does not arise from the wise and sagacious without a purpose *and* without a cause[2], (70) *in* like manner work from the unwise *and* ignorant *and* those of inconclusive understanding is all defective, without a purpose, *and* without a cause[3]. 71. And that sagacious *one* is a contriver, working sagaciously *and* methodically, for keeping away that defective work and inconclusive understanding from his own creatures.

72. He who is working defectively produced distorted[4] *and* entangled scriptures among the creatures; (73) because this is known, that it is not possible so to keep away *and* cramp[5] him who is a moving *and* living nature in a boundless void, *and*

---

[1] Sans. has 'creatures.'

[2] See § 48.

[3] See §§ 46, 47.

[4] Assuming that Pâz. far*z*înma*n*d (Sans. gumphita) stands for Pahl. par*k*în-hômand.

[5] Pâz. aw*e*fsûidan (Sans. sa*n*ko*k*ayitum); but it may be noted that the Pahlavi equivalent of this word might be easily read apasa*g*agînî*d*anŏ, 'to disorganize.'

to become without risk of injury[1]. 74. But, though he does not become entangled, fenced in, and captive, (75) *he* is spreading anguish into the entanglement and captivity, and *it* is a means of grievous punishment. 76. Only while a complete wiping away of the anguish *due to* him, and complete information as to his own ignorant activity do not arise, he *has* meditated[2] with lying falsehood on that which is connected therewith. 77. And the complete capability of the almighty creator is the wiping away of the anguish.

78. Owing to the complete wiping away of anguish, through the almightiness of the sagacious creator, he casts *him* back impotent into the boundless void. 79. *And* the good creatures thereby become fearless, immortal, *and* undistressed (80) *through* the completely methodical sagacity and discernment of means of that omniscient creator of good beings.

81. From observation of possessions the difference of things is manifest. 82. And the difference is *of* two kinds, as mentioned above[3]. 83. One is difference of operation, and the other is difference of nature. 84. Difference of operation is owing to mutual assistance and united strength[4], (85) and difference of nature is owing to want of an adapter

---

[1] From him, the evil spirit, who is said to have left his native abyss and come on towards the light, through the void which intervened (see Bd. I, 3–5, 9).

[2] So in Pâz.—Sans.; but 'he meditates' is more probable, and would be written in the same manner in Pahlavi.

[3] Perhaps referring to the 'two series of things' mentioned in Chap. VI, 13–15, but the connection is not very clear.

[4] Because co-operation in complicated work tends towards division of labour.

and *to* opposition. 86. And not in a single place is a permanence of possessions manifest.

87. If one of anything shall exist *and* one does not exist, *its* name shall exist, (88) for the sake of recognising things, one from the other, and preserving the name. 89. The bad, by separation from the good existence, is originally evolved *in* such a manner that the one is really no cause of the other. 90. Because each one is existent (aît-hômand) through its own self, (91) owing to the perpetual injury *and* antagonism which are manifestly theirs, one towards the other.

92. If any one shall say that, as the competing *formations* of the competitors are numerous—(93) such as good *and* evil, dark *and* light, perfume *and* stench, life *and* death, sickness *and* health, pleasure *and* vexation—(94) there ought to be many other such original evolutions, many *in* number and of many species; (95) then they *may* give this reply[1], (96) that, even when *there* are many names and many species of competitors, still then all are within the compass[2] of two names. 97. And these two names are their including-source, which are good and evil. 98. Their different names and different species are tokens of these two sources.

99. *There* is nothing whatever that is not *in* the compass of these two names. 100. *There has* not been and *will* not be anything which is not good or evil, or a mixture of both. 101. On which account

[1] Sans. has 'others give a reply;' but the Pâz. anyê, 'others,' is certainly a misreading of Pahl. adîn aê, 'then this,' or adînas, 'then to him,' in which latter case the phrase would be 'then they *may* give a reply to him.' The proper Pâzand for 'other' is aware or han.

[2] See Chap. IV, 12 n.

it is explicitly manifest that the original evolutions are two, *and* not more; (102) *and* also this, that it is not possible *for* good to arise from evil, and evil from good.

103. From this, too, it is possible to understand[1], (104) that it is not possible *for* complete evil to arise from that thing which is filled with goodness. 105. If it be possible, then *it* is not full; (106) because *any* one thing, when said *to be* full, is no place *for* anything else; (107) and when *there* is no place *for* anything else, other things are not improved by it.

108. If the sacred being *be* perfect in goodness and wisdom, the folly and evil of *any* one are known not to arise from him. 109. If it be possible for them to arise from him, then *he* is not perfect. 110. If *he be* not perfect, it is not proper to glorify *him* for the sacredness of complete goodness. 111. If good and evil have crept on from the sacred being, *he* is imperfect in goodness. 112. If *he be* imperfect in goodness, *he* is imperfect in good information. 113. If *he be* imperfect in good information, so also *he* is imperfect in wisdom, understanding, knowledge, intellect, and other appliances of sagacity. 114. If *he be* imperfect in wisdom, understanding, intellect, *and* knowledge, *he* is imperfect in health. 115. If *he be* imperfect in health, he is apt to become sick. 116. If he be apt to become sick, *he* is imperfect in life.

117. If any one shall speak thus: 'I always see that from one nature, such as *that of* mankind, alike good and alike evil have always crept on, through actions owing to them,' (118) that is for this reason,

[1] MH19 has 'to maintain.'

because mankind are not perfect even in one *thing*. 119. And, on account of imperfection in goodness, evil has crept on from them; (120) and also on account of imperfection, even in health, they become sick. 121. For the same reason they die, (122) because the cause of death is the struggling of two competing propensities within one nature. 123. There where two competing propensities exist within one nature, the occurrence of sickness and death is known.

124. If any one shall say that there are good and evil actions which, until they are done, do not exist, (125) then they *may* give this reply[1], (126) that the occurrence of an action apart from doing is as impossible as any propensity apart from a nature; and, as to the nature, (127) its[2] continuance and arrangement are then known thereby not to occur through its own self. 128. For when a man indulges in wrath, Vohûman[3] is far from there; (129) and when Vohûman holds the position, wrath is not there. 130. When a man tells a lie, truth is far from there[4]; (131) and when he speaks true, falsehood has no position there, and that man is called truthful. 132. So also when sickness *has* come, health is not there; (133) and when health *has* come, sickness *has* gone.

---

[1] See § 95 n.

[2] Reading adînasas, 'then its thereby' (with a double pronominal suffix), which is the original Pahlavi indicated by Pâz. ainâs (see Mkh. IX, 6 n).

[3] The archangel 'good thought,' who is said to hold the position and vanquish 'evil thought,' while the angel Srôsh does the same as regards 'wrath' (see Dînk*ard*, quoted in Dd. XCIV, 1 n; also Bd. XXX, 29).

[4] Sans. adds 'and that man is called false,' which JE also inserts in Pâzand in the margin, but all other manuscripts omit.

134. Just as a substance which is not moving can exist, (135) but movement, except in a substance, cannot exist.

136. About this chapter, too, collected as a summary, (137) do you reverently[1] and discreetly observe and instruct thereon.

CHAPTER IX.

1. Other information about the existence of the competitor, similarly testified by the Dînka*rd*[2] manuscript (nipîk), is here well noted for you. 2. For both this *which is* written above and that which is written *here* are all grown from the seed which the glorified Âtûr-pâ*d*îyâvand sowed, (3) and *from* the original thanksgiving (spâs) of the supremely learned Âtûr-frôbag, son of Farukh-zâ*d*, himself.

4. The fourth[3] subject, which is from the Dînka*rd*, is about the existence of an opponent of the creatures and of an opponent earlier than the creatures, and is from the exposition of the good religion[4].

---

[1] Assuming that Pâz. dâramaihâ (Sans. sûkshmatayâ) is a misreading of Pahl. garâmîkîhâ. It would more easily be a misreading of sharmakîhâ, 'modestly,' but this term seems rather less likely to be applied by the author to his readers.

[2] See Chap. IV, 106, 107 for the names in these §§ 1, 2.

[3] Assuming that Pâz. ard ium (Sans. balish*th*o me) is a misreading of Pahl. arbâûm. The first subject (see Chap. II, 1) consisted of the three questions of Mit*r*ô-aîyyâr discussed in Chaps. II–IV. The second subject, about the existence of God, is contained in Chaps. V, VI. And the third subject, about the existence of an evil spirit competing with the creator, is debated in Chaps. VII, VIII.

[4] The third book of the Dînka*rd*, which treats of a multitude of subjects 'from the exposition of the good religion,' does not appear

5. *That* is, a knowledge of the existence of an opponent of the creatures is obtainable from the innermost *recesses* of the body of man even to the outermost *objects* of which[1] sight is susceptible, (6) and beyond those, within the certain limits of analogy. 7. The innermost *recesses* of man are the innermost of life, (8) *and* are seen through complete observation, within the same limits.

9. This is, as ignorance is to erudition, (10) deceit to good disposition, (11) and falsehood to truth, (12) other defects of the capabilities which are the source of erudition, good disposition, and truth are the opponent, (13) and the cause of the wickedness of the soul. 14. Again, these irregularities of the rules of arrangement of the body, within the compass of the body, are the opponent, and the cause of the disintegration of the body. 15. Again, *as to* these among the emanations, cold is the opponent of heat, dryness is of moisture, *and* the other doers of mischief are *opponents* of the operations of existence.

16. Within time darkness is the opponent of light, stench of perfume, ugliness of handsomeness, unsavouriness of savouriness, poison of *its* antidote, noxious creatures and the wolf of the well-yielding cattle, *and* the vile felon (mar) of the good man. 17. Beyond time the brigand *planets* (gadûgân)[2] are the opponents of the work of the divine bestowers.

18. Beyond the knowledge obtainable of all these

to contain the materials for this chapter. The author is, therefore, probably alluding to one of the two earlier books which have not yet been discovered.

[1] Assuming that Pâz. a*n*dâ n*e* (for b*e*) thûm-i va*s* (Sans. yâvat bî*g*am asya) stands for Pahl. vad ba*r*âtûm-î a*g*a*s*.

[2] See Chap. IV, 10.

champions susceptible to sight, are those who are within the limits of analogy[1] and the certain information of multitudes, the demons who are the opponents of the sacred beings.

19. The existence of an opponent before the creation of the creatures, and his coming to the creatures (20) after the creation of the creatures, *and* also to the creator, are presented comprehensibly through reasons which are suitable[2] *and* presentable, *and* through the provision of a remedy, a creation which is for a purpose. 21. This one statement (vâkak) possesses five arguments (sâmân). 22. One is the *being* presented comprehensibly. 23. One is the *being* presented through reasons. 24. One is the reasons which are presentable *and* suitable that the creation existed. 25. One is the remedy appointed for the creation. 26. *And* one is the creation of the creatures of the creator for a purpose.

27. The existence of these five arguments is manifest through the creations *and* achievements themselves. 28. The presenting comprehensibly is wisely arranging the testimony of the effect[3] of the creatures, (29) through the reasons presented, which are a declaration owing to the same sagacity. 30. The reason obtainable, that the creation existed, (31) with the arrangement of the creation so methodically, ought to arise from the suitable *state* of the

[1] Referring to the two kinds of evidence, direct and indirect, mentioned in §§ 5, 6.

[2] So in § 24 and in Sans., though Pâz. has 'obtainable' here.

[3] Assuming that the Pâz. awar dugâê of AK stands for Pahl. bar gôkâs (or gôkâsîh). MH19 has duvâê, and PB3, JE have dusâê, while Sans. means 'about the magnitude.'

creation; (32) and the suitable design of the creation itself possesses the testimony, through *its* appearance. 33. The remedy appointed is a comprehensible *and* presentable demonstrator, (34) because it becomes a desire of knowledge and an appearance of the desire. 35. The *being* created for a purpose is manifest through the desire of activity of the creation, both severally and naturally.

36. The evidences of the existence of an opponent before the creation of the creatures are many. 37. And one of them is the suitable *state* of the creation of the creatures, (38) because the limit of suitability is not well fitted for anything except necessity. (39) That *which* is *inferred* from suitability is necessity, from necessity haste, *and* from haste the existence of an opponent who is before the suitable work which is the creation.

40. The evidence of the coming of the destroyer to the creatures, after the creation of the creatures, is the formation of the means of the creator, for encountering an opponent, before the arrival of the opponent, (41) which are omnisciently a provision before creation by the creator. 42. And there is a demonstrator of *these* same means of the creatures that is prepared, which is the struggling opposed to the opponent through the arrangement of *their* nature. 43. One duty of the nature of the creatures is the subduing of so much vexation. 44. Their preparation, too, is like a contest that is forming an enemy opposing the opponent, (45) and their natural desire for duty is removing all haste.

CHAPTER X.

1. Another subject is about the deliberating of the deliberators on unity, from which even the preparation of the duality is manifested.

2. It should be known, that whoever wishes to understand a creator, except when he gives trouble to his own life, (3) should meditate reverently[1]. 4. First, he fully understands his own body and soul, (5) that is, who produced *them*, out of what, and for what purpose? 6. Also, who is his accuser and adversary; (7) and who is his friend and helper? 8. Likewise, who instigates him to commit crime, (9) of what nature *is he*, (10) and how is it possible to escape him?

11. Then *he* is not able to understand him[2] *as* the creator through his nature and his coming to himself. 12. For when he bore the name of creator, then, with it, he brought these three creations[3]:—(13) creation, religion, and soul. 14. Because the name of creator is known from the occurrence of creation. 15. This *implies* that the creator of the creation created the creations for duty, (16) but does not release *them* from duty. 17. And the duty of the creatures is to understand *and* perform the will of the creator, (18) *and* to abstain from *what is* disliked *by him*. 19. To act by the will of the creator, and to abstain from *what is* disliked by him, is to preserve the soul. 20. The will of the creator is not under-

[1] See Chap. VIII, 137 n. [2] His accuser and instigator.

[3] All MSS. have 'he bore these three names;' but Nêr. has evidently misread *s*em, 'name,' instead of dâm, 'creature,' both words being written alike in Pahlavi.

stood, except from the religion of the creator. 21. *And* the religion is appointed by the creator free from doubt.

22. Now it is expedient to know that the sacred being appointed the religion for the understanding of his will, (23) and from the understanding of his will for the preservation of the soul are manifested the compassion and mercifulness of the sacred being. 24. From the preservativeness of the religion for the soul are manifested the grandeur and valuableness of the religion; (25) from the necessity of preserving the soul are manifested the defilement and delusion[1] of the soul; (26) *and* from the defilement and delusion of the soul is manifested a defiler and deluder of the thoughts, words, *and* deeds of mankind. 27. On the whole a corrupter of souls is manifest.

28. And now it is expedient for us to well recognise[2] and know, as to that defiler who is a corrupter of souls, of what nature *he is*. 29. Because, if the creation *and* achievement of the sacred being are said *to be* of a like nature, then how did the sacred being appoint the religion for the preservation of the soul? 30. That is not expedient for him—*if* a defiler and deluder of souls—to produce[3] as his own creation and will[4]. 31. For if he be himself the creator, and be himself the defiler and corrupter of souls, *and* nothing occurs except by his will, (32)

---

[1] Pâz. vyâwãnî (see Chap. III, 22 n).

[2] Assuming that Pâz. huzvârdan (Sans. sa*m*s*o*dhayitum) is a misreading of Pahl. hû-zinhâr*d*anŏ.

[3] Sans. 'to announce.'

[4] Because it (the religion) is opposed to his supposed work as a deluder.

then, when it is necessary for us to write of preservation from the sacred being[1], whom *shall* we make *as* a refuge[2]?

33. Now it is necessary *for* every intelligent person to understand *and* to know thus much, (34) that is, from whom it is necessary for us to flee and to abstain, (35) and with whom is the hope, and with whom the maintenance, of our protection. 36. The method for this acquisition is nothing else but to understand the sacred being in *his* nature, (37) because, as I wrote above[3], *it* is not only to know *his* existence, but it is necessary to understand *his* nature and his will.

38. And I *have* observed, in the world, the sectarian belief of all maintainers of sects who hold [the two fundamental *doctrines*][4]. 39. One is that which asserts that all the good and evil, which are in the world, are owing to the sacred being. 40. *And* one is that which asserts that all the good of the world, besides the hope of preserving the soul, is owing to the sacred being; (41) and the cause of all evil of the body, besides the risk of the soul, is owing to Aharman; (42) *and* all *things* have started from appointment *by* these two origins into various formations *and* various subdivisions.

43. Now I have been an enquirer everywhere, for understanding the sacred being, as written above[5],

---

[1] As it would be, if he were the corrupter of souls.

[2] The exclamation of the wicked soul after death, derived from Yas. XLV, 1 (see Mkh. II, 159).

[3] See Chap. V, 6–9.

[4] The words in brackets are omitted in AK, PB3, MH19, but occur in Sans. and the later MSS.

[5] Chap. I, 36, 37.

fervent-minded in the investigation of his religion and will; (44) as likewise I have wandered, for the sake of investigation, to the region without and the land of the Hindûs, and *to* many different races. 45. Because, *as to* religion, I did not admire that which *was* in supremacy[1], (46) but *I* sought that which *was* more steadfast and more acceptable in wisdom and testimony. 47. I went also into association with many different races, (48) until a time (49) when, owing to the compassion of the sacred beings, and the strength, glory, and power of the good religion, I escaped from much gloomy depth and ill-solvable doubt.

50. By the united power of knowledge of the religion (51) and the well-reflecting writing of the wise, (52) the marvellous allegorical[2] writings of the learned Âtûr-pâ*d*îyâvand[3], (53) and by that writing which the glorified Rôshan[4], son of Âtûr-frôbag, prepared—(54) for which he appointed the name of the Rôshan manuscript (nipîk)—(55) *and* likewise that *for* which the supremely learned *and* righteous Âtûr-frôbag[5], son of Farukh-zâ*d*, (56) who *was* the

---

[1] Probably a guarded allusion to Muhammadanism which it was then unsafe to disparage openly, as is evident from the rarity of its name in Pahlavi writings.

[2] Or 'the miracle-resembling.'

[3] See Chap. IV, 106.

[4] A commentator whose opinions are often quoted in Pahlavi writings (see Sls. I, 4 n). His father was probably the early editor of the Dînka*rd* mentioned in §§ 55-57, though it is hazardous to rely upon a single name for identifying an individual. In that case he must have been a younger brother of the Zaratû*s*t-î Âtûr-frôbagân who succeeded his father as 'leader of the good religion,' and revised the Dînka*rd*, as mentioned in the last paragraphs of its third book.

[5] See Chap. IV, 107.

leader of those of the good religion, (57) appointed the name of the Dînka*rd* manuscript—owing to *its* explaining the religion[1]—(58) I am saved from the many doubts, delusions, deceits, and follies of sects, (59) and, especially, from those of the deceivers, the very great *and* very mighty, very evil-teaching *and* empty-skulled[2] Manicheans[3], (60) whose devotion is witchcraft, *whose* religion is deceitfulness, and *whose* teaching is folly and intricate secret proceedings.

61. I have been deliberately confirmed by the power of wisdom and the strength of knowledge of the religion, (62) not through obstinate faith[4], but by the pure revelation opposed to the demon[5], which is the decision of Aûha*r*ma*zd* (63) that *was* taught by the creator Aûha*r*ma*zd* to the righteous Zaratû*s*t[6].

64. Zaratû*s*t came alone, on a true mission, to the lofty portal of Kaî Gu*s*tâsp[7], (65) and the religion was taught by him, with a powerful tongue, to Kaî Gu*s*tâsp and the learned, through the speech of wisdom, through manual gestures, through definite words, through explanation of many doubts, and through presentation of the visible testimony of the

---

[1] The probable meaning of dînka*rd* is 'acts of the religion.' See also Chap. IV, 107 n.

[2] Reading rat-mastarg. For rat Nêr. has read ra*d*, 'pontiff,' which is written in the same manner; his translation being Sans. guru, while his Pâz. ra*d* has become raê in AK, PB3, MH19, but has again become ra*d* in JE.

[3] See Chap. XVI.

[4] Assuming that Pâz. sakht-vîrôda*s*nihâ stands for Pahl. sakht-virôyi*s*nîhâ.

[5] That is, the Vendîdâ*d*.

[6] See Mkh. I, 10.

[7] See Mkh. XIII, 14, XXVII, 68–76.

archangels, *together* with many miracles. 66. And a greatness in power which is not the destiny of worldly existences was theirs who saw him of the vehement guardian spirit. 67. And Kaî Spend-dâ*d*[1] and Zargar[2] and other *royal* sons (zâ*d*ak), instigating the many conflicts and shedding the blood of those of the realm, accepted the religion as a yoke[3], (68) while they even wandered to Arûm[4] and the Hindûs, outside the realm, in propagating the religion.

69. Owing to *progress* onwards it came in succession to the descendants of the divinities[5], the rulers who *were* those of the Kayân race who *were* exalted ones. 70. *And* still onwards even until the achievement with melted metal pouring upon the chest of the glorified Âtûr-pâ*d*[6], son of Mâraspend, in the reign of that divinity (bagh) Shâhpûr, the king of kings who *was the son of* Aûhar*m*a*z*d[7], in a controversy with apostates of different species of many kinds. 71. *He was* preserved from those most

[1] Misread Spudâkht by Nêr. He was a son of Kaî Gu*s*tâsp, and called Spe*n*tô-dâta in the Avesta, and Isfendiyâr in Persian.

[2] Av. Zairivairi, Pers. Zarîr, a brother of Kaî Gu*s*tâsp (see Bd. XXXI, 29).

[3] Literally 'for the neck,' assuming that Pâz. ô-*k*a ôi is an erroneous reading of Pahl. va*l* *k*avarman, as in Mkh. XXXIX, 30.

[4] Asia Minor was so called from having been a portion of the Roman empire in Sasanian times.

[5] Pâz. bayãnã (Sans. mahat) is evidently a misreading of Pahl. bagânân, a term referring to the Sasanian kings who adopted the title of bagî, 'divinity,' in their inscriptions (see also § 70), and claimed to be descended from the old dynasty of Kayân kings.

[6] The supreme high-priest and prime minister of king Shâhpûr II (A.D. 309-379), who underwent the ordeal of melted metal for the sake of proving the truth of the religion.

[7] King Aûhar*m*a*z*d II (A.D. 300-309).

mighty apostates, who are called even by *the name of* their desires[1].

72. And the Arûmans[2], who have been, at various periods, termed untruthful[3], *have* asked many ill-solvable questions of this religion; (73) *but there has* been no doubtfulness of any question that is explained by this religion, (74) and the learned of the country of Irân have always been sustainers of victory among them. 75. Not like other sects whose religion is secretly progressive and deceiving, delusively for the deceived, *and* undutifully among the customs and assemblages of the less-informed, unintelligent, and demon-natured whose information was nothing whatever of knowledge and understanding of wisdom. 76. Then, so far as the assemblages that are very secretly deceived and deluded by them, nobody is presented for detection (âskârâkîh); (77) *but* afterwards, owing to the capture of the many of little knowledge and unintelligent opinions who are deluded by them, it is discovered they are *provided* with much mutually afflicting speech, falsehood, *and* disconnection, which are their religion.

78. So that I here[4] notice *some* of *their* much inconsistency and disconnection, for informing the judgment of new learners, (79) for the reason that when the writings of the learned ancients have specially minutely and reverently[5] discoursed of

[1] That is, they are called âshmôg (Av. ashemaogha, 'perplexing righteousness').

[2] The Greeks of the eastern empire of the Romans.

[3] Pâz. anâst may be either 'irreverent,' or else stand for Pahl. arâst, 'untruthful.' Sans. has 'atheistical.'

[4] In the next chapter.

[5] Or, perhaps, 'modestly' (see Chap. VIII, 137 n).

what is most astute in evil, to impel *one* to good knowledge, (80) you *should* observe with kind regards *what is* ordered.

CHAPTER XI.

1. Henceforth I write[1] *of* the inconsistency of their twaddle, and *of* just observations (2) you should estimate with wise regard.

3. First, *as to* the full consideration of that one original evolution (4) which they state thus: 'The sacred being is one, doing good works, wise, powerful, compassionate, *and* merciful, (5) so that good works *and* crime, truth *and* falsehood, life *and* death, good *and* evil are[2] owing to him[3].'

6. Now do ye ask of them (7) thus: 'Is the sacred being always compassionate *and* showing mercy, doing good works *and* judicious, and does he know all *that* is, was, *and will* be; *and* is *he* advancing the desire of *one's* wishes in everything, even *in* this where judiciousness is interference, or when such is not so? 8. Because, if *he be* compassionate, doing good works, *and* showing mercy, why then are Aharman and the demons and all these evil faiths[4] of hell admitted[5]

---

[1] Pâz. 'I have written.'

[2] Sans. and JE insert 'all.'

[3] Most of this statement can be found in the Qur'ân in isolated texts, such as 'God there is no god but he . . . He knows the unseen and the visible; the mighty, the wise . . . verily God is forgiving, compassionate . . . It is God who created you . . . and then will make you die.' (Qur'ân LXIV, 13, 18, 14, XXX, 39; SBE. vol. ix.)

[4] Assuming that Pâz. vîrôsaa (Sans. âmnâya) is a misreading of Pahl. virôyâk.

[5] Tracing Pâz. awagad (Sans. avâkirat) to Av. aiwi+gata.

by him to his own creatures, through his own compassion, doing of good works, *and* showing of mercy? 9. If not known by him, where are that knowledge and omniscience of his? 10. If he did not wish to keep misery and evil away from the creatures, and to produce only happiness *for* every one, where are that judiciousness and interference of his? 11. If it were not possible that it should not be produced by him, for what is that omnipotence of his (12) which we[1] every one, as *it were*, observe *and* well consider?'

13. Whenever they say *that* every good and evil *has* arisen from the sacred being—except when they separate from him these four attributes (hûnar), requisite for divinity, which are omniscience, omnipotence, goodness, *and* mercifulness—(14) there is then no possibility of it. 15. When, indeed, they separate from him *only* one of these four attributes, even then *he* is not complete in divinity. 16. For if a sacred being be he *who is* omniscient, omnipotent, good, and merciful, then he who is not omniscient, *or* not omnipotent, *or* not good, *or* not merciful is not a sacred being.

17. Again, *observe* this, that when *he is* a ruler, advancing desires in every person *and* thing, why are that country and empire of his own not so kept, without help, from every enemy and adversity *apart* from his own work, so that *there* would not be anything whatever of distress, oppression, injustice, and complaint for any one in his empire? 18. Since the

[1] So in Sanskrit; but, as the two Pâz. verbs end in -u*n*, the original Pahlavi termination may have been -yên (3d pers. optative), and we might read 'which every one may, as *it were*, observe.'

rule *and* empire of a man, *who is* ruler and emperor, are then commendable when *it* is possible for him so to protect *and* keep his own country *and* empire, through his own wisdom, that they *may* not assist his enemy to detract from his work, and to produce sin *and* harm. 19. Or, when his enemy covets *some* of his work, he is enabled to keep him away from his own thoughtful friends, *and* to make every one free from distress.

20. Again, *observe* this, that when *he is* triumphant, victorious, and prevailing, (21) over whom are that triumph, victory, and prevailing of his? 22. Since triumph and victory are over enemies, a competitor exists. 23. It is not expedient[1] to become himself a competitor *and* enemy to his own; (24) while when there is no enemy *and* competitor of his, over whom does he become triumphant and victorious? 25. That *sort of* triumph and victory is not spoken about, (26) because even cattle and sheep, when they have no opponent and injurer, are victorious and triumphant over themselves.

27. Again, *observe* this, is a wise *being* contented with his own divinity and grandeur, or not? 28. If the wise *being* be contented, then he *has* become contented to produce an enemy and criminal, *and* to admit all *that is* devastating into a country, through his own knowledge and will, for the benefit of the

[1] K28 inserts shâya*d*, '*and* possible,' and JE inserts Pâz. tvã, which has the same meaning; but these insertions have probably originated in a blunder of the writer of AK, who first wrote Sans. *s*aknoti, the usual equivalent of Pâz. shâya*d*, but afterwards interlined Sans. sa*m*yu*g*yate to correspond with *saze*d, 'it is expedient,' the word he had written in the Pâz. text.

country and creatures. 29. *But* why[1] is it expedient to seek a disposition of crime *and* evil, to become himself an enemy *and* curser as regards them, *and* to provide a hellish *existence*, becoming the misery of mankind?

30. Again, *observe* this, *as to* whatever he says, does he speak truly *and* credibly, or not? 31. If he speaks that truly *and* credibly which he states thus: 'I am a friend of good works and an enemy of crime,' (32) *and* always produces more crime *and* criminals than good works *and* doers of good works, (33) where is that truthful speaking of his?

34. Again, *observe* this, is his desire goodness, or vileness? 35. If his desire *be* vileness, whence is that divinity of his? 36. If his desire *be* goodness, then why are the vile and vileness more than the good and goodness?

37. Again, *observe* this, is he merciful, or not? 38. If he *be* not merciful, whence is that divinity of his? 39. If he *be* merciful, then why does he speak thus: 'The hearts, ears, *and* eyes of mankind are bent about by me, so that it is not possible for them to think, speak, *or* do *anything* but that which is wanted by me[2]; (40) be it what *has* made them great *and* noble, through *being* without want; (41) *or* be it what *has* admitted them to eternal hell, slain *and* exterminated by death of many kinds. 42. So that while those whom I force back become good *and* more active in good works, (43) yet still those who

---

[1] Assuming that Pâz. *k*i, 'what?' stands for *k*im. Sans. has 'how?' (Pâz. *k*u*n*.)

[2] 'Yet the Lord hath not given you an heart to perceive, and eyes to see, and ears to hear, unto this day' (Deut. xxix. 4).

are forced back do only a little[1], (44) *and* are much more criminal *and* more sinful than those who are forward.'

45. Again, *observe* this, that if, whatever he does, he does wisely and for a purpose, (46) then, when no opponent and adversary of his existed, why *did* the first achievement which *was* prepared by him *become* servants to demoniacal disobedience, who are perverted thereby, among mankind, to wickedness *and* a hellish *existence*[2]? 47. If *it were* not known by him that they *would* become perverted, it was expedient (sazîd) for him to order the making of a trial of them, (48) because now many thousands *and* myriads who *are* prepared by him, so that they *may* serve him and exhilarate (mastend) his rule, have become in every mode disobedient *and* unhappily advised. 49. For with that scanty knowledge that mankind *possess*, which is not so prepared *and* organized as is the wish of mankind, (50) if even anything arises, that they construct *and* prepare, which does not so come on *and* become[3] as is their wish, they do not stop again, a second *time*, for the preparation of that thing, *but* they refrain from it.

51. *As to* him, that omnipotent *and* omniscient ruler, of the abundant *and* innumerable things *he has* hitherto made and prepared not even one comes on *and* becomes such as is his wish, yet still he never refrains from the preparation *and* production of many new *things*. 52. Just as when *he was* the creator of

[1] Assuming that Pâz. khvazâr stands for khû*g*ârak; but, as Sans. has 'injury,' the Pâzand may be a misreading of â*z*âr.

[2] Referring probably to the fall of man, detailed in §§ 61–77.

[3] So in Sans. and JE, as in § 51; but AK and MH19 have 'go' here.

that *one* of his first angels whom, on account of affection, he prepared out of fire, *and for* several thousand years, (53) as they say, *they* always performed his worship; (54) at last *that one was* undone by one command that was given by him (the creator) thus: 'Offer homage to this first of mankind, who is prepared by me out of clay.' 55. And deliverance, as to *what* is not expedient to offer, *was* expressly mentioned by him. 56. Then *that one* acted scornfully *and* contemptibly as to his clay and curse and wrath; (57) and, *being* perverted to devilry and fiendishness, *he was* forced out of heaven, (58) *and was* given a life of millenniums *and* an eternal dominion, (59) so that *he said*, 'I *will* go *and* make my servants and worshippers astray *and* deluded[1].' 60. And he *was* made an injurer and adversary at his own will.

61. *At* last also that man, to whom he, the supreme angel, was ordered to offer homage with many worshippers, for the sake of affection and respect, (62) is appointed to the garden of paradise (vahist), (63)

---

[1] 'And we did create man from crackling clay of black mud wrought in form. And the ginns had we created before of smokeless fire. And when thy lord said to the angels, "Verily I am creating a mortal from crackling clay of black mud wrought into shape; and when I have fashioned it, and breathed into it of my spirit, then fall ye down before it adoring." And the angels adored all of them together, save Iblîs, who refused to be among those who adored. . . . He said, "Then get thee forth." . . . Said he, "O my lord! respite me until the day when they shall be raised." He said, "Then, verily, thou art of the respited." . . . He said, "O my lord! for that thou hast seduced me I will surely make it seem seemly for them on earth, and I will surely seduce them all together, save such of thy servants amongst them as are sincere."' (Qur'ân XV, 26-40; SBE, vol. vi.)

so that he *may* cultivate *it* and eat all the fruit, (64) except *of* that one tree of which *it* is ordered thus: 'Ye shall not eat *of it*[1].' 65. And with them (mankind) the deceiver, who is the deluder prepared by him (the creator), (66) is let into the garden. 67. There are *some* who say *he is* a serpent[2], *and* there are *some* who *say he is* Aharman[3]. 68. And an inclination *for* eating *and* greediness is given by that same *one* himself to mankind. 69. Then, being deceived *by* that deluder *saying*: 'Eat of that tree'—(70) there are *some* who say *he spoke to* Adam—(71) they ate through that inclination for eating[4].

72. After eating they became so imbued with knowledge that good and evil *were* understood and known by them[5]. 73. *Deprived* of that so-great respect and affection, through that one injunction which *was* forgotten by them—(74) and that forgetfulness *being* likewise owing to that cause—(75) they are forced out of the garden of paradise[6]—*he* with *his* wife—by grievous wrath and disrespect, (76) *and* are delivered into the hand of that enemy who is a deceiver and deluder; (77) so that he *has* propagated

[1] 'And the Lord God took the man, and put him into the garden of Eden, to dress it and to keep it. And the Lord God commanded the man, saying, "Of every tree of the garden thou mayest freely eat: but of the tree of the knowledge of good and evil, thou shalt not eat of it"' (Gen. ii. 15–17).

[2] 'Now the serpent was more subtle than any beast of the field which the Lord God had made' (Gen. iii. 1).

[3] 'That old serpent, called the Devil and Satan' (Rev. xii. 9, xx. 2).

[4] Compare Gen. iii. 1–6.

[5] 'And the eyes of them both were opened' (Gen. iii. 7).

[6] 'Therefore the Lord God sent him forth from the garden of Eden, to till the ground from whence he was taken. So he drove out the man' (Gen. iii. 23, 24).

his own will among them, *and has* fashioned *it* upon them.

78. Now which *was* unjust, the unreasonable command, the after-wisdom, *or* the scanty knowledge that *was* more faulty and more mischievous than these? 79. Also this, that is, why *was* that garden not made by him fortified and strong, so that that deluder could not have gone into *it?*

80. Even now *he* (*the deceiver*) *has* made and makes multitudes *of* his (the creator's) servants *and* worshippers deluded; (81) and, for the same reason, multitudes *of* apostles *and* prophets (vakhshvarân) are appointed by him (the creator) for the worldly *existence at* various times, (82) so that, *as he says:* 'They *may* save my servants from the hand of that deluder, (83) *and* bring *them* into the true path and way[1].' 84. And even those worshippers of his, *in* every way through their own will, have slain *and* subdued (khvâft), by a wretched death, his own apostles[2], whose diligence had brought mankind into the proper path and doctrine.

85. That original deluder and misleader is allowed an eternal life. 86. *And*, even till now, his will is more triumphant *and* absolute than that of the sacred being, through deluding *and* misleading, (87) because those deluded *and* astray are much more numerous than those *in* the true path *and* undeluded.

88. Again, *observe* this, does he do whatever he

---

[1] 'For the Lord will not forsake his people for his great name's sake; because it hath pleased the Lord to make you his people . . . but I (Samuel) will teach you the good and the right way' (1 Sam. xii. 22, 23).

[2] 'I will send them prophets and apostles, and *some* of them they shall slay and persecute' (Luke xi. 49).

does for a purpose, or not? 89. If he does *it* without a purpose, *he* is working foolishly; (90) and it is not proper to praise him who is working foolishly as a sagacious divinity. 91. If he does *it* for a purpose, (92) then, when no opponent and adversary of his existed, why is the production of all these creatures which are even like demons, disobedient men *with* the opposing will of that contentious deluder, and innumerable unprofitable creatures?

93. Again, *observe* this, that, if he knows all *that* is, was, *and will* be, it was not expedient for him to produce, through his own knowledge and will, anything of that of which he *may be* sorry, and *which* remains opposing his will and command, (94) and becomes an adversary of his apostles *and* the doers of *his* will.

95. If they say that this adversary *was* produced good and virtuous from the beginning, *and* afterwards became an evil and a misleading of the creatures, (96) that *implies*, you should say, that, when he is all-powerful, the purpose *and* will of the adversary, in changing into an evil and a misleading of the creatures, are more successful and more powerful than those of the sacred being; (97) because the evil in *any* period is stronger than the good.

98. Again, *observe* this, that when a criminal *arises* wholly through his will[1], (99) and the minds of criminals are defiled by him himself, (100) and the seed of crime is sown by him himself, (101) when[2] *it has* grown who *has* maintained *its* origin? 102.

[1] The will of the adversary is probably meant (see § 95).

[2] So in Sans. and JE, but AK has 'so that.'

And by what power of adjudication is one executed *and* one rewarded[1]?

103. Again, *observe* this, *was* this world made and created by him (the creator) for a purpose, for his own pleasure *and* for the sake of the comfort and happiness of mankind, or without a purpose, for his own discomfort and the hurry, trouble, pain, *and* death of mankind? 104. For if made by him without a purpose, *he was* acting foolishly; (105) a thing without a purpose *being* not acceptable by the wise. 106. If made by him for a purpose, and created by him for his own pleasure and the comfort and happiness of mankind, (107) why *was* it not made by him prosperous *and* full of happiness?

108. If his pleasure and happiness *arise* from the preparation of mankind and the creatures, what is the advantage from their slaughter and devastation? 109. If thoughts of crime are not given by him himself to mankind, who is he who gives thoughts of crime different from his command and will? 110. If *they* are given by him himself, and he now considers them a fault, what is that justice and arbitration of his owing to? 111. For when mankind, with little knowledge and little wisdom, even then, so far as they are able, do not let the lion and wolf *and* other noxious creatures in among their own young ones *and* pregnant *females*, (112) so long as they *can* destroy them, (113) why *has* the merciful sacred being now let[2] Aharman and the demons in upon his own creatures, (114) so that they have

[1] That is, why is the sinner punished while the adversary, who occasions the sin, remains unmolested and triumphant?

[2] AK has 'let' written above 'admitted.'

made them vile[1], defiled, wicked, *and* hellish? 115. If done for the sake of experiment, just as that which they assert, that evil *was* created by him for the sake of an experiment as regards the creatures, (116) why *was* it not understood by him before those men and creatures *existed?* 117. Because *he* whose custom[2] is experiment is not to be called omniscient.

118. The conclusion is this, that the sacred being, if *there* existed no opponent and adversary of his, was able to create all those creatures and creations of his free from misfortune; why did *he* not *so* create *them?* 119. Or was it not possible for him to wish *it?* 120. If it were not possible for him to wish *it*, *he* is not completely capable. 121. If it were possible for him not to wish *it*, *he* is not merciful. 122. If *it were* known by him that *he might say*: 'Something *or* some one *will* arise, from these creatures *and* creations which I create, that *will* not *be* according to my will,' (123) and ultimately he made *them*, (124) then to attach now all this wrath and cursing *and* casting away for punishment in hell, discontentedly to his own performance, is unreasonable.

125. Again, *observe* this, that if all the crime-meditating *and* crime-committing sin which mankind think *and* speak *and* do, as well as pain, sickness, poverty, *and* the punishment *and* misery of hell, cannot arise, except by the will and command of the

[1] Pâz. khôr, which Nêr. seems to have identified with Pers. kar, as his Sans. gives 'deaf.' It may, however, mean 'blind' (Pers. kûr), as in Chap. XII, 64, 70.

[2] The Sanskrit takes Pâz. dastûr in its more usual sense of 'high-priest.'

sacred being—(126) the will *and* power of the sacred being *being* eternal[1], (127) because his self-existence is also eternal—(128) the hopelessness of eternally saving any one whatever from misery and punishment is now certain. 129. For *it* is repeatedly declared that there is no learned teacher whatever who keeps one away from these mischievous evil desires, (130) if the worshipper *be even of* the same kind *as* those worshippers *and* high-priests who *have* issued to mankind this admonition: 'Commit no crime *and* sin.' 131. Because they wish to set aside the will *and* command of the sacred being[2]. 132. *Observe* this, too, that, as both are his will, alike crime *and* alike good works, *it* is not manifest whether he approves the good works of doers of good works more, or the crimes of criminals.

133. Likewise *observe* this, those physicians who, on account of the hope of the soul, prepare the medicine of the sick, (134) and remove *and* dismiss their pain and disease, (135) so that merit is possessed by them (the physicians) owing to that practice; (136) yet they[3] are prepared for the punishment of hell. 137. And those who, on account of affection *for* the soul, give something *to* poor, begging, suffering people, (138) and thereby scatter[4] *and* dismiss their want *and* poverty, (139) so that merit is possessed by them (the charitable)

[1] Sans. has 'the will of the sacred being *being* powerful and eternal.'

[2] Without whose will and command the sin and evil cannot arise, as assumed in § 125.

[3] The sick are probably meant, but the original text is ambiguous.

[4] Assuming that Pâz. hugâre*n*d stands for Pahl. aûkâlend.

owing to that practice; (140) yet it becomes grievous sin for them[1], through anxiety. 141. If they say that those physicians *and* the remedies which they offer, *and* also those who give something *to* the poor *and* suffering, all *exist* by the will of the sacred being, (142) it is easier, more reasonable, *and* more adapted to divinity, when the sacred being is without an adversary *and* without an opponent, for him not to create that disease *and* poverty (143) than *that*, *as to* those that *he* himself is to make sick *and* poor, he *should have* commanded mankind thus: 'Ye shall make them healthy *and* free from want.' 144. If they say that his desire is this, that he *may* occasion the happiness of those physicians *and* givers by the recompense for it, (145) and make them proceed[2] to the eternal happiness of heaven (vahist); (146) you should observe, *as to* that, since he acts injudiciously *and* incapably when, on account of the existence of a complete desire for happiness *and* prosperity[3] among others, *he* is an attainer of misery *for* multitudes *of* the innocent who are distressed, poor, necessitous, *and* sick, (147) this *may* also *be said*, that if *it be* not possible for him to occasion happiness and prosperity[4] as regards one, except by the distress, pain, and vexation of some other, (148) that *shows that* his absolute power *and* freedom from opposition are not adapted for effectual operation. 149. If they say

[1] Probably the poor, but the original text is ambiguous.

[2] Assuming that Pâz. *g*âmine*d* stands for Pahl. gâmînê*d*. The old MS. AK ends with this section, and the remaining half of the extant text has been found only in modern copies, having been formerly separated from AK and lost

[3] So in JE, but JJ has 'nobility,' and MH19 has 'pleasure.'

[4] JJ has 'nobility.'

that he makes those sick *and* poor proceed to the eternal happiness of heaven in the spiritual *existence*, as a recompense for it, (150) that *implies*, if *it be* not possible, *or* not completely possible, for him to give the recompense in the spiritual *existence*, except through the misery of the worldly *one*, (151) also this, that—his production of distress in the worldly *existence arising* unquestionably *and* unreasonably, through *its* previous occurrence, (152) *and* the recompense of the spiritual *existence arising* doubtfully *and* incredibly after the production of the distress—(153) just as the previous distress is unreasonable, the after recompense *occurs* alike unreasonably *and* foolishly. 154. This also *may be said*, that no after nobility is obtained for previous distress without a cause.

155. Again, *observe* this, that the existence of one of these three doctrines is inevitable :—(156) Every single thing that is, *or* was, *or will* be in this world is all by his will, or *it* is not, (157) or there are *some* that are by his will *and* there are *some* that are not. 158. Because nothing whatever is found which is not good, or evil, or a mixture [1] of both.

159. If they say that all *things* are *by* his will, the good and evil are both his desire. 160. If good and evil are both his desire, *he* is not of perfect will; (161) *it* is not perfect even as to a single *thing*. 162. And he who is of imperfect will must be himself imperfect, (163) as is shown above [2].

164. If nothing *be by* his will, (165) on account of nothing being *by* the will there is no will. 166. He *in* whom there is no will is working constitutionally [3],

[1] Assuming that Pâz. hamekhtaa stands for Pahl. âmîkhtak.

[2] Compare Chap. VIII, 108–116.

[3] That is, 'instinctively.'

(167) and he who is working constitutionally is constituted *and* made.

168. If there be *some things* which are *by* his will, *and* there be *some* which are not *by* his will, (169) *and* nothing is found in the world which is not good and not evil, (170) *from* that *it* is known *that*, if the sacred being *be of* good will, *he* is not desirous of that evil of it, (171) and that which is evil is not by his will. 172. If his will *be* evil *he* is inevitably not desirous of that good of it, (173) *and* that which is good is not by his will. 174. If that which is good *be by* the will of the sacred being, *it* is known *that* that which is evil arose from another will. 175. If that which is evil *be by* his will, that which is good arose inevitably from another will. 176. *And* the inevitability *of* a rival *of* the will of the sacred being is manifest.

177. If *one* says the evil springs from mankind, (178) that *implies* the inevitability—since mankind is not perpetually a self-existence—*that* evil either arose before mankind, or after, (179) or it arose with mankind. 180. If they say it arose before mankind, (181) that *implies*—since, apart from the sacred being, *there* was no other creator and producer—(182) *that* either the sacred being produced that evil, or it produced its own existence itself, or it was itself eternal. 183. If they say it arose after mankind, (184) *as to* that, when human nature is likewise a production of the sacred being, (185) and the sacred being did not produce evil in the nature of mankind, (186) how has it sprung into action from them? 187. If the evil *was* set in action by them, apart from the will of the sacred being, (188) and a knowledge, as to *their* setting about it, existed *in*

the sacred being, (189) that *implies that* the sacred being is imperfect in his own will, (190) and mankind are victorious and triumphant in setting aside the will *and* command of the sacred being, and doing the evil competing *with* the will of the sacred being. 191. Also the power of the sacred being in his own will and his own servants is manifestly unprevailing. 192. If they say that he makes them proceed afterwards to the awful punishment of hell, (193) *as to* that[1], if the sacred being *be* a powerful doer, *and* not to allow the committal of crime, *but* to convey *it* away from their minds, *be* more advantageous *and* more adapted to the compassion of a sacred being than *if* he allowed the committal, (194) *yet he has* become helplessly contented with it, (195) *and*, afterwards, contentedly punishes his own creatures, (196) *then*, as to the one matter I am well considering, either incapability, or scanty knowledge, or scanty goodness is thereby manifested.

197. If they say that the sacred being produced and created evil for the reason that so mankind *may* fully understand the value of goodness, (198) *as to* that you should observe that, if evil *be* requisite and advantageous for understanding goodness, that evil exists *by* his good will. 199. *And* if evil exists *by* his good will, and is requisite *and* advantageous for him *of* whom they say that evil is not his wish, *it* is inconsistent.

200. *As to* that also which they say, that death, pain, *and* poverty *are* produced by him for the reason that so mankind *may* much better understand the value of life, health, and opulence, (201) *and* become more grateful unto the sacred being, (202) *as to* that

[1] So in MH19 and Sans., but JE omits 'that.'

you should observe that *it* is as *it were* acting unreasonably, in the mode of him who gives poison to mankind for the sake of increasing the value *and* price of an antidote, (203) so that he *may* sell the antidote dearer *and* more costly. 204. To what is this intermeddling action owing, that, for the sake of an understanding of the value of the goodness of other *things*, he allows pain, death, *and* misery in some one else?

205. Again, *as to* that which a multitude of them say, that the sacred being is a ruler over every creature and creation, (206) because his creations are all his own. 207. *And* he acts about them as is desirable for him, because it is desirable for him, *and he* is not a causer of distress. 208. Since distress is that which they inflict upon anything that is not their own, (209) then he who, all things *being* his own, acts about them as is desirable for him, is not a causer of distress[1]. 210. *As to* that you should know that, if, on account of sovereignty, he who occasions distress is not to be called a causer of distress, (211) that is *as though* even he who is a sovereign *and* tells a lie is speaking truthfully, (212) and he who, on account of sovereignty, commits crime, sin, theft, *and* plunder is not to be called a sinner. 213. Such as that which the glorified Rôshan[2], son of Âtûr-frôbag, related as a parable (ângunî-aîtak), (214) that they saw a man who was defiling an ass, (215) when they enquired of him

[1] Compare Rom. ix. 20, 21: 'Shall the thing formed say to him that formed *it*, "Why hast thou made me thus?" Hath not the potter power over the clay, of the same lump to make one vessel unto honour and another unto dishonour?'

[2] See Chap. X, 53.

thus: 'Why dost thou commit this execrable action?' 216. And he spoke thus, in excuse: 'The ass is my own.'

217. Again, you should ask this of them, (218) that is: 'Is the sacred being a friend, or an enemy, to these creatures and creations which are made by him?' 219. If *he be* a friend of the creatures, that *implies that* it is not proper for him to desire *and* to produce the evil *and* misery of the creatures; (220) *yet*, as regards the devastation and misery of his own achievements, *he has* never even become tired of them. 221. If *he be* an enemy of the creatures, that *implies that* it is not proper for him to create *and* produce, through his own competent knowledge, that thing which is his enemy *and* disablement[1], and struggles against his will.

222. This, too, you should ask, (223) that is: 'Is the sacred being always a well-understanding, good sovereign, occasioning prosperity[2], (224) or an evil-understanding, bad sovereign, occasioning distress? 225. Or is there a time when *he is* a well-understanding, good sovereign, occasioning prosperity, (226) and is there a time when *he is* an evil-understanding, bad sovereign, occasioning distress?'

227. If *he be* always a well-understanding, good sovereign, occasioning prosperity, (228) that *implies that* there are not, in his country *and* sovereignty, *any* oppression, distress, and complaint; (229) and his affection *for* the creatures and the affection of the creatures for him are pure. 230. Owing to the

[1] Assuming that Pâz. apa*d*vâh stands for Pahl. apatûgîh; the two words being nearly alike in Pahlavi letters.

[2] Reading â*v*â*d*îh-kar instead of Pâz. â*z*âdîgar, 'producing freedom, or nobility,' which two words are alike in Pahlavi writing.

same reason *he is* merciful as regards his own creatures, (231) and his creatures are recounting *his* praise, utterers of thanksgivings *and* pure friends towards him. 232. His title of divinity, moreover, is worthily his own.

233. If *he be* an evil-understanding, bad sovereign, occasioning distress, (234) that *implies that he is* himself a pure[1] enemy to the creatures, and his creatures are also *of* a like nature towards him. 235. Owing to the same reason *he is* an injurer, destroyer, *and* deluder of the creatures, (236) and his creatures are complainers of him, strugglers concerning him, *and* pure enemies. 237. His title of divinity, moreover, is the equivalent of an unworthy name; (238) and, even on account of his eternity, the creatures are hopeless of becoming free from the risk of distress and misery for an unlimited time.

239. If there be a time when *he is* a good sovereign, well-understanding, *and* occasioning prosperity, and there be a time when *he* is turned away from this; (240) that *implies that* his affection for the creatures is mingled. 241. From a mingled affection *arises* mingled action, (242) *and* from mingled action a mingled individuality is also manifested. 243. And his creatures also are mingled friends to him. 244. Of *one's* associates *there* is none who, if a friend, is not one's enemy, no praiser who is not complaining of one, no glorifier even who is not scorning one; a character of this description is manifest among all creatures.

245. Again, *observe* this, that since all things which are in the world are not outside of these two terms,

[1] The word avêzak, 'pure,' is here used idiomatically for 'mere,' precisely as 'pure' is often used in English.

good and evil, (246) that *implies*, if good and evil are both said *to arise* from the sacred being and through the will of the sacred being, (247) *that* the troublesome Aharman is unreasonably defamed; *that*, *being* innocent *and* without an original evolution, he never was, nor *will* be, evil and headstrong[1]. 248. That which is mentioned in scripture (nipîk)[2], that Aharman became headstrong, and was put out of heaven by them, is unreasonable, (249) because even that headstrongness *and* disobedience *were* likewise through the will of the sacred being.

250. If even it be said *that* the good *arises* from the sacred being and through the will of the sacred being, *and* the evil from mankind, still Aharman is without an original evolution *and* innocent, and curses *and* scorn for him are unreasonable. 251. If all this misery and evil *be* sent down, not from a different nature, but from the individuality and individual nature of the sacred being himself, (252) that *implies* *that* the sacred being is an enemy *and* adversary to his own tendencies (rûn).

253. *Observe* this, too, that to speak of the existence of criminality apart from a nature of crime is very deluding; (254) *and* as *it* is deluding to imagine a nature of crime that is good, *is it* more deluding to imagine Aharman—who is the origin *and* original evolution of every crime—*apart* from the creation and achievement of the sacred being?

255. The conclusion is this, that if *at* first there be anything which is not within the will of the sacred being, provided everything be through the will of the sacred being, no one whatever is a sinner; (256)

---

[1] Literally 'with averted head.'

[2] Probably referring to the Qur'ân XV, 26–40 (see § 59 n).

and the apostle[1] and religion *were* appointed without a purpose. 257. If it be expedient to ruin any one for sinfulness, it is more expedient to ruin him who is the original doer, maintainer, and creator of every evil and crime. 258. And if it be said *that* evil and crime *arise* from Aharman or mankind, that *implies*, as they are likewise created and produced *by* the sacred being, *that* he is the source of them; in like manner, he who is the cause of the origin of evil (259) is worse than evil.

260. This, too, you should observe, that sects (kêshân) of every kind assert this *maxim*, handed down by their own high-priests, when *it* is mentioned and prescribed by them to their own congregation (ram), that is: 'Perform good works *and* abstain from crime.' 261. On account of delusion they do not consider this, that is, from where and what origin ought the crime to arise, about which *it* is thus commanded: 'Ye shall not commit *it, and* I *will* cast *him* who commits *it* into eternal hell.' 262. So that, if *that* same *be* owing to the sacred being, it would be easier for him not to produce it, than, after *its* production, *to have* brought *it* to notice and commanded *us* to abstain from it. 263. So far, indeed, I do not understand any advantage and motive *in* the production and creation of evil.

264. Again, in their scriptures, he speaks inconsistently about good works and crime (265) thus: 'Good works and crime are both owing to me. 266. Neither demons, nor wizards, are unrestricted in causing the ruin of any one. 267. No one *has* accepted the religion *and* done good works, and no one *has* walked in infidelity *and* committed crime, except through my will.'

[1] Zaratûst.

268. In the same scripture he adduces many *things* which *one has* to connect, and inflicts curses on the creatures, (269) thus: 'Why do mankind desire *and* commit that crime which I design for them?' 270. It occurs concerning the will and work of his own hand, and *yet* he frightens them with punishment in body and soul. 271. *In* another place he speaks thus: 'I myself am the deluder of mankind, for if it should be my will they *would* then be shown the true path by me, but *it is* my will that they go to hell[1].' 272. And *in* another place he speaks thus: 'Man himself is the causer of crime.'

273. In these three modes the sacred being gives evidence of different kinds about his own creatures. 274. One is this, that *he* himself is Aharman[2]; (275) one is this, that he is himself the deluder of the creatures[3]; (276) *and*, in the other, he makes his own creatures confederates involved with Aharman in deluding[4]; so that *he implies*: 'There are *instances* when I occasion *it*, *and* there are *instances* when Aharman *does*.'

277. Through that *which* he states, that mankind themselves occasion crime, they are made by him confederates with Aharman; *he* himself *being* at a distance from the crime. 278. For if mankind commit crime owing to their own nature and their own delusion, that *implies that* the sacred being, with

[1] Texts to this effect are numerous in the Qur'ân, such as 'whom he pleases does God lead astray, and whom he pleases he places on the right way . . . God leads the wrong-doers astray; for God does what he will . . . in hell they shall broil' (Qur'ân VI, 39, XIV, 32, 34; SBE, vol. vi).

[2] As deduced from the passage quoted in § 269.

[3] As stated in the passage quoted in § 271.

[4] As implied in the passage quoted in § 272.

Aharman, is far from the criminality, (279) because *it is* as *it were* not owing to the sacred being, nor yet owing to Aharman.

280. Again, you should ask of those whom they call Mûtazalîk[1] (281) thus: 'Is *it* the will of the sacred being *for* all mankind to abstain from crime through *their own* free will[2], to escape from hell, *and* to make *them* proceed to heaven, or not?' 282. If *one* says that *it is* not, (283) that *implies that* an[3] opinion is formed by him as to the little goodness of the sacred being *and* the evil of his will; (284) *and*, for the same reason, *it* is not fitting to glorify *him* as the divine existence. 285. If *one* says that *it is* his will, (286) that *implies that* an opinion is formed by him as to the good will of the sacred being; (287) *and*, for the same reason, *it* is fitting to glorify *him* as the divine existence.

288. *Ask* this, too, that is: 'If *it be* his will, is *he* capable of performing *it*, or not?' 289. If *one* says that *he is* not, (290) that *implies that* an opinion is formed by him as to the incapability of the sacred being as regards that will of his; (291) *and*, for the same reason, *it* is not fitting to glorify *him* as the divine existence which is almighty. 292. If *one* says that *he* is capable of performing *his* will, (293) that *implies that* an opinion is formed by him as to *his*

[1] Which is doubtless the original Pahlavi form of Pâz. muthzarî. It is an adjective, meaning 'seceding, schismatic,' derived from Ar. mu'htazil, and applied specially to Muhammadan schismatics.

[2] Assuming that Pâz. âwâ*d*-kâmî stands for Pahl. âzâ*d*-kâmîh, which would be identical with the former word in Pahlavi writing.

[3] JE has 'no' in Pâz. but not in Sans., which negative is evidently a modern blunder.

capability for that will of his; (294) *and*, for the same reason, *it* is fitting to glorify *him* as the divine existence which is almighty.

295. Again, *ask* this, that is: 'When *he* is capable of performing his will, does he perform *it*, or not?' 296. If *one* says that he performs *it*, (297) that *implies that* the abstaining from sin, escaping from hell, and bringing to heaven[1] would be manifested unto all mankind; (298) *but* this is that which is not manifest by his existence, and is falsifying even his own revelation (dînô). 299. If *one* says that *he* is capable of performing his will, but does not perform *it*, (300) that *implies that* an opinion is formed by him as to the unmercifulness of the sacred being, *his* enmity to mankind, and the inconstancy of his will. 301. For if he performs *it*, *it* is no harm to him himself and is an advantage *to* mankind; his own will is also continuous thereby. 302. *But* if he does not perform *it*, *it* is no advantage to him himself and is harm *to* mankind; his own will is also discontinuous thereby.

303. Again, *ask* this, that is: 'Does he not perform *it* through will, or without will?' 304. If *one* says that he does not perform *it* through will, (305) that *implies that* an opinion is formed by him that the sacred being is good-willed, *but* has no will to do good; (306) *and* this is even to consider *him* faulty through inconsistency. 307. If *one* says that *he* is without will, *and* therefore does not perform *it*, (308) that *implies that* an opinion is formed by him as to the weakness of the sacred being in his own self, or the existence of an injurer of his will.

309. The conclusion is this, that, *with* a manager

[1] JJ has 'saving from hell *and* escaping to heaven.'

of this worldly *existence* who may be without an opponent, without competition, and perfect in sagacity, goodness, and capability, *there* should not be all these unworthy actions, trouble and misery, pain and vexation, especially of mankind and the other creatures. 310. Because, when a manager, without an opponent, is perfect in sagacity, he knows means for evil not to occur and also remedies for carrying off evil. 311. When *he* is perfect in goodness and merciful, *he has* no wish for the occurrence of evil at first, *but* a wish for *its* extinction. 312. When *he* is perfect in capability, *he* is capable of not really becoming equally the origin of evil.

313. Now, as in the worldly *existence*, whose manager is the sacred being, the existence of evil is unquestionably visible, then thus much is not separable from this, either where the manager is *provided* with an opponent, or is without an opponent:—314. If he does not know means for evil not to occur, and remedies for carrying off evil, the imperfect sagacity of the sacred being is thereby[1] manifested. 315. Or the evil exists *with* his good will, *and* the imperfect goodness of his will is manifested. 316. Or *he* is not capable of not *allowing* the occurrence of evil, and of carrying *it* off, *and* the imperfect capability of the sacred being is manifested. 317. And when *he* is imperfect even *in* one—in sagacity, or goodness, or capability—*it* is not fitting to glorify *and* worship *him* as the divine existence who is almighty, all-good, *and* all-wise.

318. This, too, you should know, that since any existing thing, which is acting, is *provided* with a will, but *its* nature *has* not become unrestricted, (319) that

[1] Reading a*g*a*s* instead of the similarly-written a*f*a*s*, 'and by it.'

shows that, if the original existence of the creator *be* divinity, and his nature *be* light *and* beauty, fragrance and purity, goodness and sagacity, then such *things* as darkness and ugliness, stench *and* pollution, vileness *and* ignorance—the demoniacal nature itself—ought to be far from him. 320. If his original existence *be* anything demoniacal, and his nature *be* darkness *or* stench, ugliness *or* pollution, vileness *or* ignorance, then the nature of divinity remains strange to him.

321. If there be *any* one by whom indecision about all this is insinuated into his own self, that *implies that*, owing to his indecision about it, there is no discrimination *in* him as to goodness, amid his own evil. 322. Now, moreover, the hope of the hopeful is absorbed, (323) for even he who goes to heaven through doing good works is, even there, in evil and misery, (324) because there is no distinct discrimination of good from evil, even there, (325) if there be the goodness which is devoid of evil, *and* there be also the evil which is devoid of goodness, represented *as* really of the same origin. 326. This is known, that the difference of good and evil is owing to difference of nature. 327. When the two origins of their difference and distinction from the other of different nature are manifest, that hope of the hopeful is just, (328) and sagacity is their passport (parvânak).

329. This, too, you should know, that every statement which is not unconfused by its own limits is unenquiring (apa*d*-khvâh)[1]. 330. Likewise this, that the limit of divinity is specially sagacity. 331. *And* also this, that[2] the limit of sagacity is only[3]

[1] Sans. has 'undesirable.'

[2] JJ and Sans. omit these four words.

[3] Literally 'one.'

advantageous action. 332. Advantageous action is not doing injury; (333) *and* the modes of doing injury are three. 334. One is that which, *being* no advantage to oneself, is the injury of another also. 335. [One is that which, *being* no advantage to another[1]], is the injury of oneself also. 336. *And* one is that which is the injury of oneself and the injury of another also. 337. And from the creation of Aharman and the demons *there* is no advantage *to* a wisely-acting sacred being himself, *and there is* injury of others also; (338) the non-advancement of even his own will, owing to his own work, is always manifested thereby.

339. This, too, *you should know*, that if the will of the sacred being *be* goodness, (340) his will is also eternal. 341. And he should be capable of a suitable will, (342) so that, from the beginning even to the end, all the goodness *and* virtue of the will of the sacred being would have proceeded in the world. 343. Now *it* is manifest that vileness and vice always proceed much more. 344. Therefore *the cause* is one of these, either they always proceed through the will of the sacred being, or without *his* will. 345. If they always proceed through some will of the sacred being, *it* is evident that his will is also for vileness as well as for goodness, (346) or *he* is inefficient and changeable in will. 347. Since a will does not change, unless owing to a cause, or unless owing to a changer, (348) that *implies* one of these two, either *it* is through some cause, or there exists some other *being with* him *as* a changer of his will. 349. If they always proceed not through the will of the sacred being, (350) *from* that *it* is evident that the

[1] The words in brackets are omitted, both in Pâz. and Sans., by JE and JJ, the only two MSS. available.

sacred being is suffering in his own will, and his will is not perfect, (351) or there exists some diminisher of it who is a possessor *of* will.

352. *As to* this, too, which they assert, that the sacred being commanded Adam thus: 'Thou shalt not eat of this one tree which is in paradise (vahist)[1],' (353) you should ask of them (354) thus: 'Was the command which the sacred being gave to Adam, thus: "You shall not eat of this tree," good or evil?' 355. If the command were good *it* is evident that the tree was evil, (356) *and* it is not befitting the sacred being to create anything that is evil. 357. If the tree were good the command was evil, *and* it is not befitting the sacred being to give an evil command. 358. If the tree were good, and the command as to not eating *were* given by him, it is not [2] adapted to the goodness and mercifulness of the sacred being to allot a benefit *away* from his own innocent servants.

359. *As to* this, too, which they assert, that the sacred being brings every one whom he wills unto faith and the true way, and, as the recompense, he makes him proceed to the happy progress which is eternal; (360) *and* him whom he does not will he leaves in irreligion and ignorance of the sacred being, and, for that reason, he casts him into hell and eternal misery [3]; (361) you should ask of them (362) thus: 'Is he good whose desire and will are for the religion and faith of the sacred being and the true way, or he whose desire and will are for going astray, irreligion, and ignorance of the sacred being?' 363. If *one* says that he is good whose desire and will

[1] See § 64.

[2] Reading Pâz. n*e* instead of Pâz. b*e*, 'quite,' as the Sanskrit has a negative participle.

[3] See § 271.

are for the religion of the sacred being and the true way, (364) now *as to* that man about whom this is the will of the sacred being, that he *shall* leave him in irreligion, going astray, and ignorance of the sacred being, *and to whom* an apostle, or *some* other person who is a friend, recites the revelation (dînô) of the sacred being and the true way, (365) *does* that *show that* the sacred being is thereby better and more beneficial to him, or are that apostle *and* that person *so?* 366. If *one* says that the will of the sacred being about him[1] is good, it is thereby asserted by him, that not understanding the sacred being, not accepting the religion, and going astray are good; *but* this is not acceptable [and not to be taught[2]], on account of error. 367. If *one* says that his coming to the true religion and understanding the sacred being are thereby better and more beneficial, (368) it is thereby obviously asserted by one that the apostle and person are thereby better to him than the sacred being. 369. Because a person *through* whom the true way and an understanding of the sacred being are wanted among mankind, and his will is *bent* upon it, is much better than he who is a sacred being (370) *by* whose will backsliding (a*v*â*z*râsîh), misunderstanding, and irreligion *exist* among them; *and* the sacred being is much worse than that person.

371. *Observe* this, too, that if the criminal thought and criminal action of man are by the will of the sacred being, that already *implies* that the sacred being produced criminal thought, and sowed crime

[1] The man mentioned in § 364.

[2] The words in brackets have no equivalent in the Pâzand text, but are indicated by âsvâdya*ñk*a in Sans.

in his mind, (372) and Aharman merely invites and instigates him to the committal of crime; that *shows that* the criminal thought *traced to* the sacred being and also his desire for it are more violent and worse than the invitation of Aharman. 373. When, too, his listening to *what proceeds* from Aharman, *as to* the committal of crime, is likewise due to the criminal thought which the sacred being produced, and *so* also *is* his desire for it, *it* is already obvious that the sacred being is much worse and more sinful than Aharman.

374. As regards these statements, which are enumerated by us, (375) one of these two *opinions* must arise, (376) either that all are true or that all are false, (377) or there are *some* which are true and there are *some* which are false. 378. If all *be* true, every statement that is not adapted to these statements is false, *or* something *of* the two, truth and falsehood. 379. If all *be* false, every statement that is not adapted to these statements is true, *or* something *of* the two together[1]. 380. If there be *some* that are true and there be *some* that are false, (381) then of those which are true—*derived* from the nature and nucleus (nâf) of truth—(382) and of those which are false—*derived* from the nature and nucleus and original evolution of falsehood—(383) the origins are two, one from which *arises* truth, *and* one *from* which *arises* falsehood.

CHAPTER XII.

1. Again, about the inconsistency of their assertions *there* are several statements from the Dînka*rd*[2]

[1] Sans. has 'something mingled twofold.'

[2] See Chap. IV, 107. As the inconsistent statements which

manuscript, (2) *as to* that which they say, that the sacred being is around everything, *but* nothing is within him; (3) and within everything, *but* nothing is around him. 4. *That he is* above everything, *but* nothing is below him; (5) and below everything, *but* nothing is above him. 6. *That* he sits upon a throne, *but* is possessing no *resting*-place; (7) and is inside heaven, *but* is possessing no whereabouts. 8. *That* he does not exist in any place, and *yet* he does exist *there*. 9. *That* he exists everywhere, and *yet* his place does not exist. 10. Also *that* everything of his becomes *fit* for his own by his own will, (11) *his* original evolution *being both* malice and good; (12) and *he is* eternally unforgiving and compassionate, (13) preparing distress and not distressing. 14. Likewise *that* he *has* commanded him who is incapable of performing *or* neglecting the divine command, (15) and he *has* created him who is innocent for hell, not the distresser. 16. *That he is* aware of the hellish existence of mankind, owing to wickedness, and his will is for it; (17) and *he is* good-willed, or it *has* become not his will. 18. *That* he *has* produced a remedy, and is not himself distressing; (19) or no remedy, but want of remedy, is produced by him, *and yet he is* not possessing an opponent. 20. *That he is* wanting experience, and *yet* omniscient; (21) neglecting commands, and *yet*

follow in the text are not to be found in the portion of the Dînka*rd* known to be extant, they were probably contained in the first two books of that work, which have not yet been discovered. Chap. 132 of the third book (130 in Dastûr Peshotan's translation, pp. 176–178) is the nearest approach to our text in style, but not in matter. It is 'about him who is in all *and* over all, over and not lower than anything *nor* through anything, that is, even owing to management *he is* over all, and all is manageable by him.'

they are themselves his will; (22) and he who neglects, *and* provides a restricted evolution [1], is *yet* a good sovereign. 23. Also *that* his commands are all continuous, (24) and *yet* the setting aside of his commands is obtainable. 25. And *that* there is *some* of his will which is not continuous, (26) and neglect of his will is not an injurer of the will. 27. Likewise *that* he *has* commanded that which is not his will, (28) and the command *which is* not inconsistent with his will *and* also the command *which is* inconsistent with his will are both proper. 29. Also *that* his good will is not a discontinuous will, (30) and *as to* his evil will, which makes evil things, that is judicious. 31. And many other inconsistencies which are in the assertions of *various* sects.

32. If it be not possible for an orderly (pa*d*mânîk) religion to exist, without rescue from these inconsistent assertions of many kinds, (33) they then [2] say this of it, that *to* the supposers of two original evolutions [3] the work of the sacred being is weak and unresisting; (34) *and* they say *it* is not as *it were* adapted to the grandeur of the sacred being.

35. Upon this subject, too, there are *some matters*, which I *shall* clearly state, *that* should be dictated *and* known. 36. That is, does he [4] make divine things weaker and more unresisting, (37) where *it is he* who says that *the sacred being's* own achievements,

[1] Reading bandak-ga*s*tîh instead of Pâz. ba*n*daya*s*tî; compare Chap. IV, 73 n.

[2] Reading adînas, 'then of it,' for Pâz. ainâ, as in Chap. IV, 81.

[3] That is, those who hold the orthodox Mazda-worshipper's opinion, that the producer of evil is independent of the producer of good, so long as the former continues to exist.

[4] The believer in a single original evolution without any independent producer of evil. Connect §§ 36, 37 with §§ 52, 53.

which *were* created by him, have all lapsed into *being* intolerant of command *and* deaf to admonition, (38) till even the most tender-bodied creatures struggle against his will? 39. And so *they have* slain *or* impaled those many prophets (vakhshvarân) *and* apostles (pêtkhambarân) of his, who are appointed by him; (40) *and* there are *some* who *have* acted scornfully, contemptibly, and irreverently. 41. This, too, is where *he has* not only not protected his own dominion from the vile *creatures* which *were* created by him himself, but *he has* himself afflicted his own dominion also; (42) and he himself destroys his own productions without a reason, (43) and himself renders his own creations useless. 44. Through his own culpability he himself destroys his own innocent servants. 45. He himself makes his own peculiar friends weak, needy, sinful, and deluded. 46. And *his* wrath, *inflicted* upon a single innocent servant, which is like Aharman's[1], makes his own innumerable creatures unobservant *and* deluded. 47. For a sin that is limited, which is owing to his own actions, he puts the innocent to unlimited punishment[2]. 48. The door of forgiveness is finally shut up, (49) and he is not satiated with the pain, distress, and misery of his own creatures, (50) *but* maintains *them* perpetually in action and excitement. 51. And *yet* he is not able to insist upon the commands which he

[1] Aharman being supposed to be the producer of the demon of wrath, who is one of his most powerful auxiliaries.

[2] Sans. has 'he puts another unlimited punishment upon the innocent;' Nêr. having read hanŏ, 'another,' instead of avŏ, 'to,' which two words are written alike in Pahlavi. As the author's interpretation of his opponent's argument assumes that everything, including sin, is produced by the sacred being, he naturally concludes that the sinners themselves are innocent.

gives *in* the beginning, middle, *or* end. 52. Or is *it* he[1] who says that that *one* is the sacred being who is perpetually a ruler, all-knowing and almighty; (53) whose dominion and knowledge and power are perpetual *and* for unlimited time? 54. Owing to him, too, is the happiness of any goodness; (55) his actions also are for a purpose, *his* commands are advantageous, (56) *he is* compassionate and forgiving as regards his own servants, (57) and is an abundant bestower of recompense, too, *on* that servant who is a carrier *off* of victory. 58. As to him who is a sinner, who, on account of his own sinfulness, becomes captive *in* the hands of the enemy[2], *he is* forgiving upon atonement *for* the sinfulness and cleansing from iniquity and pollution. 59. *In* the end *he* is no leaver of any good creature captive in the hands of enemies[3], (60) and is their protector, maintainer, and cherisher, in body and life, amid *their* contest and struggle with enemies. 61. *He is* a complete defender of his own empire from opponents of a different nature, (62) and his champions and troops become victorious in the struggle and contest. 63. *And* in the end *he is* a bringer of victory *to* his own creatures, as regards every iniquity.

64. When it is observed *as* to light, knowledge, sight, life, health, *and* other divine creations, that *they* are fully resistant and prevailing over darkness,

[1] The believer in two original evolutions, good and evil; the producer of the latter being independent of the producer of the former for a limited period of existence. This producer of evil is not clearly described here, but is mentioned in §§ 58–61, 72 as an enemy and opponent. §§ 52, 53 are to be read in connection with §§ 36–38.

[2] The spiritual enemy, Aharman.

[3] Compare Chap. IV, 100.

ignorance, blindness, death, sickness, *and* other demoniacal peculiarities—(65) because this is known, that light is the putting aside of all darkness, (66) knowledge is victorious over ignorance, (67) and life is powerful[1] and increasing over death, (68) for, owing to the powerfulness and increase of life, the incalculable progress of the creatures arises from two persons, (69) and multitudes are confident about it; (70) so also sight and health are manifestly as much victorious and powerful over blindness and sickness —(71) *such being observed*, it is also expedient to observe this, that is, what does the opposing fiend want, *and* about what do the troops of the sacred being struggle?

72. That opponent wants this *that he speaks of* thus: 'I *will* make this earth and sky and the creatures which are luminaries[2] extinct, (73) or I *will* bring *them* into *my* possession, *and will* pervert *them* from their own nature[3], (74) so that the sacred being shall not be able to occasion the resurrection and the renovation *of the universe*, and to restore his own creatures.'

75. The troops of the sacred being struggle about this, that the opponent shall not attain to *his* will through *his* desire. 76. *Observe* this, too, that the troops of Aûha*r*ma*z*d *have been* valiant in struggling and successful in will *ever* since the original creation.

77. From this *it* is manifest, when it happens *that* this earth and sky are formed, (78) that it *would be* possible for him to make all creatures and creations extinct; but *he* is incapable of making even one of the most tender-bodied creatures of the sacred being

---

[1] Assuming that Pâz. avazman*d* stands for Pahl. ao*g*-hômand.

[2] Sans. has 'of the luminaries.'

[3] Compare Bd. I, 14.

extinct. 79. Because, if even, by reason of death, the body be separated from life, *it* is not extinction and change of nature from its own self, but decay[1] of peculiarities and a necessity of *going* from place to place, from duty to duty[2]. 80. Then each one of the qualities of one's body *and* life is to subsist again, in its own nature, for other duties, as is revealed. 81. And the existence of these creatures and creation, fully continuously *and* perpetually active, is advantageously manifest during a suitable period.

82. Thus far is considered complete upon this subject.

CHAPTER XIII.

1. Again, about the inconsistency and faulty statements of the first scripture[3], (2) which they call holy (âzâd)—(3) and as to it they are, *in* every way, unanimous that the sacred being wrote *it* with his own hand, *and* gave *it* to Moses (Mûshâê)—(4) so that, as *it* is full of delusion, I *will* here publish, for your information, a story[4] out of all *its* stupidity and of much that is in it.

5. It states, in the beginning *of* the scripture, (6) that *there* first arose earth, without form and void[5],

---

[1] Assuming that Pâz. nyârasni is a misreading of Pahl. nihârisnŏ.

[2] Compare Chap. IV, 87.

[3] The Old Testament.

[4] Pâz. nihang-*e* (Pahl. nisang-ı, Av. ni+sangha) appears to mean 'a tale, tract, or essay,' and is connected with farhang, 'learning.' Sans. has 'somewhat, a little.'

[5] Assuming that Pâz. âv khûn u tãn (which Nêr. seems to have understood as âv-i khûn-vatãn, 'water containing blood') is a misreading of Pahl. afâm va tahân. Nêr. may have been thinking of Mkh. IX, 8.

darkness, and black water; (7) and the breathing[1] of the sacred being ever yearns[2] over the face of that black water[3]. 8. Afterwards the sacred being spoke thus: 'Let *there* be light,' (9) and *there* was light[4]. 10. And stooping he considered that light below him, (11) and the light *was* transmitted by him to the day, and the darkness to the night[5]. 12. In six days this world and sky *and* earth *were* also created by him, (13) for during the seventh day he was reposing (khaspân) and comfortable[6]. 14. Through that same mystery (râz) even now the Jews are enjoying repose *on* the Sabbath day[7].

15. This, too, *is stated*, that Adam and his wife Eve (Havâê) *were* created by him, (16) *and* put into a garden of paradise (vahist); (17) so that Adam

---

[1] Reading vâyâ, 'air, breath,' instead of Pâz. vakhsh, 'growth, expanse;' these two words being written alike in Pahlavi. Sans. has 'eyes.'

[2] Reading nîyâzêd instead of Pâz. nyâved. Sans. has 'looks.'

[3] 'In the beginning God created the heaven and the earth. And the earth was without form, and void; and darkness *was* upon the face of the deep. And the Spirit of God moved upon the face of the waters' (Gen. i. 1, 2).

[4] 'And God said, "Let there be light:" and there was light'. (Gen. i. 3).

[5] 'And God saw the light, that *it was* good: and God divided the light from the darkness. And God called the light Day, and the darkness he called Night' (Gen. i. 4, 5).

[6] 'And the evening and the morning were the sixth day. Thus the heavens and the earth were finished, and all the host of them. . . . And he rested on the seventh day from all his work which he had made' (Gen. i. 31; ii. 1, 2).

[7] 'But the seventh day *is* the sabbath of the Lord thy God: *in it* thou shalt not do any work. . . . For *in* six days the Lord made heaven and earth, the sea, and all that in them *is*, and rested the seventh day: wherefore the Lord blessed the sabbath day, and hallowed it' (Ex. xx. 10, 11).

should perform cultivation in that garden, and should keep watch[1]. 18. The Lord[2], who is the sacred being himself, commanded Adam (19) thus: 'Eat of every tree which is in this garden, except of that tree of knowledge; (20) because when you eat thereof you die[3].' 21. Afterwards a serpent *was* also put by him into the garden; (22) *and* that serpent deceived Eve *and* spoke thus: '*Let* us eat of the gathering from this tree, *and let* us give *it* to Adam[4].' 23. And she acted accordingly, (24) and Adam likewise ate[5]. 25. And *his* knowledge became such that good *was* distinguished by him from evil, and they did not die[6]. 26. He also saw and knew that he was naked, (27) *and* became concealed under the trees; (28) he likewise covered over his own body *with* leaves of trees, on account of the shame of nakedness[7]. 29. Afterwards the Lord went to the

---

[1] 'So God created man in his *own* image, in the image of God created he him; male and female created he them. . . . And the Lord God took the man and put him into the garden of Eden, to dress it and to keep it' (Gen. i. 27; ii. 15).

[2] Pâz. âdînô is evidently a misreading of the Pahlavi form of Heb. adonâi, 'Lord.'

[3] 'And the Lord God commanded the man, saying, "Of every tree of the garden thou mayest freely eat: but of the tree of the knowledge of good and evil, thou shalt not eat of it: for in the day that thou eatest thereof thou shalt surely die"' (Gen. ii. 16, 17).

[4] 'Now the serpent was more subtle than any beast of the field which the Lord God had made. And he said unto the woman, . . . "ye shall not surely die"' (Gen. iii. 1, 4).

[5] 'She took of the fruit thereof, and did eat; and gave also unto her husband with her, and he did eat' (Gen. iii. 6).

[6] '"For God doth know that in the day ye eat thereof, then your eyes shall be opened; and ye shall be as gods, knowing good and evil"' (Gen. iii. 5).

[7] 'And the eyes of them both were opened, and they knew that they *were* naked: and they sewed fig leaves together, and made

garden, *and* called Adam by name thus: 'Where art thou[1]?' 30. Adam replied thus: 'Here I am, under the trees, for this reason, because I am naked[2].' 31. The Lord indulged *in* wrath, (32) *and* spoke thus: 'Who could have informed *thee* that thou art naked? 33. Mayest thou not ever yet[3] *have* eaten of that tree of knowledge, *of* which I said that you shall not eat[4]?' 34. Adam spoke thus: 'I have *been* deceived *by* this woman, who *was* given to me by thee, and I ate[5].' 35. And the Lord enquired of Eve thus: 'Why *was* it so done by thee?' 36. Eve spoke thus: 'I have *been* deceived *by* this serpent[6].' 37. And Adam and Eve and the serpent are, all three, forced out of the garden of paradise by him with a curse[7]. 38. And he spoke to Adam thus: 'Thy eating shall be through the scraping off of sweat[8]

---

themselves aprons . . . and Adam and his wife hid themselves from the presence of the Lord God, amongst the trees of the garden' (Gen. iii. 7, 8).

[1] 'And they heard the voice of the Lord God walking in the garden in the cool of the day. . . . And the Lord God called unto Adam, and said unto him, "Where *art* thou?"' (Gen. iii. 8, 9).

[2] 'And he said, "I heard thy voice in the garden, and I was afraid, because I *was* naked; and I hid myself"' (Gen. iii. 10).

[3] Assuming that Pâz. agarat stands for Pahl. akvari*k*at; see § 139.

[4] 'And he said, "Who told thee that thou *wast* naked? Hast thou eaten of the tree, whereof I commanded thee that thou shouldest not eat?"' (Gen. iii. 11).

[5] 'And the man said, "The woman whom thou gavest *to be* with me, she gave me of the tree, and I did eat"' (Gen. iii. 12).

[6] 'And the Lord God said unto the woman, "What *is* this *that* thou hast done?" And the woman said, "The serpent beguiled me, and I did eat"' (Gen. iii. 13).

[7] 'Therefore the Lord God sent him forth from the garden of Eden, to till the ground from whence he was taken. So he drove out the man' (Gen. iii. 23, 24).

[8] Sans. has 'through the spreading of sleep.'

and the panting of the nostrils, (39) until the end of thy life; (40) and thy land shall grow all bodily refuse and dung[1].' 41. He also spoke to Eve thus: 'Thy pregnancy shall be in pain and uneasy, and thy bringing forth in grievous hastening[2].' 42. And he spoke to the serpent thus: 'Thou shalt be accursed from amid the quadrupeds and wild animals of the plain and mountain; (43) for thee also *there* shall be no feet, (44) and thy movement shall be on *thy* belly, and *thy* food dust. 45. And betwixt thy offspring, with *those of* the woman, *there* shall be such hatred and conversion to enmity that they *will* wound the head of that offspring[3].'

46. This, too, they say, that this worldly *existence*, with whatever is in everything, was made and produced by him for mankind; (47) and man *was* made by him predominant over all creatures and creations, wet and dry[4].

48. Now I *will* tell *you* a story (nisang-1) about

[1] 'And unto Adam he said, "... cursed *is* the ground for thy sake; in sorrow shalt thou eat *of* it all the days of thy life: thorns also and thistles shall it bring forth to thee; ... in the sweat of thy face shalt thou eat bread, till thou return unto the ground"' (Gen. iii. 17–19).

[2] 'Unto the woman he said, "I will greatly multiply thy sorrow, and thy conception: in sorrow thou shalt bring forth children"' (Gen. iii. 16).

[3] 'And the Lord God said unto the serpent, "Because thou hast done this, thou *art* cursed above all cattle, and above every beast of the field; upon thy belly shalt thou go, and dust shalt thou eat all the days of thy life: and I will put enmity between thee and the woman, and between thy seed and her seed; it shall bruise thy head, and thou shalt bruise his heel"' (Gen. iii. 14, 15).

[4] 'And God said, "Let us make man in our image, after our likeness; and let them have dominion over the fish of the sea, and over the fowl of the air, and over the cattle, and over all the earth, and over every creeping thing that creepeth upon the earth"' (Gen. i. 26).

the contents of their twaddle and the faultiness of their statements, (49) that is, where and with what limits did that earth without form and void[1], the darkness, the sacred being and his breathing[2], and the black water arise? 50. Or *of* what description was the sacred being himself? 51. *It is* manifest that he was not light, (52) because, when the light was seen by him, (53) stooping he considered *it*[3], for the reason that he had not seen it *before*. 54. If they say that he was dark, that manifestly *implies* that the origin of darkness is uttering[4] a word *and* there is light. 55. If they say that he was not dark, but light, (56) why, when the light *was* seen by him, did he admire *and* consider it, though he was light himself? 57. And if they say that he was neither light nor dark, (58) it is necessary for such to specify that third *state* which is not light and not dark.

59. Then *as to* him whose position and abode were in darkness and black water, and light was never seen by him, how was it possible for him to look *at* that light? 60. And what *was* his divinity owing to? 61. Because even now *it* is not possible for any one who remains in darkness to look *at* the light. 62. *Observe* also this, that if his origin and abode were darkness, how was it possible for him to remain opposite the light? 63. Because this is known, that *it* is not possible *for* darkness to remain opposite the light, since *the latter* puts it aside harmless.

64. Again, *I ask* this, that is, was that earth, which

[1] See § 6 n. [2] See § 7 n.

[3] See § 10. The scripture merely says that 'God saw the light, that *it was* good;' but this difference does not really affect the author's argument as to the previous non-existence of light.

[4] Assuming that Pâz. frâi is a misreading of Pahl. parâ*s*.

was without form and void, limited or unlimited? 65. If it were limited, what was there outside of it? 66. If it were unlimited, whither did that unlimitedness of it go, (67) when, as we see, this earth and worldly *existence* are not those of the first existence?

68. *As to* that which the Lord spoke, (69) that is: 'Let *there* be light,' and it was *so*, (70) it is thereupon appropriate to understand that the Lord *existed* before the *time* that the light arose; (71) *and* when he was wishing to make the light, and he gave the command for it to arise, he then considered mentally *in* what way the light is of good appearance or evil appearance. 72. And if the light, through its own nature, reached into the knowledge and consideration of the Lord, it is evident that the light was existing alike within the knowledge and mind of the Lord, (73) and alike outside of him. 74. For it is not possible to know and obtain anything, unless *it be* a manifestation of an existence. 75. If the light was existing is it[1], on that account, a creation of the Lord? 76. And if they say that the light was not, through its own nature, within *his* knowledge, that light *was* demanded by him, who did not know of what nature *it was*, very unwisely. 77. Or how is it possible to consider in the mind that which one *has* never even thought of *or* known?

78. And *observe* this, too, that that command for the arising of light *was* given *either* to something or to nothing, (79) because this is certain, that it is necessary to give a command to a performer of commands. 80. If *it were* given by him to something existing, which *was* light, that *implies that* the light

[1] Or, perhaps, 'it is.'

itself existed. 81. And if the command *were* given by him to something not existing, then how did the something not existing hear the command of the Lord? 82. Or how did it know that the will of the Lord *was* thus, that 'I *should* become light?' 83. Because the command of the Lord is not heard *by what* does not exist, in the same manner as though *it were* not given by him. 84. Since it is not possible *for* the non-existent even to think in any way, (85) *it was* that which is appointed non-existent, so that it does not exist, but *yet* exists[1], that was really before the sight of the sage[2]; by which *it was* known *in* what manner the Lord is demanding that it *shall* arise[3], *and* in the manner which *was* demanded by him it arose.

86. If they say that the light arose from the word of the Lord, which *was* spoken by him thus: 'Thou shalt arise,' and it was *so*—(87) that *being* when the Lord and his belongings (khû*d*îh) were dark, and light had really never *been* seen by him—*in* what way is it possible *for* that light to arise from *his* word? 88. Because this is known, that speaking is the progeny of thinking. 89. If they say that his word became light, that is very marvellous, because then light is the fruit of darkness, and the source of darkness is thereby the essence of light;

[1] That is something produced as a nonentity which, being produced as nothing, is considered to be something different from nothing at all, which is not produced. Something analogous to the prototypes of the creatures, which 'remained three thousand years in a spiritual *state*, so that they were unthinking and unmoving, with intangible bodies' (Bd. I, 8).

[2] Who wrote the account of the creation in the book of Genesis.

[3] Literally 'that I *shall* arise.'

or *else it is* this, that the light was concealed in the darkness.

90. As I *have* said[1], it is evident that it is of no use to give a command, except *to* a performer of commands, (91) so that it should be *that* the light existed, *and* then the command was expedient *and* given.

92. Again, *I ask* this, *as to* these creatures and creations, sky *and* earth of his, since *they were* prepared and produced by him in six days, (93) *and* the seventh he reposed (khaspî*d*) therefrom[2], (94) then, when this world *was* not produced by him from anything, but merely arose by his command, 'thou shalt arise,' and it was *so*, (95) to what *was* that delay of his of six days owing? 96. For when his trouble is merely as much as to say 'thou shalt arise,' the existence of that delay of six days is very ill-seeming. 97. It is also not suitable for trouble to arise for him therefrom. 98. If it be possible to make the non-existent exist, and *he be* capable *of it*, it is possible to produce *it* even a long time back. 99. And if *he be* incapable of producing except in the period of a day, it is not fitting to speak of his producing it from nothing.

100. And, again, *I ask* this, that is, when the number of the days should be known from the sun, whence then is the number of the day, besides the names of the days, known before the creation of the sun? 101. For they say that the sun *was* produced by him *on* the fourth day, which is itself Wednesday[3].

---

[1] In § 79.

[2] See §§ 12, 13.

[3] Pâz. *k*ihâr *s*umba*d*, Sans. *k*atu*h*sanais*k*arîya. 'And God made two great lights; the greater light to rule the day, and the

102. *I* also *ask* this, to what *was it* owing that it was necessary for him to make *himself* comfortable *and* reposing *on* the seventh day? 103. When the delay and trouble in his creation and production of the world was *merely* so much as *that* he spoke thus: 'Thou shalt arise,' (104) how are those days accounted *for* by him, so that it was necessary to make him reposing whose trouble is recounted? 105. For if 'thou shalt arise' *were* spoken by him at once, that is his trouble, and he ought to become comfortable immediately.

106. Again *I ask* this, that is, for what purpose and cause is Adam produced by him, *together* with Eve[1], (107) so that while they practise his will[2], the purpose of it is not so presented by him that they shall not turn *away* from the performance of his desire? 108. For when it is known by him, before the fact, that they *will* not be listening *to* his command, and *yet they* are finally produced by him, that *shows that* for him now to become exhausted, and to indulge in wrath about them, is unreasonable, (109) because *it* is evident that the Lord himself was not fully proceeding *with that* which is desirable for his own will, and is manifestly an opponent and adversary to his own will. 110. If they are not understood by him before the fact, and it is not even known by him that they *will* not listen *to* his command, then he is ignorant and badly informed. 111. If they say that his will itself was for non-performance, why then is the command for performance given by him? 112. Also what is the sin in not performing

lesser light to rule the night. . . . And the evening and the morning were the fourth day' (Gen. i. 16, 19).

[1] See § 15. [2] The command mentioned in §§ 19, 20.

it, and how goes (113) a horse whom they yoke with *another* in confinement (lag) and hurry on with a whip (tâzânak)[1]. 114. From this statement signs and tokens of deceivers are manifested, (115) whose will and command are inconsistent *and* unadapted, one to the other.

116. And if his will and desire were this, that they *shall* not turn *away* from his will, (117) still their power and desire for turning *away* from his will are much stronger and more resistant than those which he *gave* for not turning. 118. If the will for their turning *away* from his will, and also the knowledge of it, were his, and the command for not turning *away were* given by him, how was it still possible *for* the distressed Adam *to act* so that they *should* not turn *away?* 119. Also, the origin and maintenance of his will ought not to exist, (120) because by turning *away* from his command *one* merely falsifies (drûg*ed*) it as a command, *while* by not turning *away* it becomes a falsification of both *his* will and knowledge.

121. Again, *I ask* this, that is, on what account and for what advantage *was* that garden, prepared by him, produced[2]? 122. And *as to* the tree of knowledge itself, about which he commanded thus: 'Ye shall not eat *of it*,' and also *as to* the injunction for not eating *of it*, which *was* issued by him, why was it necessary for him to make them?

123. *It* is also evident, from his injunction and

---

[1] Illustrating the inconsistency of determining or permitting that anything (such as the abstaining from fruit, or the trotting of a horse) shall not be done, and yet urging its performance by whip or command.

[2] See §§ 16, 17.

command, that scanty knowledge and ignorance are more loved by him, (124) and *his* desire for them is more than *for* knowledge and wisdom. 125. And *that* even his advantage from ignorance was more, (126) because while the tree of knowledge was not tasted by them they were ignorant, and not disobedient and without benefit unto him, (127) *but* just as their knowledge arose they became disobedient unto him. 128. *There* was also no anxiety for him from their ignorance, *but* just as their knowledge arose (129) he became exhausted and wrathful about them, (130) and, forced out of paradise by him, with grievous discomfort and disgrace, they are cast [1] to the earth. (131) The sum total is this, that the cause of this birth of man's knowledge, in the worldly *existence*, was owing to the serpent and deceit.

132. They also say this, that things of every kind *were* created for mankind—on account of which *it* is evident that even that tree *was* created by him for mankind—(133) and man *was* made by him predominant over every creature and creation [2]. 134. If that be so, why *were they* now to incline *their* desires *away* from that tree which was their own?

135. From this *following* statement this, too, is evident, that knowledge was not really originating with him, (136) because if he came forth to the garden [3] and raised his voice, and called Adam by name thus: 'Where art thou,' *it is* just as though he were unaware of the place where he existed; (137) *and* if he had been unanswered by him, *he would have* been unaware of the place where Adam existed. 138. If it were not owing to his (a*g*a*s*)

---

[1] Or 'admitted.' [2] See §§ 46, 47. [3] See § 29.

outcry, too, before seeing *him*, *he would have* been unaware that he *had* eaten of that tree, or not; *and of* this also, that is, *by* whom and how *it was done*, who ate and who deceived. 139. If he were aware, why *had he* to make that enquiry of him, 'mayest thou not ever yet *have* eaten of that tree, *of* which I commanded that you shall not eat[1]?' 140. And at first, when he came forth, he was not exhausted, *but* afterwards, when he knew that *they had* eaten, he became exhausted about them and was wrathful.

141. His scanty knowledge is also *evident* from this, when he created the serpent, which *was* itself his adversary, and put *it* into the garden with them[2]; (142) or *else* why *was* not the garden made so fortified by him, that the serpent, and also other enemies, should thereby not go into it?

143. Even his falsity is also evident from this, when he spoke thus: 'When you eat of this tree you die[3];' and they *have* eaten and are not dead, but have become really intelligent, (144) and good is well recognised from evil by them.

145. *I* also *ask* this, that is, how is his knowledge inconsistent *and* competing with *his* will and command? 146. For if *it were* willed by him to eat of that tree, and the command for not eating *were* given by him, the knowledge about it was that *the fruit would be* eaten. 147. Now *it* is evident that the will, knowledge, and command are all three inconsistent, one towards the other.

148. This, too, *is evident*, that, though Adam committed sin, the curse which *was* inflicted by Him (the Lord)[4] reaches unlawfully over people of every kind

[1] See § 33. [2] See § 21. [3] See § 20. [4] See §§ 37–41.

at various periods, (149) *and* I consider *it*, in every way, a senseless, ignorant, and foolish statement.

150. On this subject, on account of tediousness, thus much is considered complete.

Chapter XIV.

1. My desire is also that I write a story (nisang-i) out of the accompanying inconsistency and full delusion of the same scripture, (2) that is full of every iniquity and demonism; and I *will* disclose a summary of one *part* out of a thousand of *what is* declared thereby, (3) *so as* to notice the commands therein.

4. First, this is what he says about his own nature, (5) that is, 'I am the Lord, seeking vengeance (6) and retaliating vengeance[1], (7) and I retaliate vengeance sevenfold upon the children[2], (8) and *one* does not forget my original vengeance.' (9). Another place states that, '*having* acquired[3] wrath and grievous thoughts, (10) his lips are also full of indignation[4], (11) *his* tongue is like a blazing fire, (12) and *his* breath (vâyâ) is like a river of rapid water (arvand nâk)[5]. 13. His voice, too, as though for causing

---

[1] 'To me *belongeth* vengeance, and recompence' (Deut. xxxii. 35). Or, as it is quoted in Rom. xii. 19, 'Vengeance *is* mine; I will repay, saith the Lord.'

[2] 'Therefore whosoever slayeth Cain, vengeance shall be taken on him sevenfold' (Gen. iv. 15).

[3] Perhaps ayâftak is a misreading of âshuftak, 'distracted *by*.'

[4] Literally 'venom.'

[5] 'Behold, the name of the Lord cometh from far, burning *with* his anger, and the burden *thereof is* heavy; his lips are full of

weeping, is more resembling the shouting of a demon[1], (14) and his seat is in the gloom[2], the dew, and the cloud[3]. 15. His charger, also, is the drying (khûskâk) wind[4], (16) and from the motion of his feet is the arising of a whirlwind of dust[5]. 17. When he walks the arising of fire is behind him[6].

18. And, elsewhere, he speaks about his own wrathfulness, (19) thus: 'I have been forty years in wrath about the Israelites[7],' (20) and he said that the Israelites are defiled in heart[8].

21. Elsewhere he speaks thus: 'Who is blind[9],

---

indignation, and his tongue as a devouring fire: and his breath, as an overflowing stream, shall reach to the midst of the neck' (Is. xxx. 27, 28).

[1] 'And the Lord shall cause his glorious voice to be heard, and shall show the lighting down of his arm, with the indignation of *his* anger, and *with* the flame of a devouring fire, *with* scattering, and tempest, and hailstones' (Is. xxx. 30).

[2] Assuming that Pâz. gûam (Pers. gum, 'invisible') is a misreading of Pahl. tom, 'gloom,' as the Sanskrit is dhûmalatvam, 'smokiness.'

[3] 'He made darkness his secret place: his pavilion round about him *were* dark waters *and* thick clouds of the skies' (Ps. xviii. 11). 'Clouds and darkness *are* round about him' (Ps. xcvii. 2).

[4] 'Who maketh the clouds his chariot; who walketh upon the wings of the wind' (Ps. civ. 3).

[5] 'The Lord *hath* his way in the whirlwind and in the storm, and the clouds *are* the dust of his feet' (Na. i. 3).

[6] 'For, behold, the Lord will come with fire, and with his chariots like a whirlwind, to render his anger with fury, and his rebuke with flames of fire' (Is. lxvi. 15).

[7] Pâz. Asarâsarã is evidently a misreading of Pahl. Asrâyîlân.

[8] 'Forty years long was I grieved with *this* generation, and said, "It *is* a people that do err in their heart, and they have not known my ways;" unto whom I sware in my wrath, that they should not enter into my rest' (Ps. xcv. 10, 11).

[9] Sans. has 'whoever is needy,' both here and in § 23.

unless *it be* my servant? 22. Who is deaf[1], but the messenger (firistak) I am appointing? 23. Who is blind like the king[2]?' *And it is* declared that their king is the Lord himself[3].

24. Elsewhere it also says this, that the worshippers (parastakân) of his fire are defiled[4]. 25. Also this, that his deeds bring blinding smoke, (26) *and his* fighting is the shedding of blood[5]. 27. And this, that is, 'I pour forth mankind one upon the other, (28) *and* I sit upon the sky, over their limbs.' 29. Likewise this, that, in one night, a hundred *and* sixty thousand *were* slain by him, through a wretched death, out of the champions and troops of the Mâzendarâns[6]. 30. And, *on* another occasion, he slew six hundred thousand men, besides women and young children, out of the Israelites in the wilderness; (31) only two men escaped[7].

---

[1] Sans. has 'whoever is prosperous.'

[2] 'Who *is* blind, but my servant? or deaf, as my messenger *that* I sent? who *is* blind as *he that is* perfect, and blind as the Lord's servant?' (Is. xlii. 19).

[3] 'The Lord *is* our king' (Is. xxxiii. 22).

[4] 'About five and twenty men, with their backs toward the temple of the Lord, and their faces toward the east; and they worshipped the sun toward the east. Then he said unto me, "Hast thou seen *this*, O son of man? Is it a light thing to the house of Judah that they commit the abominations which they commit here?"' (Eze. viii. 16, 17).

[5] 'And when Joshua and all Israel saw that the ambush had taken the city, and that the smoke of the city ascended, then they turned again, and slew the men of Ai' (Jos. viii. 21).

[6] 'Then the angel of the Lord went forth, and smote in the camp of the Assyrians a hundred and fourscore and five thousand: and when they arose early in the morning, behold, they *were* all dead corpses' (Is. xxxvii. 36).

[7] 'And the children of Israel journeyed from Rameses to Succoth, about six hundred thousand on foot, *that were* men, beside

32. Again, it shows that his final result is all regret, (33) just as this which it states, that he became among the despondent (zardakân), and he spoke thus: 'I am repentant as to the making of men on the earth[1].'

34. This, too, it states, that he sits upon a throne which four angels hold upon *their* wings, from each one of whom a fiery river always proceeds, owing to the load of *his* weight[2]. 35. Now, when he is a spirit, not formed with a body, why then are those four distressed by him, who *have* to sustain with toil the grievous load of that easy *thing*?

36. Again, *it states* this, that every day he prepares, with his own hand, ninety thousand worshippers, and they always worship him until the night time, and then he dismisses them, through a fiery river, to hell[3]. 37. When trouble and injustice of this description are seen, how is it

children' (Ex. xii. 37). 'Doubtless ye shall not come into the land *concerning* which I sware to make you dwell therein, save Caleb the son of Jephunneh, and Joshua the son of Nun. . . . But *as for* you, your carcases, they shall fall in this wilderness' (Num. xiv. 30, 32).

[1] 'And it repented the Lord that he had made man on the earth' (Gen. vi. 6).

[2] 'Also out of the midst thereof *came* the likeness of four living creatures. . . . Their wings *were* joined one to another. . . . As for the likeness of the living creatures, their appearance *was* like burning coals of fire, *and* like the appearance of lamps: it went up and down among the living creatures. . . . And under the firmament *were* their wings straight, the one toward the other. . . . And above the firmament that *was* over their heads *was* the likeness of a throne, as the appearance of a sapphire stone: and upon the likeness of the throne *was* the likeness as the appearance of a man above upon it' (Eze. i. 5, 9, 13, 23, 26). 'A fiery stream issued and came forth from before him' (Dan. vii. 10).

[3] This statement may possibly be quoted from the Talmud.

expedient *for* worldly beings to exist in duty, good works, and good deeds? 38. When he casts distressed worshippers who are reverent, listening to commands, *and* pure in action, together with others *who are* sinners, into eternal hell, (39) *it is* like even that which another congregation[1] asserts, that the sacred being, *at* the day of the resurrection, gives the sun and moon, together with others *who are* sinners, to hell for the reason that there are people who *have* offered homage to them.

40. Another place also states this, that when the eyes of the aged (masâtval)[2] Abraham, who *was* the friend of the Lord, were afflicted, the Lord himself came enquiring for him; (41) and he sat *on* his cushion and asked for peace[3]. 42. And Abraham called Isaac[4], who *was* his dearest son[5], in secret, *and* spoke (43) thus: 'Go to paradise (vahist), *and* bring wine that is light and pure.' 44. *And* he went and brought it. 45. And Abraham made many entreaties to the Lord (46) thus: 'Taste one time[6] wine in my abode.' 47. *And* the Lord spoke thus:

---

[1] Probably the Christians, and referring to such texts as 'The sun shall be turned into darkness, and the moon into blood, before that great and notable day of the Lord come' (Acts ii. 20).

[2] Nêr. reads this word as a title, Mehâdar, of Abraham. It is, however, the Huzvâris of dâd-mas (for dâd-î mas, 'great age'), and appears to be a hybrid form, the first syllable being Irânian and the latter portion Semitic.

[3] Upon his host; the usual Oriental salutation.

[4] Nêr. has read Âsînak, which indicates a Pahlavi form that might be read Aîsôk, and points to Syr. 'Îs'hoq as the original of this form of Isaac.

[5] Sans. has 'his whole-blood brother's son.'

[6] Assuming that Pâz. shê stands for Pahl. gâs-1, both here and in § 49. Nêr. seems to have understood it as Ar. say, 'somewhat.'

'I *will* not taste *it*, because *it* is not from paradise, and is not pure.' 48. Then Abraham gave assurance thus: 'The wine is pure from paradise, and Isaac, who is my son, brought *it*.' 49. Thereupon the Lord, *on account of* his freedom from doubt in Isaac, and the assurance *given* by Abraham, tasted the wine one time. 50. Afterwards, when he wished to go, *he was* not allowed until one of them *had* sworn *to* the other by a serious oath[1].

51. Observe this twaddle full of delusion; not even a single *detail* is adapted to a sacred being. 52. In what way *was* his coming in bodily form to the abode of Abraham and eating bread, of which not even a single *detail* is adapted to him? 53. This, too, is evident from it, that the suffering of Abraham was not[2] from the Lord, but from another producer. 54. And even the faultiness[3] which *was* owing to his want of understanding of knowledge was such, that the purity of the wine and whence *it came* were not known by him. 55. His falsity *is* also *seen in* this, when he spoke of not drinking the wine, and *at* last drank *it*. 56. Afterwards he is confessing that it is genuine *and* pure. 57. Now, how is he worthy of worship, as a divinity that is all-knowing *and* almighty, whose nature is this?

58. And another place states that *there* was one of the sick who, with his own wife and child, *was*

[1] This tale is perhaps to be sought in the Talmud.

[2] Reading lâ instead of râî. By reading the latter Nêr. has 'the suffering, which *was* for Abraham, was from the Lord,' which is inconsistent with the context.

[3] Assuming that Pâz. bavãnî (Sans. vaikalyam) stands for Pahl. zîfânîh, which seems more probable than supposing it to be a miswriting of Pâz. dewãnagî, 'folly.'

particularly *one* that was suffering, poor, *and* without a stipend. 59. *At* all times he was very diligent and active in prayer and fasting and the worship of the sacred being. 60. And one day, in prayer, he secretly begged a favour thus: 'Give me any enjoyment that is in daily food (rôzîh), (61) that it may be easier for me to live.'

62. And an angel came down unto him *and* spoke thus: 'The sacred being has not allotted thee, through the constellations[1], more daily food than this, (63) *and* it is not possible to allot anew; (64) but, as a recompense for worship *and* prayer, a throne whose four feet are of jewels is appointed for thee in heaven (vahis*t*) by me, (65) *and*, if it be necessary, I *will* give unto thee one foot of that throne.'

66. That exalter of the apostles enquired of his own wife, (67) *and* the unfortunate *one* spoke thus: '*It is* better for us to be content with the scanty daily food and bad living in the worldly *existence*, (68) than if our throne, among *our* companions in heaven, *had* three feet; (69) but if it may occur to thee then appoint us a day's food by another mode.'

70. *At* the second coming of that angel he spoke thus: 'But if I dissipate the *celestial* sphere, and produce the sky *and* earth anew, and construct and produce the motion of the stars anew, *still* thenceforth *it* is not clear whether thy destiny *will* fall *out* good or bad[2].'

71. From this statement *it* is, therefore, manifest that he is not himself the appointer of daily food and supreme, (72) distribution is not by his will,

[1] Of the zodiac (see Mkh. XII, 5, 6, 8).

[2] This tale is probably from the same source as the last.

he is not able to alter destiny, (73) and the revolution of the *celestial* sphere, the sun and moon *and* stars, is not within the compass of his knowledge, will, and command. 74. *And* also this, that the throne, as to which *it was* announced (nivîkînî*d*) thus: 'I *will* give *it* in heaven,' is not of his formation and creation.

75. And *in* another place he speaks about his own twaddle (76) thus: 'I *have* slain, *in* one day[1], an assemblage (ram) of sinners, as well as innumerable innocents.' 77. *And* when the angels talked much of the unreasonable performance, he then spoke of it thus: 'I am the Lord, the ruler of wills, (78) superintending, unrivalled, and doing *my own* will, and no one assists *or* is to utter a murmur (dren*g*i*s*nŏ) about me[2].'

79. Especially abundant is the twaddle that is completely delusive, which *has* seemed to me tedious to write. 80. Whoever would investigate the backward opinions of these statements, should be, for that purpose of his, a high-priest speaking candidly (â*z*â*d*), (81) until he becomes aware of the nature of the same scripture, and *of* the truth of that which is stated by me.

82. Now if he *be* a sacred being, of whom these are signs and tokens, that *implies that* truth is far from him, (83) forgiveness strange to him, (84) and knowledge is not bestowed upon him. 85. Because this itself is the fiend who is leader of the hell which

---

[1] Assuming that Pâz. zumaê is a corruption of *g*umê (see Chap. IV, 101 n) and stands for Huz. yôm-i. But it may mean 'the whole of.'

[2] This seems to be quoted from the same source as the two preceding tales.

is the den (grêstak) of the gloomy race, (86) whom the devilish defiled *ones and* evil *people* glorify by the name of the Lord, and offer *him* homage.

87. About this subject is here complete.

Chapter XV.

1. Another *thing* I publish is a feeble story (nisang) about the inconsistency, unbounded statements, and incoherent disputations of Christian (Tarsâk) believers.

2. Since, inasmuch as all three[1] are from the one origin of Judaism—(3) that *implying that*, when *anything* is said within the one, it is for them mutually helping their own delusion of every kind—(4) you should know whence the original sect of Christianity came forth. 5. That in the town of Jerusalem[2] *there* was a woman of the same Jews who was known for incapacity[3], (6) *and* pregnancy became manifest in her[4]. 7. When asked by them thus: 'Whence is this pregnancy of thine?' (8) she said in reply thus: 'The angel Gabriel[5] came unto me, and he spoke thus: "Thou art pregnant by the pure wind (holy spirit)[6]."'

---

[1] The three defects mentioned in § 1.

[2] Nêr. reads Hurûsarm for Pahl. Aûrûsalem.

[3] Sans. has 'misconduct,' but this is more than Pahl. dûsâzakîh seems to imply.

[4] 'Now the birth of Jesus Christ was on this wise: When as his mother Mary was espoused to Joseph, before they came together, she was found with child of the Holy Ghost' (Mat. i. 18).

[5] Pahl. Gêprîl is misread Sparagar by Nêr. These two names would be written alike in Pahlavi.

[6] 'The angel Gabriel was sent from God . . . to a virgin espoused to a man whose name was Joseph . . . and the angel

9. *As to* that, you should observe thus: 'Who, apart from that woman, saw the angel Gabriel? *And* on what account is it expedient to consider that woman truthful?' 10. If they say that, on account of the spiritual state of that angel, no one is able to see *him*, (11) that *implies*—if the cause of not seeing that angel be *his* spiritual nature—*that* the sight of that woman also, for the same reason, is not unrestricted. 12. If they say that the sacred being made *him* visible to that woman, and on account of the worthiness of that woman, (13) no other person *being* made worthy, (14) *observe* this, where is the evidence that the woman spoke truthfully? 15. Or, if that woman were conspicuous to *any* one for truth, it is fitting for him to demonstrate that also to other persons, so that, through that evidence, she might be more fully considered as very truthful by them. 16. *But* now the showing of him (the angel), to that woman only, is not considered *by* any one as true. 17. Now you should also observe *that* the origin of their religion *has* all come forth from this testimony of a woman, which *was* given by her about her own *condition*.

18. *Observe*, again, that if they say the Messiah arose from the pure wind of the sacred being, that *implies*—if the only wind that is pure *and* from the sacred being be that one—that the other wind, which is distinct from that, is not *from* the sacred being and not pure, (19) *and* another producer is manifested inevitably. 20. If the wind be all from

answered and said unto her, "The Holy Ghost shall come upon thee, and the power of the Highest shall overshadow thee; therefore also that holy thing which shall be born of thee shall be called the Son of God"' (Luke i. 26, 27, 35).

the sacred being and sacred, it ought to be all pure. 21. If only that one wind be pure, the other wind is polluted and not sacred. 22. As there is no producer whatever except the sacred being, that pollution and impurity of the other wind are likewise from the sacred being. 23. And if the other wind be that of the sacred being and sacred, it ought to be all pure. 24. Now, that one *being* considered as purity, why was the other polluted?

25. Again, *observe* this, that, if the Messiah were the son of the sacred being for the reason that the sacred being is the father of all, through productiveness, creativeness, and cherishing, (26) that Messiah, through sonship to the sacred being, is not otherwise than the meaner creatures which the sacred being produced and created. 27. If he were born through the means of male and female, (28) that *implies*—if birth through male and female be suitable unto the sacred being—*that* it is also *so* unto the archangels *and* spirits; *in* like manner, on account of the existence of birth[1], the occurrence of death also is suitable. 29. Thus, about the arising of *that* same sacred being *there* is no doubt, (30) because there where birth of that kind *exists*, eating, drinking, *and* even death are certain.

31. And there are *some* even who say that the Messiah is the sacred being himself. 32. Now this is very strange, when the mighty sacred being, the maintainer *and* cherisher of the two existences, became of human nature, *and* went into the womb of a woman who *was* a Jew. 33. To leave the lordly throne, the sky *and* earth, the *celestial* sphere

[1] The Pâz. of JE interpolates the words 'from a mother.'

and other similar *objects* of *his* management and protection, he fell (aûpast), for concealment, into a polluted and straitened[1] place, (34) and, finally, delivered his own body to scourging, execution on the tree (dâr-kar*d*îh), and the hands of enemies, (35) while, apart from death, much brutality *and* lawlessness *were* arranged by them.

36. If they speak of his *having* been inside the womb of a woman for the reason that the sacred being exists *in* every place, (37) that *implies that being* inside the womb of a woman, through existence *in* every place, is not more antagonistic than *being in any* very polluted and very fetid place; (38) *and*, *along* with that, that the faultiness of speaking of all places *as having* been the property of the sacred being is manifold, (39) because, if *they were so*, *in* like manner the speaking of anything whatever that is devoid of the existence of the sacred being is strange[2].

40. Again, *as to* that which they say, that death and execution on the tree *were* accepted by him, as a yoke[3], for the sake of demonstrating the resurrection to mankind, (41) that *implies*—if it were not possible for him to demonstate the resurrection to mankind, except through that disgrace[4] and death and brutal treatment of himself—*that* that omnipotence of his is not effectual. 42. Or, when no opponent and adversary whatever of his arose, why

---

[1] Assuming that Pâz. u vada*n*g stands for Pahl. va tang.

[2] Assuming that Pâz. vâhar (Sans. an*ri*ta) stands for Pahl. nâhâr.

[3] See Chap. X, 67 n.

[4] Assuming that Pâz. rasûnâî stands for Pahl. rûsvâîh. Sans. has 'binding with cords.'

are they not made without doubt of that sort of clear knowledge which is *imparted* by seeing the resurrection, so that *there* would not have been a necessity for this mode of demonstrating it brutally, disgracefully[1], distressingly, *and* through the will of *his* enemies. 43. If that death *were* accepted by him, as a yoke of a new description, through his own will, (44) that *implies that* now his outcry of woe and curses for the executioners[2], *and his* considering those Jews as *it were* wrathfully are unreasonable. 45. *He ought*, indeed, not to cause curses and *imprecations of* woe upon them, but it is fitting for them to be worthy of recompense through that deed.

46. Again, *as to* this which they state, that the father and son and pure wind are three names which are not separate one from the other[3], (47) nor is one foremost, (48) *and* this, too, that, though a son, *he* is not less than the father, *but in* every knowledge equal *to* the father[4], why now is *one* to call him by a different name? 49. If it be proper *for* three to be one, that *implies that* it is certainly possible *for* three to be nine and *for* nine to be

[1] Sans. 'by binding with cords.'

[2] 'Woe unto you, scribes and Pharisees, hypocrites! . . . behold, I send unto you prophets, and wise men, and scribes: and *some* of them ye shall kill and crucify; and *some* of them shall ye scourge in your synagogues, and persecute *them* from city to city: that upon you may come all the righteous blood shed upon the earth. . . . All these things shall come upon this generation' (Mat. xxiii. 29, 34-36).

[3] 'For there are three that bear record in heaven, the Father, the Word, and the Holy Ghost: and these three are one' (1 John v. 7).

[4] 'And in this Trinity none is afore, or after other: none is greater, or less than another' (Athanasian Creed).

three; (50) *and* it is possible to speak *of* other numbers, in this sequence, unlimitedly.

51. *Observe* this, too, that if a son *be* not less than a father, that father also is not greater than the son. 52. That is possible if the father is said *to be* from the son, or the son not from the father. 53. And this is certain, that it is possible *for* every one *originating* from *any* one to be less than him from[1] whom he is, who is the essential origin[2] of himself; (54) if *he be so* in *point of* time, *and* likewise if *so* in *point of* relationship. 55. If the son *be* not less than the father, that *implies that* the maker is not before the *thing* made, nor yet is greater; (56) both must be original evolutions, (57) and the creation is not less than the creator, nor the creator greater than the creation, (58) however he *may* be said *to be* unlimited.

59. *Observe* this, too, that if the son *be* equal to the father in all knowledge, that father also is as ignorant as the son who was unaware of his own death and execution on the tree[3], (60) until *he was* slain by their capturing *him* and causing *his* wretched death, brutal treatment, *and* disgrace[4]. 61. He did not know about it because they enquired of him thus: 'When is the day of resurrection?' And he answered thus: 'Of this no one is aware but the father[5].' 62. Just as when the son is formed (tâstîk)

[1] Assuming that Pâz. vas is a misreading of Pahl. agas.

[2] Literally 'the maternal source.'

[3] This is at variance with Mat. xxvi. 2:—'Ye know that after two days is *the feast of* the passover, and the Son of man is betrayed to be crucified.' But the author explains in § 61 that he is thinking of another instance of want of knowledge.

[4] Sans. has 'binding.'

[5] 'Tell us, when shall these things be? . . . Of that day and

as *it were* ignorant, the father *must be* as *it were* just the same.

63. *Observe* this, too, that all the creatures and creation, *and* even his own adversary, being created and produced by him out of nothing, the executioners of his son are themselves deluded *by him.* 64. *And* if the sacred being himself created the executioners of his son, *and* even his own adversary, without a purpose *and* without a cause, (65) and the son *was* slain by them altogether with his knowledge, (66) that *implies that* it is now possible to be without doubt that the slayer of his son was he himself, (67) if he knew that when he produces[1] a son they *will* then slay him, and *in* the end he produced *him* foolishly and unwisely. 68. If he did not know *it*, *he* is deficient in knowledge.

69. Again, *observe* this, that, if the sacred being created these creatures and creation out of nothing, and created and produced even his adversary similarly out of nothing, that *implies that* their nature ought to be one. 70. Now, why is not the adversary preserved *in* the *same* manner as the other creatures?

71. Another *point* is about the inconsistency of the statements *derived* from the scriptures of their high-priest[2], (72) and that which he says that no *one* falls, nor anything from a tree, and no outcry arises in a district[3], nor two birds fight together

that hour knoweth no man, no, not the angels which are in heaven, neither the Son, but the Father' (Mark xiii. 4, 32).

[1] Literally 'I produce.'

[2] In § 91 Paul is called 'their high-priest,' but the term may be here applied to any other writer of the Christian scriptures.

[3] So in Sans., but the Pâz. of JE has merely 'no district arises.'

without the command of the father[1], (73) which is a demonstration[2] of these statements, that the original evolution is single and all *things* are by his will.

74. Now for what purpose *was* the Messiah appointed, who is his son; and which way is the demonstration, through that, of his (the father's) *being* unwilling; (75) when all is *by* his will, and nothing whatever is said *about* his *being* unwilling? 76. Even this is *evident* from the same explanation, that the Jews slew the Messiah, who is his son, through the will of the father.

77. Again, he speaks inconsistently about the free will (âzâd-kâmîh) of the faithful, (78) that mankind are produced by him *with* free will. 79. Thus the iniquity of the sin which mankind commit is freely willed, (80) and the freedom of will *was* produced by him himself for mankind. 81. That *implies that* it is fitting to consider him likewise a sinner who is the original cause of sin. 82. If mankind commit sin and crime by their own free will through the will of the sacred being, (83) through what free will and sin are the sin and crime of the lion, serpent, wolf, *and* scorpion—the stinging *and* slaying noxious creatures—which are the natural actions that ever proceed from them?

84. So also, who *has* maintained the origin of the deadly poison which is in the Bêsh *herb*[3] and other species of plants, the cause of which is not owing to free will? 85. If they say that those poisons

[1] Compare Mat. x. 29, 30:—'Are not two sparrows sold for a farthing? and one of them shall not fall on the ground without your Father. But the very hairs of your head are all numbered.'

[2] Literally 'demonstrator.'

[3] A poisonous plant, Napellus Moysis (see Bd. XIV, 22, XXVII, 1).

are advantageous *and* suitable in many medicines which are removers of the disease of the sick, (86) it should be asked of them thus: 'Who produced the disease itself and the harm that *arises* from it, and what is the necessity of it, (87) that, afterwards, medicine and deadly poison *were* created by him for it, and were necessary?' 88. Or, *as to* that disease, 'it would be more expedient if he had produced an antidotal (anôsh) medicine for carrying *it* away than a medicine of poison.' 89. Also this, that is, 'from what origin is the term itself "doing harm," and against whom is the advantageousness necessary?' 90. On this subject it is possible to speak abundantly for a summary compiled.

91. Another *instance* is from the words of Paul (Pâvarô*s*), who *was* their high-priest—(92) that *one* who was afflictive with[1] them at their own beginning[2]—even this, they say, (93) is thus: 'Not the good works which I desire, but the iniquity (94) which I do not desire, I do[3]. 95. And *it* is not I *that* do *so*, but that which is collected within me does *it*, (96) because I always see that *it* is striving with me day and night[4].'

97. Again, they say, from the words of the

---

[1] Reading hanbêshin, but it may be 'well-afflicting to' if we read hû-bêshin.

[2] 'As for Saul, he made havoc of the church, entering into every house, and haling men and women, committed *them* to prison. . . . Saul who also *is called* Paul' (Acts viii. 3; xiii. 9).

[3] 'For the good that I would, I do not: but the evil which I would not, that I do' (Rom. vii. 19).

[4] 'It is no more I that do it, but sin that dwelleth in me. . . . I see another law in my members, warring against the law of my mind, and bringing me into captivity to the law of sin which is in my members' (Rom. vii. 20, 23).

Messiah, that the original evolution *from* the sacred being is light and goodness; (98) evil and darkness are separate from him[1]. 99. Also this, that is, 'just as a shepherd who provides protection for his hundred sheep, (100) *and* the wolves carry *off* one from him, (101) goes after that one which the wolves carried *off* until he leads it back to the flock, (102) and leaves the ninety-nine of them in the wilderness (da*s*t)[2], (103) even so I am come to take care of the defiled, not for the just, (104) because *it* is needless to bring him who is just into the *right* way[3].' 105. That *implies*, if the original evolution *be* one, and his will *be* wholly *that* no one whatever of it *shall be* astray and defiled, (106) *that* even the wolf's slaying the sheep is likewise his will, (107) and the wolf itself *was* also created by him.

108. The word of the Messiah is specially inconsistently a demonstrator as regards the two original evolutions. 109. As they say this is one of *those* same statements of the Messiah, that there is another original evolution, 'an enemy of my father, *and* I am of that sacred being doing good works[4].' 110. From this statement *it* is evident that his own father separates from that enemy, *and* acts differently.

---

[1] 'God is light, and in him is no darkness at all' (1 John i. 5).

[2] 'What man of you, having an hundred sheep, if he lose one of them, doth not leave the ninety and nine in the wilderness, and go after that which is lost, until he find it?' (Luke xv. 4).

[3] 'For the Son of man is come to save that which was lost' (Mat. xviii. 11). 'They that are whole need not a physician; but they that are sick. I came not to call the righteous, but sinners to repentance' (Luke v. 31, 32).

[4] 'He that soweth the good seed is the Son of man: the field is the world: the good seed are the children of the kingdom; but the tares are the children of the wicked *one*: the enemy that sowed them is the devil' (Mat. xiii. 37-39).

111. This, too, *he says*, that is, 'I am produced *by* the sacred being for truth and through truth[1]; (112) and Aharman, the iniquitous, came for my death (va*d*ar*d*anŏ), (113) and I am desired by him to deceive in many ways[2].' 114. Now, if the original evolution *be* one, and there be nothing competing with it, why *was* Aharman so powerful that he desired to delude the son of the sacred being? 115. If the sacred being himself created that iniquitous *one*, then the producing of that delusion by the *latter was* with the knowledge and will of *the former* himself, (116) and the deluder of the son *was* in like manner himself.

117. This, too, it says, that, when the Jews stood disputing against *him*, he spoke to the Jews thus: 'You are from that which is a lower *region*, and I am from an upper *region;* (118) you are of this country, I am not of it[3].' 119. And he also said this, that is, 'I know that you are of the seed of Abraham, *and* he[4] who had slain mankind from aforetime (120) *has* wished to slay even me. 121. I do that which is seen of my father, *and* you do that which is seen by you as to your own father[5].' 122. This,

[1] 'And the Word was made flesh, and dwelt among us . . : full of grace and truth' (John i. 14).

[2] See the account of the temptation of Jesus in Mat. iv. 3–10.

[3] 'And he said unto them, Ye are from beneath; I am from above: ye are of this world; I am not of this world' (John viii. 23).

[4] The iniquitous one of § 125, whom he calls their father, the devil.

[5] 'I know that ye are Abraham's seed: but ye seek to kill me, because my word hath no place in you. I speak that which I have seen with my Father: and ye do that which ye have seen with your father' (John viii. 37, 38).

too, *he said*, 'If the sacred being be that father of yours, he would be a friend of me *for* your *sake*, (123) because I have sprung from the sacred being; I have not come of my own will; (124) I am appointed *by* that sacred being doing good works[1]. Why do you not hear those words of mine? 125. Only because you are from the iniquitous *one it* is not possible for you to hear them, (126) and you wish to do the will of your own father. 127. By him truth is not spoken; whatever he speaks he tells a lie of it, therefore you are false yourselves *together* with your father. 128. *As for* me, who speak the truth, you do not believe it of me[2]. 129. And he who is from the sacred being hears the words of the sacred being, but you, because you are not from the sacred being, do not hear my words[3].' 130. By all these sayings it is demonstrated by him that there are two original evolutions, 'one by which I am produced, *and* one by which the Jews *are*,' (131) and that *latter* is not his doer of good works, but is called by him the iniquitous *one*.

132. And this, too, *was* said by him, that 'not

[1] 'If God were your Father, ye would love me: for I proceeded forth and came from God; neither came I of myself, but he sent me' (John viii. 42).

[2] 'Why do ye not understand my speech? *even* because ye cannot hear my word. Ye are of *your* father the devil, and the lusts of your father ye will do. He was a murderer from the beginning, and abode not in the truth, because there is no truth in him. When he speaketh a lie, he speaketh of his own: for he is a liar, and the father of it. And because I tell *you* the truth, ye believe me not' (John viii. 43–45).

[3] 'He that is of God heareth God's words: ye therefore hear *them* not, because ye are not of God' (John viii. 47).

unrestricted (atang) is the tree of merit (kirfak) to produce the fruit of offensiveness (bazak), nor yet that of offensiveness *as to* the fruit of merit[1].' 133. This, too, *he said*, that 'he either makes the whole tree with fruit of merit, or the whole tree with fruit of offensiveness[2], (134) for every tree becomes manifest by *its* fruit, if *it be of* merit and if *it be of* offensiveness[3].' 135. And the whole tree *was* mentioned by him, not half the tree. 136. Now, how is it suitable *for* half a tree *to be* light and half dark, (137) half merit and half offensiveness, (138) half truth and half falsehood? 139. When these remain both competing together, (140) they cannot become one tree.

141. And, again, a Jewish *sect was* called by him 'the hill-serpent of the Jews[4],' (142) and he spoke thus: 'How is *it* possible for you to do good works when you are Jewish evil-doers[5]?' 143. And *it was* not his own father he called an evil-doer[6].

---

[1] 'A good tree cannot bring forth evil fruit, neither *can* a corrupt tree bring forth good fruit' (Mat. vii. 18).

[2] 'Even so every good tree bringeth forth good fruit; but a corrupt tree bringeth forth evil fruit' (Mat. vii. 17).

[3] 'For every tree is known by his own fruit: for of thorns men do not gather figs, nor of a bramble bush gather they grapes' (Luke vi. 44).

[4] 'But when he saw many of the Pharisees and Sadducees come to his baptism, he said unto them, O generation of vipers, who hath warned you to flee from the wrath to come? . . . *Ye* serpents, *ye* generation of vipers! how can ye escape the damnation of hell?' (Mat. iii. 7; xxiii. 33).

[5] 'O generation of vipers! how can ye, being evil, speak good things?' (Mat. xii. 34).

[6] As he would have implied if he considered him the father of those Jews. The author is still arguing that the New Testament really confirms the existence of two creators.

144. This, too, he says, that 'every tree which the father *has* not sown should be dug *up*, and should be cast into the fire[1].' 145. Wherefore it is fitting to understand from these words that there is a tree, which the father *has* not sown, *that* it is necessary to dig *up and* cast *away*.

146. Again, *he says* this, that 'I am come to my own, and I am not received *by* my own[2].' 147. Wherefore it is fitting to understand that *what is* his own and *what is* not his own are two *things*.

148. This, too, he says, that is, 'Our father, that *art* in the sky, let thy empire arise! And may it be thy will *that* shall take place on earth as in the sky! 149. Also give us daily bread! And do not bring us to a cause of doubt[3]!' 150. From these words *it* is evident that his will is not so unalloyed (a*v*ê*z*ak) on earth as in the sky. 151. Also this, that the cause of the doubt of mankind is not owing to the sacred being.

152. And this, too, *was* said by him at first, that 'I am not come for the *purpose* that I *may* destroy the law of Moses (Mûshâê), (153) but I am come for the *purpose* that I *may* make *it* altogether more complete[4].' 154. And *yet* all his sayings and

---

[1] 'Every tree which bringeth not forth good fruit, is hewn down, and cast into the fire. . . . Every plant which my heavenly Father hath not planted, shall be rooted up' (Mat. iii. 10; xv. 13).

[2] 'He came unto his own, and his own received him not' (John i. 11).

[3] 'Our Father which art in heaven. . . . Thy kingdom come. Thy will be done in earth, as *it is* in heaven. Give us this day our daily bread. . . . And lead us not into temptation' (Mat. vi. 9–11, 13).

[4] 'Think not that I am come to destroy the law, or the prophets: I am not come to destroy, but to fulfil' (Mat. v. 17).

commands were those that are dissipaters and afflictive for the rules and laws of Moses.

155. Upon this subject, however, as far as here is complete.

CHAPTER XVI.

1. Again, about the delusion of Mânî, one out of the thousands *and* myriads is written; (2) for I am not unrestrained (anatang) as to writing more fully of the delusion, twaddle, and deceit of Mânî and the Mânîchaeans, (3) and much trouble and long-continued daily work is necessary for me therein.

4. Now you Maz*d*a-worshippers of Zaratû*s*t should know that the original statement of Mânî *was* about the unlimitedness of the original evolutions, (5) the intermediate *one* about *their* mingling, (6) and the final *one* about the distinction of light from dark, (7) that which is much more like unto want of distinction[1].

8. Again, *he states* this, that the worldly existence is a bodily formation of rudiments of Aharman; (9) the bodily formation *being* a production of Aharman. 10. And a repetition of that *statement* is this, that the sky is from the skin, (11) the earth from the flesh, (12) the mountains from the

---

[1] Except the belief in the two original existences (whose main characteristics are, respectively, light and darkness) the account of Mânî's doctrines, given in the Fihrist of Muhammad bin Is'hâq (see Flügel's Mânî seine Lehre und seine Schriften), appears to contain none of the details mentioned in this chapter.

bones, (13) and the trees from the hair of the demon Kunî[1]. 14. The rain is the seed of the Mâzendarâns[2] who are bound on the *celestial* sphere. 15. Mankind are two-legged demons, and animals four-legged. 16. And Kunî is the commander of the army of Aharman, (17) who, to be liberated by[3] his nails from the divinity Aûharmazd *in* the first conflict, swallowed the light; (18) and, in the second conflict, the demon Kunî *was* captured by them, *together* with many demons. 19. And it is *in* binding the demon Kunî on the *celestial* sphere *he* is killed, (20) *and* these magnificent creatures are preserved from him and formed.

21. And the sun *and* moon are arranged in supremacy *in* the outer sky; (22) so that, as regards that light which the demons swallowed, they filter and excite[4] *it*, little *by* little, through the exciting and filtering of the sun and moon. 23. Then Aharman knew, through foresight, that they *would* rapidly filter and release this light through the exciting of the sun and moon. 24. *And*, for the purpose of not rapidly releasing the light from the darkness, he prepared this lesser world which, like mankind, cattle, *and* the other living creatures, is a wholly-copied similitude of the greater world

[1] So read by Nêr. in Pâz. and Kûnî in Sans. But there is little doubt that he is the demon Ku*n*da or Ku*n*di of Vend. XI, 28, 36, XIX, 138, whose Pahlavi name is Kûnd in Pahl. Vend. XIX, 138, and Kûndak in Bd. XXVIII, 42, in which latter he is said to be 'the steed of wizards.' Kûndak is written like Kûnîk in Pahl., and this latter becomes Kunî in Pâz.

[2] Who are called demons (see Mkh. XXVII, 20, 40).

[3] Sans. has 'having scratched *it* with.'

[4] Assuming that Pâz. âharâmine*n*d stands for Pahl. a-ârâmînend, 'they do not leave at rest.'

with the other bodily creations[1]. 25. He confined life and light in the body, and made *them* prisoners; (26) so that, while that light which is excited by the sun and moon is again exhausted through the cohabitation and birth of living creatures, (27) *their* release would become more tardy.

28. And the rain was the seed of the Mâzendarâns (29) for the reason *that* when the Mâzendarâns are bound on the *celestial* sphere[2], (30) whose light is swallowed by them, (31) and, in order to pass *it* from them through a new regulation, discrimination, and retention of the light of Time[3], the twelve glorious *ones*[4] show the daughters of Time *to* the household-attending male Mâzendarâns, (32) so that while the lust of those Mâzendarâns, from seeing them, is well suited to them, (33) and seed is discharged from them, (34) the light which is within the seed is poured *on* to the earth. 35. Trees, shrubs, *and* grain have grown therefrom, (36) and the light which is within the Mâzendarâns is discharged in the seed. 37. That which is within the earth is discharged from the earth as the cause of the trees.

38. Again, about the difference of nature of life and body, this *is stated*, that the life is confined and imprisoned within the body. 39. *And* as the producer and maintainer of the bodily formations of all material existences is Aharman, (40) for the same reason it is not expedient to occasion birth *and* to propagate lineage—(41) because it is co-operating

[1] The spiritual world and its inhabitants.

[2] As stated in § 14.

[3] Personified as Zurvân.

[4] The signs of the zodiac, the celestial leaders appointed by Aûharmazd (see Mkh. VIII, 18).

with Aharman in the maintenance of mankind and cattle, and *in* causing the exhaustion of the life and light within *their* bodies—nor yet to cultivate trees and grain.

42. Again, inconsistently, they also say this, (43) that the destroyer of the creatures is always Aharman; (44) *and*, for the same reason, it is not expedient to kill any creature whatever, (45) because it (killing) is the work of Aharman.

46. Again, *they say* this, that, as the world is maintained by Aharman, *and in* the end the sacred being is triumphant (47) through the departure of lives from bodies, (48) this worldly existence is dissipated in the end, (49) *and* is not arranged anew; (50) nor does *there* occur a restoration of the dead *and* a future existence.

51. Again, *they say* this, that those two original evolutions are perpetually remaining, *and* existed as contiguously as sun and shadow, (52) and no demarcation[1] and open space existed between them.

53. Now I speak first about the impossibility of the occurrence of any existing thing *that is* unlimited, (54) except only those which I call unlimited, *that is*, empty space and time. 55. Those, indeed, which are for existence within *them*—*that is* beings *and* things in locality and time—are seen *to be* limited.

56. This, too, *I say*, that, if unity and duality be spoken *of* about them, *it is* owing to this, because unity, except through the perpetual encompassing of something, does not then exist therein. 57. For the one is this, namely, not two; (58) *and* the two

[1] Reading nisânîh; Nêr. has Pâz. nisâmî (for nisîmî), Sans. âsanatvam, 'resting-place.'

are these, namely, the original *one and* the one that is the difference of *this* one from the other (59) which is not called two. 60. When the one is not understood, except through the whole compassing of unity, (61) and duality cannot occur, except through the separation of unit *from* unit, (62) the one is that one in the unity, and is steadfast in unity. 63. One and two are in the pedigree (tôkhmak) of quantity *and* numerousness; (64) and quantity, numerousness, aggregation, and separation, which, as I *have* said, cannot occur without limitation, (65) are clear even to medium understandings.

66. Again, *I say* this, the unlimited is that which is not compassed by the understanding. 67. When it is not possible to compass by any understanding, *it* is inevitable *that* it was not possible to compass in the understanding of the sacred being. 68. It is itself the peculiarity of the sacred being, *and* even that of the gloomy original evolution is not wholly compassed within the understanding. 69. To speak *of* him whose own peculiarity is not compassed within his own understanding *as* all-good and all-seeing is strange[1], (70) because it describes a whole aggregate, (71) and an aggregate is called a whole on account of encompassment *on* all sides. 72. *But what is* encompassed *on* all sides is inevitably limitedness. 73. Is it fitting to account that *as* a sacred being when aware, from all its own encompassment, *that it* is limited? 74. *And* if unlimited *it* is unaware *of it*. 75. The first knowledge of a sage is owing to his well-arranging[2] comprehension of his own pecu-

[1] See Chap. XV, 39 n.

[2] Assuming that Pâz. vas *h*vazîrasni stands for Pahl. agas

liarity, nature, and quantity; (76) *and* to speak *of him* who was unaware *of* all his own peculiarity, nature, and quantity, *and* yet wise about another nature and quantity, is strange[1].

77. This, too, *I say*, that as the unlimited, on account of non-encompassment, is not compassed by the understanding, (78) that *implies* this, that all its peculiarity *may be* wise, or there *may* be *some* that is ignorant; all *may be* light, or there *may* be *some* that is dark; all *may be* alive, or there *may* be *some* that is dead; and *one* is unaware of it.

79. Again, *I say* this, that the light and the life which I obtain here are an allotment that exists owing to the selfsame Time[2], or *they are* not. 80. If *they be* an allotment that exists owing to a peculiarity of Time, that *implies that men* should well recognise this, that anything owing to whose allotment it is possible to ordain them must be provided with allotments. 81. *As to what is* provided with allotments, except when united it is then not possible *even* for it, (82) and *as to what is* united, except through the uniter by whom that united *thing* is united it does not then determine it. 83. And when the allotment made is seen *to be* limited, the origin from which the allotment is *in* like manner made is doubtless a limited existence. 84. As regards that, since they say that all allotment of a result is a giver of evidence *as* to *its* origin, (85) that *implies*, when I obtain an allotment made *and* limited, *that* an origin even of that, except when made and united

hû-âzîrisn; the latter word can scarcely have been hû-âzîrisnîh, 'good arrangement.'

[1] See Chap. XV, 39 n.

[2] See § 31.

from allotments *and* limited, is then not possible to exist.

86. This, too, *I say*, that the unlimited is not bestowed, (87) because an allotment is bestowed from an aggregate, (88) and aggregation is an evidence as to limitation, (89) as I *have* shown above[1]. 90. So that *as to* the existence *and* nature of the origin, except by the likeness and similitude of the result, I do not then attain to them. 91. Whatever is obtained in the result (92) is certain to exist *in* like manner in the origin. 93. That *implies* likewise from *this* explanation, when the formation and limitation are obtainable in the result, *that* the origin also, from which the result *arises*, is without doubt as to limitation.

94. Again, *I say* this, that the unlimited is that which *has* an undisturbed position and an unbounded[2] individuality, (95) and there is no other position *or* resting-place for it disturbed *apart* from it. 96. That *implies*, when two original evolutions are said *to be* unlimited and of unbounded (asâmân) individuality, *that* the skies *and* earths, the rudimentary bodily formations, growths, *and* lives, the luminaries, divinities, *and* archangels, *and* the many congregations (hambarisnân) whose different names are owing to the difference of each one *of those two* from the other, cannot be limited. 97. What produced all those within them, and where *is it*, (98) when the two original evolutions have been eternally *in* an undisturbed position? 99.

[1] See § 64.

[2] Assuming that Pâz. avamãn stands for Pahl. avîmand, as it is translated by Sans. amaryâda; otherwise it might be agûmân, 'undoubted.'

Unless that individuality of theirs, which is unlimited, *be* made limited, how is it possible *for* a place to exist for all these *things that* are *and* were *and will* be made? 100. If a nature that is always unlimited can become limited, that certainly *implies that* it could even become nothing; (101) *and* that which they say about the unchangeableness of a nature is strange[1].

102. This, too, you should understand, that the unlimited becomes that which *has* disturbed it, which *was* not appointed by it *at* first; (103) nothing different from it can exist separate from it. 104. Apart from the boundary of unlimitedness it is not understood, (105) or, stupidly, *one* does not know that thing, that is, of what *it is* he always speaks and contends and bandies words about, *and* thereby deludes those with a trifle of the trifles of knowledge into *some* way *and* whither. 106. If he uncritically[2] says even this of it, that its individuality is unlimited, and its knowledge also, *being* unlimited, knows through unlimited knowledge that it is unlimited, (107) that is a strange *thing* which is twofold strange[3]. 108. One is this, that of knowledge, except about things acquired by knowledge and compassed within knowledge, (109) nothing whatever is understood until complete, except that which is wholly compassed within knowledge and acquired, (110) which knowledge of anything arises through entire understanding of the thing. 111. *And* entire

[1] See Chap. XV, 39 n.

[2] The first part of this word is a blank in JE, as if copied from an original that was illegible here. JJ has a*hv*araidihâ.

[3] See Chap. XV, 39 n.

understanding of anything arises through entire compass of the thing within knowledge[1].

. . . .

[1] The most complete MSS., yet discovered, break off at this point, without concluding the subject. It is quite uncertain how much of the work is lost, but, supposing that all existing MSS. are descended from AK, supposing that that MS. was originally complete,' and supposing that it was divided into two equal portions (the latter of which is now lost) in consequence of some division of family property, we might then conclude, if all these assumptions were correct, that very little of the work is missing, because the portion of AK still extant extends no further than Chap. XI, 145, which is very little beyond the middle of the extant text.

SAD DAR,

OR

THE HUNDRED SUBJECTS.

OBSERVATIONS.

1. The division into dars, 'chapters or subjects,' is indicated in the original manuscripts; but for that of the sections the translator is responsible, as the subdivisions of the alternating Persian-Gugarâti text are often at variance with its meaning.

2–6. (The same as on page 2.)

7. All Arabic words are quoted in parentheses on their first occurrence in the text. And the spelling of names approximates more closely to modern Persian than to the older Pahlavi.

8. The manuscripts mentioned are:—

B29 (written A. D. 1679) in a Persian Rivâyat, No. 29 in the University Library at Bombay.

J15 (undated) Persian, No. 15 in the library of Dastûr Jâmâspji Minochiharji at Bombay. It has been only occasionally consulted for this translation.

La (dated A. D. 1575) Persian, in Avesta writing, alternating with Gugarâti, No. 3043 of the Persian manuscripts in the India Office Library at London; upon the text of which this translation is based.

Lp (undated) Persian, No. 2506 of the Persian manuscripts in the same library.

SAD DAR.

Introduction.

1. *In* the name of Hôrmazd, the lord, the greatest *and* wise[1], the all-ruling, all knowing, *and* almighty.

2. This is a book (kitâb), about the proper and improper, which is extracted from the good *and* pure[2] religion of the Mazda-worshippers. 3. What is expedient (vâ*g*ib) is this, for every one to know *and* keep this in practice. 4. And it is not desirable that he become independent ('*h*âlî) of this *for* a single hour (sâ'hat). 5. Because, when *one* becomes independent, the sin for each one may become abundant; *and* when *it is* brought into practice the reward becomes abundant.

6. On this occasion (vaqt) I, a servant of the religion—like the môbad *E*rân-shâh[3], son (bin) of

---

[1] It is possible to translate the original (which is the same as in Sg. I, 1) as follows:—'The name of Hôrmazd is "the lord, the greatest wise *one*,"' as though these epithets were the meaning of Hôrmazd, which is not far from the truth; but this would not be a probable form for an invocation. Lp and B29 have a different invocation.

[2] Lp, B29, J15 omit '*and* pure.'

[3] This is the name of the writer who composed the Sad Dar Na*th*m, or metrical Sad Dar, in A. D. 1495. He calls himself, however, a son of Malik-shâh in the introduction to his verses (see Hyde's Historia Religionis Veterum Persarum, Oxon, 1700, p. 433); and in his postscript he mentions Mard-shah as his own name, which Dastûr Jâmâspji understands to mean Shah-mard, in the introduction to his Gugarâti translation of the Sad Dar-i Ba'hr-i *T*avîl, or long-metre Sad Dar (2nd ed., Bombay, 1881). The date

Yazad-yâr, son of Tis*t*ar-yâr, son of Âdar-bâ*d*, *son of* Mâraspend[1]—*have* sent a reward to their souls, unto every one who reads and is bound by duty[2]. 7. Thus much (în qadar), which *has* come written, is a good work they know, whosoever are superior; *but* it is not possible for every one inferior to know of this. 8. If it were more (ziyâdat) it is proper, but if (immâ) less than this it is not proper to know[3]; while, *in* gratitude *for* the benefits (*s*ukr-i ni'hmat) of the sacred being, they become increasing in action, and the sacred being, the most high (ta'hâlâi)[4], makes benefits occur on the spot on that account.

---

of composition of this long-metre Sad Dar is A. D. 1531, according to Dastûr Jâmâspji, and its authors state that they compiled it from the Sad Dar Nathr, or prose Sad Dar, which was composed by three celebrated Dastûrs near the time of the Arab conquest. The names in our text are found here only in La, which is either the original, or an early copy, of a version of the prose Sad Dar compiled by Râma, son of Kanhaksha, in which the Persian is written in Avesta letters, and alternates with an old Gugarâti translation composed by his son Padama. This version was prepared A. D. 1575, and the occurrence of the name of *E*rân-shâh, who lived only eighty years earlier, indicates that this part of the introduction was probably written by the editor Râma, and not copied from the original prose Sad Dar. In Lp 'the môbad *E*rân-shâh, son of Yazad-yâr,' is mentioned at the end of the work.

[1] The last two names are introduced merely to show that *E*rân-shâh traced his ancestry back either to the celebrated Âtûr-pâ*d* Mâraspend, prime minister of Shâpûr II (A. D. 309–379), or to another priest of the same name who lived about A. D. 900 (see Bd. XXXIII, 11); but very many intermediate names have been omitted in this genealogy.

[2] J15 omits the whole of § 6, and Lp, B29 have merely 'and a reward is sent to their souls, &c.,' to be read in connection with § 5.

[3] Lp, B29, J15 have 'so that no hesitation arises' instead of 'to know.'

[4] Lp, B29, J15 omit this epithet.

9. And, secondly, the kindness (lu*t*f) and generosity (karm) of the sacred being, the most high[1], are manifest from this, that he created us with each member (âlat) complete (tamâm), and did not keep anything from the maternal *nature*. 10. And whatever was necessary for use he gave us. 11. At the head, likewise, he appointed a master, which is[2] the wisdom for the purpose that they *may* keep these members in action.

12. May the peace of the sacred being, the most high, be on the souls of those acquainted with the religion of the pure Zaratu*s*t, the Spitamân, and of those *who are* pure *and* virtuous. 13. For the souls of those persons it is desirable that every duty they perform they *shall* perform through the authority (dastûrî) of the wisdom of the high-priests[3].

CHAPTER I.

1. The first subject is this, that it is necessary that they become steadfast in the religion, and do not introduce any hesitation (*s*akk) and doubt into the heart. 2. And *that* they make a statement ('haqîqat) with confidence (i'htiqâd), that the good religion, the true and perfect, *which* the Lord sent into the world ('*h*alq), is that which Zaratu*s*t has brought; which is this I hold[4].

3. Every time[5] that mankind are like this, and do

---

[1] Lp, B29, J15 omit this epithet. [2] J15 has 'who possessed.'

[3] For §§ 12, 13 Lp, B29, J15 have merely the following:—'And peace is possible for that person who does every duty that he performs, through the authority of the high-priests.'

[4] Lp, B29 omit these five words.

[5] Lp, B29 have 'for every time.'

not introduce any hesitation *and* doubt into the heart, of every duty *and* good work that *others* have done, from the days of Zaratust until these days, and of whatever *one* does after this until the resurrection, *there* is a share[1] *for* that person. 4. When the soul, on the fourth night[2], arrives at the head of the *K*invad bridge, the angel Mihir and the angel Rashn[3] make up its account ('hisâb) and reckoning. 5. And, if the good works it has done *be* deficient *in* quantity, of every duty *and* good work that those of the good religion have done *in* the earth of seven regions they appoint it a like portion (naꞩîb), till the good works become more in weight[4]; and the soul arrives righteous in the radiant locality of heaven.

6. For it is declared in revelation, that of the duty[5] *and* good work which they perform in doubt—that is (ya'hnî), they entertain a suspicion like this, that 'I do not know that this faith, which I possess, is better *in comparison* with other faiths'—no merit whatever comes to their souls. 7. Therefore, the first (avval) thing is to become steadfast in the religion; and this is the chief of all good works.

Chapter II.

1. The second subject is this, that it is necessary to make an effort (*g*ahd), so that they *may* not

---

[1] Lp, B29 have 'an equal share.'

[2] The older books say at dawn on the fourth day (see Mkh. II, 115).

[3] See Mkh. II, 118, 119.

[4] Lp adds, in the margin, '*by* one filament of the hair of the eye-lashes;' but this phrase seems to have been taken from Chap. II, 3.

[5] Lp, B29 have 'of every duty.'

commit any sin. 2. If even a trifling sin occurs it is not desirable to assume that this small quantity does not possess harm hereafter.

3. For it is said in revelation, that if such *be* the quantity of sin that the sin is one filament of the hair[1] of the eyelashes more in weight than the good works are, that person arrives in hell. 4. And if such a quantity of good works be in excess, he arrives righteous in the radiant locality of heaven.

5. Therefore, even if a sin be trifling it is not desirable to commit *it*; and it is requisite to refrain, so that they *may* not commit *it*, and *may* become without doubt as to the religion.

Chapter III.

1. The third subject is this, that it is necessary *for* man that he be continuously employed (mas*gh*ûl) on his own work, and then the work becomes his own.

2. For it is declared in revelation, that every one who hereafter becomes employed[2] *on* his own work, if in the midst of that work any trouble and discomfort happen to him, obtains in that *other* world twelve recompenses[3] for every single *instance*. 3. If he becomes employed *on* iniquity (fasâd), and in the midst of that work any trouble and harm happen to him, he so[4] obtains in that *other* world only torment ('huqûbat) and punishment.

4. Similarly (maTHalâ*m*), if any one be himself going, employed on his own work, and a robber falls

---

[1] Compare Mkh. II, 121.

[2] B29 has 'hereafter may be.'

[3] La omits 'recompenses.'

[4] Lp, B29 omit 'so.'

upon him on the road, and carries off his property (qumâs), or he be slain[1], they give him back in that *other* world four *things* for each one[2] of whatever they have carried off. 5. If he be slain he becomes righteous, any sin that he has committed goes clean *away* from him, *and* they convey him to heaven. 6. But (ammâ) if he becomes faulty (bâtil) in any duty, and a robber falls upon him on the road[3], and carries off his wealth (mâl), or he be slain, when he descends to that *other* world[4] all the property that *other* carried off from him becomes just as *though it were* his who has carried it off from that person[5]; and, besides, *there* occur, as a substitute ('hivaz) *for* that property, the punishment and torment they give him. 7. *And* if he be slain it is just as *though* he who has carried it off from that person *were one* who had innocently slain that person who arrives in hell as retribution (mukâfât) for sin.

Chapter IV.

1. The fourth subject is this, that it is not desirable for any one that he *should* become hopeless of the pity (ra'hmat) and forgiveness of Hôrmazd, and fix *his* heart outwardly[6] on this, that our sin is excessive *and it is* not possible to arrive in heaven. 2. Because it happens that a small quantity of duty *and* good work is performed, *and* it may be that for that

---

[1] Lp, B29, J15 have 'or they shall slay him anywhere.'

[2] Lp, B29 omit the rest of this sentence.

[3] Lp, B29 omit 'on the road.'

[4] That is, to hell.

[5] That is, the person robbed loses all claim to his property, on account of his neglect of duty.

[6] Lp, B29 omit 'outwardly.'

quantity Hôrmazd, the good *and* propitious, *may* have pity on him *and may* make *him* arrive in heaven.

3. For it is declared in revelation[1], that one time when Zaratust was in conversation *with* the sacred being, the most high, he saw a man whose whole[2] body was in hell, and one foot—the right *one*[3]—was outside of hell. 4. Zaratust enquired of the sacred being, the most high[4], thus: 'What person has this man been?' 5. Hôrmazd, the good *and* propitious, gave a reply (*g*avâb) thus: 'He has been a king, and possessed the sovereignty of thirty-three towns, and was conducting that sovereignty many years. 6. And he never did any virtuous action, but was committing much oppression, lawlessness, and violence (*th*ulm). 7. By chance (qa*z*ârâ) he was one day going on the chase, *and* arrived out at a place (maû*z*a'h) *and* saw a goat *that* was tied. 8. A morsel of hay *was* placed very far *off*, and that goat was hungry. 9. Owing to this the goat was trying to eat the hay, but did not reach the hay. 10. This the king saw, *and* kicked *his* foot at that hay *and* cast *it* in front of the goat. 11. Now, in recompense for that, that one foot of his is outside of hell, and the remaining (bâqî) limbs[5] are in hell.'

12. Therefore, although a sin has happened to any one, it is not necessary *for him*[6] to become hopeless. 13. And whoever has the power (*t*âqat)

[1] The Spend Nask (see Sls. XII, 29). The story is also told in AV. XXXII.

[2] Lp, B29 omit 'whole.'

[3] Lp, B29 have 'and his right foot.'

[4] Lp, B29 omit this epithet.

[5] Lp has 'the rest,' and B29 has 'the whole body.'

[6] Lp, B29 have '*for* the same.'

is to endeavour to perform good works, so that *there* may be an atonement for the sin thereby; because the sacred being, the good *and* propitious, is kind to every one.

Chapter V.

1. The fifth subject is this, that it is necessary for all those of the good religion that they make a thorough effort, so that they celebrate the ritual and become Navazûd[1].

2. For in our religion there is no good work more ample than this. 3. And it is declared in revelation, that, although much duty and good work be performed, it is not possible to attain to the supreme heaven (garôdmân)[2], except *on* that one occasion when the Navazûd *ceremony* is performed, or they have celebrated a Gêtî-kharîd[3]. 4. And *on* any occasion ('hâl), if they are not able to perform *it* with their own hands, it is requisite to order *it; and* then it is inevitably necessary that the celebration of[4] the Gêtî-kharîd should be *in* the same manner as they *would* have performed *it* with their own hands.

---

[1] Apparently 'newly born' (see Sls. XIII, 2 n), a term applied to one who has been duly initiated. After preparatory performances of the Bareshnûm purification and the ordinary ceremonial, the ceremonies are carried on four days longer by two priests. The first day's ceremony is that of the Nônâbar, the second is the Srôsh yast, the third is the Sîrôzah, and the fourth is the Visparad (see Vigirkard-î Dînîk, ed. Peshotan, p. 147).

[2] Ordinary good works, when in excess of the sins, are a passport only to the ordinary heaven (vahist).

[3] Literally 'purchased *in* the worldly *existence*' (see § 11). A ceremony somewhat resembling the Navazûdî (see Bd. XXX, 28 n), but celebrated either late in life, or after death.

[4] Lp, B29 have 'that they celebrate.'

5. Man and woman are both[1] equal in this good work; therefore[2], it is not proper to neglect this duty, for it is the chief of all the good works of the religion. 6. Because it is declared in revelation, that on the day that they are performing the Navazûd *ceremony*, or are celebrating a Gêtî-kharîd on his account, three times the soul of that person arrives at heaven, and they show it a place therein, and offer it a profuse greeting (niTHâr)[3].

7. The explanation (tafsîr) of the Gâhs[4] is this, that a Gâh—that is, that his own place—becomes visible to him[5] in heaven that day.

8. And if *one* does not perform a Navazûd *ceremony*, or does not order the celebration of a Gêtî-kharîd, it is the same as when a poor (*gh*arîb) man makes *for*[6] a town, and does not obtain a spot where he *may* alight *in* that place. 9. Although it is his own town he is in this trouble. 10. Therefore, it is not possible to bring to hand a place in heaven through any good work, except by the performance of the Navazûd ceremony, or *by* ordering the celebration of a Gêtî-kharîd.

11. And a Gêtî-kharîd is this, that heaven is purchased in the world, and one's own place brought to hand in heaven.

---

[1] Lp, B29 omit 'both.'

[2] Lp omits 'therefore,' and B29 has 'certainly.'

[3] Lp, B29, J15 add 'and, afterwards they bring the Gêtî,' and Lp continues thus: 'the meaning is adduced in Pâzand.'

[4] This explains 'the heavenly Gâhs' of Bd. XXX, 28. The Sad Ḍarband-i Hush (as quoted in B29, fol. 458 b) says that it is stated in revelation 'that the day when one celebrates the Gêtî-kharîd of any one, the soul of that person seizes upon the heavenly Gâhs three times in that one day, *and* is conveyed to heaven and the supreme heaven.'

[5] Lp, B29 have 'is brought into sight.'

[6] Lp, B29 have 'arrives at.'

Chapter VI.

1. The sixth subject is this, that of the many good works there are those which, when they accomplish *them*, obtain great ('h*a*t*h*îm) rewards; *and* if *one* does not perform *them* severe punishment seizes upon *one* at the head of the *K*invad bridge[1]. 2. One is *the celebration of* the season festivals[2]; the second is keeping *the days* of the guardian spirits[3]; the third is *attending to* the souls of fathers, mothers, *and* other relations[4]; the fourth is *reciting* the Khûrshê*d* Nyâyi*s*[5] three times every day; the fifth is *reciting* the Mâh Nyâyi*s*[6] three times every month, once when it becomes new, once when it becomes full, and once when it becomes slender[7]; *and* the sixth is celebrating the Rapithwin[8] *ceremony* once every year. 3. If not able to celebrate *them* oneself, it is requisite to order *them*, so that they *may* celebrate them every single time[9].

4. These six good works are things indispensable unto every one. 5. When any one *of them* is not *performed*—be it that which, if omitted at its own time[10], it is not possible to accomplish, or if it be that one time *one* omits an occasion, *and* another time[11] they accomplish twice as much—*one should* consider[12] that as an advantage, *which* occurs in retri-

[1] See Sls. XII, 31.
[2] See Mkh. IV, 5 n.
[3] See Mkh. LVII, 13 n.
[4] See Chap. XIII.
[5] The salutation of the sun (see Chap. XCV).
[6] The salutation of the moon.
[7] In Gugarâti 'on the last day.'
[8] The mid-day period.
[9] Lp, B29 have 'celebrate them on his account.'
[10] B29 inserts 'or if it be that which, one time omitted.'
[11] B29 has merely 'if another time.'
[12] Lp, B29 have '*one* does not consider;' the copyists having

bution for it, or *as* atonement for the transgression. 6. Because they call the transgression of each of these six a bridge-sin; that is, every one *through* whom a transgression of these may have arisen they keep back, at the head of the *K*invad bridge, till punishment for it happens to him, and no good work is possible[1] in this place, which is torment and punishment for him[2].

7. Therefore it is necessary to make an effort, that they *may* be performed each one at its own time, so that they *may* obtain a recompense, *and* not a severe punishment.

Chapter VII.

1. The seventh subject is this, that, when a sneeze ('ha*t*sat) comes forth from any one, it is requisite to recite one Yathâ-ahû-vairyô[3] and one Ashem-vohû[4]. 2. Because there is a fiend in our bodies, and she is an adversary who is connected with mankind, and strives so that she *may* make misfortune ('hillat) and sickness predominant (mustaûlî) over mankind. 3 And in our bodies there is a fire which they call a disposition—in Arabic they say *t*abî'hat—and they call *it* the sneezing instinct (*gh*arîzî). 4. *It is* connected with that fiend, *and* they wage warfare, and it keeps her away from the body of man. 5. Then, as the fire becomes successful over

failed to notice that retribution and atonement are advantageous in this case, because they save the soul from punishment.

[1] Lp, B29 have 'no good work resides.'

[2] Lp, B29 have 'which will liberate him from torment and punishment.'

[3] See Mkh. XXVII, 70 n, Sls. XII, 32.

[4] A formula in praise of righteousness, which begins with these two Avesta words, and is in constant use (see Bd. XX, 2).

that fiend, *and* puts her to flight (hazîmat), a sneeze comes because that fiend comes out.

6. Afterwards, because it is necessary, they recite these *inward* prayers[1] and perform the benediction (âfrîn) of the fire, so that it may remain *for* a long period while thou art keeping[2] this fiend defeated. 7. When another person hears the sneeze, it is likewise requisite for him to utter the said prayers, and to accomplish the benediction of that spirit[3].

Chapter VIII.

1. The eighth subject is this, that it is necessary to maintain the religion by rule (dastûr), and to practise obedience to the commands of the high-priests; *and* every duty that *people* perform they *should* perform by their authority.

2. For it is declared in the good religion, that, if they accomplish as many good works as the leaves of the trees, *or* the sand-*grains* of the desert, *or* the drops (qa*t*rah) of rain, which they do not perform by command of the high-priests, *or* to their satisfaction, no merit whatever attains to their souls, and *for* the good works they have done they obtain sin *as* a recompense. 3. While *such a one* is living it is not proper to call him righteous, and when he dies he does not attain to heaven, and not a single archangel comes[4] near him. 4. He does not make his escape from the hands of the demons and Aharman, and he

[1] The formulas are muttered as a spell.

[2] B29 has 'it is making.'

[3] In some parts of Europe it is still the custom to invoke a blessing, by means of some formula, on hearing a sneeze.

[4] Lp, B29 have 'goes.'

does not obtain a release from hell. 5. Because duties *and* good works[1] attain to the soul *on* those occasions when they perform *them* with the authority of the high-priests and those acquainted with the religion, and *when* they give them one-tenth of those good works[2].

CHAPTER IX.

1. The ninth subject is this, that it is necessary to practise abstinence from committing *or* permitting unnatural intercourse[3]. 2. For this is the chief of all sins *in* the religion: there is no worse sin than this in the good religion, and it is proper to call those *who commit it* worthy of death in reality.

3. If any one comes forth to them, and shall see them in the act, *and* is working with an axe[4], it is requisite *for him* to cut *off* the heads or to rip up the bellies of both, *and* it is no sin for him. 4. *But* it is not proper to kill any person without the authority of high-priests and kings, except on account of committing *or* permitting unnatural intercourse.

5. For it says in revelation that unnatural intercourse is on a par with Aharman, with Afrâsiyâb[5], with Dahâk[5], with Tûr-i Brâ*d*ar-vakhsh[6] who slew

---

[1] That is, the merit of performing them.

[2] The principles of blind submission of the laity to the priesthood, and complete abnegation of private judgment, which pervade the whole of the Sad Dar, are especially conspicuous in this chapter. They are the ideas prevalent in the darkest ages of the religion, which have now nearly disappeared with the spread of true knowledge as in other faiths.

[3] *G*h*ulâmbâragî u mûâ*g*arî.*

[4] B29, J15 have 'takes a look,' and J15 adds 'he shall kill *them*.'

[5] See Mkh. VIII, 29 n.

[6] One of five brothers of the Karap tribe (see Byt. II, 3, Dd. LXXII, 8).

Zaratust, with Malkôs[1] who will arise, with the serpent Sruvar which existed in the days of Sâm Narîmân[2], and as many sins as are theirs. 6. And Aharman, the evil *one*, becomes more joyful, owing to this practice, than owing to the other sins *which* have made high-priests necessary[3]; for the soul itself of that person becomes extinct.

7. And when they commit *the sin* with women, it is just the same as that with men.

Chapter X.

1. The tenth subject is this, that it is incumbent on all those of the good religion, women and men, every one who attains to fifteen years, to wear the *sacred thread*-girdle[4]. 2. Because the *sacred thread*-girdle is to be a girding of the loins and to preserve obedience (*t*â'hat) to the Lord, may he be honoured and glorified ('hazza va *g*alla)!

3. The first person who set the wearing of this *sacred thread*-girdle in view was Jamshê*d*[5]. 4. And it may be the whole (*g*umlah) of the demons and fiends who are made extinct by the glory of wearing the *sacred thread*-girdle.

5. Every one who *has* tied the *sacred thread*-girdle *round* the waist is out of the department of Aharman, and is established in the department of

---

[1] See Mkh. XXVII, 28 n.

[2] Sâma and Naremana*u* are two titles of the hero Keresâspa who slew the serpent Srvara (see SBE, vol. xviii, pp. 369–371). In the Shâhnâmah he is called Sâm, son of Narîmân.

[3] J15 has '*which* the high priests have made manifest.'

[4] See Dd. XXXIX, 1 n. A modification of the age is recommended in Chap. XLVI.

[5] Av. Yima khshaêta (see Mkh. XXVII, 24 n).

Hôrmazd. 6. And also, while he keeps the *sacred thread*-girdle on the waist, *there* is a share *for* him of all those duties and good works which they perform in the earth of seven regions. 7. It is like that *which occurs* when they are performing hamâ zôr and hamâ ashô[1], and have put *on* this *sacred thread*-girdle on that account, *or* when, similarly, some one in Kasmîr, or *Ê*rân-ve*g*, or Kangdez, or the enclosure formed by Jam[2], performs a good work, *and* we are not able to perform *it* with hamâ zôr, then they and we, *who* wear the *sacred thread*-girdle on the waist, are mutually connected and equally meritorious, one *with* the other. 8. As no good work attains to him *who* does not wear a *sacred thread*-girdle—excepting that which he performs himself—it is therefore necessary that any one of mankind *should* not put *it*[3] away from the waist on any occasion, so that the associated good works of those of the good religion *may* attain to him.

9. And those four knots[4], *with* which they tie *it* on, are on this account, that it *may* give four attestations.

---

[1] These words form part of a benedictory formula which concludes certain ceremonies (see Haug's Essays, pp. 407, 409), and the recital of them implies that the ceremony, which is a good work, has been fully and satisfactorily completed. If this good work be in excess of what is wanted to balance its performer's sins, it can be imputed to any other member of the good religion who may be in want of it, provided he wears the girdle. The MSS. have hamā for hamâ.

[2] These four localities are considered to be isolated from the seven regions to some extent (see Bd. XXIX, 4), probably implying that they were supposed to contain Mazda-worshippers independent of Iranian rule, or that their position had become unknown. (See also Mkh. XXVII, 27–31, 58, 62, XLIV, 17–35, LXII, 13–19.)

[3] Lp, B29 have 'that mankind *should* not put the girdle.'

[4] That is, two double knots, one before and the other behind (see SBE, vol. xviii, pp. 386, 387).

10. The first knot is that which preserves[1] constancy (qarâr), and gives attestation as to the existence, unity, purity, and matchlessness of the sacred being, the good *and* propitious. 11. The second knot is that which gives attestation *that it is* the good religion of the Mazda-worshippers which is the word of the sacred being. 12. The third knot is that which gives attestation as to the apostleship and mission (rasûlî) in the just ('haqq) Zaratust, the Spitamân. 13. The fourth knot is that which adduces more pleasantly, gives assurance (iqrâr), and openly accepts that I *should* think of good, speak of good, and do good. 14. And from the whole I become established; and the pure, good[2] religion is this, that I persist in those *views.*

15. And, again, when the archangels came meeting Zaratust they likewise wore the *sacred thread*-girdle on the waist; and the distinctive *characteristic* (farq) amid the laws of the sacred being is the wearing of the *sacred thread*-girdle. 16. It is incumbent both on woman and on man, *and* it is altogether (albattah) improper when they do not wear *it.*

CHAPTER XI.

1. The eleventh subject is this, that it is necessary to maintain the fire-place[3] properly, and to keep watch[4], so that *the fire shall* not die *out*, and *that* nothing polluted and impure *shall* attain to the fire; and it is necessary to make a menstruous woman avoid *being* within three steps *of it.*

---

[1] Altered into 'brings' by a later hand in La, and so written in Lp, B29.

[2] Lp, B29 omit 'good.'

[3] Or, perhaps, 'the house-fire.'

[4] B29 omits these four words.

2. Because every time that they maintain a fire properly, which is within a dwelling, every fire which is in the earth of seven regions becomes pleased with those persons, and, when they ask a favour, or beg a necessity ('hâgat), it becomes quickly operative. 3. And every time that *one* does not maintain *it* properly, every fire which is in the earth of seven regions receives injury from that person, and the necessity he begs does not become operative. 4. If any one does not maintain the fire-place properly, if he gives a hundred dînârs[1] to the fire Gusasp[2] *there* is no acceptance *of it*, and that sin does not depart from him.

5. For it is declared in revelation[3], that the creator Hôrmazd has given sovereignty in heaven to Ardibahist[4], the archangel, and has spoken thus: '*As to* every one with whom thou art not pleased, do not let him escape into heaven.' 6. And this is also declared in revelation, that, every time that they do not maintain the fire properly, pregnancy becomes scarcer for the women, fewer male children are born, and honour ('hurmat) in the vicinity of the king becomes less for the men, and *there* is no approbation (qabûl) of *their* words.

7. *For* every single fire which dies out in a dwelling a loss of three dirhams and two dângs[5] falls

---

[1] The dînâr is a gold coin which, if it contained a dirham weight of gold, and if the dirham were 63 grains (see Dd. LII, 1 n), was equal to about half-a-sovereign.

[2] One of the three most sacred fires (see Bd. XVII, 7).

[3] Lp, B29 have 'in the good religion.'

[4] Av. asha vahista, 'perfect rectitude,' who is supposed to protect fire (see Bd. I, 26, Sls. XV, 12).

[5] That is, three dirhams and a half in silver, or nearly one rupee and a quarter.

on the property of that person, or it becomes the loss of this dwelling, or it does not reach him from the place whence wealth comes to him.

CHAPTER XII.

1. The twelfth subject is this, that, when any one dies, an order is necessary[1] *that* how much soever scantier[2] clothing they are able to make a beginning *of*, the better they act. 2. Beside (illâ)[3] something become old *and* washed, anything new is not proper for *the purpose* that they *may* let *it* go upon a dead body.

3. For in the commentary of the Vendîdâ*d*[4] it asserts that, if they *shall* pass on to a dead body as much as a woman's spindle makes for a single thread, with the exception of that which is unavoidable, for every single thread a black snake hangs, in that *other* world, on to the liver of that person who has made a beginning of the clothing. 4. Likewise, that dead *person* becomes his antagonist ('*h*aȝm), and hangs similarly[5] upon *his* skirt, and speaks thus: 'This clothing, which thou hast put on my body, devours *me*, *having* become worms and noxious creatures. 5. *My* name *was* put upon a sacred cake[6], the fourth *day*, with a Yast, so that *there*

---

[1] B29 has 'it is necessary to utter two orders.'

[2] Lp, B29 have 'older.' Compare Sls. XII, 4.

[3] Lp, B29 have 'that is.'

[4] Pahl. Vend. V, 170–177, where, however, the penalty here mentioned is not now extant.

[5] Lp, B29 omit 'similarly.'

[6] Referring to the cake consecrated to the righteous guardian spirit on the fourth day after death (see Chap. LXXXVII, 2, Sls. III, 32 n, XVII, 5 n).

might be alike a benefit therefrom for my soul, and it might be alike unnecessary for thee to bear this torment ('haᴅʜâb).' 6. Owing to that, many sorrows come to that person, and he has no advantage from it. 7. Therefore, it is necessary to act *with* caution (i'htiyâ*t*), so that, how much soever the clothing be scantier[1], they *may* make a beginning *of it*.

8. And as many as shall be able to walk after the bier (tâbût) and corpse shall walk. 9. Because every step that they go after a corpse is a good work of three hundred stîrs[2]; *and* every stîr is four dirhams, in such manner that three hundred stîrs are a thousand *and* two hundred dirhams[3]. 10. For every single step *there* is thus much good work.

CHAPTER XIII.

1. The thirteenth subject is this, that it is necessary to maintain the souls of fathers, mothers, and relations properly. 2. And, when any day of theirs[4] occurs, it is necessary to make an endeavour, so that they *may* accomplish the ceremonial (yazi*s*n), the sacred feast (myazd), *the consecration of* the sacred cakes (drôn), and the benedictions (âfrîngân).

3. For it is declared in revelation, that, every time that any day of theirs occurs, they will bring with

---

[1] Lp, B29, J15 have 'older.'

[2] An amount which would counterbalance a Tanâvar or Tanâpûhar sin (see Sls. I, 2).

[3] B29 omits these fourteen words.

[4] That is, on the monthly and annual anniversaries of their deaths, when ceremonies are requisite (see Sls. XVII, 5 n). Compare Chap. XXXVII.

themselves 9999 guardian spirits of the righteous, like that *case* when any one goes home himself, and brings people (qaûm) in hospitality. 4. And, when they utter[1] *the consecration of* the sacred cakes and sacred feast and the benedictions, those people become joyful and utter blessings on that house and master of the house, and on the house-mistress and any persons who are in that house.

5. But if they do not celebrate the sacred feast, *the consecration of* the sacred cakes, the ceremonial, and the benedictions, *the spirits* will remain for them *in* that place from dawn as long as the period of a day, and are maintaining a hope that 'perhaps they *will* have us *in* remembrance.' 6. Then, if they do not bring them[2] *into* remembrance, the souls turn upwards from that place, go very quickly on high, and will say, 'O creator Hôrmazd! they do not know that we are such as we are[3], *and that* it is necessary for them[4] to come into this world, and in this world they will not give any one acquittal. 7. For them there is need of the good works in *consecrating* the sacred cakes and *celebrating* the sacred feast and benedictions; there is no need of them for such as we. 8. Yet (va lîkin), if they would have maintained a place *for*[5] the duty of those days, we should have turned away from them misfortunes of various kinds; but, as they have not maintained[6] observance of us *in* the day's duty, we are not able to come in friendship *to* this house.'

[1] B29 has 'celebrate.'

[2] Literally 'us.' Lp, B29 omit this and the next two words.

[3] Lp, B29 have 'that just like us are they.'

[4] Lp, B29 omit 'for them.'

[5] B29 has 'maintained observance of us *in*.'

[6] B29 inserts 'proper.'

9. Thus much they say, and turn *away* in anger, and go away from that place.

Chapter XIV.

1. The fourteenth subject is this, that, when the nails *are pared* according to custom (ba-'*h*ilâl)[1], it is necessary that they put *the parings* into a paper. 2. And it is further necessary to take the Srôsh-bâ*z*[2] *inwardly*, and *to utter* three Yathâ-ahû-vairyôs[3]. 3. And for the speaking *of this*—to say with each Yathâ-ahû-vairyô[4]—the Avesta is this:—Paiti tê, meregha Ashô-zu*s*ta! im*au* srv*au* vaêdhayêmi, im*au* srv*au* âwaêdhayêmi; im*au*se tê srv*au*, meregha Ashô-zu*s*ta! hyâre ar*s*tayas*k*a, karetayas*k*a, thanvare*k*a, ishavas*k*a erezifyô-parena, asna*k*a fradakhshanya paiti daêvô-Mâzainyãn[5]; ashâ vohû mananghâ yâ sruyê par*e* magaonô[6]. 4. Afterwards, *one* completes the Bâ*z* in the manner that *it was* taken *inwardly*.

5. At those two Yathâ-ahû-vairyôs, *with* which *one* completes the Bâ*z*, at each one, he makes lines ('*h*a*tt*hâ) *in* a little dust in the midst of the nail-

---

[1] B29 has 'when the nails and a toothpick ('*h*ilâl) *are* pared;' and the Gugarâti translator takes '*h*ilâl in the same sense.

[2] A particular form of prayer.

[3] See Mkh. XXVII, 70 n.

[4] B29 omits these eleven words.

[5] Vend. XVII, 26–28:—'Unto thee, O bird Ashô-zu*s*ta! do I announce these nails, do I introduce these nails' (or, according to the Pahlavi, 'do I make known these nails, these nails do I make *thee* known to'); 'may these nails be such for thee, O bird Ashô-zu*s*ta! *as* spears and knives, bows, falcon-feathered arrows, and sling-stones against the demon Mâzainyas.'

[6] Yas. XXXIII, 7b:—'Through the righteous good thought, by which I am heard before the mighty *one*.'

parings. 6. And, if he does not know this Bâ*z*[1], on uttering the Srôsh-bâ*z* and those three Yathâ-ahû-vairyôs *he is* to furrow three lines, with the nail-cutter[2], around the nail-*parings*, *and* then *he is* to complete the Bâ*z* with those Yathâ-ahû-vairyôs, *and* to put the dust, with the end of the nail-cutter, into the midst of the nail-*parings*, and carry *them* to a desert *spot*. 7. It is necessary that he *should* carry *a hole* down *through* four finger-*breadths* of earth, and, *having* placed *the nail-parings* in that spot, he puts the soil overhead.

8. For Hôrmazd, the good *and* propitious, has created a bird which they call Ashô-zu*s*t[3], and they call *it* the bird of Bahman[4]. 9. They also call it the owl, *and* it eats nails.

10. It is altogether necessary that they do not leave *them* unbroken, for they *would* come into use as weapons (silâ'h) of wizards[5]. 11. And they have also said that, if they fall in the midst of food, *there* is danger of pulmonary consumption.

Chapter XV.

1. The fifteenth subject is this, when *one* sees anything that is welcome to the eyes, it is requisite to say 'in the name of the sacred being.' 2. Because, if they do not say 'in the name of the sacred being,' and an injury happens to that

---

[1] The formula quoted in § 3.

[2] B29 omits these four words.

[3] See Bd. XIX, 19, 20.

[4] The archangel Vohûman (see Bd. I, 23, 26 n). His bird is the cock according to Sls. X, 9.

[5] See Sls. XII, 6.

thing, or a disaster occurs, *one* becomes a sinner; so far is notorious (ma'hlûm).

Chapter XVI.

1. The sixteenth subject is this, that, when a woman becomes pregnant in a house, it is necessary to make an endeavour so that *there may* be a continual fire in that house, and to maintain a good watch *over it.* 2. And, when the child becomes separate from the mother, it is necessary to burn a lamp *for* three nights *and* days—if they burn a fire it would be better—so that the demons and fiends *may* not be able to do any damage and harm; because, when a child is born, it is exceedingly delicate *for* those three days.

3. For it is declared in revelation[1], that, when Zaratust, the Spitamân, became separate from *his* mother, every night, *for* three nights, a demon came on, with a hundred and fifty *other* demons, so that they *might* effect the slaughter (halâk) of Zaratust, *and*, when they had beheld the light of the fire, they had fled away, and had not been able to do any damage and harm.

4. During forty days it is not proper that they *should* leave the child alone; and it is also not proper that the mother of the infant *should* put *her* foot over a threshold in the dwelling, or cast *her* eyes upon a hill, *for* it[2] is bad for *her* menstruation.

---

[1] Lp, B29 have 'in the good religion.' This is quoted probably from the Spend Nask (see Sls. X, 4, XII, 11).

[2] B29 has 'which they have said.'

Chapter XVII.

1. The seventeenth subject is this, that when they cut a toothpick (*kh*ilâl), or a splinter which they wish to apply to the root of the teeth, it is necessary that they retain no bark. 2. For if a small quantity of bark be on it when they apply *it* to the teeth, and they cast *it* away, if a pregnant woman puts *her* foot upon it, the danger of that may be that the child comes to harm[1].

Chapter XVIII.

1. The eighteenth subject is this, that it is necessary for mankind to make an endeavour, so that they *may* espouse a wife in *their* youth and beget a child. 2. And for women, in like manner, it is necessary that *there* should be a longing (ra*gh*bat) for espousing a husband.

3. Because it is declared in revelation[2], *that* every duty and good work a child performs becomes the father's and mother's, just like those which they have performed with their own hands. 4. The meaning (ma'hnî) of pûr ('a son') is that which signifies pûl ('a bridge')[3], for by this bridge they arrive at that *other* world. 5. If *there* be no child for any one they call *him one with* a severed bridge, that is, the

---

[1] Owing to her fear of having stepped on dead matter (see Sls. X, 20, XII, 13).

[2] In the Spend, Nihâ*d*ûm, and Dâmdâ*d* Nasks (see Sls. X, 22, XII, 15).

[3] This fanciful explanation must be derived from a Pahlavi source, as it is only in that language that the two words are written precisely alike.

way for him *to* that *other* world is severed, and he is not able to attain to that world. 6. At the head of the *K*invad bridge he shall remain; although he has performed much duty and good works he is not able to make a passage over the *K*invad bridge, and they do not make up his account and reckoning. 7. And every archangel that comes forward *to* that place first asks these words, that is, 'Hast thou brought thy own substitute visibly into the world, or not?' 8. When he has not brought *it*, they will pass over him, and his soul will remain, *in* that place[1], full of anguish and grief (*gh*am).

9. A similitude (miTHâl) of it is like that which *happens when* any one may be in a wilderness, and *there* may be fear of wild animals and creatures, and near to him may be his own town, *but* a river of water is in front[2], and it is not possible to make a passage over that river, *as* a bridge is fallen in, and he is not able to arrive at that town, *but* he is always upon the bank (sar*t*) *speaking* thus[3]: 'Would that the bridge would become perfect!'

10. The duty as to children[4] is in this aggregate[5]. 11. Therefore, the creator Hôrmazd *has* granted unto men that, if *there* be any one to whom sickness from heaven may occur, and *there* be no provision of a child for him, he *has* commanded him that he *should* make some one a son of his own, as[6] a friend of *his* soul, and *should* receive a child, because every duty *can be* delegated. 12. That person is in place of a

[1] Lp, B29 add 'on the bridge.'
[2] La omits these eight words.
[3] Lp, B29 have 'always in regret ('hasrat) thus.'
[4] Lp has 'as to the command.'
[5] Lp has 'manner,' and J15 has 'endeavour.'
[6] Lp, B29 have 'some one through his own affection.'

child, and every duty and good work that he performs shall be just like that *which* is performed by one's own hand.

13. And, finally, if any one departs from the world (dunyâ)[1] and possesses no adopted child, it is incumbent on the priests and high-priests and his relations to appoint his adopted son, and it is necessary to bring some one in sight on that account, so that his soul *may* spring away from the torment of hell. 14. Because, every time that his relations do not pay attention *to this*, when they proceed to that *other* world, the soul of that person hangs about them and speaks thus: 'I left with you something that I had collected and borne trouble for in many years, and you seized upon *it*, and put *it* into your own expenditure (*'h*ar*g*), and did not seek for[2] mercy (*s*afqat) on my soul. 15. *In* the same manner as I have remained, delayed (maûqûf) *in* this place, I *will* not let you pass; so that you *will* make no passage over the *K*inva*d* bridge till the sacred being takes my rights away from you.' 16. Then the angel Rashn and the angel Mihir[3] make up their reckoning, *and, as to* whatever those persons have seized upon from the *other's* property[4], for every single dînâr the account makes four, and they take away the equivalent. 17. And, *as* in that world *there* are no gold and silver, they take away from their souls the good works that they have done, and they give *them* to the soul of this *other*. 18. Still, while *others* do not appoint the adopted son, they are not able to pass over the *K*inva*d* bridge, nor to arrive at their own station.

---

[1] La omits these nine words.
[2] B29 has 'bring.'
[3] See Mkh. II, 118, 119.
[4] Lp, J15 insert 'and have expended.'

19. There is no duty whatever more incumbent on relations than this duty, and every time that they appoint an adopted son *for* any one it is just as though they have made the deceased alive; and there are no limit ('hadd) and end (nihâyat) of their good works.

Chapter XIX.

1. The nineteenth subject is this, that the performance of agriculture is like that when some one is performing the ceremonial of the sacred beings, and it is necessary to maintain much respect *for* agriculturists; it is also necessary to keep trouble and strife far from them.

2. For it is declared in revelation, that, *as to* every one who replants a shrub, while that shrub *or* tree exists at the place, every good work that every one, who eats of that shrub, does in that *state of* repletion becomes the agriculturist's, just like those which are done by his own hand. 3. If any one orders *it*, just as that good work occurs[1] much new repose (râ'hat) and comfort reach his soul[2]. 4. *As to* corn and grain ('hubûb) and whatever they sow, it is just like this[3], because, *as regards* every one who eats wheat, barley, and other grains, and performs duty *and* good works, they become *those* of the sower of[4] those grains, just as those which are performed by his own hand. 5. Because, for the life of mankind a crop was necessary, the creation of a

---

[1] Lp, B29 have 'is performed.' [2] Lp, B29 add 'therefrom.'

[3] B29 adds 'way.'

[4] La omits the rest of this chapter, as well as the words 'they become,' by mistake.

creator[1] after the sacred being, the most high[2], owing to the work of the agriculturist. 6. For every one who eats anything dies, therefore, *as regards* that person by whose work the life of mankind is established, it is necessary to consider him valuable and precious.

Chapter XX.

1. The twentieth subject is this, that it is incumbent on those of the good religion that they continually give something to the worthy to eat, on account (*g*ihat) of that which it says in revelation[3] thus: 'When thou givest things to some one that he *may* eat, every duty and good work that he performs in that *state of* repletion become *those* of that person, who has given that bread or food to him, just like those which he has performed with his own hand.' 2. And if he commits a sin, he who may have given food to him is innocent. 3. But it is necessary that he be of the good religion and worthy; they *should* give something to *one of* a different religion only in case of extreme necessity (ẓarûrat), lest it become as a sin.

Chapter XXI.

1. The twenty-first subject is this, that, when they eat bread, it is necessary that *one should* recite

[1] B29, J15 omit these five words.

[2] J15 has 'after its creation *by* the sacred being, the creator.' The alteration of this sentence, in B29 and J15, seems due to their writers' reluctance to attribute the power of creating, even figuratively, to the mere producer of a crop.

[3] In the Nihâ*d*ûm Nask (see Sls. X, 23, XII, 16).

the Ithâ-â*d*-yâzamaidê[1] and three Ashem-vohûs[2], especially (ba-'*h*â*zz*ata*m*) in the benediction-ceremonies (âfrîngân).

2. For it is declared in the good religion of the Mazda-worshippers, that, when they wish to celebrate the sacred feast (myazd) and benediction-ceremonies, it is necessary that all persons who are seated at the feast *should* take up the *inward* prayer. 3. For each man an angel is stationed, on the right-hand *side*, and two angels for the priests. 4. *But* when they eat chatteringly, *or* relate the news ('hadîTH)[3], the angels depart from them, and a demon seizes on the place of each angel[4].

5. And in former times the custom ('hâdat) of the people would have been in this manner, that, if any one should have come to the door in the middle of the feast, that person whose Âfrîngân-precinct it might have been, *or* whoever should have gone to the expense of that Âfrîngân, would have had words with that *intruding* person[5], and would have also spoken thus: 'As thou hast brought my feast to harm, give me back whatever has been the cost[6].'

6. And *in* one place in revelation *it is* declared

---

[1] Yas. V, 1, 2, of which these are the first three words. This, with the three Ashem-vohûs, constitutes the inward prayer, or grace, before eating (see Dd. LXXIX, 1 n).

[2] See Chap. VII, 1 n.

[3] By which they commit the sin of breaking the protective spell of the inward prayer.

[4] Lp, B29 have 'a demon is (B29 stands) in place of the angel.'

[5] B29 has 'would have spoken to that person who had uttered words, would have taken *something* away from him.' Lp merely adds 'would have taken *something*' to the words in the text.

[6] B29 has only, 'As it is my feast, give *it* back.' The interruption having destroyed the merit of the ceremony.

that from eating chatteringly itself is the sin, for[1] every one who is chattering during the eating of bread is just like him who is smiting and harassing the angels of the spiritual *existences.*

7. Therefore, if *there* be any one who is not able to consecrate a sacred cake[2], it is necessary to eat bread with the *inward* prayer of Hôrmazd, that is, the archangels. 8. And, if he does not altogether know *it*, he recites the Ithâ-â*d*-yazamaidê[3] and three Ashem-vohûs, and eats up the bread. 9. Afterwards he makes *his* mouth clean, and, four Ashem-vohûs and two Yathâ-ahû-vairyôs *being* spoken out[4], *he is* then to utter words.

10. For, every time that this custom (qâ'hidat) is carried *on* in a place, through the first Ashem-vohû so much good work *has* arisen that it has propitiated the sacred being, the good *and* propitious; through the second Ashem-vohû so much good work *has* arisen that it has reverenced and[5] propitiated Srôsh, the righteous[6]; through the third Ashem-vohû so much good work *has* arisen that it has reverenced and[5] propitiated Khurdâ*d and* Ameredâ*d*[7], the archangels; and through the fourth Ashem-vohû so much good work *has* arisen that whatever the creator Hôrmazd has created becomes reverenced and propitiated. 11. And with each mouthful (luqmah) that is eaten, while the *inward* prayer subsists, they

[1] B29 has 'from eating chatteringly is so much sin that.'

[2] See Mkh. XVI, 17 n.

[3] See § 1 n.

[4] These formulas begin the grace after eating, and, being uttered aloud, break the spell of the inward prayer now no longer necessary; after them the eaters are at liberty to speak.

[5] B29 omits these two words.

[6] See Mkh. II, 115 n.

[7] See Horvada*d* and Amerôda*d* (Mkh. II, 34).

proclaim a blessing *for* Khurdâ*d* and Ameredâ*d*, the archangels. 12. *But*, if *it be* eaten without the *inward* prayer, as demons are *in* that place[1], they say, 'Thou mightest have eaten the poison of a serpent.' 13. Therefore, take notice as to which is the better of these two.

CHAPTER XXII.

1. The twenty-second subject is this, that the performance of *G*âda*n*gôî[2] ('intercession') is like that when some one is occasioning the ceremonial of the sacred beings. 2. Therefore, it should be expedient that it be continuous, *and that*[3] they perform *G*âda*n*gôî as regards the priests and high-priests and the worthy.

3. For, in the commentary of the Hâdôkht *Nask*, it says that every one who performs *G*âda*n*gôî, and extracts anything from a person on their account, and conveys *it* to them, is as much without dishonesty (*'h*iyânat), towards them[4], as he who may

---

[1] See § 4.

[2] The original Pahlavi of this word can be read either dâ*d*ô-gôbîh, 'a speaking of the law,' or yêdatô-gôbîh, 'a speaking of the sacred being;' in either case it implies 'pleading for the proper observance of religious duties,' especially the duty of supporting the priesthood and the poor, and it is for such purposes that the 'intercession' with those possessing property must be understood as being exercised. As the traditional mode of reading Pahl. yêdatô is *g*âtan, or *g*â*d*an, it is evident that the Pâzand inventors of the word in the text must have understood the Pahlavi in the latter of the two meanings mentioned above.

[3] Lp, B29 have merely 'that continuously.'

[4] Lp, B29 omit these two words. But the meaning of La seems to be that he who bestows charity out of the contributions of others, without mentioning the contributors, does not act dishonestly towards the recipients.

have given to them out of his own property. 4. And *in* the spiritual *existence* they take[1] account of that profit for him, and just as they make *out* the account of the good work of that person who may have given *it*, even so much is his good work.

CHAPTER XXIII.

1. The twenty-third subject is this, that it is requisite to restrain a tethered *animal* from misbehaviour, and to keep watch *over* one's own *creatures*, especially *at* the time when they have eaten meat.

2. Therefore, if they have eaten meat *and* they commit an assault, every offence that the animal ('haivân) commits may be that person's whose meat may be eaten. 3. For example, if a horse lashes *out* a kick (lakad) at any one, the offence may be that person's whose food may be eaten and caused the offence.

4. Therefore it is necessary to make an endeavour that they *shall* commit no offence whatever, especially at a time when they have eaten meat.

CHAPTER XXIV.

1. The twenty-fourth subject is this, that when an infant is born from *its* mother it is necessary that they give *it* the consecrated Hôm-juice[2], on this account, that understanding ('haql), wisdom, and

[1] Lp, B29 have 'the spirits take.'

[2] See Mkh. LVII, 28 n, Sls. X, 16.

knowledge *may* more abundantly get to it, and the want (ablat) of them *may* come more scantily upon *it*[1].

2. If, at that time, they do not perform the consecration, they *should* take forth a little Hôm for it[2], and recite[3] a Yathâ-ahû-vairyô[4], and put a trifle of water into *it*, and make Hôm-juice of that, and give *it* to the infant, and afterwards[5] milk.

CHAPTER XXV.

1. The twenty-fifth subject is this, that any agreement and promise (qaûl) they make with any one it is necessary so far to perform and bring to pass. 2. Although many things *may* go[6] to harm by means (sabab) of it, it is not desirable to perform that agreement with duplicity.

3. Because, in our religion, they call this a Mihir-drug ('breach of promise'), *and* in revelation it decrees, *as to* any one *who* commits a Mihir-drug, that the way *to* heaven becomes closed for him, and that person himself goes discomforted out of this world, so that a warning ('halâmat) becomes quite manifest unto him.

4. And a Mihir-drug is attached[7] *in* such a manner that, *if* fortune (*t*âli'h) may have befallen any one[8]

---

[1] B29 omits these eleven words.

[2] B29 adds 'in the Hôm-mortar.'

[3] B29 adds 'and utter.'

[4] See Mkh. XXVII, 70 n.

[5] Lp, B29 insert '*they are* to give.'

[6] Lp, B29 have 'come.'

[7] Lp, B29 have 'understood,' and another copy in B29 has 'considered.'

[8] Who has broken his promise.

happily, or an insufficient quantity of his life ('humr) may have remained, the Mihir-drug extends to his children without opposition ('*h*ilâf). 5. And every household that becomes extinct, or race whose issue fails, or *any of* the great misfortunes that happen to mankind—from which misfortune *one* obtains release with difficulty—may all be owing to the *fact* that they have committed a Mihir-drug.

6. If *committed by* oneself, it is declared, *in* one place in revelation, that the glorified Zaratust, the Spitamân, enquired of Hôrmazd, the good *and* propitious, thus: 'Of any of the sins that mankind commit which is the worst?' 7. Hôrmazd, the good *and* propitious, decreed thus: 'No sin whatever is worse than this, that two persons make a covenant with one another *in* such a manner that no one whatever is between them, except me who am Hôrmazd; *and*, afterwards one of those two persons deviates *from it*, and says, "I have no knowledge ('*h*abar) *of it*," and no one whatever is a witness, for that *other* person, except me.' 8. No sin whatever is worse than that, and that person himself *will* not go out of this world until retribution overtakes him, and in that *other* world his punishment is more severe than all; *so* that person becomes unfortunate *in* both worlds. 9. And it is the same *if* this covenant *be* with a righteous *person or* a wicked *one*.

CHAPTER XXVI.

1. The twenty-sixth subject is this, that the wise and the ancients say that when a man becomes fifteen years *of age* it is necessary that he takes

one of the angels[1] as his own protection[2], *that* he takes one of the wise as his own sage, and *that* he takes one of the high-priests and officiating priests as his own high-priest. 2. So that, if, any time, a bereavement (âstânah) approaches, he *may* beg a favour from the archangels[3], in order that it *may* furnish[4] an escape *from that* bereavement. 3. And[5], any time any affair comes forward, and *he has*[6] to have opinion (râî) *and* advice (masvarat), he holds a consultation with that sage, while the sage tells him *his* opinion (tadbîr). 4. And, if any *question as to* proper and improper comes forward, he speaks with that high-priest, so that he *may* tell him *in* reply.

5. When the instructions of these three persons are brought to pass, carrying *out* the commands of the sacred being is accomplished. 6. Especially the instructions of the high-priests, because their satisfaction is connected with the satisfaction of the sacred being; and the high-priests possess so much dignity (martabat) *in* the presence of the sacred being, the good *and* propitious, that they are quite able to forgive *any* trivial one of the sins of mankind[7], and Hôrmazd, the good *and* propitious, quickly[8] forgives that sin for the high-priest. 7.

[1] La, Lp have 'ancients,' but this seems inconsistent with § 2.

[2] La has 'ancestor,' having read ba-niyâh instead of panâh.

[3] Lp, B29, J15 add '*and* they *may* provide health of body and safety.'

[4] Lp, B29, J15 have 'that they *may* furnish him.'

[5] Lp, B29 insert 'if.'

[6] Lp, B29 have 'it is necessary.'

[7] B29 has 'to forgive one-third of the sins which mankind commit.'

[8] Lp has 'likewise.'

Therefore, carrying *out* the commands of the high-priests becomes[1] incumbent on every one; and the fulfilment of this maxim is *better* than *that of* a whole assemblage of maxims.

Chapter XXVII.

1. The twenty-seventh subject is this, that is, if any affair comes forward, that they *should* thoroughly understand[2] whether it be a good work, or a sin. 2. In that manner it becomes better that they make an evasion on the spot[3], until a time *when* they make *it* known with accuracy[4] that that affair is a sin or a reward. 3. If they perform any affair without knowing *this*, although it be a good work, it becomes a sin for them.

4. For it is declared in revelation, that, except that which they enquire of the high-priests, no affair whatever is proper to perform. 5. Whatever wisdom *there be* for any one from his own head is only one; then, *as* two wisdoms are more than one[5], it therefore makes *it* expedient to enquire of the high-priests.

Chapter XXVIII.

1. The twenty-eighth subject is this, that, when they teach the Avesta, it is *in* like manner neces-

[1] Lp, B29 have 'is.'

[2] Lp has 'that they *should* be told,' and B29 has 'that *one should* realise.'

[3] See Sls. X, 25, 27.

[4] Lp adds 'and truly,' and B29 has 'make known *that* it is false *or* true.'

[5] Lp, B29 omit these eight words.

sary that they teach *it* properly and truly, *and* recite *it* with deliberation and composure (sâkinî). 2. And it is necessary *for* those who are taught to recite *it* connectedly, and to keep *it* ever *in* remembrance.

3. For it is declared in revelation, that the sacred being *has* decreed thus: '*As to* every one who puts the Avesta away from *his* memory, I *will* put his soul as far from heaven as the width of the earth[1].' 4. And in the commentary of the Avesta it is related *that*, in former times, *as to* any one who had been taught the Avesta and had put *it* away from *his* memory, until the time he had again made *it* easy, they would have given him bread like that which they give to the dogs. 5. *And in* another place I have read that they would have given bread to him *on* the point of a spear.

Chapter XXIX.

1. The twenty-ninth subject is this, that, when they provide any munificence (sa'*h*âvat) *or* liberality, it is necessary that they provide *it for* the worthy; and *one is* to consider thus: 'Is this person, to whom I am giving this thing, worthy or not?'

2. Therefore it is necessary to make an effort, so that they *may* not give to the unworthy. 3. For in revelation, as regards[2] that person who provides any munificence for the unworthy, they call *it* a vain work *and* a gift without advantage; and day by day *it* is[3]

---

[1] Compare Chap. XCVIII, 3.

[2] Lp, B29 have 'for in the good religion it is declared.'

[3] Lp, B29 have 'it increases.'

the punishment *and* torment of that person. 4. And, whatever they give to the unworthy, they have made that thing extinct.

Chapter XXX.

1. The thirtieth subject is this, that it is not proper to pour *away* water at night, especially from the northern side (*g*ânib) which would be the worst[1]. 2. Therefore, if it become a necessity in the end (ba-'*k*atam)[2], it is requisite to recite one Yathâ-ahû-vairyô[3], and, *when* they make a light ready ('hâ*z*ir)[4], to pour *away* the water gently.

3. *In* like manner it is not proper to swallow water at night, because it is a sin. 4. *But*, if a necessity arises, it is necessary to make a light ready, and *one* first eats some morsels of food (*t*a'hâm) so that the sin may be less.

Chapter XXXI.

1. The thirty-first subject is this, that, every time they eat bread, it is necessary to withhold three morsels from their own bodies, and to give *them* to a dog. 2. And it is not desirable to beat a dog. 3. For, of the poor no one whatever is poorer than

[1] Lp has 'side it would be,' to which B29 adds 'bold.' The reason of the impropriety is that the demons are supposed to come from the north, and anything thrown out northwards might be of use to them (see Sls. X, 7, XII, 18, 19).

[2] B29 has 'necessity to pour.' [3] See Mkh. XXVII, 70 n.

[4] Lp, B29 omit these seven words. Both the recitation and light are supposed to frighten away any demons.

a dog, *and* it is necessary to give a tethered *animal* bread, because the good work is great.

4. And in revelation it is declared in this manner, that, if a dog is asleep upon the road, it is not proper that they put a foot violently on the ground, so that he becomes awake. 5. And, in former times, an allowance (râtib) of bread would have been made every day for the sake of the dogs, three times in summer *and* twice in winter, on this account, that *one* wishes *them* to come to the assistance of his soul at the *K*inva*d* bridge.

6. In the worldly *existence* they are the guard of men and cattle. 7. If *there* had not been a dog they would not have been able to keep a single sheep. 8. Every time that he barks, just as his bark goes forth, the demons and fiends run away from the place.

Chapter XXXII.

1. The thirty-second subject is this, that, when a hen utters a crow in a house, or the cock crows unseasonably, it is desirable that they do not kill it[1], and do not consider *it* a bad habit (fa'hl). 2. Because it is uttering that crow *for* the reason that a fiend has found a way into that house, and the hen or the cock, *alone*, does not possess the power (*t*âqat) that *would* keep the fiend away from that house, and the hen is going to give the cock assistance, and utters the crow. 3. Therefore, if any time the chance (ittifâq) happens in that manner, it is requisite to bring another cock, so that they

[1] See Sls. X, 30.

may drive away that fiend through the assistance of one another. 4. And if a cock crows unseasonably it is likewise not desirable to kill *it*, because the reason may be this which I have stated.

5. For it is declared in the good religion, that there is a fiend whom they call Sê*g*[1], *and*, in every house *where* an infant exists, that *fiend* strives that she *may* cause some misfortune to come upon that house. 6. *So* it is necessary that they *should* keep a cock *on* the watch for her, so that it *may* smite that fiend and force *her* to the road *away* from that house.

Chapter XXXIII.

1. The thirty-third subject is this, that, when *there* is a place and any risk *or* fear exists that a corpse[2] is concealed beneath the ground, *one is* to make *it* apparent *and* visible[3], because it is a great good work.

2. For it is declared in the good religion, that, *when* they conceal a corpse beneath the ground, Spendârma*d*[4], the archangel, shudders; it is just as severe as a serpent *or* scorpion would be to any one in private sleep[5], and i is also just like that to the ground. 3. When thou makest a corpse

---

[1] Av. ithyê*g*ô, Pers. sî*k*. In Pahl. Vend. XIX, 4, 6 she is said to be 'a secret-moving deceiver;' in Bd. XXVIII, 26 she is said to 'cause annihilation.'

[2] Or 'dead matter.'

[3] B29 has 'it is necessary to make *it* apparent.'

[4] Av. spe*n*ta ârmaiti, 'bountiful devotion,' the female archangel who is supposed to have special charge of the earth (see Sls. XV, 20–24).

[5] B29 has 'in a sleeping garment.'

beneath the ground as *it were* apparent, thou makest *the ground* liberated from that affliction.

CHAPTER XXXIV.

1. The thirty-fourth subject is this, that it is greatly necessary to refrain from much slaughter of animals and the cattle species[1]. 2. Because it says in revelation[2] that, *for* every one who slaughters many animals *and* cattle[3], every fibre of the hair of a goat becomes, in that *other* world, like a sharp sword, *and* adheres in the soul of that person.

3. And there are several things the slaughter of which is very bad, and the sin very abundant, *as* the lamb, the kid, the ploughing ox, the war horse, the swallow bird that catches the locust, and the cock; and of the whole of these the sin is most *as regards* the cock. 4. If it becomes a necessity[4], it is proper to kill a cock *that* does not crow[5], and it is necessary to consecrate their heads. 5. Any head of an animal, not consecrated, it is not desirable to eat, so that it becomes so far[6] a righteous gift. 6. If *one* be not able to consecrate the head, it is requisite to consecrate one kidney *as* a substitute (badal) for it.

---

[1] Lp, B29, J15 omit 'species.'

[2] In the Stûdgar Nask (see Sls. X, 8, 9).

[3] Lp has 'slaughters much.'

[4] Lp, B29 have 'if it becomes inevitable.'

[5] Lp has 'that has not crowed.'

[6] Lp, B29 have 'when it is not *along* with.'

Chapter XXXV.

1. The thirty-fifth subject is this, that, when they wish to wash the face[1], they *should* recite one Ashem-vohû[2], *and* set the mouth firmly closed, so that the water, not staying *away* from it[3], *shall* not go into the mouth. 2. *And*, as *one* washes over the face, they *should* recite the Kem-nâ-mazdâ[4], so that the fiend Nasrust[5] *may* become smitten.

Chapter XXXVI.

1. The thirty-sixth subject is this, that it is strictly incumbent on mankind, on man[6] and woman, to perform the Bareshnûm *ceremony*[7], because mankind feed on menstruous *matter* in the womb of the mother. 2. For that reason it is necessary to perform the Bareshnûm once, so that *one may* become pure from that pollution. 3. For if *one* becomes fifteen years *of age*, and does not perform the Bareshnûm, whatever he puts a hand on, the glory and purity of that thing will diminish; and it

---

[1] Compare Chaps. L, LXXIV.
[2] See Chap. VII, 1 n.
[3] B29 omits these five words.
[4] A stanza of the Ustavaiti Gâtha (Yas. XLV, 7) beginning with those three words (see SBE, vol. xviii, p. 443).
[5] Or nisrûst, 'contamination' (see Sls. X, 32); probably the same as the demon Nas or Nasu (see Bd. XXVIII, 29). Also mentioned in Chap. XXXVI, 7.
[6] B29 omits 'on man.'
[7] A tedious ceremony of purification that lasts nine nights (see SBE, vol. xviii, pp. 431–453). Its name is Av. (acc.) bareshnûm, 'top' of the head, the first part of the body to be washed.

is not proper that they put a hand on a sacred cake *or* any *thing* washed *with ceremony*.

4. In revelation it says, if any one *who has* not performed the Bareshnûm shall die, the demons make *him*[1] as though *he were* a corpse *kept* one month in the hot season. 5. And, when the soul arrives at the head of the *K*inva*d* bridge, the archangels and angels complain of the stench of that soul, *and* are not able to make *up* its account and reckoning. 6. It remains at the *K*inva*d* bridge *and* is not able to pass; it experiences much repentance and has no advantage from it.

7. If it be necessary for any one to perform the Bareshnûm of the head, and he be able to do *it*, *but* does not do *it*, if he performs the *ceremonial* ablution of the head a thousand times, it does not become pure from that pollution[2], and that is the pollution of Nasru*s*t[3], which is amid the veins and sinews, and the flesh and bones; it does not become pure *through* any other thing except through *the liquid consecrated by* the religious formula[4].

8. And *as to* that person, also, who performs the Bareshnûm *for* mankind[5], it is necessary that he be a man, a friend of the soul, a truthful speaker, *and* an abstainer, because through chastity and modesty (mastûrî) he becomes employed. 9. If complaint of any perfidy in him is publicly diffused[6], in that disgrace (malâmat) it is necessary that the high-priests

[1] B29 has 'it makes his soul.'

[2] Lp omits 'pollution.'

[3] See Chap. XXXV, 2. B29 has 'that is bodily refuse (hî'har) and pollution.'

[4] That is, bull's urine, the liquid that is first used, in a consecrated state, for sprinkling the body in the Bareshnûm purification. Compare Chap. LXXVII, 9, 10.

[5] That is, the purifying priest.

[6] B29 has 'publicly comes *on*.'

should dislocate his joints one by one, and it is requisite that they give him as food to the dogs. 10. So that by this action they *may* make a man observe more chastely and continently, that this result ('hâsil) of sin *may* not occur.

Chapter XXXVII.

1. The thirty-seventh subject is this, that, when *the days of* the guardian spirits[1] come on, it is necessary that all persons, among their own food and devotion, *should* order *and* provide the sacred cakes and ceremonial, the sacred feast and benedictions (âfrîngân). 2. *For* these ten days it is incumbent on every one; *and* those are better which they prepare in their own houses, because the souls[2] go every one to its own house. 3. And they *should* have an ear for them[3], so that they *may* prepare the sacred cakes and feast and benedictions.

4. Those ten days any one of all the souls—*that* are in this *way*[4] in every house where they provide the feast more abundantly—proclaims, as to that master of the house[5], that family, and the whole who are in that house, and the year's affairs of every kind, *that* they are very good, and their entry (da'*h*l) and coming in are very good. 5. And every single

---

[1] See Mkh. LVII, 13 n.

[2] Which are supposed to revisit the earth during those days.

[3] Or 'for these *words*,' as the Gugarâti translator assumes.

[4] Lp, B29 have 'those ten days all the souls are in this worldly *existence*.'

[5] Lp omits these five words, and B29 adds 'the mistress of the house.'

good work, on account of which we have spoken of the souls of the departed, becomes just like those we have done for our own souls. 6. And, when they pass away from this worldly *existence*, those souls come again, meeting them, and cause gladness, maintain[1] their courage, and also render *them* honour in the presence of the creator Hôrmazd, and speak *thus*: '*These* righteous souls did not put us away from remembrance while they were in the world, *and* we have been satisfied with them; now we are unanimous that thou *shouldest* provide them equal shares of those good works of ours, *and* make their souls attain to the position of the righteous.' 7. They utter these words, and give those souls confidence, while they make out their account. 8. Afterwards, with them, they make the passage of the *K*inva*d* bridge, till they arrive at their own position, *and* then they return.

9. Therefore it is necessary to make an effort, so that they *may* maintain the guardian spirits properly, and the souls of *their* fathers and mothers and relations *may* exist with honour from them. 10. For if they retire with dissatisfaction they utter a curse, *and*, as the soul departs from this world, they administer reproaches to it, and speak *thus*: 'Thou thinkest that they wish continually to make a way[2] for thee *to* that place, *but* it is not necessary for thee to come into this world[3]. 11. Now, hadst thou performed duty *and* good works on our behalf, and hadst thou recollected us, we would also have come to thy assistance, and would have released thee from

---

[1] Lp, B29 have 'restore.' [2] Lp, B29 have 'an escape.'
[3] That is, into heaven. Compare Chap. XIII, 6, 8.

this fearful position.' 12. And that *soul* experiences much repentance, and has no advantage whatever *from it*.

Chapter XXXVIII.

1. The thirty-eighth subject is this, that, so far as effort and endeavour prevail[1], it is requisite to abstain from the same cup as those of a different religion, and it is not desirable to drink the water of any goblet of theirs. 2. And if the goblet be of copper or of tin[2], it is requisite[3] to wash *it* with[4] water, so that it *may* be proper to drink the water[5]. 3. If the goblet be of earthenware *or* wooden, it is altogether improper[6].

4. Because, when[7] any one drinks with a stranger, it makes *his* heart inclined (maîl) towards him, for it would be a sin; and, on account of the sin committed, he becomes bold, and *his* soul has an inclination for wickedness.

---

[1] Lp has 'are necessary,' and B29 has merely 'with the endeavour necessary.'

[2] B29 has 'of metal.'

[3] Lp inserts 'to expose *it* to fire, to polish *it* with ashes, *and* afterwards;' J15 inserts 'to polish *it* with fire, and, afterwards.'

[4] B29, J15 insert '*ceremonial* ablution and.'

[5] Lp, J15 add 'if the cup or goblet be of copper or of brass, *one* makes the water *that is* drunk likewise pure in this *manner*; if it be earthen *or* wooden, *one* puts *it* far *away* from the house, *or* they present *it* to *one of* a different religion; just like that *one* performs the *ceremonial* ablution of *what is* altogether polluted.' (J15 has '*what is* polluted like a metal *one*.')

[6] J15 adds 'to drink.'

[7] Lp, B29, J15 have 'every time that.'

CHAPTER XXXIX.

1. The thirty-ninth subject is this, that it is necessary to properly maintain the sacred fire[1] which they have established in a town or village. 2. And *at* night it is necessary to make *it* blaze up once, and by day twice.

3. For it is declared in revelation, that, if *there* had been no sacred fire, no one would have been able to go from town to town; because it is *owing to* the glory of the sacred fire that no one on the roads is able to commit an excess upon any one *else*.

4. It is necessary that they *should* present the whole of the firewood; and, *as to* the person who makes *it* blaze, they *should* give him bread and a salary (nafaqah). 5. For, every time that that fire is satisfied, and they maintain *it* properly, every fire that may exist in the earth of seven regions becomes satisfied with that person.

CHAPTER XL.

1. The fortieth subject is this, that it is not desirable to distress *one's* priest, *or* father, *or* mother; and, if *people* perceive much trouble, disquietude, and harm *arising* from them, it is certainly not desirable that they *should* give them back a reply with any aggravation. 2. Because their satisfaction is connected with the satisfaction of the sacred being, *and* every time that *people* distress them they have

---

[1] Literally 'the fire of Bahirâm.' Compare Chap. XCII.

distressed Hôrmazd, the good *and* propitious. 3. It is not possible *for* any duty *or* good work to extend to the spiritual *existences* while *one* does not make those *guardians* satisfied, and it is not possible (mumkin) that any one *should* repay these three persons all *their* dues.

4. In the commentary of the Hâdôkht *Nask* it says:—Mâ âzârayôis, Zarathustra! mâ Pourushaspem, mâ Dughdhôvãm, mâ aêthrapaitis[1], 'it is not desirable that thou, O Zaratust! *shouldest* distress *thy* father, *or* mother, *or* priest.'

5. Therefore, three times every day it is indispensable *for one* to fold *his* arms[2] in the presence of these three persons, *and* to say:—'What is your will (murâd)? So that I *may* think and speak and do it. 6. If *what* was not proper has come from me of itself, it is necessary that you make a righteous gift on our behalf.'

Chapter XLI.

1. The forty-first subject is this, that it is greatly requisite to avoid a menstruous woman, while they give *her* bread and food moderately. 2. As soon as

---

[1] This Avesta passage is not known to be extant elsewhere, and its orthography has been corrected in accordance with the translation attached to it by the author of Sd. In La, Lp, J15 the first two names are in the genitive, and the third is accusative; B29 differs by putting the third name also in the genitive; the last word being accusative in all. Pourushaspa and Dughdhôva (?) were the names of the father and mother of Zarathustra, and the latter name has not previously been found in the Avesta texts, but is known only from Pahlavi and Persian writings.

[2] That is, to stand in an attitude of obedient reverence.

she is not able to eat[1] they *should* not give *her* more, and *in* the same manner *as regards* water, on this account, that whatever remnant comes from that menstruous *woman* does not come to any use[2].

3. When they wish to provide[3] bread they put the hand into the sleeve, or they place something on the top of the sleeve, *and* it is necessary that her bare hand *should* not come *forth* again in any place. 4. Because every drop of water that trickles on to a limb of a menstruous woman becomes a sin of three hundred stîrs[4]. 5. And it is requisite *for* a menstruous woman to avoid everything that is washed *with* ceremony by fifteen steps. 6. It is *also* necessary *for her* to be *at least* three steps distant from a righteous man, and on whatever her eye casts a look it diminishes the glory[5] of that thing.

7. And on every woman the twelve ceremonials[6], *atoning for* the offence of menstruation, are incumbent. 8. One on account of the offence that has occurred as regards the spiritual *existence*[7]. 9. The second on account of the offence that has occurred

---

[1] That is, as soon as her hunger is satisfied.

[2] Lp, B29 have 'it is not possible to make of any use.'

[3] Lp, B29 have 'bring.'

[4] The amount of a Tanâvar or Tanâpûhar sin (see Sls. I, 2).

[5] Lp, B29 add 'and purity.'

[6] These resemble the celebration of the Hômâst, but are shorter and less onerous. The Hômâst consists of a Yasna each day for 144 days in honour of twelve angels, each angel being reverenced for twelve successive days. The angels are nearly the same as stated in the text, but the celebration of the Hômâst is twelve times as long. The cost of this latter is said to be 350 rupis (see Byt. II, 59 n). Occasionally a still more onerous celebration is said to be incumbent on such women as can afford it (see Chap. LXVI).

[7] Lp has 'the spirits,' and B29 has 'mankind.'

as regards the stars[1]. 10. The third on account of that which[2] has occurred as regards the sun. 11. The fourth on account of that which has occurred as regards the moon. 12. The fifth on account of that which has occurred as regards the spirit of fire. 13. The sixth on account of that which has occurred as regards the spirit of water. 14. The seventh on account of that which has occurred as regards the spirit of earth. 15. The eighth on account of that which has occurred as regards the spirit of the wind. 16. The ninth on account of that which has occurred as regards Khurdâ*d*[3]. 17. The tenth on account of the offence that has occurred as regards Ameredâ*d*[3]. 18. The eleventh on account of the offence that has occurred as regards meal-time ('*h*urdak gâh)[4]. 19. The twelfth on account of the offence that has occurred as regards bodily refuse *and* dead matter. 20. Therefore it is incumbent on every one *in* this manner[5]; if any one be more opulent eighteen *ceremonials* are indispensable, and if she has silver in excess (ba-*gh*âyat) *there should be* twenty-one, *and in* one place I have read that twenty-four are indispensable; but, for lesser people, this that I have noted is necessary.

21. That which they provide in *their* lifetime is better[6]; *and*, just as would occur when any one

[1] B29 has 'the rain.'

[2] Lp, B29 use the same form of words in §§ 10–16 as in §§ 8, 9.

[3] See Mkh. II, 34.

[4] Doubtful, and not understood by the Gugarâti translator.

[5] Lp, B29 have 'thus much.'

[6] The author evidently implies, by this paragraph, that the celebration of these ceremonials was only occasional, perhaps once in a lifetime, but the earlier the better, so as to admit of a larger growth of merit before death.

plants a tree anew, *and* is eating the fruit of it every year, even so much is that good work increasing every year. 22. If she shall live ten years, *or* if a hundred years, even so long it is becoming every year much more[1]. 23. If they provide *it* after her *lifetime*, that which would be the increase departs; and in *her* lifetime, also, that occurs which every one, who *has* done a duty on his own account, has seen, that *the thing* itself *which others* accomplish after his *lifetime* is very different; so that she *should* provide *it* with her own hands, not after her decease (vafât).

CHAPTER XLII.

1. The forty-second subject is this, that it is necessary to practise strict abstinence *from* that sin *which affects* accusers[2]. 2. That would be when any one slanders (buhtânad)[3], or any one commits a rape on the wife of some one[4], or causes a woman *to occupy* a separate bed from her own husband.

3. These are sins *for* which there is no retribution, except when thou beggest forgiveness of that person whom thy sin has assailed. 4. Afterwards, they keep back the soul, *at* the *K*invad bridge, till the time when its antagonist arrives and exacts justice from it; then it obtains release.

5. Every time that any one applies a falsehood or a slander to some person, so that *people* are after-

[1] Lp, B29 have 'it is proceeding every year to a head.'

[2] Any sin that injures another party who, thereupon, becomes an accuser and must be satisfied, by atonement, before the sin can be expiated (see Sls. VIII, 1 n).

[3] Lp, B29 have 'applies falsehood and slander to any one.'

[4] See Chap. LXIII, 11. Lp omits these twelve words.

wards telling that falsehood again, and it vexes the heart of that person, they are bringing punishment ever anew on the soul of that *former* one. 6. The sin does not depart through *the performance of* duties and good works, so long as he does not make *his* antagonist satisfied.

7. This is a grave sin, *and* it is requisite to be careful that they do not commit *it*.

Chapter XLIII.

1. The forty-third subject is this, that it is necessary to make an endeavour to kill noxious creatures *and* reptiles ('hasarât) of the earth; because, in revelation[1], it is put *forth as* a great good work.

2. Especially these five things:—One is the frog in the water, the second is the snake and scorpion, the third is the ant (markis)[2] that flies, the fourth is the *common* ant (môrkah), and the fifth is the mouse. 3. Therefore[3], every time that they bring a frog up, out of the water, and make *it* dry, and, after (ba'hd) that, kill it, it is a good work of a thousand *and* two hundred dirhams *in* weight[4]. 4. And every time that they kill a snake, and recite the Avesta that is *appointed* for that *occasion*[5], it is

---

[1] See Vend. XIV, 9–17, XVIII, 144–146.

[2] If markis were Pahlavi, it would mean 'the deadly thing.' Possibly 'the locust' (mala'h) is meant, but the description in § 6 is rather perplexing.

[3] Lp omits 'therefore,' and B29 has 'and.'

[4] See Chap. XII, 9 n. The frog is considered noxious because it is supposed to injure the water, being generally found in stagnant pools which are unwholesome.

[5] An Avesta passage of about thirty words, to be used on such occasions, is to be found in the Rivâyats, but is still unedited.

just as though they have slain an apostate (âshmôgh). 5. *For* every one who kills a *flying* ant (markis) it is as much good work as *for* any one who is reciting *inward* prayer *for* ten days. 6. Among the creatures of Aharman nothing whatever is more harmful than this; for, if it dies in the air (havâ) it becomes a gnat, if it dies in the dust it becomes a worm, if it dies in the water it becomes a leech[1], if it dies among the excavators of flesh it becomes a venomous snake (mâr-i af'hai), and if it dies in dung it becomes creeping *things*. 7. *For* every one who kills a corn-dragging ant it is as much good work as *for* any one *who* recites the Hôrmazd Yast. 8. And *for* every one who kills many noxious creatures it is as much good work as *for* a priest who performs the ceremonial of the sacred beings; both good works are equal. 9. *For* every one who kills a mouse it is as much good work as *if* four lions are killed[2]. 10. Therefore, it is incumbent on every one to make an effort to kill a noxious creature.

CHAPTER XLIV.

1. The forty-fourth subject is this, that it is not desirable *for* those of the good religion, so far as they are able to manage *it*, to put a bare foot upon the ground[3], because it is a sin, *and* injury[4] occurs to Spendârmad[5], the archangel. 2. And they call that the sin of running *about* uncovered.

[1] B29 has 'hedgehog.'

[2] Ants and mice (or rats) are considered noxious on account of the damage they do to certain crops and farmers' stores.

[3] See Sls. X, 12.

[4] Lp has only 'because injury.'

[5] See Chap. XXXIII, 2 n.

CHAPTER XLV.

1. The forty-fifth subject is this, that it is continually necessary that *people should* keep in remembrance the accomplishment of repentance (taûbat). 2. Every time that a sin leaps from control it is necessary to act so that they go before the priests, high-priests, and *spiritual* chiefs, and accomplish repentance.

3. And[1] in accordance with the sin *should be* the good work, just as though the good work *were* due to that occasion when they accomplish *it*. 4. While mankind are living, it becomes every year a further benefit. 5. Sin is also, *in* like manner, going *on* to a head every year; and when they accomplish repentance, so that it *may* not increase further, it is just like a tree that becomes withered, and they extirpate its further growth.

6. And that repentance is better which they accomplish before high-priests and *spiritual* chiefs, and when they accomplish the retribution that the high-priest orders every sin that exists departs from them. 7. The repentance *that* high-priests accomplish they likewise call repentance[2]. 8. If *there* be no high-priest it is necessary to go before some persons who are commissioned *by* high-priests; and if those, also, do not exist, it is necessary to go to a man *who is* a friend of the soul, *and* to accomplish the repentance.

---

[1] Lp, B29 have 'for.'

[2] Here and throughout the rest of the chapter B29 has patit, 'renunciation *of sin*,' instead of taûbat. The outward form of repentance consists of the recitation of the patit, in which all imaginable sins are mentioned and renounced.

9. At the time when *one* shall depart from the world it is incumbent on sons and daughters and relations, that they give repentance into the mouth of the afflicted *one, and that* they give the Ashem-vohû[1] into *his* mouth. 10. For the high-priests have said that, when they have accomplished repentance because they have committed many sins, they do not arrive in hell, *but* they administer punishment *to them* at the head of the *K*invad bridge, and afterwards conduct *them* to their own place.

11. Repentance is that when they accomplish repentance of the sin which they have committed, and do not commit that sin a second *time;* if they do commit *it*, that *first sin* then comes back[2].

CHAPTER XLVI.

1. The forty-sixth subject is this, that, when people become fourteen years *of age*, it is necessary to tie on the *sacred thread*-girdle[3], because the high-priests have said that it is likewise necessary to take into account those nine months that they have been in the womb of the mother.

2. For in our religion there is no duty better than wearing the *sacred thread*-girdle, and it is incumbent

[1] See Chap. VII, 1 n.

[2] That is, repentance is not a mere penance, but requires a change of will, a veritable renunciation of that sin for the future; otherwise it is useless.

[3] See Chap. X, which mentions fifteen years in accordance with Vend. XVIII, 115, 120. But Sls. X, 13 recommends fourteen years and three months as more prudent, no doubt for the reason stated here in the text.

on man and woman. 3. And, in former days, if any one should have become completely fifteen years *of age*, and should not have worn the *sacred thread*-girdle, they would have done for him by stoning, as bread and water are forbidden ('harâm) for him.

Chapter XLVII.

1. The forty-seventh subject is this, that, when a child of seven years shall die, an order is necessary *that* it is requisite to perform a ceremony (yast) *for* Srôsh[1] on account of it, *and* to consecrate the sacred cake of the fourth night[2].

2. For it says in revelation that the souls of children go with the souls of *their* fathers and mothers; if the father is *fit* for heaven *the child* goes to heaven with him, if he be *fit* for hell it arrives in hell; if the mother be *fit* for heaven it reaches heaven with her, if she be *fit* for hell it reaches hell with her[3].

3. Therefore, every time that they accomplish the ceremony *for* Srôsh, the soul of that child becomes separated from the souls of *its* father and mother, and goes to heaven, and is imploring intercession (sifâ'hat) for *its* father and mother in the presence of the sacred beings in that *other* world.

---

[1] See Mkh. II, 115 n.

[2] That is, most of the ceremonies requisite after the death of an adult, as detailed in Chap. LXXXVII, are also to be performed in this case, for the reason here given.

[3] Lp omits these twenty-three words.

CHAPTER XLVIII[1].

1. The forty-eighth subject is this, that, when they boil a cooking-pot, it is necessary to make the water two parts of one-third *each*, that one-third of the pot may be empty; so that, if *at* any time the pot shall boil, *the water* shall not go to the top[2]. 2. For if they do not act so, and the[3] water, owing to not stopping, goes into the fire[4], it is a sin of a thousand and two hundred dirhams *in* weight[5]; therefore it is necessary to keep watch that this sin does not arise.

CHAPTER XLIX[6].

1. The forty-ninth subject is this, that, when *one*

---

[1] There is some confusion in the MSS. as to the arrangement of a few of the following chapters. The order here adopted is that of B29, J15, which is here in accordance with the metrical MSS., although Chaps. 48–56 are numbered 52–60 in the latter, owing to variations in the earlier part of the work. In La Chaps. 48–50 have been originally omitted, but part of 48, prefixed to a portion of 50, has been afterwards inserted in the margin, and Chap. 49 has been similarly added after the last chapter in the book. In Lp the chapters are arranged as follows:—48, 51–53, 49, 54, 56, while 50, 55 are omitted.

[2] Lp, B29, J15 add '*and* the water not go into the fire.' La, Lp add '*at* least one-third *should be* water [*in* such a manner that it becomes wet from ear to ear. It is necessary to keep the mouth continually closed, so that the water *shall* not go into the mouth],' but the passage in brackets is clearly a portion of Chap. L, 2, 3; it was originally written also in J15, but has been struck out of that MS.

[3] La has 'if a drop of.'

[4] La has 'mouth;' the passage in that MS. being evidently the end of Chap. L, 3.

[5] La has 'of three hundred stîrs,' as in Chap. L, 3, and omits the rest of the text. The two amounts are identical, and are equivalent to a Tanâvar or Tanâpûhar sin (see Sls. I, 2).

[6] Inserted in La after the last chapter in the book, and numbered C. In Lp it is numbered LII.

gathers up a fire, it is requisite to leave *it for* a time, so that the ash-bed (bûm) of the fire *may* become cold; afterwards, *one is* to take *it* up and carry *it* to the precinct of fire. 2. It is not proper that they carry the ash-bed (zamîn) of a hot fire to the precinct of fire; so far is notorious.

Chapter L[1].

1. The fiftieth subject is this, that, every day *at* dawn, when they rise up from sleep, it is not proper to wash the hands first with water.

2. The *ceremonial* ablution is to wash the hands, face, nose, eyes, and feet thoroughly, either with fruit (mîvah)[2] or some grass upon which no water has come; afterwards, to make *them* dry, *and* to wash *them* three times with water *in* such a manner that it becomes wet from the face as far as the ear[3]. 3. It is necessary to keep the mouth closed, so that the water *shall* not go into the mouth; for if a drop, owing to not stopping, goes into the mouth, it is a sin of three hundred stîrs[4]. 4. Afterwards, *one is* to wash the hands three times with water, as far as the *upper* arms; first the right hand, *and* afterwards the left hand; and, *in* like manner, *he is* to wash the right foot and left foot.

---

[1] Omitted in La, Lp, though the former contains a portion of this chapter annexed to part of Chap. XLVIII, and most of its contents are repeated, in other words, in Chap. LXXIV.

[2] Perhaps mîvah may be taken as an adjective from mîv, 'hair;' in which case we should have 'with *something* either hairy or grassy.' According to the long-metre Sad Dar, the liquid to be used for this first wetting is either goat's or bull's urine.

[3] La has 'from ear to ear' (see Chap. XLVIII, 1 n).

[4] A Tanâvar or Tanâpûhar sin (see Sls. I, 2).

5. Then they recite the Kem-nâ-mazdâ[1], for, every time that they wish to recite anything as an *inward* prayer, it is necessary that the hands be washed with *ceremonial* ablution[2], and, if *they are* not, the Avesta is not accepted, and the fiend of corruption (nasus) does not rush *away*, *and* it becomes a Tanâvar sin.

Chapter LI.

1. The fifty-first subject is this, that it is incumbent on every one to send a child to school, and to teach *it* something. 2. Because every duty and good work that a child performs is just as though the father and mother had performed *it* with their own hands. 3. Therefore it is necessary to make an effort, so that they *may* teach them something good, and make *them* aware of good works and sin; for they are doing that on account of their own souls, so that those *children may* be courageous in doing good works.

4[3]. If they are not taught, they then perform less duty *and* good works, *and* less reaches the souls of the father and mother. 5. And it also happens that if they do not deliver children to school, and do not teach *them* anything, and they become bold in committing sin, that sin[4] becomes *fixed* on the necks of the father and mother.

6. Therefore they have decided rightly who[5] teach

---

[1] See Chap. XXXV, 2 n, which chapter, as well as Chap. LXXIV, treats of nearly the same subject.

[2] As described in §§ 2–4.

[3] Lp, B29 insert 'because.'

[4] B29 has 'that commission of sin.'

[5] B29 has 'rightly for the children, *at* the time when they.'

them something, especially *what* is proper and improper according to revelation; because the chief principle is this, whether, through the duty of this world, a good *or* bad result is coming hereafter.

CHAPTER LII.

1. The fifty-second subject is this, that it is incumbent on every one that, every year *when* the month Fravardîn comes on, *he is* to provide a sacred cake *on* the day Khurdâ*d*[1], and whatever they are able to bring to hand, *a little* of everything, *they are* to place by that sacred cake, and to consecrate *it* with the dedicatory *formula* Ayaranãm*k*a[2], so that

---

[1] That is, on the sixth day of the first month of the Parsi year, a day which is called Khurdâ*d*-sâl and kept sacred, because it is said to be the anniversary of many remarkable events, of which the following are mentioned in a Pahlavi tract that is also translated in the Persian Rivâyats (B29, fol. 401):—On that day worldly life was created, Gâyômar*d* came into the world and slew Arezûr, Mashya and Mashyôî grew up from the ground, Hôshâng appeared, Takhmôrup made Aharman his steed, Yim made the world free from death and decay, brought on a truce (? pa*d*mânak) with hell, and established depositories for the dead and new year's day, Frê*d*ûn divided the world between his three sons, Mânû*sk*îhar slew two of them, and rescued the world from Frâsyâk, Sâm the Narîmânian slew the demon Gandarêpak (?), Kaî-Khûsrôî slew Frâsyâk and went to heaven, leaving the sovereignty to Lôrâsp, Zaratû*s*t came to converse with Aûha*r*ma*z*d and received the religion from him, Kaî-Vi*s*tâsp accepted the religion, eighteen things come in eighteen years to Khûsrô son of Aûha*r*ma*z*d, Vâhrâm the Var*g*âvand comes from the Hindûs, Pêshyôtanû, son of Vi*s*tâsp, comes from Kangde*z*, Hûshê*d*ar comes to converse with Aûha*r*ma*z*d, Sâm slays A*z*-î Dahâk and rules till Kaî-Khûsrôî reappears to reign for fifty-seven years, with Sôshâns as supreme high-priest, after which Kaî-Vi*s*tâsp resumes the sovereignty, and Zaratû*s*t the priestship, and the resurrection takes place on the same day of the year.

[2] Corrected from airyanãm*k*a in all MSS. See Âf. I, 1 as far as saredhanãm*k*a, then gâthâbyô, &c. (Âf. II, 1).

the affairs of that year may be better through that day's provision and the entry and coming in *of guests*.

2. For it is declared in revelation[1], that, every year, when the day Khurdâ*d* of the month Fravardîn comes on, they allot a daily provision *for* mankind, and whatever *one* wishes to pass to the lot of mankind in that year they write down that day. 3. Therefore, when they shall consecrate this sacred cake, the archangel Khurdâ*d*[2] is making intercession for that person.

Chapter LIII.

1. The fifty-third subject is this, that, when, in former[3] times, any one wished to go on a journey (safar) that might have been at least[4] twelve leagues (parasang), they would have consecrated a sacred cake, so that no affliction might happen in that journey, and affairs might be according to *their* wish, and employments (sug*h*l)[5] cheerful. 2. And it is *still* incumbent on every one that, when they wish to go on a journey, *they are* to consecrate this sacred cake.

3. *And*, while the person is on the journey, he *should* order the consecration of this sacred cake, in his house, every Bahirâm day[6], so that that person *may* arrive in safety (salâmat) at *his* house. 4.

---

[1] B29 has 'in the good religion.'
[2] See Horvada*d* (Mkh. II, 34).
[3] La, Lp omit 'former.'
[4] B29 has 'less than.'
[5] Lp, B29 insert 'might become.'
[6] The twentieth day of the Parsi month.

The dedicatory formula is this—Amahê hutâstahê[1] —*and* is known to the priest himself.

Chapter LIV.

1. The fifty-fourth subject is this, that if any one has a serving wife[2], *and* if the acquisition of a male child results[3] from her, it is suitable for adoption *by* that person[4], and the bridge[5] is not severed *for* that person. 2. *But* if it be a female *child* it is necessary that the man *should* not be negligent (ghâfil) in appointing an adopted son for his own sake. 3. He *should* himself appoint a son of some relation, *who is* a friend of the soul, so that the bridge may not be severed *for* his soul.

Chapter LV[6].

1. The fifty-fifth subject is this, that when a Navazûd[7] *ceremony* is performed, and it happens that it is not possible to consecrate a sacred cake, it is necessary that *one should* eat bread with the Hôrmazd *inward* prayer; *and*, afterwards, he *should*

[1] The dedication to the angel Bahirâm, which begins with these words (see Sîr. I, 20).

[2] A childless widow who has married again, and half of whose children, by her second husband, belong to her first one, to whom she also belongs in the other world (see Bd. XXXII, 6 n).

[3] B29 has 'if a male child be born.'

[4] The child being considered to belong to its mother's first husband, can be only an adopted son of her second husband.

[5] The Kinvad bridge, which is the passage to heaven.

[6] Lp omits this chapter.

[7] See Chap. V, 1 n.

complete the prayer just as when they complete *it* as regards the sacred cake, so that the sin *may* be less.

CHAPTER LVI.

1. The fifty-sixth subject is this, that, when any one wishes to make an evacuation of water, it is necessary that he *should* not make the evacuation of water *while standing* on *his* feet. 2. Because, in the commentary of the Vendîdâ*d*[1], it is said, concerning that, *that it is* a serious sin.

3. When they squat for evacuating water it is necessary that *it extend only*[2] from the heel as far as the end of the toes; for, if it be more, every drop is a Tanâvar sin. 4. And, when they wish to squat for the evacuation of water, *they are* to utter one Yathâ-ahû-vairyô[3]; *and*, when the action is over, *they are* to recite the Ashem-vohû[4] three times, the Humatanãm[5] twice, the Hukhshathrôtemâi[6] three times, the Yathâ-ahû-vairyô four *times*, and the Ahunem-vairîm[7] to the end. 5. Because, every time that they act like this, they are pleasant in the eyes and hearts of mankind, and their words are more approved *in* the vicinity of kings.

---

[1] Pahl. Vend. XVIII, 98.

[2] Lp, B29 have 'that they do not make the evacuation of water more *than*.'

[3] See Mkh. XXVII, 70 n.

[4] See Chap. VII, 1 n. The recitation of this and the four following formulas is commanded in Vend. XVIII, 97.

[5] Yas. XXXV, 4–6.

[6] Yas. XXXV, 13–15.

[7] Yas. XIV, end.

Chapter LVII.

1. The fifty-seventh subject is this, that it is not proper to kill a hedgehog; and, everywhere that they see *it*, it is necessary to take *it* up and carry *it* into the wilderness (sa'hrâ), so that it *may* go into a hole, which is ever considered a great good work. 2. Because, when a hedgehog is in *their* nest[1], some ants will die; it will *also* catch and eat thousands of snakes and[2] other harmful *creatures*, and it eats all noxious creatures. 3. Therefore, owing to the whole *of this*, these words are expedient.

Chapter LVIII.

1. The fifty-eighth subject is this, that it is ever necessary that those of the good religion *should* make an effort that they *may* celebrate *a ceremony for their* living souls. 2. *For* the soul, *for which* they have celebrated *a ceremony*[3], just as much good work as it then becomes each year, it is twice as much good work the second year. 3. So that, *in* this manner, the merit of *the ceremony for* the living soul is increasing just so much every year, while the man is living. 4. And, after that, this also occurs, that, if at the time when that person becomes an immortal soul *there* be no one *at hand*—Srôsh[4] *being* the angel when *the ceremony for* the living soul is celebrated—Srôsh, the righteous, receives the soul by

[1] Lp, B29 have 'goes into an ant's nest.'

[2] B29 omits these four words.

[3] B29 has 'for every time that they have celebrated *a ceremony for* the living soul.'

[4] See Mkh. II, 115 n.

himself, and is keeping watch *over it* during the three days[1], and does not forsake *it*, so that no danger *or* harm happens to it. 5. And the fourth night he is a helper, with the angel Rashn[2], at the *K*invad bridge, while they make up its account and reckoning, and it goes *to* its own place.

6. And this *ceremony for* the living soul is appointed for the reason that, just in the manner *that*, when an infant becomes separated from the mother, a midwife (qâbilat) is necessary for it, so that they *may* keep watch over it, *and* just in the manner that she takes up the infant[3] from the ground—and, *at* the time when it is born, it is ever necessary that *there* be a woman present ('hâʒirat), or they *may* perform work *for* the infant at a time *fit* for the demon—*in* this same manner, when the soul is becoming separated from the body it is like an infant (*t*ifl), *and* does not know any way to its place. 7. When they celebrate *a ceremony for* the living soul, and have propitiated the righteous Srôsh, the righteous Srôsh becomes like the midwife, so that he receives that soul by himself, and keeps watch *that it is* out of the hands of Aharman and the demons. 8. When they do not celebrate *a ceremony* for the soul *when* living, *but*, after that[4], the priests perform *it* before Srôsh, it is like that *which occurs* when a woman brings forth a child[5], *and* after that they set *her* before the midwife. 9. And it happens that while some one is coming in, who takes up that child and wraps *it* up, it has perished.

---

[1] While it is supposed to stay near the body.

[2] B29 adds 'and the angel Mihir.' See Mkh. II, 118, 119.

[3] Lp, B29 have merely 'and she takes *it* up.'

[4] Lp adds 'it is necessary that.'

[5] Lp adds 'they make no enquiry (*t*alab) about it before her.'

10. Therefore, as she does the needful which they *should* do earlier by the hand of some one, *in* this same manner it makes *it* incumbent on every one to celebrate *a ceremony for* his own living soul, so that it *may* be free (îman) from these misfortunes. 11. *And*[1] that, if his decease occurs *in* any place where *there* may be no one who *will* celebrate *a ceremony for* his soul, since *a ceremony for* the living soul is celebrated, *there* are no arrears for him, and he is free. 12. And, in many things, it is that *ceremony for the* living soul which is expedient, especially in these times when the priests have remained few *in* number; *and*, when it is celebrated by one's own hands, it is a great duty.

Chapter LIX.

1. The fifty-ninth subject is this, that, in the good *and* pure religion of the Mazda-worshippers, they have not commanded the women to perform the Nyâyises[2]. 2. And[3] their Nyâyises are these, that three times every day, *at* dawn, mid-day[4] prayer, and evening prayer, they stand back in the presence of their own husbands, and fold their arms and speak thus: 'What are thy thoughts, so that I *may* think them; what is necessary for thee, so that I *may* speak it; and what is necessary for thee, so that I *may* do it?'

3. For, any command, and whatever the husband

---

[1] B29 adds 'this also happens.'

[2] Periodical salutations of the sun and moon (see Chap. VI, 2), fire and water.

[3] Lp, B29 have 'for.'

[4] Literally 'former, early.'

orders, it is requisite to go about that day. 4. *And*, certainly, without the leave (riẓâ) of the husband *she is* to do no work, so that the Lord *may* be pleased with that wife. 5. For the satisfaction of the sacred being is in a reverence (yast) for[1] the satisfaction of the husband; so that every time that they perform work *by* command of the husband they call them righteous in the religion; and if not, what do they call them?

Chapter LX.

1. The sixtieth subject is this, that we are keeping the good *and* pure religion of the Mazda-worshippers with us[2], so that escape from hell *may* be possible for our souls[3]. 2. And we are completely united in hope, and through investigation (ta'hqîq) we fully understand that, when we are steadfast in the good religion, we arrive in heaven. 3. And we know that arrival in heaven occurs through virtuous actions, and through them we are saved; so that we think of good[4], speak of good, and do good.

4. And no doing of good is better than that which *offers itself* when a difficult duty comes before one of the good religion as his soul wishes to depart. 5. Since it comes to thee, do thou give help *to* that which has escaped *his* hand, so that he *may* come out of that hindrance; and do thou not forsake *him*

[1] Lp has merely 'is in,' and B29 has 'is connected with.'

[2] Lp has 'through hope.'

[3] B29, J15 have 'that in the good *and* pure religion of the Mazda-worshippers it is declared that we are maintaining a hope that the soul *may* obtain escape from hell.'

[4] La puts the thinking of good last of the three.

so that he relinquishes the religion. 6. For after that, while he is in the religion, *and* while his children, after him, are in the religion[1], every duty and good work that he does—and *his* children—is just like those which are done by *thine* own hand.

7. And *it is* just like that with regard to poll-tax, it is also indispensable to give *it* in semblance of help, so that they *may* give that person *his* release (*'h*alâ*s*), and he *may* stay in his own place, *and* the advantage of a good work (THavâb) *may* come to that *other person*.

CHAPTER LXI.

1. The sixty-first subject is this, that it is requisite to abstain strictly from speaking falsehood; so that, every time that mankind indulge in the speaking of falsehood with fondness[2], it is not proper to do *so;* and[3] falsehood is the chief[4] of all sins.

2. Zaratu*s*t enquired of Hôrmazd thus: 'Who is a liar like?' 3. Hôrmazd, the good *and* propitious, said: 'A liar is a co-operator with Aharman.'

4. In revelation it says that *there* is no hereafter (â'*h*irat) for the speakers of falsehood, and in the midst of mankind they are contemptible ('haqîr). 5. If *such* a man be powerful (mu'hta*s*im), *and there* be no avoiding ('haDHar) him in the vicinity

[1] B29 omits these ten words.

[2] Lp omits these fourteen words.

[3] B29 omits these twenty words.

[4] This seems to have been the meaning intended, judging from §§ 2–6; otherwise it might be translated 'end' or 'result,' especially as the writer has characterised other sins as 'the chief' (see Chaps. IX, 2, XXV, 8).

of mankind, they do not have any respect *for him*, and he is clearly (farȝâ*m*) an evil liar. 6. Although he possesses much wealth, it will all depart from his hands, and, finally ('hâqibat), begging of mankind occurs to him, and his progeny also becomes scanty[1].

Chapter LXII.

1. The sixty-second subject is this, that it is necessary to take early to the speaking of truth and doing of justice, and to maintain oneself therein, for nothing whatever is better among mankind than truth.

2. Owing to truth Hôrmazd created this world and that *other* world, and truth has remained on the spot, and on account of truth it becomes pure. 3. And the accursed Aharman, *being devoid* of anything good, does not issue from that which is owing to truth. 4. It is requisite to occasion the resurrection owing to truth; and, *as to* every place where truth is not taken up, the glory in that place *has* found a way *out*, and *as to* every household where much *of this* resides, it is on account of truth, and Aharman does not find a way into that place.

5. It is said in revelation that one truthful man is better than a whole world ('hâlam) speaking falsehood; and Gâvah of Ispahân[2]—when he kept *his* stand upon the truth, and was speaking words with truth until *the time* when Dahâk[3], who possessed the

[1] Lp omits these six words.

[2] B29 adds 'he was a blacksmith.' His revolt against Dahâk is detailed in the Shâhnâmah.

[3] See Mkh. VIII, 29 n.

whole realm, *and* the whole of the demons and mankind have been afraid of him, through the truth of the words spoken—was bold with them in every speech, and became victorious (mu*th*affar) over them, by reason of the true words that he was speaking.

6. The accursed Aharman, when he perceived the spirit of truth, had fallen senseless three thousand years[1]. 7. From fear of truth he never managed to hold up *his* head, and from fear of truth he did not manage to come into this world[2]. 8. And everything that thou settest *thy* gaze (na*th*ar) *upon* therein, that has remained on the spot when thou seekest again an examination of it, has remained through truth. 9. And the interpretation of the Ashem-vohû[3] is in truth, *and*, for that reason, they recite the Ashem-vohû frequently.

Chapter LXIII.

1. The sixty-third subject is this, that it is necessary to practise strict abstinence from adultery on this account, that *through* every one who beguiles the wife of another, and commits iniquity with her, that woman becomes, in a moment, unlawful as regards *her* husband. 2. And, after that, every time her husband comes round about her, it is just as though she had gone near to a strange man. 3. The righteous bestowal[4] *of herself* on her own husband, in this

[1] See Bd. I, 22. The spirit of truth was his opposite, the spe*n*tô mainyu*s* or 'bountiful spirit' of Hôrmazd.

[2] See Bd. III, 1–5.

[3] See Chap. VII, 1 n.

[4] Lp inserts 'he shall wish.'

situation, is always worse *than his going*[1] with women of a different religion, on this account, that, if that wife becomes pregnant, it is just as though one of the good religion had fallen *away* into a different religion, and[2] thereby that man becomes worthy of death.

4. And it also happens, when that wife becomes pregnant, *that* she *may* effect the slaughter of the infant, from fear of a bad reputation. 5. Then, *for* that person whose child it is, it is just as though he had effected the slaughter of the child with his own hand; therefore, he is worthy of death. 6. If the infant be born, and it remains[3] in the religion, every sin that that child of his commits is, for that person, just as though it were committed by his own hand.

7. And if a woman of those of the good religion commits *adultery*, she becomes in a condition unlawful as regards *her* husband; *and* if an infant be born it is illegitimate. 8. And the sin owing to this will depart *at* the time when that person goes near to her husband *and* shall say: 'What is *there* in me befitting thy wife? 9. A calamity (âk) *has* occurred, and a crime ('*h*a*t*â) *has* come into *my* body; thou knowest if thou *wilt* exercise forgiveness ('hafû), and if not, when *it is* not for me, do thou kill *me*; my blood is lawful ('halâl) unto thee.' 10. If he shall kill her, her sin will depart owing to this;

---

[1] B29 has 'it never becomes a righteous bestowal of herself on *her* husband, and if, in this situation, he is also.'

[2] B29 omits 'and.'

[3] Lp, B29 have 'it does not remain,' but the text seems to be assuming that the illicit origin of the child is unsuspected, in which case it would undoubtedly remain in the religion, as it would probably do in any case.

otherwise, this sin will not depart from her in any manner (navaî)[1].

11. And *one* calls this sin a sin *affecting* antagonists[2], *and*, so long as the antagonist does not become satisfied, the sin flows on[3], *and* they keep his soul back at the head of the *K*invad bridge, till the time that its antagonist shall arrive and himself accomplishes *his* antagonism, and they give him back a reply[4].

Chapter LXIV.

1. The sixty-fourth subject is this, that it is necessary to practise great abstinence from committing theft[5] and seizing anything from mankind by force.

2. For it is declared in revelation that, *as to* every one who steals one dirham[6] away from another, when they really know *it*, it is necessary to take two dirhams away from him; one dirham *being* that which *was* carried off, and one dirham as the fine of him who committed the theft. 3. It is also requisite to cut *off* one ear, and it is necessary to strike ten *blows with* a stick, and to detain *him* one period in prison.

---

[1] B29 omits these eleven words.

[2] Or accusers (see Chap. XLII, 1, 2).

[3] B29 has 'it flows on,' if we read bi-rêzad; but the Gugarâti translator seems to take gunâh-barêza*d* (Av. bereza*n*t) as a technical epithet for the soul, as though he would say 'they keep back the soul of him *whose* sin is rampant.'

[4] That is, the investigating angels announce their decision as to the proper fate of the soul they have detained.

[5] B29, J15 have 'violence.'

[6] A silver coin of 63 grains in weight, or about 5⅜ annas (see Dd. LII, 1 n); say, seven-pence.

4. And if he shall steal another[1] dirham, in the same manner *one* is to take away two dirhams[2], to cut *off* the other ear, to strike twenty *blows with* a stick, and to detain *him* two periods[3] in prison. 5. And if he shall steal three dirhams and two dângs[4], it is requisite to cut *off his* right hand. 6. If he shall steal five hundred dirhams[5], it is requisite to hang *him*.

7. *On* the spot the punishment is this, and among the spirits it brings punishment on the soul itself. 8. And, if the *other* person does not know *it*, they take away twice as much good work, among the spirits, from that *thief*, and give *it* to the soul of this person. 9. If *the thief* possesses no good works, they give the compensation from the constantly-beneficial treasury[6], and exhibit the punishment *on* the soul of that *thief*.

10. *As to* that person who has seized anything

---

[1] Lp has 'two.' [2] Lp has 'to take four.'

[3] The Gugarâti translator takes 'one period' as 'one ghadî (24 minutes),' but 'two periods' as '2½ ghadî (one hour).' The word sâ'hat, 'period,' means also 'an hour,' but so short a term of imprisonment seems improbable.

[4] That is, 3½ dirhams, nearly 1¼ rûpî, or, say, two shillings.

[5] That is, 175 rûpîs, or, say, £14 12*s*.

[6] Where all supererogatory good works are supposed to be kept in store by the angels, for the purpose of granting them to souls who deserve them, but have been unable to acquire a sufficiency. It is said to be situated in the 'endless light' of heaven, and is the misvânô gâtus *hv*adhâtô, 'ever-benefiting place, the self-sustained,' of Vend. XIX, 122. Perhaps gang, 'treasury,' may have been originally gung, 'space,' which would better suit the idea of a 'self-sustained place' (see Dd. XXVI, 3, XXXI, 24, XXXVII, 22, 24, XXXVIII, 3). The term 'treasurer,' applied to the female personifications of conscience who meet the soul with the stores of its good works and sins (see Sg. IV, 92–96), seems to have no connection with this treasury of other people's good works.

from another by force, among the spirits they seize back four *things*[1] as compensation for every single one. 11. And if, *on* the spot *where people* capture him, he makes *it* convenient to return four *things* in compensation *for* one, when they have fully understood, as they capture that person who is committing highway-robbery, *that* he makes *it* convenient[2], they *may* kill him at once.

Chapter LXV.

1. The sixty-fifth subject is this, that every one is to practise thanksgiving continually, *and* it is requisite *that* he maintains *it* through good and bad; and *he is* to keep in view[3] the benefits of Hôrmazd. 2. Because the creator[4] Hôrmazd demands two things from mankind, the one is that *one should* not commit sin, and the other is that *one should* practise thanksgiving. 3. And how much soever more grateful mankind become, through virtue *and* worthiness as regards him, they[5] grant more abundant daily provision for the grateful than that which is for other persons. 4. And *as to* every one who is not grateful *to* him, the bread that he eats becomes unlawful, and it is not proper for any one to do good *in connection* with him.

---

[1] Twice as much as in cases of theft without violence (see § 2).

[2] So that they may not interfere with such benefit for his soul as he may obtain by atonement. These old priestly laws having much more consideration for the soul than for the body.

[3] La has 'to portray.'

[4] Lp omits these fourteen words.

[5] The angels.

5. And it is declared in revelation that when an unthankful person dies, wherever they deposit his corpse, the archangel Spendârmad[1] is trembling like a sheep that sees a wolf. 6. And *as to* a bird that eats that corpse, on whatever tree it rests and settles, it makes that tree wither away, and the person *who* sits down in the shadow of the tree becomes ill.

7. There are different things that it is necessary for those of the good religion to make predominant over themselves. 8. One is to exercise liberality *in connection* with the worthy; the second is to do justice; the third is to be friendly unto every one; and the fourth is to be sincere and true[2], and to keep falsehood far from themselves. 9. And these four habits (ʻhaẕlat) are the principles (aẕl) of the religion of Zaratust, and it is necessary, when thou listenest *to them* thyself, *that* thou dost not listen to any one *else*[3]. 10. Because the creator Hôrmazd says, 'O Zaratust! if thou wilt that thou become pure and saved, *and that* thou arrive at the place of the pure, do thou accomplish these two duties:—11. One is this, that thou prefer the friendship of the spiritual *existence to that of* the worldly *one*, and consider the things of the world as contemptible and those of the spirit precious; on this account the glory of the world is sought[4] with scorn, and do not thou let the spirit escape. 12. The second is this, that thou speak truly with every one and act justly with me,

[1] See Chap. XXXIII, 2 n. Lp, B29 omit 'archangel.'

[2] Lp omits these nine words.

[3] Lp has 'that what thou listenest *to* thyself, thou listenest *to* as regards any one *else*.' B29 has 'that what thou dost not approve *for* thyself, thou dost not do to any one *else*' (see § 12).

[4] B19 has 'on this account the world is sought again.'

that is, whatever thou dost not approve for thyself do not approve[1] for any one *else;* when thou hast acted in this manner thou art righteous.'

CHAPTER LXVI.

1. The sixty-sixth subject is this, that it is incumbent on all women[2] to order the days (ayyâm) of the Dvâzdah-hômâst[3], because the whole of any sin that may have arisen during menstruation, and *at* other times, becomes cleared away *thereby*.

2. And in the commentary of the Vendîdâd it says *that* every one becomes sanctified in the days of the Dvâzdah-hômâst, and all sins become cleared away from her, like that which *occurs at* harvest time, when a great wind comes on and carries it off; just like this the sin departs from her, and the person becomes clean *and* pure.

3. And, for women[4], there is no duty more indispensable than this; for it is declared in revelation that, when they celebrate a Dvâzdah-hômâst, it is a good work of a hundred thousand Tanâvars[5], and if

[1] B29 has 'perform.'

[2] B29 has 'on the wives of every one,' and J15 has 'on every one.'

[3] In the Gugarâti version (p. 310) of the long-metre Sad Dar Dastûr Jâmâspji states, in a foot-note, that the Dvâzdah-hômâst consists of a Yazisn ceremony every day for 144 days, in honour of twelve angels, so that each angel is reverenced for twelve successive days. He stated formerly (see Byt. II, 59 n) that this celebration was a Hômâst, and that a Dvâzdah-hômâst was a similar celebration for 264 days in honour of twenty-two angels for twelve days each. It appears, however, from Chap. XLI, 7, 20, that the number of ceremonies may vary with the wealth of the individual.

[4] Lp omits these thirteen words.

[5] See Sls. XVI, 6.

it be the days of the Dvâzdah-hômâst it is a good work of a thousand thousand Tanâvars, and when they celebrate *it* by day it is a good work just like this.

Chapter LXVII.

1. The sixty-seventh subject is this, that it is necessary for women to practise great abstinence from committing adultery. 2. For it is declared in revelation, *as to* every woman who *has* lain with a strange man, thus: 'What is it necessary to call her, and why is the explanation[1] that she is of one nature with all wizards and sinners?'

3. And in the commentary of the Vendîdâd[2] it says '"every woman who consorts with two strange men is the first *down* upon me, who am Hôrmazd. 4. For if she takes a look into a river of water it will make *it* diminish, if she takes a look[3] at a tree *or* shrub the fruit of the trees becomes scanty, and if she speaks a word with a righteous man it will make the glory[4] of the man diminish." 5. Zaratust enquired of Hôrmazd, "What occurs on[5] her account?" 6. The creator Hôrmazd spoke thus: "It is necessary to kill her sooner than a biting serpent and similar creatures and wild beasts, because she is more harmful to my creatures."'

7. Therefore, since she is like this, it is necessary for women to keep themselves *with* great effort, so that they *may* not become unlawful unto their own

---

[1] B29 has 'and it is by reason of that fault.'

[2] What follows is a free paraphrase of Vend. XVIII, 123–132.

[3] Lp omits these four words.

[4] Lp, B29 add 'and purity.'

[5] Lp, B29 have 'what is necessary.'

husbands. 8. For, every time that *one of them* gives herself four times to another person, she is, after that, unlawful as long as[1] she may be *in* the house of *her* husband[2], and new sin is increasing *in connection* with her soul[3].

Chapter LXVIII.

1. The sixty-eighth subject is this, that for a menstruous woman who casts an eye upon a fire it is a sin of twelve dirhams *in* weight[4]; and if she goes *within* three steps of the fire it is a sin of a thousand *and* two hundred dirhams[5] *in* weight for her; and when she puts her hand *to* the fire it is a sin of fifteen Tanâvars for her.

2. In like manner, if she takes a look *at* running water it is a sin of twelve dirhams *in* weight for her[6]; if she goes *within* fifteen steps of running water it is a sin of fifteen dirhams *in* weight for her; and when she sits down in running water it is a sin of fifteen Tanâvars for her. 3. And when she walks in the rain, through every drop that drops upon her limbs *there* arises a sin of one Tanâvar for her.

4. *If* she comes to a Khûrshê*d* Nyâyi*s*[7], to observe *it*, it is not proper *for her* to speak a word with a

[1] B29 has 'unlawful when.'

[2] This seems to be the author's interpretation of the following commentary (Pahl. Vend. XVIII, 124*a*):—'And it is no matter to her; for, when cohabitation is three times conceded by her, *she is* worthy of death. Gôgô*s*asp said that this is an adulteress who is *kept* within bounds.'

[3] B29 has 'increasing as to water and fire.'

[4] About 756 grains, possibly four Farmân sins (see Sls. XI, 2).

[5] A Tanâvar or Tanâpûhar sin (see Sls. I, 2).

[6] B29 omits this clause.

[7] Or salutation of the sun.

righteous man[1]. 5. It is not proper *for her* to put a bare foot on the ground. 6. It is not proper *for her* to eat any food with a *bare* hand; it is not proper *for her* to eat bread *when* satisfied[2]. 7. It is not proper *for* two menstruous women to eat together; it is not proper for them to sleep *so*[3].

8. And so long as three days *have* not elapsed it is not proper to wash the hands[4], and three days after that, if she *has* perceived herself clean, it is requisite to remain another day, and *so* until the lapse of nine days, *when*, if she *has* perceived herself clean, it is not necessary *to remain* to the end of[5] another *interval of* time. 9. If menstruation occurs *for* twenty-nine days, it is necessary[6] to consider that she is menstruous a second time, and during three other days it is not proper to wash again, and it is necessary to exercise care, just like that which[7] I first wrote *about*.

10. If she be doubtful whether menstruation is come to her, it is requisite *for her* to strip off *her* dress, and then to take notice if she has become menstruous, *or if* the dress that is stripped off be clean. 11. If she has an infant *to feed* with *her* milk,

---

[1] § 4 in B29 is as follows:—'It is not proper *for her* to take a look at the sun, *or* at a righteous man.'

[2] La, B29 have sêr, but Lp has *s*îr, 'milk,' which is also the reading taken by the Gugarâti translator who must have understood the clause as follows:—'It is not proper *for her so* to eat bread *and* milk.'

[3] B29 adds 'and it is not desirable *for their* limbs to touch each other.'

[4] B29 has 'head.'

[5] B29 has 'it is requisite to remain for.'

[6] La omits these ten words, as well as 'a second time' further on.

[7] B29 has merely 'the care which.'

one puts away the dress from the infant, and gives *it to* the mother till it *has* fed *on* the milk, *and* then it is proper to give *it* to other persons. 12. It is pure, but when the mother washes *her* head she also washes[1] the head of the infant.

13. And it is necessary *for* a menstruous *woman* that she *should* not pass by the end of[2] anything ceremonially washed, for, if it be a thousand cubits (gaz) *in length*, she makes the whole *of it* polluted, *and* it becomes unclean. 14. With any one *who* holds a sacred-twig stand[3] she *should* not speak a word; *and* if a priest holds the sacred twigs in *his* hand, *and* a menstruous *woman* speaks some (ba'hụ̄ê) words[4] from afar, or he walks within three steps of a menstruous woman, she makes *it*[5] unclean.

Chapter LXIX.

1. The sixty-ninth subject is this, that it is not proper that sunshine *should* fall on a fire, for, every time that sunshine falls upon a fire[6], it is a[7] sin. 2. If thou expose a fire to the sun it is a sin of three

[1] Lp, B29 have 'it is also requisite to wash.'

[2] B29 has 'pass a look over.'

[3] This consists of two metal tripods with crescent-shaped tops, to support the small faggot of sacred twigs or wires that are bound together by a girdle of narrow strips of a date-palm leaflet; the girdle being tied on the faggot in the same manner as that on the waist of a Parsi (see Sls. III, 32 n). The sacred twigs must always be present at ceremonies, sometimes held in the hand of the officiating priest, and sometimes lying on their stand.

[4] B29 has '*and* if she speaks words with him.'

[5] B29 has 'it becomes.'

[6] B29 omits these eight words.

[7] B29 has 'much.'

stîrs[1]; and, if thou set down anything on the top of the fire, it is necessary that it *should* not have any hole—so that the light (nûr) and strength of the fire *might* become less—so far as thou knowest.

CHAPTER LXX.

1. The seventieth subject is this, that, *as to* any persons, when they carry a corpse to the appointed place, it is necessary that two suits of clothes be put on, on account of this work. 2. It is requisite *for* those clothes to be on[2], and it is necessary[3] to make a dog gaze at the corpse twice, once *at* the time when life becomes separated *from* it, and once *at* the time when they wish to take *it* up.

3. Then it is necessary that both those persons be connected, *and each of them is* to tie a cord on one of his own hands, so that the hand *may* go away[4] from *that of* the other one. 4. And, when they are moving, it is necessary for him to be prepared and not to speak a word with any one. 5. And if it be a pregnant woman *they are* to take *her* up by four persons, because there are two corpses[5].

6. When, avoiding dead matter, *one* comes again upon it, *he has*, in the end, to wash[6] with *ceremonial* ablution[7], and that is requisite for the reason that he

---

[1] The same as the twelve dirhams in Chap. LXVIII, 1, 2.

[2] Lp, B29 have 'to dress in those clothes.'

[3] B29 omits 'it is necessary.'

[4] That is, the cord must hang quite slack, though B29 states that 'the hand *may* not go apart.'

[5] See Sls. X, 10.

[6] B29 has '*he has* to wash *his* head and body.'

[7] Lp, B29 add 'and water.'

may not thereby be rapidly a *cause of* wickedness or death for any one[1].

7. And if *one* does not show a dog to the corpse, *and* they take *it* up, how many soever *there* be, the whole *of them* become polluted[2]. 8. In the commentary of the Vendîdâd it is asserted, that every one who takes up a corpse that a dog *has* not seen is polluted and worthy of death[3], and never becomes clean; his soul *also* would be wicked.

Chapter LXXI.

1. The seventy-first subject is this, that, forasmuch as it is not desirable *for* any one to eat dead matter for the sake of medicine and remedy, *let them* beware (zinhâr) when they eat *it*[4].

2. For it asserts, in the commentary of the Vendîdâd[5], that it is requisite to demolish the habitation, house, and abode of any one *who* has[6] eaten dead matter, and to fetch his heart out of *his* body, and it is necessary to scoop out his eyes. 3. And *along* with these torments, which they accomplish on him, his soul is in hell till the resurrection.

Chapter LXXII.

1. The seventy-second subject is this, that when any one carries dead matter to water, *or* to fire, he is

[1] Lp, B29 omit 'for any one.'

[2] B29 has merely 'and if, to make a dog gaze at the corpse, they take *it* up, *it is* on how many soever *there* be.'

[3] Compare Sls. II, 65.

[4] B29 has 'beware that they do not eat *it*.'

[5] Perhaps alluding to Pahl. Vend. VII, 59-64.

[6] B29 has 'to demolish his house and abode if any one has.'

worthy of death[1]. 2. And[2] it asserts in revelation, that *any* year when the locust comes profusely[3], it comes for the reason that dead matter is brought to water and fire. 3. And, *in* like manner, the winter is colder, and the summer is hotter.

Chapter LXXIII.

1. The seventy-third subject is this, that, when a cow or a goat *has* eaten dead matter[4], in any place, nothing whatever of *its* flesh, *or* milk, *or* hair, *should* come into use for one year. 2. After that one year it is clean: and, if it be pregnant, its young one is likewise not clean *for* one year.

3. And if a domestic fowl *has* eaten dead matter, its flesh and eggs are, *in* like manner, not clean *for* one year.

Chapter LXXIV.

1. The seventy-fourth subject is this, that *at* dawn, when they rise up from sleep, it is first necessary to throw something[5] on the hands, that is the hand-

---

[1] See Pahl. Vend. VII, 65–71. [2] Lp, B29 have 'for.'

[3] La has sâl, and B29 san for 'year;' Lp has 'that when the bê*s* and locust come profusely.' The bê*s* may be either a poisonous plant (*Napellus Moysis*), or 'distress.'

[4] See Pahl. Vend. VII, 189–192, Sls. II, 109.

[5] According to the long-metre Sad Dar this 'something' (as in Chap. L) is Nîrang, the ritualistic liquid or consecrated bull's urine (see Chap. XXXVI, 7 n). This chapter is, to some extent, a repetition of Chap. L.

cleansing[1]. 2. Afterwards, *they are* to wash the hands quite clean with water, *in* such manner that *they are* to wash the hands three times from the forearm (sâ'hid) to the end of the hand; and the face is washed from behind the ears to below the chin *and* up to the crown of the head; and *one* washes the feet three times thoroughly, as far as the leg (sâq); then *one* recites the Kem-nâ-mazdâ[2].

3. If it be a place where *there* is no water, and the risk be that *the time for* the Nyâyis[3] *should* pass by, it is requisite to cleanse[4] the hands three times *with* dust, and to perform the Nyâyis. 4. Afterwards, when *one* arrives at water, *he is* to wash the hands and face a second time, and to accomplish the Nyâyis[5].

5. Before *the time* when *one* throws something on the hands it is not proper to wash the hands and face, *and* it is a Tanâvar sin; it is also not possible to work at anything whatever *with* the hands and face not washed.

Chapter LXXV.

1. The seventy-fifth subject is this, that, when they wish to provide a supply of water *for* any cultivated *land*, it is first necessary that they make

---

[1] Lp adds 'or some grass upon which no water has come, or fruit, is also to go into the nose *and* eyes, *and* make *them* clean' (see Chap. L, 2).

[2] See Chap. XXXV, 2 n.

[3] The salutation of the sun (see Chap. VI, 2).

[4] B29 inserts 'the face and.'

[5] B29 omits § 4.

an inspection through every course *and* channel[1] of the water, *to ascertain* whether there be dead matter therein, or not; *and*, after that, *through* the water *in* like manner. 2. If they be in the middle of it, when the water is within their cultivated *land*, *and* dead matter comes in sight, if it be possible to ward *it off* *one* wards *it off*, and if it be possible to divert the water *one* diverts *it*. 3. And if the water arrives with dead matter unawares, it is no sin for them. 4. *But* if no inspection of the stream and cultivated *land* be made, and the water arrives with dead matter, those people are polluted, and it is necessary to perform the Bareshnûm *ceremony*[2] *as regards* their heads.

Chapter LXXVI.

1. The seventy-sixth subject is this, when a woman brings forth, it is necessary that she *should* not wash *her* head *for* twenty-one days, nor put *her* hand again on anything, nor walk on a terrace-roof, nor put *her* foot on a threshold in *her* habitation. 2. And after the twenty-one days, if she sees herself *in* such a state that she is able to wash *her* head, she washes *her* head. 3. And, after that, until the coming on of the fortieth day, it is requisite to abstain from the vicinity of a fire and anything that is wooden[3] *or* earthen; it is also requisite to abstain from everything of her cooking and pot-boiling[4]. 4. Afterwards, when it is forty days, *she is*

---

[1] B29 has 'when any one wishes to enter into participation of a cultivated field, it is first necessary to observe in every course.'

[2] See Chap. XXXVI, 1 n.

[3] La '*h*as, B29 *k*ôbîn; Lp has '*h*ûri*s*, 'food.'

[4] B29 omits these thirteen words.

to wash *her* head, and it is proper *for her* to do every *kind of* work.

5. Till the lapse of a second[1] forty days it is not proper *for her* husband to make an approach to her, for it is a great sin, and it is possible that she *may* become pregnant a second time, as within a *period of* forty days women become very quickly pregnant[2].

6. And if after the *first* forty days she sees herself impure, unless she knows with accuracy that it has come from the infant, it is necessary to consider if *she be* menstruous.

Chapter LXXVII.

1. The seventy-seventh subject is this, that, when a woman's infant is still-born, it is necessary to give *her* first something washed with ceremony *and* brought *with* fire-ashes[3], so that it *may* make the heart within her pure. 2. After that, *for* three days, it is altogether improper to give *her* water, *or* anything in which *there* is water or salt. 3. And these three days are from period to period[4], *in* such a

---

[1] Only B29 and the Gugarâti have 'a second.'

[2] B29 omits these twelve words.

[3] So in B29, which agrees with Vend. VII, 163, but La, Lp are defective. The 'something' means consecrated bull's urine, as in Chap. LXXIV, 1; this, mingled with ashes, is prescribed as the first thing to be tasted by the woman.

[4] That is, from the given hour to the same hour on the third day, although, from what follows, it appears that, if the given hour were in the middle of any period of the day, the third day would expire at the beginning of the third similar period. Whether the three days are to be inclusive, or exclusive, of the day when the term begins, that is, whether the term is to be nearly 48 or 72 hours, is not very clear.

manner that, if the duty of mid-day[1] prayer has occurred, they extend till the mid-day prayer itself, *and she is* to pass over one other hour *and* it is *then* proper to swallow water. 4. After that, till the lapse of forty days, *she is* to sit apart again, and, afterwards, to undergo the Bareshnûm *ceremony*[2].

5. *On* the infant's becoming a four-months' *child*, whenever it is *still*-born it is a dead *body*[3], for the reason that so long as it does not reach the fourth month life does not come to it. 6. And if after three months this affair occurs, *one is* to exercise great caution (i'htiyâ*t*) and to insist strictly on this matter.

7. For our religion has reiterated on this matter that, if *one* be polluted and do not keep himself pure, so long as he is living he never becomes clean from that pollution. 8. That, if he wash *his* head ten thousand times in *ceremonial* ablution, he certainly does not any *way* become pure from it[4]. 9. Because this pollution is not from without; it is from within every bone and vein and tendon; *and* water makes clean *only* anything that is on the skin. 10. Impurity which is *in* the bones, except *through the liquid consecrated by* the religious formula[5], does not otherwise become clean.

CHAPTER LXXVIII.

1. The seventy-eighth subject is this, that in every habitation *where* any one departs, passing away from

---

[1] Literally 'former, early.' [2] See Chap. XXXVI, 1 n.

[3] And, therefore, to be treated with all the precautions necessary in dealing with a corpse to avoid the pollution alluded to in §§ 7–10. Hence the necessity of careful enquiry in doubtful cases, as recommended in § 6.

[4] B29 omits § 8. [5] See Chap. XXXVI, 7 n.

the world, it is necessary to endeavour that they *may* not eat and not consecrate fresh meat *for* three days therein[1]. 2. Because the danger is that some one else *may* depart, passing away; *so* the relations of that *former* person *should* not eat meat *for* three days.

Chapter LXXIX.

1. The seventy-ninth subject is this, that it is necessary to make an effort that they *may* exercise munificence and liberality towards the good and the worthy. 2. For the exercise of liberality is grand, *in* such manner as it is better and pleasanter, *in* like manner, for the ground on which a liberal man walks, better for the wind that blows upon a liberal man, better for the horse on which a liberal man sits, better, *in* like manner, for the cow and goat that[2] a liberal man eats, *and*[3] pleasanter for the sun and moon and stars that shine upon a liberal man.

3. To such an extent is a liberal and munificent *man* precious ('hazîz), that Hôrmazd speaks[4] thus: 'I have wished that I *might* give a recompense *to* a munificent man, if it be suitable for him, *but* I have not found any recompense and happiness that are suitable for him, except a blessing.' 4. And virtuous men and the united archangels are perpetually uttering blessings on account of the liberal man who maintains no refusal of his own things to a stranger.

[1] See Sls. XVII, 1, 2.

[2] B29 has 'whose milk,' and Lp further adds 'and butter.'

[3] B29 inserts 'better and.'

[4] Lp, B29 have 'asserts.'

5. For it is declared in revelation, that the creator Hôrmazd spoke to Zaratust, the Spitamân, thus: 'I have created the supreme heaven of heavens for the sake of any of the liberal who provide for the worthy and give them something; and gloomy hell is for all those persons who give anything to the unworthy.'

6. *In* like manner it is declared in revelation, that there are thirty-three ways to heaven, besides *that of* the souls of the liberal. 7. If the soul be of any one else, it is not able to arrive in heaven[1] by that way. 8. Besides *this* happy[2] way, a soul of the liberal is able to arrive in heaven by means of the thirty-three ways. 9. For no one is it easier to arrive in heaven than *for* the liberal.

CHAPTER LXXX.

1. The eightieth subject is this, that there is a time when thou recitest one Ashem-vohû[3], *and* the merit of it may be as much as *that of* ten. 2. There is a time when thou recitest one Ashem-vohû, *and* the merit of it may be as much as *that of* a hundred. 3. A time may be when thou recitest one[4], *and* the merit of it may be as much as *that of* a thousand. 4. A time may be when the merit of one Ashem-vohû[5] may be as much as *that of* ten thousand. 5.

---

[1] B29 omits 'in heaven.' [2] B29 has 'besides by the one.'

[3] See Chap. VII, 1 n. The contents of this chapter are derived from Hn. I, 11–35 (Yt. XXI, 6–15).

[4] B29 adds 'Ashem-vohû.'

[5] La omits 'the merit of;' and B29 has 'when thou recitest one Ashem-vohû, *and* the merit of it,' both here and in § 5.

A time may be when the merit of one Ashem-vohû is as much as the value (qîmat)[1] of this world and that *other* world[2].

6. As for that Ashem-vohû whose nature[3] is as much as ten, that is when they recite *it* as they eat bread. 7. That which is, from nature, as much as a hundred is when they recite *it* after eating[4]. 8. That which is so much by nature that, *having* turned side over side, they recite *it* correctly may be a merit of a thousand[5]. 9. That which is of the nature of ten thousand is that which thou recitest when thou risest up from sleep[6]. 10. And that whose nature is as much as this world and that *other* world[7] is when they recite *it* at the time of the dissolution of life; for, if he be not able to recite *it* himself, friends and relations give *it* into his mouth. 11[8]. If he be fit for hell he becomes fit for the ever-stationary, if he be fit for the ever-stationary he becomes fit for heaven, *and* if he be fit for heaven he becomes fit for the supreme heaven[9].

CHAPTER LXXXI.

1. The eighty-first subject is this, that every duty and good work, which it is requisite to perform, they *should* accomplish while within that day, and not postpone for the morrow.

---

[1] So Lp, B29, Hn., but La has qismat, 'share, destiny.'
[2] B29 omits these four words.
[3] B29 has 'value,' both here and in §§ 7, 9, 10.
[4] La has 'sleeping.'
[5] B29 omits § 8.
[6] La omits § 9.
[7] B29 has merely 'is the price of this world.'
[8] Lp, B29 insert 'for.'
[9] See Pahl. Hn. I, 35 *a*.

2. For it is declared in revelation, that the creator Hôrmazd spoke to Zaratust thus: 'O Zaratust! I have created no one better than thee in the world, and after thee I *shall* likewise not create *one;* thou *art* my chosen one, and I have made this world apparent on account of thee. 3. And all[1] these people ('*h*alâîq) whom I have created, and the whole of these monarchs who have existed and do exist, have always maintained the hope that I *should* create thee in their days, so that they *should* accept (qabûl kunand) the religion, and their souls *should* attain to the supreme heaven.

4. 'Nevertheless I have created *thee* at the present time, in the middle period; for it is three thousand years from the days of Gayômard till now, and from now till the resurrection are the three thousand years that remain; therefore, I have created thee in the middle. 5. For whatever is in the middle is more precious and better and more valuable, *in* the same manner as the heart is in the middle of the whole body *and* is unquestionably (lâ-*g*arm) very precious[2], *in* the same manner as the land of *E*rân[3] is more valuable than other lands, for the reason that it is in the middle. 6. And the country of *E*rân, which is *in* the fourth climate (iqlîm)[4], is better than other places, for the reason that it is in the middle. 7. Therefore, I have created thee in the middle, in the manner of *what is* precious, and I have given thee the apostleship, and have sent *thee* to a monarch, a friend of knowledge and a friend of religion.

8. 'Afterwards, I have sent thee, with thus much

[1] B29 omits 'all.' [2] B29 omits these twenty-five words.
[3] The Gugarâti pronunciation of Irân.
[4] The middle one of the seven.

preciousness, to the people; and the knowledge of the good works that mankind perform[1] in life, and have not been able to bring to hand without trouble (mi'hnat), I have made clear *and* plain unto thee; and I have made thee aware of the whole of knowledge. 9. I have taught *it*[2] to thee in the Avesta, in a language that no one in the world considers plain *and* easy; and I have told thee its interpretation (zand) in a language that is more current among mankind, and thou likewise hast more eloquence (faẕ'h) therein.

10. 'While *thou hast* all this greatness that I have given to thee, O Zaratust! I enact a precept for thee, that "every good work which thou art able to do to-day do not postpone for to-morrow, and accomplish with thine own hand the counsel of thine own soul." 11. Do not be proud (*gh*arrah) on the *score* that it is still *the time of* youth, *and* it is quite possible to do *it hereafter*, while thou thinkest thus: "I will do *it* after this." 12. For *there* have been many people whose *remaining* life was one day, and they have been taken *away* in the presence of fifty years' work[3].'

13. Therefore, make an effort, so that thou *mayest* not postpone to-day's duty for to-morrow. 14. Because Aharman, the evil wicked *one*, has intrusted two fiends with this matter, the name of one is Tardy (dêr) and the name of the other is Afterwards (pas). 15. Both these fiends are united, *and* they

[1] B29 has 'the knowledge that mankind practise.'

[2] Lp, B29 have 'taught the whole of knowledge.'

[3] It is quite uncertain whether Hôrmazd's exhortation ends here, or elsewhere.

make an effort and exertion[1] with man, so that his duty falls back behindhand[2]. 16. For, *as to* every duty and good work which comes forward, that fiend whose name is Tardy speaks thus: 'Thou wilt live long, and it is possible to perform this duty *at* all times;' and that fiend whose name is Afterwards says: 'Pass on now; it is possible to perform *it* afterwards.' 17. And these two fiends united keep the soul away from its own duty, till the end arrives; all duties have fallen back behindhand, and *it has* to experience regret ('hasarat) and penitence. 18. It has no benefit through duty *and* good works, *and* departs from this world.

Chapter LXXXII.

1. The eighty-second subject is this, that, when thou risest up from the bed-clothes, it is necessary to tie the *sacred thread*-girdle[3] again *at* that same place, and it is not desirable to put *forth* a step without the girdle.

2. For it is declared in revelation, that every single step which *one* puts forth without the *sacred thread*-girdle is a Farmân sin[4], *and* through four steps it becomes a Tanâvar sin which would be a weight of a thousand *and* two hundred dirhams[5]. 3. Therefore, it is necessary to keep watch *over* oneself, as regards this sin, and to tie on the *sacred thread*-girdle.

---

[1] Lp has 'conflict.'

[2] B29 omits 'behindhand.'

[3] See Chaps. X, XLVI.

[4] See Sls. I, 2, IV, 10, XI, 2.

[5] The dirham being probably about 63 grains (see Dd. LII, 1 n).

Chapter LXXXIII.

1. The eighty-third subject is this, that it is requisite to abstain from the keeping of fasts. 2. For, in our religion, it is not proper that they *should* not eat every day *or* anything, because it would be a sin *not to do so.*

3. With us the keeping of fast is this, that we keep fast from committing sin with *our* eyes and tongue and ears and hands and feet. 4. Some people are striving about it, so that they *may* not eat anything all day, and they practise abstinence from eating anything. 5. For us it is also necessary to make an effort, so that we *may* not think, *or* speak, *or* commit any sin; and it is necessary that no bad action *should* proceed from our hands, *or* tongue, *or* ears, *or* feet, which would be a sin owing to them.

6. Since I have spoken *in* this manner, and have brought forward the fasting of the seven members of the body, that which, in other religions, is fasting owing to not eating is, in our religion, fasting owing to not committing sin.

Chapter LXXXIV.

1. The eighty-fourth subject is this, when they wish to sleep, it is requisite to utter one Yathâ-ahû-vairyô *and* one Ashem-vohû[1], and to accomplish repentance *one is* to speak thus: 'I am sorrowing for, and repentant and in renunciation of all that sin which I have spoken and *was* imagined by

---

[1] See Chap. VII, 1 n.

me, and *has* assailed me; of these actions I am in renunciation[1].'

2. Afterwards *one is* to lie down; and every time that *one* acts *in* the manner that I have mentioned, and wears the *sacred thread*-girdle on the waist—while *he is* equally sharing the whole of the good works which they are performing in all the world during that night, *and he is* of similar merit[2]—every single breath that he inhales and exhales is a good work of a weight of three dirhams. 3. *And* when he turns from side to side he *should, in* like manner, recite one Ashem-vohû[3].

Chapter LXXXV.

1. The eighty-fifth subject is this, that, *in* every matter that comes forward, it is necessary to enquire of the wise and relations, so as to have their advice, and not to transact any business according to one's own idea *and* opinion.

2. For it is declared in revelation, that the sacred being, the good *and* propitious, spoke to Zaratust thus: '*As to* every business that thou wishest to transact, do thou receive wisdom and knowledge at one place with the wise *who* reply, and cast away *what is* unconsidered, so that Aharman *may* not reach *it* midway, and injury (*h*alal) *may* not occur to that business.'

---

[1] This is the general form of a Patit or renunciation of sin.

[2] B29 omits these six words.

[3] See Chap. LXXX, 8. This chapter nearly corresponds to Sls. X, 24.

3. *In* like manner the archangel Spendârma*d*[1], *at* the time when *her* gaze passed on to Minô*k*ihar[2], issued to him this admonition *and* precept (vazîyat), *and* said: 'O Minô*k*ihar! although *there* be deliberation *in* an affair, this may be no reason for it as regards the spirits[3]; although a horse may be good, *there* may be no resource *except* a whip for it; and although *one* may be a wise man, *there* should be no retreat on his part from having advice, so that his business *may* become complete.'

Chapter LXXXVI.

1. The eighty-sixth subject is this, that it is not proper to kill a beaver[4]; *but*, if they see *it in* any place, it is necessary to take *it* up and carry *it* to running water. 2. For, in the commentary of the Vendîdâ*d* it is ranked[5] *as* a great sin for the *killer*[6]; and, *as to* every one who kills a beaver, the source of his seed becomes exhausted.

Chapter LXXXVII.

1. The eighty-seventh subject is this, that, when

[1] See Chap. XXXIII, 2 n.

[2] Pahl. Mânûs*k*îhar (see Mkh. XXVII, 41 n). It appears from Sls. X, 28, where a portion of this tale is quoted, that it comes originally from the *K*î*d*ras*t* Nask.

[3] B29 has 'although a knife be sharp, *there* may be no resource except a whetstone for it,' which follows the next clause in Sls. X, 28. In the original text this change of meaning is produced by a difference in only four words, and the author of the Sad Dar has probably misunderstood the Pahlavi original when translating it.

[4] Literally 'a water dog.'

[5] B29 has 'decreed.'

[6] As shown by the excessive atonements prescribed in Vend. XIV, in default of which he is said to go to hell till the resurrection.

any one departs from the world[1], it is necessary to make an effort, in those three days, so that they *may* continuously perform the ceremonial of Srôsh[2] and make the fire blaze, and *may* recite the Avesta; because the soul is three days in this world[3].

2. The fourth night it is requisite to consecrate three sacred cakes; one *with* a dedication *to* Rashn[4] and Âstâd[5], one *with* a dedication *to* the spirit Râm[6], *and* one *with* a dedication to the righteous guardian spirit; *and one is* to consecrate a dress and something *as* a righteous gift for that soul[7].

3. It is necessary that the dress be new and of uniform quality (gins), and such as turban, shirt, vest, girdle, trowsers, shoes (pasandil)[8], and mouth-veil. 4. Since they give those among the spirits a counterpart of those garments, therefore, whatever is more beautiful, *and* more surpassing *in* grandeur for the soul *in* that place, is necessary where that place is, because our fathers and mothers and the whole of *our* relations are *in* that place. 5. *And* since the souls recognise and ask after one another in that world, they are, therefore, more joyful on account of every one whose dress[9] and grandeur are more surpassing. 6. In a similar manner, when the dress is old and ragged, they are ashamed, and exhibit heaviness of heart.

---

[1] La omits 'from the world.'

[2] See Mkh. II, 115 n, Sls. XVII, 3. [3] See Mkh. II, 114, 158.

[4] See Mkh. II, 118, 119, Sls. XVII, 4.

[5] Av. arstâd, 'uprightness;' the angel whose name is given to the twenty-sixth day of the Parsi month.

[6] The angel of the upper air, often called Vâê the good.

[7] B29 has 'on that cake.'

[8] B29 has mûzah, 'boots,' and places them last.

[9] B29 inserts 'is more beautiful.'

7. They call that dress a righteous gift because they consecrate *it;* and it is necessary to give *it to* the priests and high-priests, as it is a righteous gift on account of their position. 8. And it is suitable for them to keep *it* for the reason that the souls are nearer to them; *people should also* make an effort that the dress may be stitched like the dress of a priest.

9. The sacred beings make up the account *and* reckoning for the soul when the priest recites frasasti ahurahê mazdau[1] and removes the Frasast[2] from this side to that side. 10. The soul passes over the *K*inva*d* bridge when, *on* the fourth night, it arrives from the world *at* the *K*inva*d* bridge. 11. First it goes to the abode of fire (âta*s*-gâh)[3]; afterwards, one step reaches to the star station, the second step reaches to the moon station, the third step to the sun station, *and* with the fourth step it reaches the *K*inva*d* bridge[4], *and* they convey it to its own place.

---

[1] 'Glory *be* to Ahura-mazda.' Lp adds 'ahunahê vairyêhê as far as ashaya nô paiti-*g*amyâ*d*,' that is 'to the Ahuna-vairya *formula*,' &c. as far as 'may he come to us in righteousness' (Yas. VIII, 1–3).

[2] A Frasast is a sacred cake marked on the upper side with nine superficial cuts (in three rows of three each) made with a finger-nail while repeating the words humat hûkht huvar*s*t, 'well-thought, well-spoken, well-done,' thrice, one word to each of the nine cuts. It is placed before the consecrating priest, but to his right, while the ordinary sacred cakes are to his left (see Haug's Essays, pp. 396, 407, 408).

[3] That is, when it leaves the vicinity of the body, after hovering about it for three nights (see Sls. XII, 5).

[4] In other accounts the soul has to pass over this bridge before it steps forwards to the stars and moon and sun (see Mkh. II, 123, 145, VII, 9–12, Dd. XXXIV, 3, AV. V, 2, VII–IX, 1).

Chapter LXXXVIII.

1. The eighty-eighth subject is this, that, *as to any piece of* wood on which they carry a corpse, or on which they wash *it*, and that which may be defiled with blood and impurity, that on which menstruous *defilement*, or a bare limb, is deposited by a *menstruous* woman, and that on which they impale a human being, it is necessary to avoid the whole of these *pieces of* wood, and not to work with[1] them again, because one's dress becomes impure; and it is not proper to burn *them*. 2. It is necessary to put *them* in a place where any one, *who* pulls *them* up and stirs *them*, *will* not[2] bring *them* into the use of mankind.

Chapter LXXXIX.

1. The eighty-ninth subject is this, that[3] Hôrmazd keeps watch when any one, through imposition ('hîlat) *and* unawares, eats dead matter, *or* gives *it to* one of the good religion, or throws dead matter upon one of the good religion. 2. While his will and command are, *that* it is necessary that *such a person should* undergo the Bareshnûm *ceremony*[4], and accomplish repentance[5] before the *spiritual* chiefs and high-priests. 3. So that, after that, *one may* indicate to him the sin in these *actions*, *and* he *may* perform the retribution which the high-priest mentions, in order that, owing to this, his sin *may* depart.

---

[1] La has 'to eat on,' Lp 'to buy with,' B29 'to touch on.'

[2] B29 has 'any one *will* not take *them* up and not stir *them* about, so that he does not.'

[3] B29, J15 insert 'the religion of.'

[4] See Chap. XXXVI, 1 n.

[5] See Chap. XLV, 7 n.

Chapter XC.

1. The ninetieth subject is this, that it is not proper that they *should* give anything to a sinful person *or one* worthy of death, because[1] it is like that they have placed in the jaws of a destructive serpent (azdahâ). 2. And, if this be food which he devours *and* they give, they pass into the committing of sin; *and* that person *who* may have given food to him is a participater with him. 3. In eating food, if *there* be no danger and fear of them[2], it is not desirable to give anything to them, for it would be a great sin.

Chapter XCI.

1. The ninety-first subject is this, that is, *in* what mode is it necessary to wash everything that becomes polluted by dead matter?

2. Gold *one is* to wash over once with *ceremonial* ablution[3] to make *it* dry once with dust, and to wash *it* over once with water. 3. Silver (nuqrah) *one is to do* twice; copper, tin, lead, and brass *articles* three times; steel four times; stone *articles* six times; turquoise, ruby (yâqût), amber, carbuncle, cornelian ('haqîq), and, like these, whatever is from a mine (ma'hdan) are all to be washed six times in the manner which I have stated. 4. Afterwards they are clean *in* that manner, when every single time *one* washes *them* over with *ceremonial* ablution, makes

[1] B29 omits these six words.

[2] That is, if the sinners begging assistance be not dangerous.

[3] That is, with consecrated bull's urine (see Sls. II, 112–117).

them dry with dust, and washes *it* off[1]; and just like this *on* the occasion of the other times—up to three times, or four, or six—as far as whatever is ordered.

5. For pearls two modes[2] are ordered, but the conclusion is this, that they *should* wash *them* six times, just like stone *articles*. 6. The whole of wooden and earthen *ware* it is requisite to throw *away*. 7. All clothing of the body it is requisite to wash six times *in* the manner that I have stated, *and*, after that, to put *them* in a place where the sun and moon must *shine* on them *for* six months[3]; after that they are fit for a menstruous woman.

Chapter XCII.

1. The ninety-second subject is this, that it is necessary to properly maintain the sacred fire[4] and some one who *will* work with assiduity (kahdân) to provide[5] maintenance and sympathy for it. 2. And the supply of its firewood is entirely *in* such a manner that they burn this year the firewood of last year[6]. 3. *At* midnight they make *it* blaze up, *and* put incense upon *it in* such a manner that the wind carries off its scent.

4. The demons and fiends rush away, because there is the glory of the sacred fire that we are able to make a living existence in the midst of this

[1] Lp, B29 add 'with water.'

[2] Pahl. Vend. VII, 188 gives three opinions.

[3] See Pahl. Vend. VII, 36.

[4] Literally 'the fire of Bahirâm.' Compare Chap. XXXIX.

[5] Lp, B29, J15 have 'so that some one *may* keep watch over it, and is to provide proper.'

[6] So that it may be quite dry, as to put anything damp into a fire would be considered sinful (see AV. X, 6–14).

people. 5. For, if no fiend[1] and the glory of the archangels and the day of the sacred fire had not existed, it would not have been possible to produce the living existence any day. 6. And, therefore, it makes *it* expedient that they supply a fire-attendant to maintain the firewood and fire, so that a seeking for *its* safety ('hâfiyat) *may* come into *operation*, and they *may* know a support and protection for it that would be acceptable.

Chapter XCIII.

1. The ninety-third subject is this, that it is necessary for all those of the good religion to practise abstinence from uttering slander (*gh*aîbat) behind *one's* back[2].

2. In the commentary of the Vendîdâ*d* it states, that[3] slander is the greatest of all sins. 3. Every one who perpetrates slander *about* any one is like him who has eaten dead matter—and the eating of dead matter is a sin[4] *that* has likewise been mentioned, before this, in this book[5]—but the statement is like this, while they do not indicate *any* punishment for it in this world[6], it does not go *without it* in that *other* world. 4. Therefore it is necessary for those of the good religion to make an effort, so that they *may* guard themselves from this slander.

5. In order that they *may* show thy soul, *when*[7] resigning life, the satisfaction (i*g*zâ) for the sin, it

---

[1] That is, the absence of fiends. B29 has 'if the splendour.'
[2] Literally 'face.'
[3] B29 inserts 'the perpetration of.'
[4] B29, J15 have 'a great sin.'
[5] See Chap. LXXI.
[6] Thereby differing from the sin of eating dead matter.
[7] Lp, B29 have 'show at the time of.'

states, in the commentary of the Vendîdâd, *as to* any one by whom slander is perpetrated, if *the injured person* goes before him *and* begs a righteous gift from him, and he provides a righteous gift for that *person*, the sin departs from him.

CHAPTER XCIV.

1. The ninety-fourth subject is this, when a person confers a benefit *or* kindness upon any one, it is necessary that *the latter should* understand the value of it, and lay the obligation (minnat) upon himself; and, if he be able, he *should* provide a benefit to that amount (miqdâr) for that *person*.

2. It is declared in revelation, *that*, when a person confers a benefit upon any one, Hôrmazd[1] gives him ten times as much, *as* an equivalent. 3. And, if *the other* be not understanding[2] the justice *of this*, it is related in the commentary of the Avesta *in* this manner, that it is a great sin for him. 4. And Aharman[3] speaks like this, namely: 'That sinner is akin to me; *in* the end he will come into my hands; I will not give him into the hands of any demon, *but* I *will* inflict punishment *with* my own hands.' 5. *And* the chief priest[4] says it is necessary for all Zaratustians that they keep themselves far from this sin.

CHAPTER XCV.

1. The ninety-fifth subject is this, that it is necessary that it be expedient for all those of the

---

[1] Lp, B29 add 'the good *and* propitious.'
[2] Lp, B29 have 'praising.' [3] Lp, B29 add 'the accursed.'
[4] Probably meaning the commentator.

good religion to perform the salutation of the sun[1] three times every day.

2. If *one* performs *it* once, it is a good work of one Tanâvar[2]; if he performs *it* twice, it is twice as much; *and* if he performs *it* three times, it is thrice as much. 3. And if he does not perform one repetition, it is a sin of thirty stîrs[3]; if he does not perform two repetitions, it is twice as much sin; and if he does not perform three repetitions, it is thrice as much sin.

4. And it is the same as this with regard to *the salutations of* the moon and fire[4]. 5. Therefore it is expedient, in the religion, for every one of the good religion to bring the salutations *into* practice.

Chapter XCVI.

1. The ninety-sixth subject is this, when any one departs to that *other* world it is not proper for others that they *should* utter an outcry, maintain grief, *and* make lamentation *and* weeping. 2. Because every tear *that* issues *from* the eyes becomes one *drop* of that river[5] before the *K*inva*d*

[1] The Khûrshê*d* Nyâyi*s* (see Chaps. VI, 2, LXVIII, 4).

[2] That is, sufficient to counterbalance a Tanâvar or Tanâpûhar sin (see Sls. I, 2).

[3] Equivalent to an Aredû*s* sin, or blow with a weapon (see Sls. I, 1, 2).

[4] The Mâh and Âtash Nyâyi*s*. B29 also interpolates 'the Mihir' Nyâyi*s*.

[5] 'This river is the many tears that men shed from *their* eyes, as they make lamentation and weeping for the departed. They shed those tears unlawfully, and they swell to this river. Those who are not able to cross over are those for whom, after their departure,

bridge, *and* then the soul of that dead *person* remains *at* that place; it is difficult for it to make a passage there, and it is not able to pass over the *K*inva*d* bridge. 3. It is therefore necessary that they recite the Avesta and celebrate the ceremonial, so that the passage of that place *may* become easy for it.

Chapter XCVII.

1. The ninety-seventh subject is this, that it is expedient for[1] those of the good religion, that they converse, according to their own ability, *in* the presence of officiating priests, high-priests, *spiritual* chiefs, and priests, and hearken cordially to whatever they say. 2. And they *should* understand *their* statements, and, during them, they *should* not utter any reply *or* question (sûâl).

3. For in the commentary of the Avesta it says, *as to* every one who brings altercation ('hu*gg*at) into any statement of the elders of the religion, '*one* breaks out his tongue, or he goes out from this world abortively (mubaʈʈalâ).'

Chapter XCVIII.

1. The ninety-eighth subject is this, that it is necessary for all those of the good religion, that they learn the Avesta characters *in* the presence of

---

much lamentation and weeping were made; and those *who cross* more easily are those for whom less was made' (AV. XVI, 7–10).

[1] Lp, B29 insert 'all.'

priests *and* teachers, so as to read, *and that* no error *may* continue *in* the Nyâyises and Yasts.

2. And it is still more expedient for priests *and* teachers, that they teach the Avesta characters to all those of the good religion[1]; and if a priest, while teaching, shows incompetence (taqsîr), it is a great sin for him. 3. For Hôrmazd, the good *and* propitious, spoke to Zaratust thus: '*As to* every priest and teacher *who* commits a blunder in teaching[2] those of the good religion, I make him just as far from heaven as the width of the earth[3].'

Chapter XCIX.

1. The ninety-ninth subject is this, that it is not proper for officiating priests, high-priests, *spiritual* chiefs, and priests, that they teach Pahlavi to every one.

2. For Zaratust enquired of Hôrmazd thus: 'To whom is it proper to teach Pahlavi?' 3. *And* Hôrmazd, the good *and* propitious, gave a reply thus: '*To* every one who is of thy family (nasl), an officiating priest, a high-priest, a *spiritual* chief, and every one who is an intelligent priest. 4. [4] Besides these that I have mentioned, if *one* teaches *it* to others[5] it is a great sin for him; *and* if he has performed many duties *and* good works, the end for him may *still* be hell.'

[1] B29 omits these seven words.

[2] Lp, B29 insert 'the Avesta to.'

[3] Compare Chap. XXVIII, 3.

[4] B29 inserts 'it is not proper for any other person.'

[5] Lp has 'if *there be* any one of the others, it is not proper that *one* teaches *him*.'

CHAPTER C.

1. The hundredth subject is this, when a person molests or smites any one *who is* innocent, it is a sin of one Tanâvar every day for that *person*, as long as he lives[1]. 2. *And*, when he departs from this world, the angel Mihir and the angel Rashn make up his account and reckoning. 3. *He is*[2] full of affliction, and experiences much regret and penitence, and has no advantage from it[3]. 4. It is *therefore* necessary to keep oneself far from this sin[4].

---

[1] See Sls. X, 17.

[2] Lp, B29, J15 have 'afterwards, he remains *in* that place.'

[3] B29, J15 add '*in* that place.'

[4] B29, J15 add 'and to do good to every one.' In La this chapter was originally numbered XCIX, and Chap. XLIX was subsequently inserted after it, and numbered C. In Lp it was numbered XCVIII, and occurs again as Chap. C, while Chap. XCIX is a repetition of XLIX (which is numbered LII in Lp). The discrepancy in the numbering of the chapters, of one in the case of La, and two in Lp, extends backwards as far as the confusion mentioned in p. 311, note 1, and was evidently due to that confusion.

INDEX.

OBSERVATIONS.

1. The references in this index are to the pages of the introduction, and to the chapters and sections of the translations; the chapters being denoted by the larger ciphers.

2. Though different forms of the same name may occur in the translation only one form is usually given in the index, to which the references to all forms are attached; except when the forms differ so much as to require to be widely separated in the index.

3. Abbreviations used are:—Av. for Avesta; com. for commentary or commentator; Dr. for Doctor; Gug. for Gugarâtî; Hâd. for Hâdôkht; Int. for Introduction; m. for mountain; Mkh. for Dînâ-î Maînôg-î Khirad; MSS. for manuscripts; n. for foot-note; Pâr. for Pârsî; Per. for Persian; Pl. for Pahlavi; Prof. for Professor; Pz. for Pâzand; rev. for revelation; scrip. for scripture; Sd. for Sad Dar; Sg. for Sikand-gûmânîk Vigâr; Sk. for Sanskrit; Test. for Testament; Vd. for Vendîdâd.

INDEX.

TRANSLITERATION OF ORIENTAL ALPHABETS ADOPTED FOR THE TRANSLATIONS OF THE SACRED BOOKS OF THE EAST.

CONSONANTS.	MISSIONARY ALPHABET. I Class.	II Class.	III Class.	Sanskrit.	Zend.	Pehlevi.	Persian.	Arabic.	Hebrew.	Chinese.
Gutturales.										
1 Tenuis	k	...	...	क	𐬐	[illegible]	ک	ک	כּ	k
2 „ aspirata	kh	...	...	ख	𐬑	[illegible]	...	...	כ	kh
3 Media	g	...	...	ग	𐬔	[illegible]	گ	...	גּ	...
4 „ aspirata	gh	...	...	घ	𐬖	[illegible]	...	...	ג	...
5 Gutturo-labialis	q	...	...	...	...	...	ق	ق	ק	...
6 Nasalis	ṅ (ng)	...	...	ङ	{ 𐬧 (ng) 𐬣 (N) }	...	...	...	...	...
7 Spiritus asper	h	...	...	ह	𐬵 (𐬒 *hv*)	[illegible]	ه	ه	ה	h, hs
8 „ lenis	’	...	...	...	...	[illegible]	ا	ا	א	...
9 „ asper faucalis	‘h	...	...	...	...	...	ح	ح	ח	...
10 „ lenis faucalis	’h	...	...	...	...	...	ع	ع	ע	...
11 „ asper fricatus	...	‘*h*	...	...	...	...	خ	خ	ח	...
12 „ lenis fricatus	...	’*h*	...	...	...	...	...	...	...	...
Gutturales modificatae (palatales, &c.)										
13 Tenuis	...	*k*	...	च	𐬗	[illegible]	چ	...	...	*k*
14 „ aspirata	...	*kh*	...	छ	...	...	...	...	...	*kh*
15 Media	...	*g*	...	ज	𐬘	[illegible]	ج	ج	...	...
16 „ aspirata	...	*gh*	...	झ	...	...	غ	غ	...	...
17 „ Nasalis	...	*ñ*	...	ञ	...	...	...	...	...	...

CONSONANTS (*continued*).	MISSIONARY ALPHABET. I Class.	II Class.	III Class.	Sanskrit.	Zend.	Pehlevi.	Persian.	Arabic.	Hebrew.	Chinese.
18 Semivocalis	y	...	...	य	𐬫, init. [illegible]	[illegible]	ي	ي	י	y
19 Spiritus asper	...	(ẏ)	...	...	...	...	...	...	...	...
20 „ lenis	...	(ẏ)	...	...	...	...	...	...	...	...
21 „ asper assibilatus	...	*s*	...	श	𐬱	[illegible]	ش	ش	...	...
22 „ lenis assibilatus	...	*z*	...	...	𐬲	[illegible]	ژ	...	...	*z*
Dentales.										
23 Tenuis	t	...	...	त	𐬙	[illegible]	ت	ت	תּ	t
24 „ aspirata	th	...	...	थ	𐬚	...	...	...	ת	th
25 „ assibilata	...	...	TH	...	...	...	ث	ث	...	...
26 Media	d	...	...	द	𐬛	[illegible]	د	د	דּ	...
27 „ aspirata	dh	...	...	ध	𐬜	...	...	...	ד	...
28 „ assibilata	...	...	DH	...	...	...	ذ	ذ	...	...
29 Nasalis	n	...	...	न	𐬥	[illegible]	ن	ن	נ	n
30 Semivocalis	l	...	...	ल	...	[illegible]	ل	ل	ל	l
31 „ mollis 1	...	*l*	...	ळ	...	...	...	...	...	...
32 „ mollis 2	...	...	L	...	...	...	...	...	...	...
33 Spiritus asper 1	s	...	...	स	𐬯	[illegible]	س (ث)	س	שׂ	s
34 „ asper 2	...	...	s (ʃ)	...	...	...	...	...	ס	...
35 „ lenis	z	...	...	...	𐬰	[illegible]	ز (ذ)	ز	ז	z
36 „ asperrimus 1	...	...	z (ʒ)	...	...	...	ص	ص	צ	ʒ, ʒh
37 „ asperrimus 2	...	...	ẓ (ʒ̣)	...	...	...	ض	...	...	...

Dentales modificatae (linguales, &c.)										
38 Tenuis	...	*t*	...	ट	...	...	ط	ط	ט	...
39 " aspirata	...	*th*	...	ठ	...	...	ظ	ظ	...	...
40 Media	...	*d*	...	ड	[illegible]	[illegible]	...	...	...	...
41 " aspirata	...	*dh*	...	ढ	...	...	...	ض	...	...
42 Nasalis	...	*n*	...	ण	[illegible]	...	...	...	...	...
43 Semivocalis	r	...	...	र	[illegible]	[illegible]	ر	ر	ר	...
44 " fricata	...	*r*	...	...	...	...	...	...	...	*r*
45 " diacritica	...	...	R	...	...	...	...	...	...	...
46 Spiritus asper	sh	...	...	ष	[illegible]	[illegible]	...	...	...	sh
47 " lenis	zh	...	...	...	...	...	...	...	...	...
Labiales.										
48 Tenuis	p	...	...	प	[illegible]	[illegible]	پ	...	פּ	p
49 " aspirata	ph	...	...	फ	...	...	...	...	פ	ph
50 Media	b	...	...	ब	[illegible]	[illegible]	ب	ب	בּ	...
51 " aspirata	bh	...	...	भ	...	...	...	...	ב	...
52 Tenuissima	...	*p*	...	...	...	...	...	...	...	...
53 Nasalis	m	...	...	म	[illegible]	[illegible]	م	م	מ	m
54 Semivocalis	w	...	...	...	[illegible]	...	...	...	...	w
55 " aspirata	hw	...	...	...	...	...	...	...	...	...
56 Spiritus asper	f	...	...	...	[illegible]	[illegible]	ف	ف	...	f
57 " lenis	v	...	...	व	[illegible]	[illegible]	و	و	ו	...
58 Anusvâra	...	*m*	...	अं	[illegible]	...	...	...	...	...
59 Visarga	...	*h*	...	अः	...	...	...	...	...	...

VOWELS.	MISSIONARY ALPHABET. I Class.	II Class.	III Class.	Sanskrit.	Zend.	Pehlevi.	Persian.	Arabic.	Hebrew.	Chinese.
1 Neutralis	0	...	....	...	....	...	...	...	ְ	ă
2 Laryngo-palatalis	ĕ	...	....	...	....	...	...	...	...	...
3 „ labialis	ŏ	...	....	...	....	𐭠 fin.	...	...	...	...
4 Gutturalis brevis	a	...	....	अ	𐬀	𐭠 init.	ـَ	ـَ	ַ	a
5 „ longa	â	(*a*)	....	आ	𐬁	𐭠	ـَا	ـَا	ָ	â
6 Palatalis brevis	i	...	....	इ	𐬌	...	ـِ	ـِ	ִ	i
7 „ longa	î	(*i*)	....	ई	𐬍	𐭉	ـِي	ـِي	ִי	î
8 Dentalis brevis	*li*	...	....	ऌ	....	...	...	...	...	...
9 „ longa	*lî*	...	....	ॡ	....	...	...	...	...	...
10 Lingualis brevis	*ri*	...	....	ऋ	....	...	...	...	...	...
11 „ longa	*rî*	...	....	ॠ	....	...	...	...	...	...
12 Labialis brevis	u	...	....	उ	𐬎	...	ـُ	ـُ	ֻ	u
13 „ longa	û	(*u*)	....	ऊ	𐬏	𐭅	ـُو	ـُو	וּ	û
14 Gutturo-palatalis brevis	e	...	....	...	𐬆(e) 𐬇(*e*)	...	...	...	ֶ	e
15 „ longa	ê (ai)	(*e*)	....	ए	𐬈, 𐬉	𐭉	...	...	ֵ	ê
16 Diphthongus gutturo-palatalis	âi	(*ai*)	....	ऐ	....	...	ـَيْ	ـَيْ	...	âi
17 „ „	ei (ĕi)	...	....	...	....	...	...	...	...	ei, êi
18 „ „	oi (ŏu)	...	....	...	....	...	...	...	...	...
19 Gutturo-labialis brevis	o	...	....	...	𐬊	...	...	...	ָ	o
20 „ longa	ô (au)	(*o*)	....	ओ	𐬋	𐭅	...	...	וֹ	...
21 Diphthongus gutturo-labialis	âu	(*au*)	....	औ	𐬃𐬎 (*au*)	...	ـَوْ	ـَوْ	...	âu
22 „ „	eu (ĕu)	...	....	...	....	...	...	...	...	...
23 „ „	ou (ŏu)	...	....	...	....	...	...	...	...	...
24 Gutturalis fracta	ä	...	....	...	....	...	...	...	...	...
25 Palatalis fracta	ï	...	....	...	....	...	...	...	...	...
26 Labialis fracta	ü	...	....	...	....	...	...	...	...	ü
27 Gutturo-labialis fracta	ö	...	....	...	....	...	...	...	...	...